BEYOND COMMUNITY ENGAGEMENT

Transforming Dialogues in Art, Education, and the Cultural Sphere

---

Edited by
Kim Snepvangers and
Donna Mathewson Mitchell

Part of the Curated Series:
Transformative Pedagogies in the Visual Domain

Series Curators:
Dr. Arianne Rourke and
Dr. Vaughan Rees

BEYOND COMMUNITY ENGAGEMENT

Transforming Dialogues in Art, Education, and the Cultural Sphere

---

Edited by
Kim Snepvangers and
Donna Mathewson Mitchell

Part of the Curated Series:
Transformative Pedagogies in the
Visual Domain

Series Curators:
Dr. Arianne Rourke and
Dr. Vaughan Rees

COMMON GROUND RESEARCH NETWORKS 2018 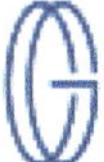

First published in 2018
as part of the Image Book Imprint
http://doi.org/10.18848/978-1-86335-001-3/CGP (Full Book)

Common Ground Research Networks
2001 South First Street, Suite 202
University of Illinois Research Park
Champaign, IL
61820

Library of Congress Cataloging-in-Publication Data

Names: Snepvangers, Kim, editor. | Mathewson Mitchell, Donna, editor.
Title: Beyond community engagement : transforming dialogues in art, education, and the cultural sphere / edited by Kim Snepvangers and Donna Mathewson Mitchell.
Description: Champaign, IL : Common Ground Research Networks, 2018. | Series: [Transformative pedagogies in the visual domain] | Includes bibliographical references.
Identifiers: LCCN 2018026157 (print) | LCCN 2018028106 (ebook) | ISBN 9781863350037 (pdf) | ISBN 9781863350013 (hardback : alk. paper) | ISBN 9781863350020 (pbk. : alk. paper)
Subjects: LCSH: Art--Study and teaching. | Art and society.
Classification: LCC N85 (ebook) | LCC N85 .B49 2018 (print) | DDC 701/.03--dc23
LC record available at https://lccn.loc.gov/2018026157

Cover Photo Credit: Bernadett Butson, Zeeshan Khan, Arianne Rourke, Vaughan Rees and Kim Snepvangers

Table of Contents

Acknowledgements xi
List of Figures xiii
List of Tables xix
Endorsement Statement xxi
Curators' Essay xxiii

Chapter 1 1
Transforming Dialogues through Ecologies of Practice in Art, Education, and the Cultural Sphere
Kim Snepvangers and Donna Mathewson Mitchell

Chapter 2 23
Bodies of Water, Bodies at Sea: The Sea is All Around Us
Margaret Woodward

Chapter 3 41
#MuseumEdOz: Facilitating Socially Distributed Meaning Making through Twitter
Narelle Lemon

Chapter 4 59
Windows and Frames on Young People's Artwork
Jonathan Cooper and Maureen Ryan

Chapter 5 85
Communal Luxury and the Universal Republic of the Arts: Transcultural Flows of Art Pedagogy
Angela Giovanangeli

Chapter 6 101
The Company It Keeps: Arts-based Research as Assemblage
John Rae

Chapter 7 117
Medical Imaging, Modern Clinical Practice, and the Art of Exploration
Gregory Turner-Rahman

Chapter 8 137
Connective Understanding: Traditional Materiality & Contemporary Installations
Jamie-Lea Hodges and Eleanor Venables

Chapter 9 161
Collaboration or Cooperation: Peer-led Learning and Institutional Partnerships through Two Case Studies
Jo Higgins and Sarah Coffils

Chapter 10 193
Digital Storytelling and Organic Theater: Pedagogies in 21st Century Learning
Marty Otañez and James Walsh

Chapter 11 215
Cicada Press: Transforming Dialogues and Applications of Distributed Leadership
Michael Kempson

Chapter 12 251
Changing platforms: How Supported Studios Help Artists with Intellectual Disability Fast-Track their Career
Gabrielle Mordy

Chapter 13 271
The Process of Collaboration and Contemplation in Examining Public Pedagogies in a Local Makerspace
Lisa Hochtritt

Chapter 14 291
Reflections on Transformative Pedagogies and Ecology in the Cultural Sphere
Kim Snepvangers and Donna Mathewson Mitchell

Contributor Information 309

ACKNOWLEDGEMENTS

Editors Dr Kim Snepvangers and Dr Donna Mathewson Mitchell would like to sincerely thank all the authors for their contribution to this book and most specifically the sharing of their experience and knowledge regarding art, education and the cultural sphere.

The contributors to this book have provided significant insights into their practices as academics, researchers and practitioners, located in a range of sites. Their work crosses boundaries in a variety of ways, engaging in important transformative dialogue across the spheres of art, education and culture.

The editors would also like to sincerely thank the series editors Associate Professor Arianne Rourke and Associate Professor Vaughan Rees and Common Ground Research Networks for their professional support from manuscript to published book.

List of Figures

Chapter 2

Figure: 2.1 - We are leaving Busan right now and heading to Xingdao, China (2016). Image credit: Jonathan Pacifico.
Figure: 2.2 - Customised souvenir mugs with QR codes. (2015) Margaret Woodward. Image credit: Justy Phillips.
Figure: 2.3 - Visiting seafarers from the ship LUCKY LIFE. (2015). Margaret Woodward. Image credit: Justy Phillips.
Figure: 2.4 - Cake and Mugs. (2015) Margaret Woodward Installation view *The Sea is All Around Us* (2015), Dome Gallery, Mission to Seafarers Victoria, Melbourne. Image credit: Justy Phillips.
Figure: 2.5 - Departures. (2015). Margaret Woodward. Installation view *The Sea is All Around Us* (2015). Dome, Gallery, Mission to Seafarers Victoria, Melbourne. Image credit: Margaret Woodward.
Figure: 2.6 - Seafarers and Souvenirs, October (2015). Image Credit: Deanna Duffy, Spatial Analysis Data Network, Charles Sturt University.
Figure: 2.7 - Shipping Routes, May. (2016). *Marine Traffic Website* www.marinetraffic.com.
Figure: 2.8 - Shipping Routes. (2012). Image Credit: Kiln. Digital and University College London (UCL).
Figure: 2.9 - Jonathan Pacifico. *(2016). Port of Singapore.* Image Credit: Jonathan Pacifico.

Chapter 4

All Figures are photographs of images held on the Gallery Sunshine Everywhere website: all copyright is held by GSE (2016).

Figure: 4.1 - Connecting youth and adult worlds through artistic expression. (2016). Gallery Sunshine Everywhere ©
Figure: 4.2 - A moment in time holistically connected. (2016). Gallery Sunshine Everywhere ©
Figure: 4.3 - Deer Park History Mosaic Mural (communal art project). (2016). Gallery Sunshine Everywhere ©
Figure: 4.4 - Engaging with popular culture. (2016). Gallery Sunshine Everywhere ©
Figure: 4.5 - Little aesthetics. (2016). Gallery Sunshine Everywhere ©
Figure: 4.6 - Young people's perspectives on their worlds. (2016). Gallery Sunshine Everywhere ©
Figure: 4.7 - Self, family and home – children expressing themes of home, family and self across a range of GSE experiences. (2016). Gallery Sunshine Everywhere ©

Figure: 4.8 - Responses to 2009 Victorian Bushfires. (2016). Gallery Sunshine Everywhere ©
Figure: 4.9 - Here where people meet Sunshine (a collaborative installation where members of the community arrange ceramic words, letters and objects into meaning). (2016). Gallery Sunshine Everywhere ©
Figure: 4.10 - I love Sunshine. (2016). Gallery Sunshine Everywhere ©
Figure: 4.11 - Big things come in small packages Rey Mysterio. (2016). Gallery Sunshine Everywhere ©
Figure: 4.12 - Concrete poetry in collaboration with local artist Debbie Qadri, Brimbank festival. (2016). Gallery Sunshine Everywhere ©
Figure: 4.13 - Never fear the future and don't be afraid to fly and see after all I'm not perfect, la, la, la, la. (2016). Gallery Sunshine Everywhere ©

Chapter 5

Figure: 5.1- This engraving describing an introductory page appears in the letter addressed to the Minister for Public Instruction and was part of the prospectus for the book *Australian Decorative Arts* (Henry 1890b).
Figure: 5.2- This engraving titled *Kookaburra electric lamp for bedroom* appears in the letter addressed to the Minister for Public Instruction and is part of the prospectus for the book *Australian Decorative Arts* (Henry 1890b).
Figure: 5.3 - This engraving titled *Stained Glass Window, Town Hall, Sydney* appears in the letter addressed to the Minister for Public Instruction and is part of the prospectus for the book *Australian Decorative Arts* (Henry 1890b).

Chapter 6

Figure: 6.1 - Connections (2010). John Rae.
Figure: 6.2 - Immersion, John Rae.

Chapter 7

Figure: 7.1 - Student-defined conceptual map regarding the clinical gaze (2015).
Figure: 7.2 - Sketch complementing Foucault's text (2015). Photograph by the author.
Figure: 7. 3 - Student's project listing the value of body parts on the black market (2015). Photograph by the author.
Figure: 7.4 - A mid-term project: girl scout cookies as drug delivery system (2015). Photograph by the author.
Figure: 7.5 - A final project: medical instruments made from industrial re-bar (2015). Photograph by the author.
Figure: 7.6 - Composited images describing the evolution of the clinical gaze (2015). Photograph by the author.
Figure: 7.7 - A static documentary on the challenges of dealing with a health issue (2015). Photograph by the author.

Figure: 7.8 - Data about the average woman is overlaid upon one another (2015). Photograph by the author.

Chapter 8

Figure: 8.1 - *Connective Understanding*, 2014, Aboriginal artists from Outback Arts, various materials, 15m long. Connective understanding: a focus on String through contemporary Aboriginal art - Collateral event at 56th Venice Biennale 2015. Outback Arts, Boolarng Nangamai and Galamban.
Figure: 8.2 - Country: Installation view (detail) - Connective understanding: a focus on String through contemporary Aboriginal art - Collateral event at 56th Venice Biennale 2015. Image: Courtesy of the artists' and *Outback Arts.*
Figure: *8.3* - The Murray-Darling Darling Basin by Ben Spraggon
http://www.abc.net.au/news/rural/specials/murray-darling-basin-plan/
Courtesy of ABC Retrieved 21 July 2016
Image page: http://www.abc.net.au/site-archive/rural/murraydarling/map-large.png
ABC copyright agreement signed by author Eleanor Venables.
Figure: *8.4* - Artists harvesting Emu Foot Sedge grass on the banks of the Namoi River, Walgett. Image: Courtesy of Jamie-Lea Hodges and *Outback Arts.*
Figure: *8.5* - Aboriginal Country Map NSW (detail) - Map of the Kamilaroi and Wailwan nations of NSW. Original image sourced and modified from: http://www.curriculumsupport.education.nsw.gov.au/shared/abmaps/nsw.htm#
Figure: 8.6 - Detail: freshly harvested Emu Foot Sedge grass. Image: Courtesy of Jamie-Lea Hodges and *Outback Arts.*
Figure: *8.7* - String piece packed for transportation and storage. Image: Courtesy of Jamie-Lea Hodges and *Outback Arts.*

Chapter 9

Figure: 9.1 - The Academy Goes Public, 2012. Louis Vuitton Young Arts Project. Image credit: Richard Eaton. Courtesy: REcreativeUK.com/South London Gallery
Figure: 9.2 - Kaldor Public Art Projects Pilot Regional Engagement Project, weekend workshop, May 2015. Image credit: Paige Williams / Orana Arts. Courtesy: Kaldor Public Art Projects
Figure: 9.3 - A visit to Frieze Projects, part of The Academy Goes Public, 2012. Louis Vuitton Young Arts Project. Image credit: Richard Eaton. Courtesy: REcreativeUK.com/South London Gallery
Figure: 9.4 - The Academy Goes Public, 2012. Various venues. Louis Vuitton Young Arts Project. Image credit: Richard Eaton. Courtesy: REcreativeUK.com/South London Gallery
Figure: *9.5* - Caitlyn Coman-Sargent, *Pruning Time - A collection of private and public rituals*, 2015. Presented as part of "What It Means To Be Me", Saturday 26 July 2015, Western Plains Cultural Centre, Dubbo. Photo: Alex Wisser. Courtesy: Kaldor Public Art Projects

Figure: 9.6 - Kaldor Public Art Projects Pilot Regional Engagement Project, weekend workshop, May 2015. Image credit: Paige Williams / Orana Arts. Courtesy: Kaldor Public Art Projects
Figure: 9.7 - The Academy Goes Public, 2012. Various venues. Louis Vuitton Young Arts Project. Image credit: Richard Eaton. Courtesy: REcreativeUK.com/South London Gallery
Figure: 9.8 - Kate Hagan, *Five Performances for Imagination,* 2015. Presented as part of "What It Means To Be Me", Saturday 26 July 2015, Western Plains Cultural Centre, Dubbo. Image credit: Alex Wisser. Courtesy: Kaldor Public Art Projects
Figure: 9.9 - Grace Farmilo, *Grace,* 2015. Presented as part of "What It Means To Be Me", Saturday 26 July 2015, Western Plains Cultural Centre, Dubbo. Image credit: Alex Wisser. Courtesy: Kaldor Public Art Projects
Figure: 9.10 - The Academy of Youth Mythology, Southbank, 2011. Louis Vuitton Young Arts Project. Image credit: Richard Eaton. Courtesy: REcreativeUK.com/ South London Gallery
Figure: 9.11 - Workshop with Marina Abramović, Saturday 4 July, Pier 2/3 Walsh Bay. Image credit: Kaldor Public Art Projects

Chapter 10

Figure: 10.1 - Students performing Molly Maguire skit (2006). Image credit: Jim Walsh
Figure: 10. 2 - Students in Irish in America course prepare for a performance (2006). Image credit: Jim Walsh
Figure: 10.3 - The Romero Theater Troupe, one of the largest and most diverse arts collectives in the U.S. (2013). Image credit: Michael Kilman

Chapter 11

Figure: 11.1 - Printing plates for Chris O'Doherty aka Reg Mombassa's *Pine Hedge* (2012) etching and aquatint. Image credit: Ben Rak.
Figure: 11.2 - Noel McKenna (left) and visiting Canadian artist Mark Bovey develop their printing plates in the etching studio at UNSW A&D (2016). Image credit: Michael Kempson.
Figure: 11.3 - Michael Nelson Jagamara (left) working collaboratively with Michael Kempson at Cicada Press (2006) during the first Sydney based Papunya print workshop. Image credit: Kasumi Ejiri.
Figure: 11.4 - The Cicada Press stand in the Paper Contemporary section of *Sydney Contemporary 2015* at Carriageworks, Sydney. Image credit: Michael Kempson.
Figure: 11. 5 - Michael Kempson (left) interacts with UNSW A&D students around a printing press (2015). Image credit: Sally Marks.
Figure: 11.6 - Chris O'Doherty aka Reg Mombassa with BFA student Kasumi Ejiri (2006). Image credit: Michael Kempson.
Figure: 11.7 - Norman Hetherington aka Mr. Squiggle (right) with Michael Kempson and BFA student Tess Barnard (2005). Image credit: Georgina Gye.

Figure: 11.8 - UNSW A&D casual academic Ben Rak and Director of Indigenous Programs Tess Allas review a screenprinted layer on Laurel Nannup's *Quiriu,* (2016) linocut and screenprint. Image credit: Michael Kempson.
Figure: 11. 9 - Ramesh Mario Nithiyendran *One Hung Bitch* (2013), etching, aquatint and viscosity roll, image size 60 x 50.5 cm, printed at Cicada Press UNSW A&D. Image credit: Sue Blackburn.
Figure: 11.10 - Noel McKenna *Horse* (2011) lithograph, image size 38 x 45.5cm, printed at Cicada Press UNSW A&D. Image credit: Sue Blackburn.
Figure: 11.11 - Artist and musician Maytee Noijinda (left) discusses options for his print with Yuttana Sittikan, Yuree Kensaku and Kitikong Tilokwattanotai (right) at Chiangmai Art on Paper in Thailand (2011). Image credit: Surachet Wonghun.
Figure: *11.12* - Guy Warren signing *Bora Dance* (2006) etching and aquatint. Image credit: Michael Kempson.
Figure: 11.13 - Fiona Hall *Lying in the Dark* (2012) etching, aquatint, open-bite and screenprint, image size 50.5 x 101 cm, printed at Cicada Press UNSW A&D. Image credit: Sue Blackburn.
Figure: 11.14 - Michael Callaghan *Operation Iraqi Freedom* (2009), digital, aquatint and screenprint, image size 136 x 107 cm printed at Cicada Press UNSW A&D. Image credit: Sue Blackburn.
Figure: 11.15 - Norman Hetherington aka Mr. Squiggle *The Pied Piper* (2005), etching and aquatint, image size 30 x 22.5 cm, printed at Cicada Press UNSW A&D, photography – Sue Blackburn.
Figure: 11.16 - Mathew Calandra (left) develops an image while working alongside Chris O'Doherty aka Reg Mombassa at the Cicada Press studio in UNSW A&D (2012). Image credit: Michael Kempson.
Figure: 11.17 - Gregory O'Brien *Raoul Island Whale Survey with shipping containers, Astrolabe Reef* (2012-13) etching and aquatint, image size 51 x 41cm, printed at Cicada Press UNSW A&D. Image credit: Sue Blackburn.
Figure: 11.18 - Dame Robin White *Braveheart* (2011) etching and aquatint, image size 19.5 cm diameter, printed at Cicada Press UNSW A&D. Image credit: Sue Blackburn.
Figure: 11.19 - Road to Papunya, Northern Territory, Australia (2008), photography – Ben Rak
Figure: 11.20 - Reduction block linocuts drying after a session of printing at the Papunya School (2007). Image credit: Kasumi Ejiri.
Figure: 11.21 - Michael Kempson (left) with Jess Bulger, Sian McIntyre and Ben Rak with children from the Papunya School after a print workshop in Papunya (2008).
Figure: 11.22 - Doris Bush Nungarrayi *Untitled* (2011), aquatint, image size 33.5 x 50 cm, printed at Cicada Press UNSW A&D. Image credit: Sue Blackburn.
Figure: 11. 23 - Vernon Ah Kee *ABC* (2012), aquatint, image size 32 x 31 cm, printed at Cicada Press UNSW A&D. Image credit: Sue Blackburn.
Figure: 11.24 - Laurel Nannup signs prints with the support of son Brett Nannup (2015). Image credit: Michael Kempson.
Figure: 11.25 - Director of Indigenous Programs Tess Allas (left) documents Ryan Presley working on a lithographic stone (2015). Image credit: Michael Kempson.

Figure: 11.26 - Participants and visitors in the Aboriginal Print Workshop 2016. Image credit: Tess Allas.
Figure: 11.27 - Tony Albert *Greetings from Appin,* (2016) etching and aquatint, image size 50 x 50.5 cm, printed at Cicada Press UNSW A&D, photography – Sue Blackburn
Figure: 11.28 - Tahjee Moar assists with editioning Ryan Presley's *dominium* (2015) etching and aquatint. Image credit: Michael Kempson.
Figure: 11.29 - MArt students Rachel Dooris and Ruth Saveka review a proof of 'Uncle' Vic Chapman's *Hebel Hotel* (2016) etching and aquatint. Image credit: Michael Kempson.

Chapter 12

Figure: 12.1 - Ramsay Street (2015) Nadia Lolas. Mixed media on paper, 38 x 56cm. Image credit: Studio A.
Figure: 12.2a - Man with Facial Hair 1 & 2 (2014) Robert Thom Smith, 21 x 30cm (each work), Posca pen on transparency paper. Image credit: Studio A.
Figure: 12.2b - Man with Facial Hair 1 & 2 (2014) Robert Thom Smith, 21 x 30cm (each work), Posca pen on transparency paper. Image credit: Studio A.
Figure: 12.3 - Studio A artist Daniel Kim working on portrait (2011). Image from Studio A.
Figure: 12.4 - Mo Baby (2011) Daniel Kim. Pencil on paper, 140 x 180cm. Image credit: Studio A.
Figure: 12.5 - Nicola's Return from the Grave (2015) Greg Sindel. Four-colour screenprint on paper, 70 x 100cm. Image credit: Studio A.
Figure: 12.6 - Studio A Mentor Printmaker Michael Kempson working with Studio A artist Meagan Pelham in Cicada Press, College of Fine Arts, University of New South Wales (2013) Image credit: Gabrielle Mordy.
Figure: 12.7 - City Circle Arrives at Cloud Heaven at Underbelly Arts Festival (2015) Thom and Angelmouse installation. Image credit: Studio A
Figure: 12.8 - Mathew Calandra, Ghost Movie, 2013, Etching Acquatint by Cicada Press. 19 x 24.5cm (print size). Image credit: Studio A.
Figure: 12.9 - Judith Scott's assemblages on exhibition in Judith Scott – Bound and Unbound at Brooklyn Museum (2015). Image credit: Emma Johnston.
Figure: 12.10 - Looking at Judith Scott's work on exhibition in Judith Scott – Bound and Unbound at the Brooklyn Museum (2015). Image credit. Emma Johnston.
Figure: 12.11 - Nick Pagan's sculptures in process at Creative Growth March (2015) Photo by Gabrielle Mordy, taken with permission of Creative Growth and artist.
Figure: 12.12 - Creative Growth gallery space (2015). Image credit: Gabrielle Mordy.

Chapter 13

Figure: 13.1 - Research team in graduate student Michael Barrett's school bus that often doubled as our classroom (2016). Image credit: Lisa Hochtritt.

Figure: 13.2 - Class members in the basement of the Makerspace (2016). Image credit: Misha Burstein.
Figure: 13.3 - Participants in the Education and Public Pedagogy group meet to discuss the mapping of findings, data analysis, and research outcomes (2016). Image credit: Lisa Hochtritt.
Figure: 13.4 - The Education and Public Pedagogy group's chalkboard outline for writing the program evaluation review report for makerspace organisers (2016). Image credit: Lisa Hochtritt.

List of Tables

Chapter 3

Table: 3.1 - Lines of digital becoming demonstrated through the #MuseumEdOz online community facilitated through Twitter.

Chapter 10

Table: 10.1 - Key activities in courses designed to promote contemplative pedagogies

Endorsement Statement

This is a thoughtful and thought-provoking compilation that both reflects and challenges contemporary practice. For those involved in higher education whose interest is in visual communication and associated pedagogy, this book is essential; others working in related fields will find much of great value. The editors, Dr Donna Mathewson and Dr Kim Snepvangers, have done an excellent job in bringing together a wide range of well-informed authors. It examines, in a rigorous and informed way, fundamental issues associated with art, education and culture and the complex relationships between each.

The editors' introductory chapter, 'transforming dialogues in art, education and the cultural sphere' sets the stage with an insightful account that introduces the reader to ideas such as the notion that cultural practices are 'living' phenomena that are interdependent and connected through 'ecologies of practice', reminiscent perhaps of the 'rhizome' metaphor, much used in a/r/tographical writings.

There are several chapters that I found to be particularly apposite innovative in a book of this kind, but if I were to single out one as an example of this text's pioneering approach, it would be the chapter entitled 'medical imaging, modern clinical practice and the art of exploration' by Dr. Gregory Turner-Rahman. This chapter, in keeping with others in the volume, adopts a case study approach; it examines the potential of image making to serve as an exploratory act of visual reasoning. In doing so, it reflects the potential for trans-disciplinary research. This is an important dimension to the book and is a tacit but fundamental theme: the principle that all knowledge is connected.

The final chapter, written by the editors, applies a critical lens to view the theoretical framework of ecologies of practice; this is done to re-evaluate, in an analytical way, the relationship between communities and visual culture. This concluding chapter (entitled 'reflections on transformative pedagogies and ecology in the cultural sphere') rounds off the book in an elegant manner, making the whole a well-informed addition to the field. Overall, this innovative book provides an eclectic yet coherent vision for the future of art in education and in communities at large.

Professor Richard Hickman
University of Cambridge

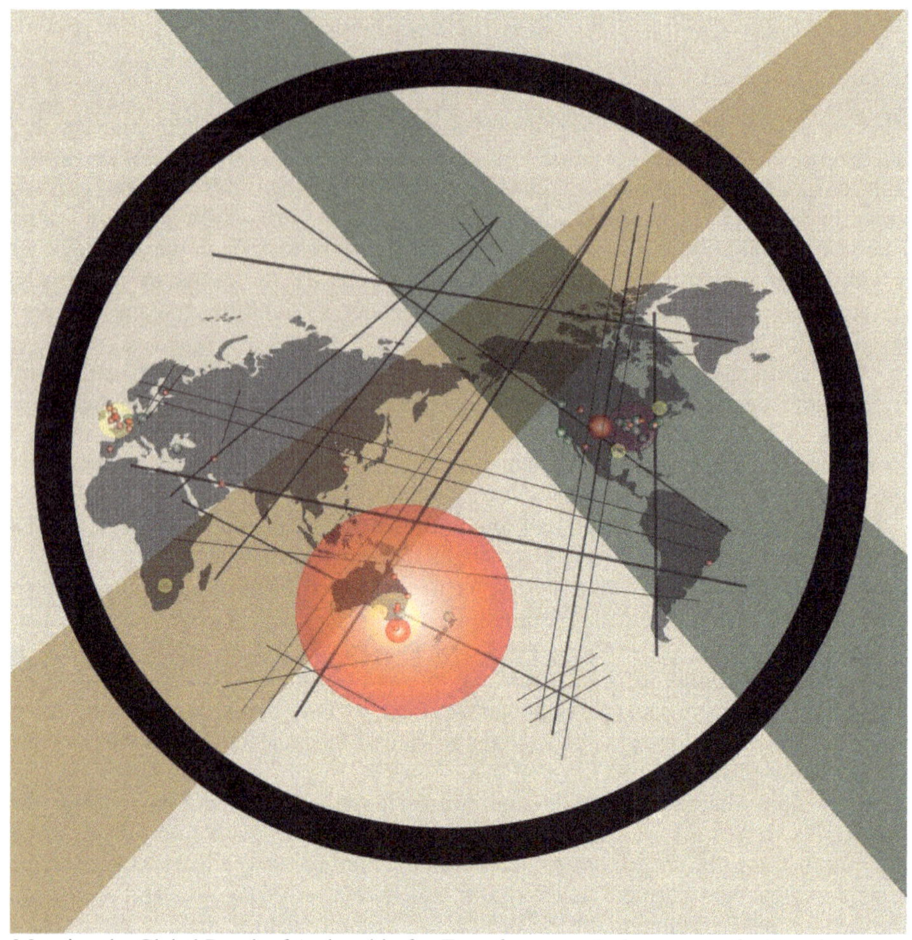

Mapping the Global Reach of Authorship for *Transformative Pedagogies in the Visual Domain*

Curators' Essay

Dr Arianne Rourke and Dr Vaughan Rees

The Editors of *Beyond Community Engagement: Transforming Dialogues in Art, Education, and the Cultural Sphere,* Dr Kim Snepvangers and Dr Donna Mathewson Mitchell, in the fourth book of eight in the Curated Series: *Transformative Pedagogies in the Visual Domain,* explore how ideas may be considered as ".living things that are interdependent on other practices and connected in ecologies of practice." Snepvangers and Mathewson Mitchell have selected prime examples of visual art, design and media projects that give the unique view of researcher as main instrument (Piantanida & Garman, 1999) or "insider-practitioners" engaging in communities.

The potential for knowledge exchange between various stakeholders such as academic institutions and the large professional cultural industries provides a porosity through which to foster opportunities for engagement. Relationships that are charged with reciprocal understanding, and challenges in-situ provide a feedback loop to keep research relevant, applied and constantly interrogated. This dynamic relationship also spawns new ways of perceiving participatory practice, theory and more robust and situation specific research methodologies.

The central driver of Snepvangers and Mathewson Mitchells' book is contemporary community practice and giving primacy to the view of the cultural practitioner. The value presented here comes from an informed reflective collection of practitioners deeply involved in the transformative knowledge of those who engage in practice. Practitioners are simultaneously immersed within their practice yet, they are also able to step back and articulate the meta-narrative with all its epiphanies, pitfalls and potential. This book celebrates the individual voice of the practitioner rather than those who often speak for them. Therefore, assumptions about practice and community engagement are challenged, unpacked, and ideas emerge about types of participation, how participation is performed and received and, how practitioners and those interested in learning and education might reflect on the experience.

These reflective encounters value intuition, emotive and innovative responses in the creative and communicative process. Here ideas are collectively mobilised and the process of engagement becomes a valued dialogue of reciprocity, where lived experience is shared and the focus is less on an end goal or on establishing a predetermined social/community group. The richness of these relationships is explored and self-reflection is seen in this process as a valued component of transformative learning. Here according to Mezirow (2009), learning "transforms problematic frames of reference to make them more inclusive, discriminating, reflective, open, and emotionally able to change" (p.22). In the process 'like-minded people' engage and form 'authentic' collaborations that are respectful, sharing and evolving. Where as Kucukaydin and Cranton's (2012) suggests, "adults experience a deep shift in perspective that leads them to better justified and more open frames of reference" (p. 11).

Snepvangers and Mathewson Mitchell propose a theory of 'practice encounters' to reflect newly charted territories and transitions revealed in this book. The projects and authors value "the character of improvisation in relation to practice and its surprises" (Yanow & Tsoukas, 2009, p. 1339) as well as the quality of encounters where emphasis is on according to Snepvangers and Mathewson Mitchell "care, respect, reciprocity, trust, the capacity to shape relationships, discovery and engagement." The notion of an 'ecology of practice' is explored, which according to Siemens (2007) are "Adaptive, dynamic and responsive - the ecology enables (or more specifically fosters) adaptation to the needs of the agents within the space" (p. 62-63). This is a space where Staron (2013) suggests: "We need to trust ourselves to establish a learning ecology that is meaningful, authentic and supportive of our growth and personal wellbeing" (p. 7). This is described as a 'value adding' correlative relationship that facilitates the establishment of a 'sense' of community. This book provides a valuable contribution to the book series, providing many thought-provoking perspectives on ways of mobilising emergent transdisciplinary participatory practices to explore the nexus between contemporary educational pedagogies and community engagement contexts.

The genesis for this series *Transformative Pedagogies in the Visual Domain* came from The Curators' observing and experiencing how a fertile field of higher educators were strategically creating visual material to ignite both a knowledge transfer and indeed knowledge exchange, between the educator and the student. One of the advantages of working in higher education is the opportunity to observe throughout the various disciplines and modes of delivery, the extraordinary variety of pedagogical practices where visual material is an important primary ingredient for promoting an engaging rich educational environment. For the last few years both Curators have identified examples of best practice within their professional network and created a place to publish where a practitioner can reflect on practice and share examples of best practice to a wider, critical and appreciative international audience. This opportunity creates an ongoing practice of discipline specific practitioners not only exhibiting, researching and creating outcomes within their main focus but also to contribute to the scholarship of pedagogy about how practice and higher level thought is communicated and shaped within a creative learning environment.

During this time the network formed into a Community of Practice that crossed professional disciplinary boundaries, geographical locations, cultural constructs, contemporary and traditional methods, varied research methodologies and theories. This community is corralled within a framework of overlapping territories of higher education, pedagogy and the visual. Taking on the premise of a Community of Practice as Wenger, McDermott and Snyder (2002) argued, where: "Groups of people …share a concern, a set of problems, or a passion about a topic, and …deepen their knowledge and expertise in this area by interacting on an ongoing basis" (p.4). As our network expanded we were able to see naturally forming clusters of knowledge and sufficient depth within the Community of Practice to create this series with eight separate books with each focussing on the visual, higher education and pedagogy within: the environment, Asia region, contemplation, community engagement, innovation and entrepreneurship, innovative learning, work integrated learning and, the embodied.

The legacy of Donald Schön (1983, 1987) pivotal work on the modelling reflective practice and educating the reflective practitioner created scholarly guidelines, that seem to naturally fit with many visual educators as his notion of a purposeful reflective mode resonates with those in the creative industry education sector. Sellars (2012) when commenting on Schön's (1983, 1987) reflective practice model, argued the importance of educators beginning this process by reflecting on their "own individual experiences and perspectives", believing there is a need to "consider these in their contextual variations and draw upon the theoretical, professional strategies that they have encountered or plan to explore" (p.466). This approach permeates throughout the book series where many point of views and theories as well as practices are shared and united under the visionary core idea of recognising the important role visuals play in the communication, engagement as well as 'meaning' of learning.

Through case study examples, theories and personal reflections, authors have provided a visual lens for observing and studying the thought processes and actions of their students, audiences and participators whose lives have been enriched through their unique visions, creative approaches and experiences. With technology bombarding our tertiary learning spaces with its avalanche of visual imagery, there has risen an imperative need to develop multi-modal literacy (Kress & van Leeuwen, 2001) skills to understand the complex ever-evolving interconnected visual world, this series envisages to contribute further knowledge and understanding to this field.

The series of eight books would not have been possible without the dedicated work of sixteen book Editors, who reviewed and then selected 163 authors from all over the globe to contribute their reflections and transformative pedagogical approaches to assist in understanding the visual world. Authors from twenty-one countries and ninety-eight different educational institutions and businesses have contributed to the series their expertise from fields as varied as lyrical prose writing to sports psychology, with educators from health sciences to cultural anthropology and business entrepreneurship.

The global contribution of so many authors and editors, their geographical location and associated institutions offered the opportunity to present visually the numerical and locality data generated by the authorship of this book series. Graphic designers Bernadett Butson and Zeeshan Khan working with the Series' Curators, visually mapped the global reach and the critical mass of the authorship. A graphic language of colour saturation and intensity, organic and mechanical shapes, structuring and focusing lines and the relationship between these elements (influenced by Russian artist Wassily Kandinsky 1866-1944, and his 1923 highly graphical painting, *Circles in a Circle*) present the visual overview seen on the previous page and acts as a basis for the various coloured and cropped versions that are printed on the covers of the eight books.

Current international developments in social data visualisation have identified the need to establish new forms for representing identity in terms of research networks and connectivity. Together with Dr Kim Snepvangers, the Curators have been addressing research questions of the unstable nature of relationships, deliverables, outcomes and impact in the cultural sphere. The graphical visualisation of the eight books in the Curated Series, gives new insights and potentialities to identify questions of local, national and international research strength in the visual, creative arts and humanities comprising the titles and subjects of the eight books. Visualisation is the premise underlying the series and so the significance of the cover design and related design identities is that it seeks to overcome barriers to connectivity and the complex nature of collaboration. Visual adaptation of hotspots, hubs and moments of intensity as a graphical articulation of participatory academic practice, highlights the significance of this Curated Series as a collaboration stepping stone for future research potentialities in the visual domain.

This inclusive series brings together practitioners from all stages of academia from Early Career Researchers to Emeritus Professors, from beginning teachers to retired educators with many years' experience who have come together to contribute their inspirational insights for the *Transformative Pedagogies in the Visual Domain* book series.

References

Kress, G. & Van Leeuwen, T. (2001). *Multimodal discourse.* London: Routledge.

Kucukaydin, I., & D. Cranton, P. (2012). Critically questioning the discourse of transformative learning theory, *Adult Education Quarterly*, 63, 43-56.

Langer, E.J. (1997). The power of mindful learning. Cambridge, MA: Persesus Publishing.

Mezirow, J. (2009). Transformative learning theory. In J. Mezirow & E. W. Taylor (Eds.), *Transformative Learning in Practice: Insights from Community, Workplace, and Higher Education* (pp. 18-32). San Francisco, CA: Jossey

Piantanida, M. & Garman, N. B. (1999). The qualitative dissertation: a guide for students and faculty. London: Sage.

Schon, D.A. (1983). *The Reflective Practitioner*, San Francisco: Jossey-Bass.

———. (1987). *Educating the Reflective Practitioner*, San Francisco: Jossey-Bass.

Sellars, M. (2012). Teachers and change: The role of reflective practice, *Social and Behavioral Sciences*, 55, 461-469.

Seimens, G. (2007). Connectivism: Creating a learning ecology in distributed environments. In Theo Hug (Ed.) *Didactics of Microlearning: Concepts, Discourses and Examples*, (pp. 53-68), Münster: Waxmann.

Staron, M. (2011) Connecting and integrating life based and lifewide learning. In N. J. Jackson (Ed.) *Learning for a Complex World: A lifewide concept of learning, education and personal development* (pp.137-159), Bloomington: Authorhouse.

Wenger, E., McDermott, R. & Snyder, W. M. (2002). *Cultivating communities of practice.* Boston Massachusetts: Harvard Business School Press.

Yanow, D. & Tsoukas, H. (2009). What is reflection-in-action? A phenomenological account, *Journal of Management Studies, 46*(8), 1339-1364.

CHAPTER 1

Transforming Dialogues through Ecologies of Practice in Art, Education and the Cultural Sphere

Kim Snepvangers and Donna Mathewson Mitchell

ABSTRACT

This chapter prefaces some of the key ideas and emergent practices in contemporary community engagement with a focus on 'lived experience' and practice. Kemmis, Edwards-Groves, Wilkinson and Jardy (2012) explore the idea that practices are living things that are interdependent on other practices and connected in 'ecologies of practice.' Kemmis further draws on Schatzki, to show that practices can be seen as orchestrated arrangements that are evident in the projects people pursue. Researching ecologies of practice anticipates the theoretical framework for the chapter by privileging events, networks and relationships. A discussion of how these ideas engage with contemporary art, design and media is illuminated by exemplar projects, research and field-work from the perspective of 'insider-practitioners', as presented within the following chapters in this book. Building on these ideas, we consider how practices, or clusters of transdisciplinary arrangements focused on community engagement prefigure the social world that those involved in projects related to art, education and the cultural sphere engage in. We further examine the implications of this practice framework in terms of participatory practice and research creation methodologies. In this sense we trace the visual terrain, and identify spaces for a re-imagining and a re-orientation of approaches to research and ecologies of practice in community engagement. Case studies of community and educational initiatives, research projects and partnerships that explore the role and place of individual identity within collective social exchange are the focus of this chapter. Re-considering community connectivity is explored using concepts relevant to participation as co-presence with a focus on ecologies of practice. Contingency, chance elements coupled with well-designed 'encounters' conceived as the beginning of new experiences have particular educational and transformative value. Accepting the unforeseen and improbability of outcomes and innovation provides a counterpoint to socially static ways of working with communities. Emergent practices structure the discussion and focus on how interventions and a decentering agenda can act against neoliberal agendas and institutional practices in the visual and performative domain. Exemplars of working "with" rather than "for" a range of diverse communities are disclosed. Localised and contextual practices, highly valued in arts based research co-creation are juxtaposed with international methodologies to reveal new possibilities in transformative pedagogy.

Community, Engagement, and Relations

The relationships between art, artefacts and a range of identified communities within the cultural sphere form a key focus of this book. In addressing the primacy of relationships in the interstice of cultural community engagement, we and the authors in this book, are interested in how the potentialities of new practices, relationships, projects and research approaches which we have termed 'practice encounters" lead to transformation. Following Connolly (2013) the following summary outlines the approach and concept of community that the authors are applying to the cultural sphere. Community engagement when partnered with, for example, educational/cultural agencies, universities, and community based public projects, is perceived to have a strong base in social justice and the process of empowerment. It aims to build the capacity of local people to respond to educational and structural disadvantage and to participate in decision making and policy creation. Other authors (Smith, 2009) describe "education for the community within the community", beyond geographical or place/context conceptions. This sense of building communities, is the process of "working on relationships between members of the community, in order to enhance their lived experience" (Connolly, 2013). Lived experience and an examination of prefiguring processes inform the chapters as they unfold. Examples include projects from formal education contexts, informal education in social networks, public art agencies, companies and community projects, as well as non-formal sites and settings. Aspects of participation are explored that link the individual person with the social and communal understandings of diverse perspectives. In projects and research that foster high levels of participatory co-authoring and presence, connecting ideas with life experience provides a powerful process of political action.

In addition, the scope of the book describes visual and performative 'encounters' with a range of diverse communities by exploring key terms such as engagement, participation and ecologies of practice. From the perspective of the authors of this chapter, two academics engaged in the tertiary education and research sector, community engagement is a term often linked with concepts of social impact which most often involve aspects of measurement. Typically employed by business, government agencies, universities and smaller alliances, associations and social groups, engagement by contrast often refers to contemporary 'requirements' to engage with publics beyond the confines of institutional or organisational boundaries. For example, the recent Federal Department of Education and Training, Australian National Innovation and Science Agenda (NISA) "Engagement and Impact Assessment Consultation Paper" (2015), suggests that in terms of research:

> Engagement describes the interaction between researchers and research organisations and their larger communities/industries for the mutually beneficial exchange of knowledge, understanding and resources in a context

> of partnership and reciprocity (Publicly Funded Research Agencies (PFRA) in Research Engagement for Australia Summary Report, 2015, p.4).

Such examples of principles of partnership, reciprocity and interaction for mutual beneficial exchange are also an attempt to bring the research from universities into the public sphere, supported by a stronger recent theme of 'knowledge exchange' which brings an economic dimension and a demand for dialogic reciprocity to the debate. Beyond mutual benefit, the larger significance of social capital in terms of understanding how educational equity, and mobility of citizens is related to socio-economic factors in taken up by Putnam (2015, 2001, 1993), Yussen et al, (2016) and Cox (1995). Putnam initially outlines some dilemmas of collective action (1993) and suggests enhancing individual social capital through an analogy with physical capital and human capital (p.1). "Putnam makes a compelling argument that the social investments we make on one another (our social capital investments) pay off handsomely for those who receive them and conversely create mighty impediments for those who do not" (Yussen, 2016, p. 465). Putnam's recent 2015 book, continues the theme by comprehensively proposing a range of 'levers' (p. 464) to address inequality, particularly focused on youth/kids and ongoing related issues such as "weak economic growth, a failed democracy with lack of civic engagement, and lack of meeting our moral obligation to fairness in opportunity." The levers detail "inequality on dimensions of family experiences, parenting differences, schooling opportunities, and community resources" (ibid) and are mainly focused on children. Yet, for the purposes of this chapter the section on possible interventions in the community sphere to respond to inequality is of most import. For example, Putnam's suggestions can be broadly understood as strategies to increase community mentors, increase opportunities for extra-curricular activities by eliminating fees that disadvantage the poor, and investing in services for families (Yussen, 2016, p. 464). These ideas also have salience to central questions in this work regarding how inequality and difference in wealth and class 'impact opportunity and social mobility' (ibid).

Community engagement is often a mandated public good, which needs careful articulation and consideration in the context of organised institutions and public agencies. "Unlike conventional capital, social capital is a 'public good' that is not the private property of those who benefit from it" (Putnam, 1993, p.4). Ties, norms and trust are hallmarks with poetic-expression and enjoyment vicariously increasing social fabric and the chapters in this book set out to explore how social capital can be created.

Whist referring to conceptions of community within Nation states, Anderson's (2006) concept of 'Imagined Communities' alerts us to the tensions in assuming that a community pre-exists. When working with students/community, Kallio-Tavin (2014) uses Nancy (1991) to critique the idea of "performative experimental communities" (p. 342) as outlined by Ileris (2013) together with subjectivities traditionally ascribed to art and design educational goals. Kallio-Tavin reminds us of the impossibilities of community when pre-determined goals are in place with "presupposed" (p.343) conceptions of an already existent physical and geographical community. The transient aspects of community are also highlighted by Kallio-Tavin, who signals that "it is more relevant to talk about a *sense* of community than anything that could be thought of as a practicing community" (Kallio-Tavin, 2014, p. 343). Kallio-Tavin also alerts us to the possibilities of 'being' as an aim in working with communities, considering that "art education might not include any presupposition of time, quality, subjectivity or form of art practice in community-based projects" (p.344). Through Kallio-Tavin and the work of Nancy (1991) we aim to interrogate tensions in community based art education projects. For example, a clear tension is when subjectivity aims to be shared and made common to all participants, yet some theorists believe that there is already a fixed view or understanding. What lies beyond this tension in concepts of community is the possibility of relations existing as an ecology, especially "if we sense that they [the words communism or community] carry something completely different than what could be common to those who would belong to a whole, to a group" (Nancy, 1991, p.42). This explanatory device foregrounds relations that have a 'sense' of community without suppositions or predetermined forms of practice.

Social mobility and the significance of developing social networks and connectedness capabilities in the digital age (Bridgstock, 2016) also have high salience within studies of university partnerships and career/workplace communities and pathways. In addition, scholars in business ethics have noted some of the key terms of community engagement with (Bertland, 2011) for example, providing a focus on how "people need to explore all of the ways in which people share with each other rather than just those ways that that advance a narrow set of goals" (p.1). Bertland is interested in the limits of perceived community building in workplace settings providing examples of how to address Jean-Luc Nancy's argument that "the hope of fully unifying a community through work is problematic" (ibid). Bertland concludes that the richness of relationships needs to take primacy over the goal of shared work experiences.

As the title of the book proclaims, within the range of projects and approaches outlined in this book, the contributors have engaged with tensions in seeking to go beyond assumptions of the value of commonalities within community engagement. Ideas about how participation is sought, undertaken and reflected upon as well as the role of tangible artefacts in ecologies of practice is the focus. Given this ecological emphasis and the range and scope of the inquiry the authors do not attempt to also engage important contemporary innovations and new approaches to consultation in community engagement settings, such as the 2016 "Leapfrog Project" in the United Kingdom, and the artist and creative practitioner focus of artist/community/schools engaged in creative partnerships through "The Signature Pedagogy Project" (Thomson et al, 2012). Also, beyond the scope of the book is the politics and approach to impact studies particularly within cultural measurement studies (MacDowell, Badham, Blomkamp & Dunphy, 2015); Community Cultural Development (CCD) and Collective Impact in contemporary Indigenous sites (Woolcock, 2015) or visualisation and affect studies of shared experience that prioritises a visual matrix over discourse (Froggett, Manley & Roy). Another key report, the Warwick Commission Report (2015) from the UK is particularly insightful, although also beyond the scope of the chapters in this book. The report focuses on future value, scalability and the role of cultural and creative industries in securing greater value for the nation of Britain from the cultural and creative sector. Whilst focused on the role of cultural industries in building nationhood, the key headings from the report (Ecosystem, Diversity and Participation, Education and Skills Development and Digital Culture and Making the Local Matter), resonate with the concerns of university and government sectors in thinking about community engagement as a commitment with future value. The report also resonates with the ecological approach (relationships, participation and practice) of the authors. Finally, the following quote from the forward of the report, has a striking similarity with Putnam's social capital approach to inequality and disadvantage noting that:

> The key message from this report is that the government and the Cultural and Creative Industries need to take a united and coherent approach that guarantees equal access for everyone to a rich cultural education and the opportunity to live a creative life. There are barriers and inequalities in Britain today that prevent this from being a universal human right. This is bad for business and bad for society (Vicki Heywood in Neelands, 2015, p. 8).

THE CULTURAL SPHERE

In recent years, there has been a rapidly growing movement of artists, curators and educators choosing to engage with timely issues by expanding their practice beyond the safe confines of the studio and/or the gallery, into the complexity of the unpredictable public sphere. The book brings together fields that are related but often not brought together to address important questions. In doing this it advances site-ontological studies of practice in art, education and cultural studies. The authors are representative of a community of scholars and creative practitioners with a common interest in art, learning and education. In bringing these authors and their ideas together a qualitative social research approach to engaging with participants, artefacts, methodologies and ecological relations is developed that focuses attention on the novel role of "insider-practitioners" (Kemmis, 2012, p.893). The significance of this approach is outlined from a cultural economic perspective by Newsinger & Green (2016) as they note that:

> One important though overlooked element of the significance of cultural value is therefore as a record of the performance of power within the cultural sector, an 'official transcript' that represents dominant discourse of cultural value in opposition to the 'hidden transcripts' that correspond to cultural practitioners. We argue for a research agenda that represents cultural value from practitioners' point of view (Newsinger & Green, 2016, p. 382).

In prefacing the book, this chapter is addressing the potential for transforming dialogues in art, education and the cultural sphere through revealing 'hidden transcripts' that signal intangible cultural value. In our focus on this area, we frame the questions that are explored in the following chapters. In the following section of this chapter, we specifically examine the notion of practice/praxis with respect to art, education and the cultural sphere. We then explore the notion of transformative dialogues and mobility and how they transform diverse communities. As we do this we develop a conceptual framework informed by theories of encounters, encountering and practice to develop a theory of 'practice encounters.' Following this we outline how these overarching themes relate to the chapters in the book and the respective foci of authors, foregrounding their respective contributions.

PRACTICE

In engaging with the concept of practice, we are elaborating on discussions of practice that contribute to what has been termed the "practice turn in contemporary theory" (Schatzki et al., 2001, p. 7). This chapter will consider the implications of a practice-theoretical approach for the theorisation of community engagement and connections between art, education and the cultural sphere. In examining the area of practice and learning, we examine the concept of practice and approaches to the theorisation of practice and then engage specifically with the theories of practice architectures and ecologies of practice as having particular relevance to the ideas explored in this book.

As Hager, Lee and Reich (2012) and Reich and Hager (2014) note, the term practice is often co-located with different domains, where focus is on the domain and the term practice is assumed to be understood. For example, Hager et al (2012) give the examples of yoga practice, teaching practice and legal practice. Practice in relation to learning is likewise collocated in terms such as professional practice, pedagogical practice, vocational practices. Within such terms, practice remains the concept that is assumed and often undefined, is taken for granted and is under-theorised. Given the fundamental importance of practice, the authors argue for the greater attention to theorisation and problematisation of the concept. In thinking through the meaning of the term practice, Kemmis, Heikkinen, Fransson, Aspfors and Edwards-Groves (2014) provide a particularly comprehensive definition of practice as follows:

> We define a practice as a form of socially established cooperative human activity that involves characteristic forms of understanding (sayings), modes of action (doings), and ways in which people relate to one another and the world (relatings), that 'hang together' in a distinctive project. …The project of a practice encompasses (a) the intention (aim) that motivates the practice, (b) the actions (sayings, doings and relatings) undertaken in the conduct of the practice, and (c) the ends the actor aims to achieve through the practice (although it might turn out that these ends are not attained) (2014, p. 155–156).

In examining how the concept of practice is theorised within practice theory, Hager, Lee and Reich (2012) suggest 5 principles are evident:

1. Practices are knowing-in-practice
2. Practices are socio-material
3. Practices are embodied and relational
4. Practices exist and evolve in historical and social contexts
5. Practices are emergent

Reich and Hager (2014) note that these principles are drawn from research and theorisation within practice theory and identify them as common threads in the theorising of professional practice. In doing this they look across the work of prominent practice theorists including Schatzki (2012, 2006, 2002), Gherardi (2012, 2009) and Reckwitz (2002) as well as researchers who have applied these theories to areas such as professional practice (Green, 2009; Kemmis, 2005) and workplace learning (Fenwick, 2009). In developing their framework, they add one additional principle by splitting principle 3 to consider embodied and relational as separate threads explored in literature.

Common to the theorisations of practice explored briefly above, is a conception of practice as not being linear. Practice is noted as encompassing dynamic interconnections and interplays that relate to how practices emerge, are stabilised, are maintained and sustained and how they change in response to social change. However, the authors also note that practice theorisations differ in terms of how they consider change in relation to practice. On one hand, Hager et al (2012, p.10) note that there are theories that emphasize the relationship between practice, learning and change, asserting that in specific times, spaces and circumstances, all practice is emergent and involves change. Learning is thus seen as commensurate with change as it involves activity, movement and difference. However, other theorists, such as Schatzki argue that activities happen and that happenings are not equivalent to change. Therefore, the performance of an action does not necessarily lead to change and can in fact act to maintain. Many contemporary practice researchers have continued to attempt to understand this issue of the dynamics of practice change. Kemmis (2009) for example, argues that "changing practices requires changing things frequently beyond the knowledge or control of individual practitioners, and frequently outside the individual practitioner's field of vision" (2009, p. 38).

Importantly there is an acknowledgement that practices are not entirely intentional and do not exist in the action of individual human beings. Kemmis (2005) explains them as shaped by 'extra-individual' arrangements that can exist beyond the intentional actions of human beings. These arrangements shape practices and can be shaped by practices. Schatzki calls these 'practice arrangement bundles.' Drawing on these ideas, Kemmis, Wilkinson, Edwards-Groves, Hardy, Grootenboer and Bristol (2014) argue that the intersubjective spaces where people encounter one another are always shaped by the practice arrangements that already exist. The authors argue that these intersubjective spaces exist in shared language (cultural-discursive), in space-time in the material world (material-economic) and in social relationships (social-political). These intersubjective spaces are termed practice architectures. According to the theory of practice architectures, to understand particular kinds of practices, we must understand how they are enmeshed with the particular kinds of arrangements (cultural-discursive, material-economic, social-political) that make them possible. Thus, practice architectures offer an analytical resource to view and understand practices in terms of the languages, activities and resources and relationships involved. Importantly, particular practices are enmeshed with particular practice architectures and practice can be enabled by particular kinds of practice architectures.

Extending from the concept of practice architectures, Kemmis et al (2014) have also developed a theory of ecologies of practice. This theory recognises that practices are connected ecologically and impact on one another, through practice-changing, by constraining or enabling. As Edwards-Groves and Kemmis (2016, p.90) note: The notion of ecologies of practices provides a framework for understanding how education is locally constituted in sites, not only in a physical or geographical sense but also as nexuses of intersubjective spaces – semantic space, physical space–time and social space – that are always entwined with one another and enmeshed with arrangements to be found at (or brought to) the site in which they exist, in site-specific ways. Thus, different, lived and living practices sometimes form relationships of interdependence with one another in ecologies of practices, nudging against one another as they unfold (not always harmoniously, and not always in relation to all of the others.

Nick Hopwood (2014) uses practice theory to understand practice as related to child and family health. His approach has much to offer in his examination of Schatzki's (2003) site ontology and Kemmis' practice architectures and ecologies, within a sociomaterial approach. It provides a way to think about new accountabilities as they come into being in specific instances through practices bundled with material arrangements. Hopwood argues that partnership can be understood as a particular form of coproduction. He states that: "Coproduction highlights particular kinds of relationships between professionals and service users, such that practice is not done by professionals on or for others, but is jointly produced. Arguably professional practices are always coproduced in some way" (p.2). Drawing on Schatzki (2003), Hopwood observes that individuals perform practices but their organisation and prefiguring is a matter of social practice, thus the actions of individuals relate to wider processes and arrangements. Relationships between practices and material arrangements (humans, artefacts, organisms and things) are elaborated as bundles: practices respond and react to material states of affairs or changes in them.

Drawing on Kemmis' (2009) and Kemmis et al (2012) practice architectures and ecologies of practice, Hopwood discusses the idea that practices are not only interconnected, but that these connections shape responsive adaptations and evolutions, just as living things co-exist and respond to each other. He notes that Kemmis returns to the idea of the site: practices arise in relation to one another in a particular site, and their interdependence is to a large extent site-specific. He further uses these ideas as a way to consider what Nicolini (2009, 2012) refers to as "zooming out" —understanding specific events as instantiations and parts of wider sociomaterial assemblages. Nicolini (2012, 2009) argues that to understand practices we need to both "zoom in" and focus on particular instances at a local level, and "zoom out" to understand ways that practices are always inevitably shaped by other practices with which they "hang together" (Schatzki 1996, 2002).

Practice architectures and ecologies of practice are particularly helpful in clarifying and extending the work of "zooming in" and "zooming out" (Nicolini, 2009, 2012). The chapters in this book can be seen as articulations of partnership-based approaches to art, education and culture that are co-produced. The projects, partnerships and instances examined in the chapters are located in practice architectures, comprising material-economic, cultural discursive and socio-political dimensions. The nature of practices in each case are defined by and expressed through the doings, sayings and relatings that occur at any particular site and in relation to the specific practice architectures with national or international connectivity. The examples in the chapters can be understood as part of ecologies of practices, where relations of interdependence shape responses and adaptations. Through accounts of practice, the authors have elucidated features of professional knowing, epistemic and relational work in partnership-based professional practices, in relation to aspects of transformation and mobility. The significance of the mobility of ideas in developing social mobility as well as mobilities in a traditional sense of transportation, travel and cultural movement as experience is highlighted by Cresswell (2013, 2010). Creswell is a well-known author in human geography and mobility studies, yet in his latest research he suggests that:

> Most mobilities research to date has focused on the movements of people and things and the relation between them. ... There is also a clear sense of the role of mobility in the production of social hierarchies. Other areas are less well developed. The 'new mobilities paradigm' has been promoted as an integrated approach to the mobility of people, things and ideas across all scales. The last developed of these has been the mobility of ideas (Cresswell, 2012, p. 651).

Significantly, the authors and contributors to this book describe methods and practices (sayings, doings and relatings) that prefigure how participants and examples access ideas. The social mobility of participants in, through and with each project and approach is a key concern of each author. For example, within the chapters we gain insight into: the mobile seafarers who visit Melbourne's Mission to Seafarers; social media and art/museum professional in the Galleries, Libraries, Archives and Museum (GLAM) sector; "little publics' in Gallery Sunshine Everywhere, Lucien Henry the first Instructor in the Department of Art at Sydney Technical College and exhibitions that travel from Australia across the world to share ideas in Venice. What is significant are the ways in which these participants move from an initial encounter towards the possibility of transformation and efficacy in a specific site ontology of ideas for mobility.

Transformative Practice

Prefiguring possibilities that anticipate transformative practice is at the heart of this book, ricocheting across art, design and media projects in the context of educational interventions focused on the cultural sphere. Transformation and the transformative practice of individuals and groups is a key component of both artistic and educational discourses and in this book we make manifest interdisciplinary practices that respond to diverse subjective and intersubjective experiential spaces (Kemmis, 2012). Following Kemmis (2012) we argue that a focus on practice as research through lived experience described as the "living practice of education" (p.893) is a priority in community engagement projects. Privileging this aspect of research practice in the cultural sphere 'recognises, reflects, respects and engages with their [practitioner] *interpretive categories*, their *lived realities*, and their *experience* (ibid). As Kemmis, (2012, p.893) notes, "The 'practice' which is the object of detached observation, the one seen only by the spectator, is not the same 'practice' that the insider-practitioner sees." The authors and practitioners in this book contribute both novice and expert experiences, working in an array of artworld agencies, units and roles across the tertiary academy and in gallery/community settings to enable participant engagement with knowledge and mentors in situ. The contribution of the book with regard to the "beyondness" of community engagement invokes ecological understandings of educational, conversational and dialogic spaces for example in university courses, regional arts development projects and exhibitions within hubs, collectives, and makerspaces. Rather than a traditional or "spectator" research perspective, which "like a naturalist's interest in observing the behaviour or practices in relation to one another – it aims to show that practices are inside the sites in which they are situated, and that practitioners, too, are inside these sites" (Kemmis, 2012, p.890), the ecological perspective aims to provide insight into site ontologies through the perspective of the practitioner – the *insider* in those sites.

The insider-practitioners contributing to this discourse include academics, artsworkers, public program managers and consultants who interweave their research, curatorial and teaching methodologies with the experiential transformational potential of particular, situated learning sites. The insider-practitioners focus on diverse participants, the role of artefacts and both static and mobile "site ontologies" (Kemmis, 2012). Creating co-presences and co-authoring (Cornwall, 2008; Literat, 2012) with a focus on both traditional representational practices and forms of non-representational experience discloses the depth of wisdom required of creative and culturally attuned practitioners. The primacy of building community relationships and shared connectivity in the design and co-production of projects and experiences is gradually revealed as types of engagement. The focus is on the sustainability of ideas rather than ongoing formation of social/community groups.

This chapter's interest in diverse, often overlooked or disenfranchised communities extends concepts of transformation beyond cognitive individual achievement in educational contexts through methodologies of dialogue, assemblage, meshing, interweaving and entanglement. For example, a focus on individual empowerment is the focus of Mezirow's (1998) description of how critical self-reflection is a necessary process of transformative teaching where "learning to think for oneself involves becoming critically reflective of assumptions and participating in discourse to validate beliefs, intentions, values and feelings" (p. 197). Transformative learning for Mezirow aligns well with Kemmis et al's (2012) description of "practice architectures" as "elaborating existing frames of reference, learning new frames of reference, transforming habits of mind, and transforming points of view" (Mezirow in Kitchenham, 2008, p. 118).

Self-reflection is utilised in many of the projects described within this book, as a necessary component of community engagement, including the self-reflection of individual insider-practitioners in relation to professional gallery/public arts/exhibition and museum programs. Through consideration of experience, histories and reception of ideas by audiences and participant groups new frames of reference and the personal, professional and contextual factors that contribute to conceptions of transformation within the learner are represented. Adding to the literature on transformation in educational contexts, Arnold and Ryan (2003) define transformative experiences as "those, which occur with sufficient emotional intensity to be meaningful, and with sufficient cognitive patterning to organize thinking and learning in deeply significant ways" (p. 5). Transformative experiences are characterised by four factors:

1. Quality of engagement with knowledge;
2. The deepening of teachers' functions, especially as learning mentors;
3. Enhanced capacity for imagination, innovation and creativity;
4. The primacy of relationships as part of the transformative capacity of new learning (Arnold & Ryan, 2003, p. 5).

As markers of transformation, these four concepts are helpful in the context of developing capacity for new learning as they provide a narrative structure to investigate existent qualities of community orientated projects and research methodologies. They are characteristics that are discussed throughout the chapters as the authors examine how their various projects: engage with knowledge formation; deepen understandings of pedagogical practice, engage with creativity and create space for imaginative and emergent experiences; and foreground relationships. Many of the approaches discussed in the ensuing chapters, juxtapose the transformative potential of visually conceived projects, with understandings of artefacts and knowledge/content as an ecological system to anticipate enhanced capacities for innovation in the cultural sphere. Emotional intensity is another quality identified by Arnold and Ryan (2003) as being a contributing factor in eliciting personal change. While not foregrounded in the exemplars in this book, emotions are components of the experiences evident through references to challenge, intensity, disappointment, joy experienced before, during and after the projects undertaken, as transformational change occurs. It is further evident in the examples of the work of artists, designers and media practitioners used throughout the book as they combine material and conceptual ideas in new and innovative ways.

This focus on individual learning capacity within systems of learning and teaching is important to note at this stage. Whilst acknowledging the need to understand the transformative capacity of learning, authors such as Connell (2013) provide a succinct discussion of an increasingly homogenised market agenda in education. Anticipating a need for re-invention, Connell suggests coalitions of social groups and the creation of spaces for educational invention and experimental forms of inquiry across both formal and informal educational sites. In many ways the examples provided in this book evidence transformational actions that counter restrictions imposed by external factors, presenting pedagogical projects that embrace emergence. As Atkinson says, "my purpose here is to argue for an educational project that prioritises an immanence of learning which is not controlled or constrained by established knowledge of practice" (p. 8). Atkinson (2015) clearly positions learning in a space of becoming, linked to creating and extending what already exists. Entanglement and ecologies of truthfulness are connected in many ways in this book actively concerned with "puncturing assimilated ways of knowing, thinking and doing and the emergence of a new or reconfigured world for the learner" (Atkinson, 2015, p.1).

Practice Encounters

Encounter is a key term in this research implying a range of practices, phenomenon and ideas. As described by Snepvangers and Bulger (2016) "an encounter can mean coming up against something, perhaps through serendipity or as a considered response and either with an agreeable or conflicting set of engagements or outcomes." So far the authors have been referring to the concept of 'prefiguring' community engagement. It is in the context of developing a sense of encountering and "practice encounters" that we wish to use the term prefiguring. Rather than having a preconceived of fixed notion of formation of a specific community or planning using a predetermined set of goals or pre-specified engagements we use the term encounter to set up a theoretical emphasis on how engaging individuals liminally eventuates. Meyer and Land characterise liminality as a "liquid space, simultaneously transforming and being transformed by the learner as he or she moves through it" (Meyer & Land, 2005, in Land, Rattray & Vivien, 2014, p.201). Typically, liminal spaces engage troublesome and contested domains, which is an approach well suited to many of the projects and communities described in the following chapters. We argue, using a similar approach to Meyer and Land's work in learning and teaching contexts, that a liminal approach to working with communities will significantly enhance both the "insider-practitioners'" and participants' loci of control. The insider-practitioner's choice of content, use of artefacts and forms of engagement act as "conceptual gateways" (Meyer & Land, 2005 in Land, Rattray & Vivien 2014, p.200) and "transformative" portals of experiences in working with participants. The authors suggest that fluid states of liminality, suspending goal driven accounts and making artefacts in new and fluidly formed ecologies, create possibilities to "re-author" forms of beliefs and practices (Ross, 2011, in Land, Rattray & Vivien, 2014, p.201).

Many of the projects and approaches discussed in future chapters are about ideas that involve possibilities of environmental or "worldly sensibilities", rather than human 'agent-centred perception" (Hansen, 2015, p.5). Hansen's focus is on how environments, contexts and the "operational present of sensibility" (p.6) gives unprecedented "access to events outside the scope of our conscious attention and perception." Human and non-human agency therefore are not distinct, rather they "exist as dimensions of a larger production of a complex environmental process" (p.9). Although Hansen is interested in media networks, this way of conceiving content as environmental complexity and sensibility is also salient when thinking about the interrelatedness of community engagement.

The term "encounter" and "encountering" have been used recently to address neo-liberal "human capital" agendas (Connell, 2013). For Connell, "the creative development of social practice through time" (p.104) combined with the concept of encounter, act a counterpoint to stable conceptions of social reproduction, that in many educational settings can mean lack of action, complacency or despair. For Connell, an emphasis on 'encounter' as intervention and interruption acts as a counterpoint to bland versions of transformation conceived as a social process. Significantly Connell recognises nurturing and "encounter(s) between persons ... involves care" (p.104) as well as complexity, all of which are salient features of many of the chapters involving projects and participants. Encounter has the following qualities:

- people capable of encounter, with autonomy to explore power relations for diagnosis and contestation;
- mutual respect, reciprocity and engagement as a condition of complex communication and complex learning;
- equality or citizenship in educational situations conceived as *social labour* through trust building, (which is easily damaged);
- multiple numbers, structures and diversity of people involved in shaping educational relationships (class, gender, race, regions) as an inclusive practice;
- calibrated to reality, not denying an encounter by omission or need;
- cognitive intellectual excitement, learning through discovery and engagement with truth. (Connell, 2013, p. 104-105).

These qualities of encounter, particularly exploration of care, respect, reciprocity, trust, the capacity to shape relationships, discovery and engagement, link well to the 5 principles of practice already identified by Hager, Lee and Reich (2012). Linking encounter with practice brings together the significance of socially derived coalitions with principles of relational emergence. For example, Hager et al identified qualities of practice as knowing-in-practice, socio-material, embodied and relational, evolving in historical and social contexts and having emergent qualities. Thus far we have provided a set of theoretical resources for thinking about the following chapters of this book. We have examined the concepts of community, engagement and relations to consider ecological understandings and to move beyond some traditional assumptions about community engagement. In doing this we have engaged with notions of trans-disciplinarity, advancing site-ontological studies of art, education and the cultural sphere. We have taken a practice-theoretical approach to further theorise community engagement by meshing practice architectures, ecologies of practice and the concept of encounter. These theoretical insights provide a research approach with the potentiality to examine the affordance and constraints of sayings, doings and relatings. Further to this we have conceptualized transformation and transformational learning in relation to change.

As we have engaged in this thinking, we have spoken of 'practice encounters.' While the term practice encounters is most often used in relation to medicine, we are applying it here to refer to engagement with practice in terms of the lived experience. Practice encounters encompasses visual, verbal and performative engagement and various levels and degrees of participation. They are situated in practice architectures and ecologies of practice that inform actions and response. The activities, experiences and ideas that are evidenced in the research, projects, case studies of teaching and learning, exhibitions and artworks, discussed in the coming chapters provide examples of rich and diverse practice encounters. In the following section of this chapter we provide a necessarily brief summary of the contribution of each of those chapters.

Research Approach to Community Engagement

The following research approaches to community engagement entail aspects of ecologies of practice as a suite of prefigured encounters within the cultural sphere. In Chapter 2, Margaret Woodward provides a fascinating insight into the transformative possibilities of a project titled *The Sea is all Around Us.* This project focused on the global and mobile community of seafarers, using a souvenir as a vehicle of welcome and connection. This souvenir, an aesthetic object integrates a QR code, effectively utilising technologies in ways that allow for the tracking of the souvenir as well as the tracking of the movement of the respective seafarer. Initiated through a performative installation, the project continues to trace the life of seafarers on a dedicated website that reveals the ways in which relational objects can hold and carry meaning and forge connections between people and place. This project illustrates a creative research approach that incorporated local/global mobility and connectivity, drawing, installation, design, interaction, writing and mobile technology within an interdisciplinary theoretical framework. The framework is informed by cultural geography and tourism and the work of theorists such as Appadurai (1986), Gibson (2014), MacCannell (1976) & Ramsey (2009), allow an examination of how a designed artefact can activate social networks crossing geographic boundaries.

In Chapter 3, Narelle Lemon explores how social media has and is transforming communication, connections and social engagement with a particular focus on practice in the GLAM sector. Drawing on data gathered through an ongoing digital ethnography project, #MuseumEdOz, Lemon examines this as an online community uniting teachers, museum educators and cultural organisations, in Australia and internationally. Her discussion of digital interaction is framed by Ingold's (2015) notion of lines, intersections and meshworks. Data is explored through the entanglement of digital becoming, visibility and connecting and reciprocity. As such issues of emergent participatory cultures, collaborative problem solving and empowered citizenship are examined (Trembacj & Deng, 2015).

In Chapter 4, Jayson Cooper and Maureen Ryan use the example of Gallery Sunshine Everywhere, located in the western suburbs of Melbourne to examine how 'little publics' (Hickey-Moody, 2014) speak with and to larger public identities enabling a shared dialogue. They examine aesthetic reasoning (Juncker, 2012) as an everyday practice, suggesting that little and big publics meet at the intersection- the contact zone- of little and big aesthetics. Relational interactions between youth and adults are enabled through the structures of GSE that frame the transformative components of visual arts experiences. Examples of such transformative experiences are provided and illustrated through artworks and discussion of a collaborative public pedagogy (Savage, 2014; Springgay & The Torontians, 2014) and an ethics of care (Noddings, 2015).

In Chapter 5, Angela Giovanangeli examines Lucien Henry, a French artist, convicted of treason, and banished to the penal colony of New Caledonia, ending up in Australia after being granted a pardon. As the first Instructor in the Department of Art at Sydney Technical College Henry's teachings and decorative work mirrored revolutionary ideas evidenced in France in the second half of the 19th century. Using a transcultural framework informed by Pratt (1992) and Ray (2012) Giovanangeli suggests that this historical case study illustrates how the relationship between community engagement, art and education can be associated with the cultural flow of ideas. Her examination clearly shows the significance of Henry's work and how his pedagogical work changed the ways that Australians understood and represented national and local identity.

In Chapter 6, John Rae investigates Sandvik's (2012) notion of 'assemblage' drawing on the theoretical resources of Deleuze and Guattari (1987) to examine how it can inform arts-based research. He explores connections between artist, researcher, artwork and material aspects of the research context as assemblages. Two cases are presented as illustrations of how artworks were used within research to facilitate deep thinking and to further research conversations. The arts-based assemblage approach is proposed as generating insight and creating new ways of knowing that cross boundaries between art, research, higher education and health care.

In Chapter 7, Gregory Turner-Rahman provides a description of project work as a type of abductive visual reasoning that facilitates student-directed investigations of interwoven theories and topics. In the context of a visual studies course he examines how analysis, evaluation and critique can be used in relation to science, technology, medicine, art and design. In the case presented students mapped the domain of the visual in medical technologies from the 1700s to the late 1900s informed by the theories of Foucault (1973) and conceptual and artistic representations of the body. This study culminated in creative projects that reveal a deeper discourse and higher order thinking about medicine, disease and health. They further reveal the use of abductive visual reasoning, as outlined by Peirce (1958) as a creative form of discovery in which material artifacts are manipulated and representations are cognitive strategies in learning.

In Chapter 8, Jamie-Lea Hodges and Eleanor Venables provide a fascinating insight into a contemporary art installation titled *Connective Understanding* which was co-created in Indigenous communities in regional and rural Australia and exhibited at the 2015 Venice Biennale. The discussion addresses the materiality of the work in terms of ancient string making methods to create collaborative weaving. The cultural knowledge, ecological embeddedness and ethnobotanical understandings underpinning the development of the artwork are examined and documented both verbally and visually in the chapter. The chapter illuminates the transformative role of arts workers and communities and the role of public exhibitions in providing facilitation and sites for presenting alternative realities of human experience and the landscape to geographically diverse international audiences. It draws on the theories of new materialism, (Barrett & Bolt, 2013), understandings of community development (Kay, 2000; McGonagle, 2007) and Indigenous learning ecologies, (Snepvangers and Allas, 2013) to examine the nature of materialism, the role of the artefact and the relationship between knowledge, production and habitation.

In Chapter 9, Jo Higgins and Sarah Coffils provide an examination of collaboration, cooperation, agency and outcomes as explored in education partnership projects located in the UK and Australia. They examine the Louis Vuitton Young Arts Project (LVYAP) that involved Londoners aged 13-25, bringing together five of the city's most recognisable art institutions over a period of years and ending in 2013. This partnership is related to the Regional Youth Engagement program that was part of the Kaldor Public Art Project in 2015. This was a 12-week program involving the Western Plains Cultural Centre (WPCC) in Dubbo, in New South Wales, Australia. Both authors were involved in these programs, providing an insider-perspective to reflect on the experience. They provide excerpts from a conversation about these programs with a focus on collaboration, cooperation, agency and outcomes. This is supported by data gathered from those involved in these projects, providing insights into the challenges and opportunities involved in working with youth and in partnership.

In Chapter 10, Marty Otanez and James Walsh present an approach to teaching at university level using digital storytelling and organic theatre. Both are collective processes where individuals build on experiences to explore ideas through storytelling. In discussing approaches to the application of digital storytelling and organic theatre, the authors present cases from their respective experiences to show how they facilitate peer-to-peer teaching and contribute to a culture of trans disciplinary scholarship.

In Chapter 11, Michael Kempson uses an analytical framework of distributed leadership (MacBeath, 2004) to examine the activities of Cicada Press, a research group at the University of New South Wales, Art and Design. Cicada Press began as a pedagogical experiment involving artists in an educative relationship with students engaging with their creative process and in doing so, developing a creative partnership. Artist, student and course lecturer play integral roles in producing research outcomes. The printed artwork that is generated in this relationship facilitates further engagement with diverse artists and projects that explore a range of transdisciplinary issues and enables local and international curatorial collaborations for the exhibition of artworks. This process results in a rich series of collaborations, partnerships and community building networks focused on the visual that extend beyond the university classrooms and workshops, reinforcing the importance of experience in learning. The chapter highlights the intuitive alignment of educational philosophies and instructional methods with the distributed leadership model and provides an overview of the various forms this takes as is empowers creative leaders of the future.

In Chapter 12, Gabrielle Mordy explores issues related to disability in the arts sector and identifies a range of obstacles faced by artists with disabilities. She further examines policy initiatives and research that demonstrates a community focus on inclusion and creating access to the creative sector and employment pathways through education, training and mentoring. Mordy goes on to examine the supported studio model as one solution to problems of access and representation. Such studios offer adults with disabilities the opportunity to explore and develop their skills and provide professional pathways. In addition, they provide the opportunity to work with professional artists who act as mentors and facilitators. The role of supported studios and aspects their work are explored through the examples of Studio A in Sydney, Australia and Creative Growth in San Francisco, USA. Success stories are examined as cases that illustrate the power of supported studios as drivers of change, enabling artists with disabilities to develop their talent and have their work seen by audiences, and ultimately connecting people, changing perceptions and transforming lives.

In Chapter 13, Lisa Hochtritt discusses the experiences of ten graduate students and the teacher of a public pedagogy course in art and visual culture. Centred on a collaborative experience with a non-profit local maker and hacker community space, students engaged with research in self-directed ways in a student-centred approach to learning. The approach was informed by theory and research in relation to public pedagogy (Sandlin, Schultz and Burdick, 2010) and a learner-centred framework drawing on Weimer (2013). The site of the curriculum experience is significant given the increasing importance of makerspaces, (Dougherty, 2012; Rosenfeld, Halverson & Sheridan, 2014) as contemporary community sites of public pedagogy. Personal learning vignettes capture the voices and contemplative thoughts of students and the challenges they faced as they directed their own learning. Accounts indicate the nature of collaboration and explore feelings of unease encountered during the process. The importance of practice-based projects, student driven decision making and learner-centred teaching in universities is highlighted in this example. In addition, it highlights the importance of moving beyond classroom walls as designated spaces of inquiry to embrace exciting learning communities.

Final Remarks

This chapter has examined the diversity of factors that the authors of this chapter and insider-practitioners perceive as transformational. The contribution of this chapter extends such individual transformational experiences to include representational and non-representational dialogic methodologies described by Kemmis as living systems as "ecologies of practice." The cognitive dimensions of practice have encompassed principles of ecology as networks, nested systems, interdependence, diversity, cycles, flows, development and dynamic balance. Moving beyond subjective individual experience signals a wordly sensibility and an interest in developing connectedness capabilities to enable not just the transformation of people and things but the mobility of ideas (Cresswell, 2012). The mobility of ideas explained in each of the following chapter signals emergent, yet significant practices without a necessarily fixed goal in mind. Encountering is suggested as a serendipitous yet, well connected approach to how communities engage. The theoretical concept of "practice encounters" has been introduced as a transformational way to connect learning through lived experience in communities of engagement across diverse participants and populations not traditionally perceived as connected.

REFERENCES

Anderson, B. (2006). *Imagined communities: Reflections on the origin and spread of nationalism*. Revised Edition. Verso: London.

Arnold, R., & Ryan, M. (2003). *The transformative capacity of new learning*. Discussion Paper, Australian Council of Deans of Education (ACDE).

Atkinson, D. (2015). The blindness of education to the "untimeliness" of real learning. J. Burke Symposium. Retrieved: http://freepdfs.net/the-blindness-of-education-to-the-untimeliness-of-real-learning/bbffe51ef16608f88cb10e5573379b35/

A Summary to the Australian Academy of Technology and Engineering (ATSE) Report Research Engagement for Australia (REA) (2015). Australian Academy of Technology and Engineering.

Australian National Innovation and Science Agenda (NISA) (2015). *Engagement and Impact Assessment Consultation Paper*. Federal Department of Education and Training.

Bertland, A. (2011). The limits of workplace community: Jean-Luc Nancy and the possibility of teambuilding. *Business Ethics, 99*(1), 1-8.

Bridgstock, R. (2016). *Graduate Employability 2.0: Social networks for learning, career development and innovation in the digital age*. Paper for Discussion. GE2.0.

Connell, R. (2103). The neoliberal cascade and education: an essay on the market agenda and its consequences. Critical Studies in Education, *54*(2), 99-112.

Connolly, B. (2010). Community Based Education in *Community Based Adult Education: International Encyclopaedia of Education 3rd Edition.* Peterson, Penelope; Baker, Eva; & McGaw, Barry. [Eds] Elsevier UK, 120-126.

Cornwall, A. (2008). Unpacking 'Participation': Models, Meanings and Practices. *Community Development Journal*, *43*(3) July, Oxford University Press, 269–283.

Cox, E. (1995). The dark side of the warm inner glow: Family and Communitarians. Chapter 3 in *A Truly Civil Society*. 1995 Boyer Lectures. ABC: Sydney.

Cresswell, T. (2010). Towards a politics of mobility. *Progress in Human Geography, 36*(5), 645-653. Sage.

———. (2012). Mobilities 11: Still. Environment and Planning D: Society and Space, 28, 17-31.

Edwards-Groves, C. and Kemmis, S (2016). Pedagogy, education and praxis: Understanding intersubjectivity through action research and practice theory. *Educational Action Research, 24*(1), 77-96.

Fenwick, T. (2006). Work, learning and education in the new economy: A working class perspective. *Curriculum Inquiry, 36*(4), 453-466.

Froggett, L., Manley, J., & Roy, A. (2015). The Visual Matrix method: Imagery and affect in a group-based research setting. *Forum: Qualitative Social Research, 16*(3). Retrieved: http://www.qualitative-research.net/index.php/fqs/article/view/2308

Gherardi, S. (2009). Knowing and learning in practice-based studies: An introduction. *The Learning Organization, 16*(5), 352-359.

Green, B. (2009). *Understanding and researching professional practice*. Rotterdam: Sense Publishers.

Hager, P., Lee, A., & Reich, A. (2012), *Practice, learning and change: Practice-theory perspectives on professional learning*. Dordecht: Springer.

Hansen, M. (2015). Feed-Forward: On the future of twenty-first century media. The University of Chicago Press: Chicago.

Hopwood, N. (2014) A Sociomaterial Account of Partnership, Signatures and Accountability in Practice. *Professions and Professionalism*, *4*(2), 1-14.

Illeris, H. (2013). Potentials of togetherness: Beyond individualism and community in Nordic art education. *Studies in Art Education, 55*(1), 79-83.

Kallio-Tavin, M. (2014). Impossible practice and theories of the impossible: A response to Helene Illeris's "Potentials of Togetherness." *Studies in Art Education, 55*(4), 342-344.

Kemmis, S. (2012). Researching educational praxis: spectator and participant perspectives. *British Educational Research Journal*, *38*(6), 885-905. British Educational Research Association, Routledge Taylor & Francis Group.

———. (2005). Knowing practice: Searching for saliences. *Pedagogy, culture & society, 13*(3).

———. (2009). Understanding professional practice: A synoptic framework. Chapter 2 (pp.19-38) in B. Green (Ed.). *Understanding and researching professional practice.* Rotterdam: Sense Publishers.

———. (2012). Ecologies of practice (Chapter 3, p.33-49), in Lee, A., Hager, P., & Reich, A. Practice, learning and change. Netherlands: Springer.

Kemmis, S., Edwards Groves, C., Wilkinson, J. & Hardy, I. (2012). Ecologies of practices: Learning practices. In P. Hager, A. Lee & A. Reich (Eds.). *Practice, learning and change*. London: Springer.

Kemmis, S., Wilkinson, J., Edwards-Groves, C., Hardy, I., Grootenboer, P. & Bristol, L. (2014). *Changing practices, Changing Education*. Singapore: Springer.

Land, R., Rattray, J., & Vivien, P. (2014). Learning in liminal space: as semiotic approach to threshold concepts. *Higher Education*, *67*, 199-217.

Leapfrog: Transforming public sector engagement by design (2016). Lancaster University. Retrieved:http://imagination.lancs.ac.uk/activities/Leapfrog_transforming_public _sector_engagement_design

Literat, I. (2012). The Work of Art in The Age of Mediated Participation: Crowdsourced Art and Collective Creativity. *International Journal of Communication*, *6*, 2962–2984.

MacDowell, L., Badham, M., Blomkamp, E., & Dunphy, K. [eds] (2015). *Making culture count: The politics of cultural measurement.* New Directions in Cultural Policy Research. Basingstoke, UK: Palgrave.

Meyer, J. & Land, R. (2003). Threshold concepts and troublesome knowledge: Linkages to ways of thinking within the disciplines. *Occasional Report*, 4 May. Universities of Edinburgh, Coventry and Durham.

Nancy, J. (1991). *The Inoperative Community*. Edited by Peter Connor. Theory and History of Literature, Volume 76. University of Minnesota Press: Minneapolis.

Neelands, J., Belfiore, E., Firth, C., Hart, N., Perrin, L., Brock, S., Holdaway, D., & Woddis, J. (2015). *Enriching Britain: Culture, Creativity and Growth*. The 2015 Report by the Warwick Commission on the Future of Cultural Value. The University of Warwick: The Warwick Commission, UK.

Newsinger, J., & Green, W. (2016). The infrapolitics of cultural value: cultural policy, evaluation and the marginalisation of practitioner perspectives. *Journal of Cultural Economy*, *9*(4), 382-395.

Nicolini, D. (2009). Zooming in and out: studying practices by switching lenses and trailing connections. *Organization Studies*, *30*(12), 1391-1418.

———. (2012). *Practice theory, work and organization: An introduction*. Oxford: Oxford University Press.

Putnam, R. D. (2015). *Our kids: The American Dream in crisis.* Simon & Shuster: New York, NY.

———. (2001). *Bowling alone: The collapse and revival of American community*. Simon & Shuster: New York, NY.

———. (1993). The prosperous community. *The American Prospect*, March 21, *4*(13), 1-11.

Reckwitz, A. (2002). Towards a theory of social practice: A development if cultural theorizing. *European Journal of Social Theory,* 5(2), 243-263.

Reich, A. and Hager, P. (2014). Problematising practice, learning and change: Practice-theory perspectives on professional learning, *Journal of Workplace Learning, 26*(6/7), 418-431.

Rourke, A., & Snepvangers, K. (2016). Ecologies of practice in tertiary art and design: a review of two cases. *Higher Education, Skills and Work-Based Learning*, *6*(1), 69-85.

Schatzki, T. (1996). *Social practices: A Wittgensteinian approach to human activity and the social.* Cambridge/New York: Cambridge University Press.

———. (2002). *The site of the social: A philosophical account of the constitution of social life and change*, Pennsylvania: Pennsylvania State University Press.

———. (2003). A new societist social ontology. *Philosophy of the Social Sciences*, *33*(2).

Smith, M. K. (2009). Community Education. Retrieved http://www.infed.org/community/b-comed.htm

Snepvangers, K., & Bulger, J. (2016). Learning in liminal spaces: Encountering Indigenous Knowledge and artworks in professional education. *fusion Special Issue - Professional education in the e-learning world: Scholarship, practice and digital technologies*. Issue 8. Published by Charles Sturt University. Retrieved: http://www.fusion-journal.com/learning-in-liminal-spaces-encountering-indigenous-knowledge-and-artworks-in-professional-education/

Thomson, P., Hall, C., Jones, K.,* & Sefton Green, J. (2012). *The Signature Pedagogies Project: Final Report. Creativity, Culture and Education.* The University of Nottingham: UK and * Goldsmiths College, The University of London: UK.

Woolcock, G. (2015). *Shredding the evidence: Whose collective impact are we talking about?* A Community Cultural Development Critique of Beyond Empathy's Maven Project. Beyond Empathy – art for community capacity (BE-http://be.org.au/). Retrieved: http://be.org.au/wp-content/uploads/2015/11/BE_shreddingtheevidence_paper.pdf

Yussen, R., Allen, T., Cronin, S., Dienhart, C., Martyr, M., Song, W., & VanMeerten, N. (2016). A growing chasm of opportunity for American children: A Review of Putnam. *Educational Researcher*, *45*(8), 463-465.

CHAPTER 2

Bodies of Water, Bodies at Sea: The Sea is All Around Us

Margaret Woodward

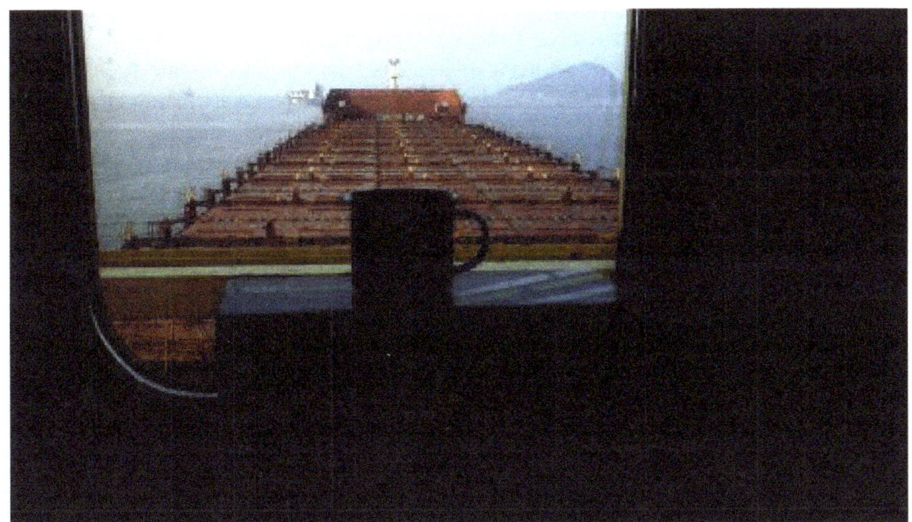

Figure: 2.1 - We are leaving Busan right now and heading to Xingdao. China (2016). *Image credit: Jonathon Pacifico*

ABSTRACT

"Once again, we came back here in Fremantle, and as usual, we grabbed every opportunity to go out, whenever possible, and we are so blessed that there are seaman's mission like Flying Angels and Stella Maris, that cares for seamen, we got free rides to the city, and entertainment as well at the seaman's mission." (Comment from a seafarer left on project website http://sensingtheremote.net/)

The Sea is All Around Us aims to make a personal connection with a mobile community of seafarers, by using an aesthetic object — a souvenir — as a vehicle of welcome and connection. The continuing project was initiated through a performative installation at the Mission to Seafarers in Melbourne's Docklands in 2015, and continues through a website which traces the mobile life of seafarers using customised and track-able souvenirs (www.sensingtheremote.net). The ongoing life of the project reveals ways in which objects can hold and carry meaning, trigger intangible, affective qualities and forge connections between people and place. Combining creative practice as research approaches, of drawing, interaction, writing and design together with an interdisciplinary theoretical framework from cultural geography and tourism, the project tests the potential for a designed artefact to activate social networks that cross geographic boundaries and borders of occupational isolation.

INTRODUCTION

The focus of this chapter is the artwork *The Sea is All Around U*s (2015), a multi-layered project that acknowledges and raises awareness of the often difficult and dangerous working lives and journeys of seafarers by making visible their role in transporting commodities, materials and objects to and from Australia's shores. *The Sea is All Around U*s (2015) is comprised of several relational elements including a participatory installation, a designed souvenir, a floor drawing and a project website. From the outset this artwork is concerned with the life of the seafarer and the seafaring souvenir.

I open this chapter by presenting the artwork *The Sea is All Around Us* and the creative practices employed as research strategies that were to welcome, map and track a mobile community of seafarers. Here, I will speculate on the potential for creative practice research to connect aesthetic objects, spaces and audiences in socially engaging ways across globally dispersed networks. I will argue that through its process of participant engagement, the project's initial aims of welcoming, mapping and tracking are unfolding a broader set of political and social concerns. Later in the chapter these will be considered using the work of other artists, performers and designers whose focus is contemporary seafaring. In doing so, the chapter aims to demonstrate how artists, communicators and designers can attend to social issues and communities through a creative project which follows seafarers, traverses the local through modes of global connectivity, and crosses borders in a range of synchronous and asynchronous modes.

By way of introducing the voice of the seafarers who are participating in the artwork the *Sea is All Around Us*, I want to allow a "third space" to emerge through the writing of this chapter. Multi-media artist Randall Packer conceives of the third space as a networked space. He describes this third space as "the fusion of the physical (first space) and the virtual (second space) into a networked place that can be inhabited by remote users simultaneously or asynchronously (third space)" (http://www.randallpacker.com/third-space/). Following Packer (2014) I propose that the first space of this artwork is one of seafaring work, the second space is the more remote maritime space, and third space is the relationships which are forged through the creative project and the technology it uses. By activating a third space, this chapter aims to make present that which is absent from the dialogue of logistics, mapping and tracking. This third space is a human one, incorporating comments from seafarers, extracts from the project blog and the daily writing that continues to form a critical part of the artwork, allowing the experience of the seafarers to "float" though the chapter.

> *"I am so excited because I am signing off here in Malaysia, and I will travel to Singapore by car and tomorrow midnight I will fly going home to the Philippines. I am about to fly home! And I am so excited to see my loved ones.*
> *"3 days after departure Geelong, we were experiencing rolling due to strong wind, rough seas but we arrived safe to our destination Singapore. Keep praying to Jesus Christ. Thank u so much for this project. Very Appreciated!"*
>
> *(Comments from seafarers left on project website http://sensing theremote.net/)*

The Sea is All Around Us

The Sea is All Around Us was activated during a residency at the Mission to Seafarers Victoria (MTSV) in Melbourne, Australia. This mission is one of a global network of 200 "Flying Angel" missions who "provide help and support to the 1.5 million men and women who face danger every day to keep our global economy afloat" (http://www.missiontoseafarers.org/about-us). The Port of Melbourne is Australasia's largest container and general cargo port, handling around 36% of the nation's container trade, similar in capacity to Oakland (US) and Osaka (Japan). Annually over 3,000 Ships visit the port each year and 30,000 seafarers are welcomed at the MTSV facilities in Melbourne, Portland and Geelong.

The Mission is located in a heritage listed building in the Docklands area of Melbourne which has welcomed seafarers continuously for nearly 100 years. Its fine Spanish mission architecture accords with its function as a mission, offering respite from the port and the city. Inside is a complex which feels like a village, enclosed within stucco walls and complete with a courtyard, garden, kitchen, chapel, dining room and what was once a circular gymnasium, and is now a gallery space. The Mission offers free transport to and from the port; the Seafarers' Flying Angel Club offers social and recreational facilities, tourist information, currency exchange and phone and Internet services for seafarers to contact their families often after long periods of isolation at sea. During my residency, conversations with volunteers and ex-seafarers at the mission highlighted the loneliness and isolation of contemporary seafaring – a result of quick turnarounds and short stays in port, dangerous conditions at sea including piracy, shipwreck and abandonment, the regimented working life and the impact of these factors on seafarers' families.

I developed *The Sea is All Around Us* in consultation with the Mission's management and volunteers, working closely with port workers to welcome visiting seafarers to Melbourne and invite them to participate in a global project that witnessed their journeys and traced the mobile life of seafarers and souvenirs. I designed two hundred limited edition souvenir enamel mugs and commissioned a

Polish traditional enamelware manufacturer Waldemar Brzozowski, to produce them through his company Emalco. In doing so I was continuing the Polish tradition of producing high quality souvenir items from enamel and linen The design incorporated the geographic co-ordinates of the MTSV (37 ° 49'21" S and 144° 57'03"E) as well as referencing Melbourne's waterway Port Phillip Bay, and the Sassafras leaf, the ingredient for a uniquely flavoured bush tea, set against an orange background representing Australia's ochre earth. These design elements were intended to combine and serve as a memento of their visit and the hospitality shown to them at the Mission where they were gifted to seafarers, along with tea and cake as gestures of welcome and a memento of their visit (see Figure: 2.1). By offering each visitor a traditional cup of tea and some freshly baked cake each day, the souvenir mug was also the centrepiece of a welcome rich in Australian tradition. Printed on the base of each numbered mug was a QR code with the capacity for both artist and participant to trace the onward mobile life of the souvenir.

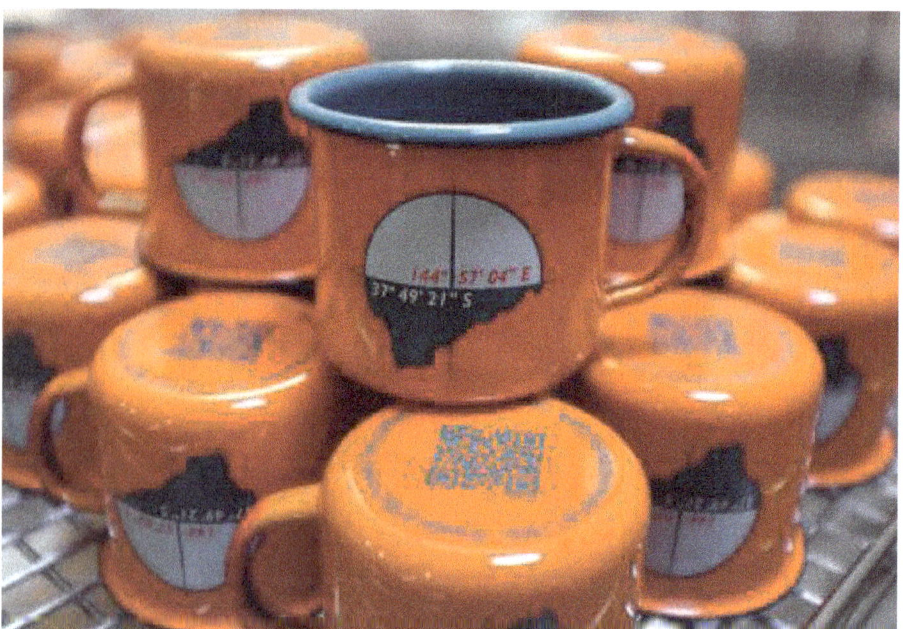

Figure: 2.2 - Customised souvenir mugs with QR codes. (2015) Margaret Woodward.
Image credit: Justy Phillips.

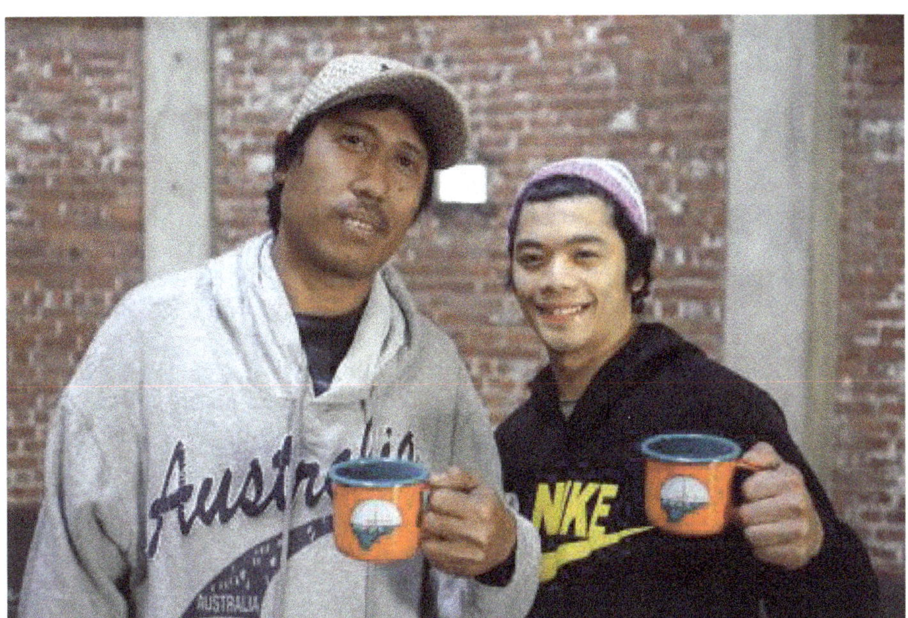

Figure: 2.3 - Visiting seafarers from the ship LUCKY LIFE. (2015). Margaret Woodward.
Image credit: Justy Phillips.

The stunning circular space of the Mission's Dome Gallery, immediately inspired me to draw a large scale compass on the floor — the intersection of its latitude and longitude co-ordinates marking the centre of the former gymnasium (see Figure: 2.4). As the days passed visitors and volunteers would gather around a central tea urn tea urn to talk and chart their collective journeys. As seafarers were welcomed to the Dome Gallery I mapped their journey on the floor compass recording their ship's name, their next destination and ongoing ports. Over a fortnight this compass became the base layer of a large floor chalk drawing, 17 metres in diameter, which accumulated marks, recordings and stories mapping ports, waterways and ships. The participatory, performative aspect of the installation generated many exchanges with visiting seafarers, photos taken, cake and tea consumed and mugs gifted. I was even invited on board a bulk carrier as a ship's visitor and was welcomed by some of the crew who had come to the gallery the day before. This visit gave me a glimpse of the working and living spaces of a ship's interior and an insight into the lives of the visiting seafarers.

> *"Day 4 Thursday 13 May 2015*
> *Ships visitor to Appelton Wharf. PAN EIDELWEISS. Up the gangplank, clear security. Meet the captain. Korean. Go upstairs to the crew's mess, see Adrian and Hercules who had visited the gallery the day before. From gallery to galley. Entering another world, a liminal space on-board, unsettling, work like, hi-vis vests, step into another country's ship, rules,*

> *jurisdictions. Traditions, customs, maleness, trust, floating off shore tethered by rope, relieved to be back in Melbourne" (Project Diary notes)*

As well as recording the ship's destinations the circular map also incorporated my own creative writing capturing the experience of this unusual activation of the Dome. I wove together seafarers' narratives, stories from volunteers and visitors, and the daily ritual of drawing and writing as a poetic memoir of the two-week event. Unexpectedly, this act of drawing, writing and mapping released some emotional stories from my own history, linked to memories, to loss, to distant journeys and tragedies at sea. This floor drawing became what I have come to call an "affictive cartography", tracing past and future journeys, weaving writing, memories, drawing, marking an erasure and blurring the lines between mapping, fiction and affect. After two weeks the Dome floor drawing was erased ceremoniously with a mop, reminiscent of washing the deck.

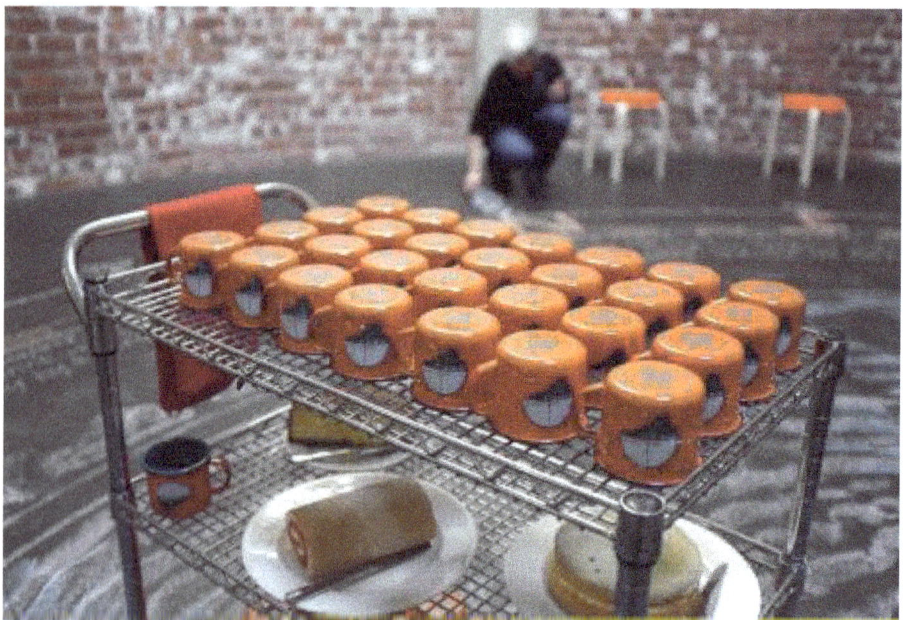

Figure: 2.4 - *Cake and Mugs. (2015)* Margaret Woodward Installation view *The Sea is All Around Us* (2015), Dome Gallery, Mission to Seafarers Victoria, Melbourne.
Image credit: Justy Phillips.

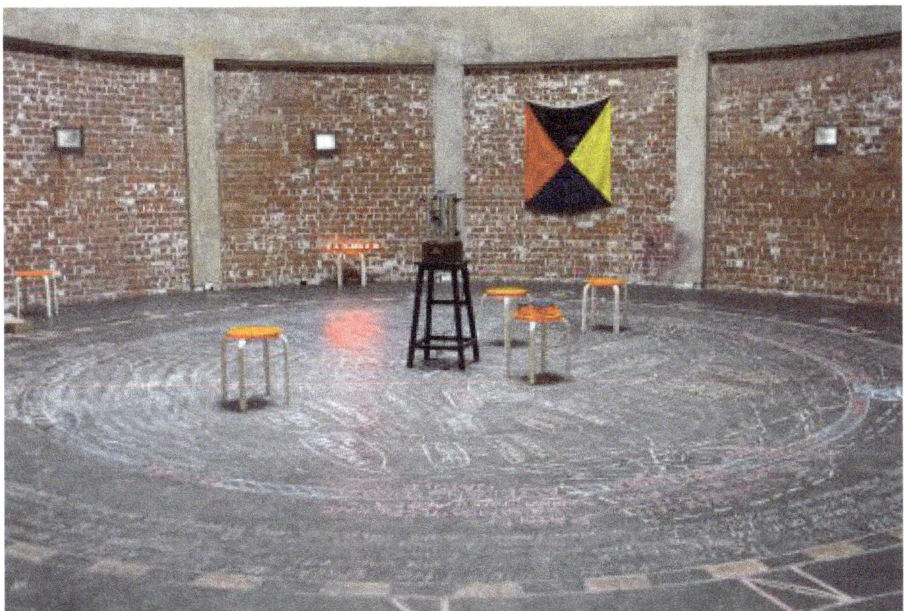

Figure: 2.5 - *Departures. (2015).* Margaret Woodward. Installation view *The Sea is All Around Us* (2015). Dome, Gallery, Mission to Seafarers Victoria, Melbourne.
Image credit: Margaret Woodward.

On leaving Australian shores the seafarers were invited to record their journeys by scanning a QR code printed on the base of their mug. Scanning the QR code with a smartphone connects the seafarer to the project's website, whereby they can register their current location and are invited to share something about their journey. In the year since the project commenced this mobile fleet of souvenir mugs is creating its own cartographic narrative. Participating seafarers scan their mugs when they dock (tele-communication is limited at sea), some send photos and messages of destination ports, with their short comments revealing the nature of their work, conditions and life at sea. Using the website data and in collaboration with cartographer, Deanna Duffy, from the Spatial Analysis Data Network at Charles Sturt University, the progress of the seafarers' souvenir mugs is mapped (see Figure: 2.5). As the lines on these maps fan out around the globe from the Port of Melbourne, the following of souvenirs, seafarers and vessels continues in constant motion as they navigate between land masses, islands, waterways and oceans. These *affictive* cartographies are works in progress, their fluidity springs from lines that are constantly being drawn and redrawn.

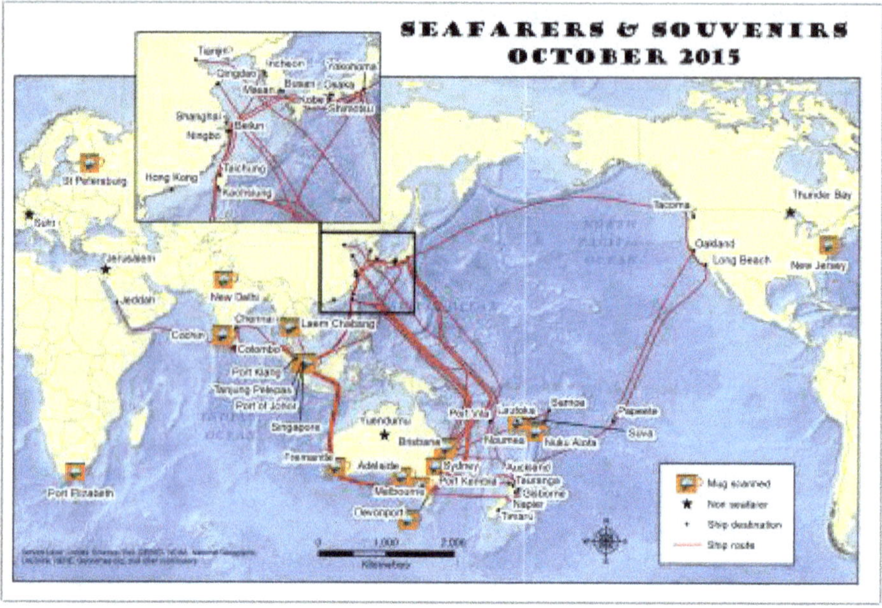

Figure: 2.6 - *Seafarers and Souvenirs, October (2015).*
Image credit: Deanna Duffy, Spatial Analysis Data Network, Charles Sturt University.

Welcome, Following, and Mapping

> *"It was great tho the waves really made their presence felt again. Still the journey we had was remarkable and I hope we can go back to Australia sometime soon before we finish our contract. A good place with good people. Definitely one nation worth remembering in my book.*" (Comment from a seafarer left on project website http://sensingtheremote.net/)

The literature emerging from Tourism studies, Geography and Cultural Studies recognises that souvenirs are entangled geographically, economically, mythologically and personally (Ramsay 2009) and that an understanding of both the affective qualities of souvenirs, along with their materiality is significant (Ramsay, 2009; Gibson, 2014). *The Sea is All Around Us* started as a welcoming, following and mapping project. The research focus of the project was initially aimed at understanding souvenirs as objects of place communication and carriers of imagined geographies. As the project unfolded the focus now encompasses understanding them as relational objects with a capacity to connect individuals and communities. As relational objects they possess what Ramsay (2009) calls "a will to connect" an ability to forge connections between people and places, and people with other people. One visitor to the installation observed that the project had many "tendrils of concern", a comment that stayed with me during and after the project. What started as a project of welcome, following and mapping, over time has revealed some unexpected tangents extending out from the souvenir object. These tendrils highlight the nature of contemporary seafaring as a profession both enabled by and vulnerable to the forces of globalisation, technology and exploitation. In later sections of the chapter I will return to this discussion of how the work of other creative practitioners has raised questions and concerns about the profession of contemporary seafaring.

As mnemonic objects souvenirs compress experience and geography using a "symbolic shorthand" (Gordon, 1986), as "relational objects" they forge connections between people and places (Ramsay, 2009), and as designed objects their material and symbolic aspects exhibit a rich and complex "social life" (Appadurai, 1986). Beyond their representational role, souvenirs also trigger intangible, affective qualities. Understanding souvenirs not only simply as representational objects, but as more complex relational objects allows for multiple meanings and tendrils of concern to entangle them. Susan Stewart, in her seminal work, *On Longing: Narratives of the miniature, the gigantic, the souvenir, the collection* proposes that things, everyday objects, also have a "secret life", which can "reveal a set of actions and hence a narrativity and history outside the given field of perception" (1993, p.54). This less visible, private side of souvenirs which connects with memory, personal identity and attachment provides insights for researchers into how souvenirs can simultaneously be emotionally charged, as well as banal (Peters, 2011). Following Stewart (1993) and Appadurai (1996), I argue that souvenirs have an emotional life that triggers intangible, "affective" qualities, offering reminders of journeys and places and new associations with tastes, sounds and people, thereby becoming objects which focus and hold memories from places and situations that move and affect us. Souvenirs intersect in multiple ways in the performance of tourism, as evidence of having "been there", as objects of validation and witnessing, and as multisensory triggers for remembering sometimes difficult and uncomfortable experiences.

Like seafarers, souvenirs have complex social and geographical lives. Some souvenirs are crafted and made in the place they are purchased, but more commonly they are produced somewhere entirely different and inscribed with words which connect them to a location. Their association with place makes them what Beverly Gordon (1986) and Dean MacCannell (1976) call tourist "markers." They carry the mark of the place they represent, through image or text or invisibly through memories associated with a particular place. This quality as a marker makes it possible to map their place of purchase and representation. However, the souvenir's place of production is less easy to map and frequently bears no relation to the place they represent. Shipped to Australia, the geographic life of the souvenir mug in this project is typical of most souvenirs, and indeed most commodities that we accept into our lives. Manufactured by Polish enamelware company Emalco in Seidlce, Poland, these mugs were then shipped via Lomianki, Warsaw, Paris, Guangzhou, Singapore, Derrimut, Brighton East to the Mission to Seafarers in Docklands, Melbourne.

Tourism Telemetry

The Sea is All Around Us forms the third stage of *Tourism Telemetry*, an ongoing research project which seeks to reveal the mobile "life" of souvenirs. This artwork builds on two recent projects in which I use creative practice to activate souvenirs as a strategy for research generation. In *Greetings from Aggaw Aggaw,* a sculptural installation at Wagga Wagga Art Gallery (2011), I created a "fictive" destination complete with its own customised souvenir cloth badges, engraved pencils, postcards and footstools. In *Tabletop Cairns*, Reykjavik (2012), I compared the islands of Iceland and Tasmania through souvenir objects that travelled between the two locations. This artwork explored the capacity of souvenirs to transmit messages about remote places to distant audiences. The *Tourism Telemetry* project uses the concept of telemetry to understand how souvenirs as portable artefacts have the capacity to carry and send messages about places, remotely. Telemetry is used in science to measure and send data through transmitters back to distant monitoring stations. It is used for example to track the movements of wildlife that have been tagged with radio transmitters, or to transmit meteorological data from weather balloons to weather stations. Extending the notion of telemetry to souvenirs allows us to understand their potential as transmitters of information about destinations and places. Purchased at a distance and then sent as gifts to others or carried home, souvenirs transmit representations and myths about places to their receiving "stations" in the domestic settings of everyday life. Where the previous creative works in the *Tourism Telemetry* series explored telemetry through the symbolic and representational aspects of souvenirs, telemetry in *The Sea is All Around Us* has extended the notion of telemetry using scanning and mapping technologies afforded by shipping, mobile phone and website technology.

From the outset, the intention of this project has been to follow souvenirs, asking where do souvenirs go, where do they end up after they are given or purchased as gifts? In *The Sea is All Around Us*, the idea of recording and tracing seafarers' journeys across bodies of water was inspired by the process of "following" which has developed as a research strategy from the work of Appadurai (1986). More recent work has used following as a strategy to show how the consumption of commodities is connected to global networks flows and also to identify sites of exploitation of workers and communities through the process of trade and production (Cook, 2004; Cook 2006). Ramsay used a following approach in relation to souvenirs and maintains "that following souvenir-objects as a research process is well positioned to explore the complex relations between people, things and their spatiality" (2009, p.38). As well as using the process of "following" to track the journey of the souvenirs, I quickly understood the potential of the "following" process to render visible previously invisible or ignored patterns of circulation of commodities, material and of people.

Artist, photographer and theorist, Allan Sekula was committed to making visible the maritime space occupied by the invisible workforce of seafarers. Sekula (2012) argues against the overbearing domination of ubiquitous telecommunications and instead reminds us of the materiality (and the invisibility) of the maritime industry that transports a staggering 90% of the world's cargo). In Australia as an island highly dependent on shipping, this statistic is even higher. Sekula's writing and images in the book *Fish Story* (1995) and later the moving images in the film *The Forgotten Space* (2010) co-produced with film critic Nöel Burch serve to critique the vast material flows of commodities and globalisation. Sekula argues eloquently for the continued importance of maritime space, and ships and the work of seafarers who are at risk of becoming invisible in a world dominated by air and computer space and communication. He identifies the invention of the shipping container in America in the late 1950s as key to the rise of globalisation and transformations in seafaring professions.

Mobile tracking technology and logistics allow shipping containers to be tracked using computerized systems with some being fitted with Global Positioning System (GPS) devices so clients can also track them. The BBC project *The Box* illuminated international trade and globalization issues by following a single standard shipping container on its journey around the world. During 2008 and 2009 the branded BBC container used a Global Positioning Systems (GPS) transmitter enabling its progress to be followed via BBC correspondents filing reports on the production and consumption of the goods it carried as well as economic, environmental and social issues such as the impacts of piracy and inter-dependency created through globalisation. Visitors to a BBC website could also track the progress of the container on a mapping interface. In just over a year it made 2.08 laps of the earth and travelled 75,761 km by sea and a further 7,368 by land. Its voyage was conducted amidst volatile conditions in the global economy, during the first global recession in 60 years which saw its passage slowed when global trade almost came to a standstill (http://news.bbc.co.uk/2/hi/business/8314116.stm). In Australia, The Port of Melbourne handles almost 2.5 million containers annually and most of the seafarers who visit the Mission to Seafarers work on containerised shipping freighters. During *The Sea is All Around Us* installation seafarers from 22 ships visited, of them 72% were container vessels, the rest were bulk carriers, oil tankers and vehicle carriers. This artwork shifts the focus beyond the inanimate objects of material freight to the living experience of the workers who navigate it and on whose manual work global economies rely.

> *"Day 4 Thursday 13 May 2015*
> *Tour the port with Tony. Palettes of orange, rusted red, blues, shipping brands and logos set against a grey sky. Cranes and gantries, chutes, trucks, skels (empty containers), tracking. Precision logistics. Orange. Eyes drawn to hi-vis. Walls of colour." (Project diary notes)*

Following ships and vessels carrying containers and cargo is now also made possible through freely available websites and apps that incorporate Geographical Information Systems (GIS), satellite imagery and GPS. In tandem with the Universal Shipborne Automatic Identification System (AIS) – a telemetry system used on vessels for identifying, locating and tracking shipping traffic – these systems and technologies work in consort to deliver live shipping data on public sites such as Marine Traffic (www.marinetraffic.com). Data on ships' location, itinerary, cargo, type, size, capacity, speed, draught and more are available at all hours, in ports all over the world. Photographs of the vessel are included in the data, the ships previous names and importantly the "flag" of the country under which it is registered. As I write this chapter the Marine Traffic website hosts live data on 86,334 ships worldwide, including cargo ships, passenger and recreational vessels. The density map function on the Marine Traffic website illuminates the passage of ships to and from Australia with a fluorescent glow, rendering the invisible, visible.

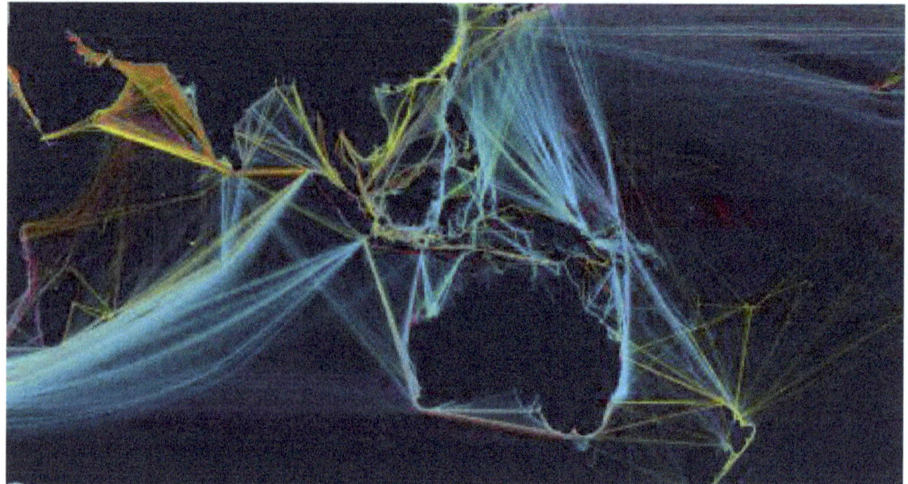

Figure: 2.7 - Shipping Routes, May, (2016).
Source: Marine Traffic Website www.marinetraffic.com.

A dynamic web based visualisation of shipping movements has been produced using Clarkson's Research UK World Fleet Register and the European Climate Foundation data in conjunction with (AIS) shipping movement data. This mesmerising interactive presentation, developed by designers at Kiln.digital (www.shipmap.org) in collaboration with researchers from University College London (UCL) shows 250 million global shipping data points. Such recent visualisations of shipping routes afforded by large data sets and layered mapping technologies allow views of the shipping routes with the land-masses layers turned off. This capacity illustrates in sharp focus Sekula's observations about the now inversed relationships of sea and land:

> Factories become mobile, ship-like as ships become increasingly indistinguishable from trucks and trains, and seaways lose their difference with highways. Thus the new fluidity of terrestrial production is based on the routinization and even entrenchment of maritime movement. Nothing is predictable beyond the ceaseless regularity of the shuttle between various end-points. This historical change reverses the "classical" relationship between the fixity of the land and the fluidity of the sea (Sekula, 2012, p.12).

While large data sets picture the global activity in one screen, *The Sea is All Around Us* focuses on the personal, intimate and everyday gestures of human activity and the relational cartographies of life on the sea.

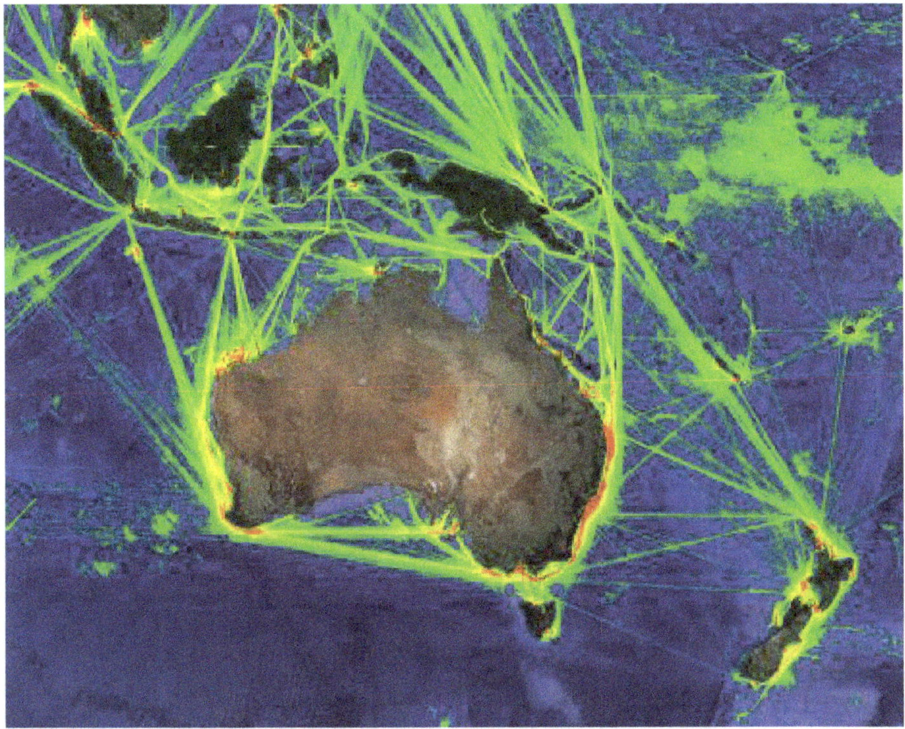

Figure: 2.8 - Shipping Routes. (2012).
Image Credit: Kiln. Digital and University College London (UCL).

Printed on the base of the souvenir mugs, is the now ubiquitous QR code. This user-friendly consumer tracking technology remains intrinsically linked to the operations of manufacturing and globalisation. Invented to track vehicles during manufacture and to allow high-speed component scanning employed in just-in-time (JIT) automobile manufacturing, the QR code was created to service the on-demand market. Sekula likens ships to just-in-time factories and again inverts the functions of ships and factories:

> As ships become more like buildings—the giant, floating warehouses of the "just-in-time" system of distribution—factories begin to resemble ships, stealing away stealthily in the night, restlessly searching for ever cheaper labour. A garment factory in Los Angeles or Hong Kong closes; the work benches and sewing machines reappear in the suburbs of Guangzhou or Dacca. In the automobile industry, for example, the function of the ship is akin to that of conveyor systems within the old integrated car factory: parts span the world on their journey to the final assembly line (Sekula, 2012, p.17).

Whilst Sekula is critical of the subjugation of maritime space to airmail and computer space, in the "ceaseless regularity of the shuttle between various end-points" (2012, p.12), I argue that the same technology that affords the relentless tracking and tracing of cargo and ships can also make visible the merchant shipping activity that surrounds us. With the click of a mouse it is possible to visualise global shipping traffic at any given time, at any scale, from individual vessels to entire fleets. With the assistance of a scanning app, QR codes are now widely used in conjunction with mobile phone technology to scan codes that are linked to information held on websites. *The Sea is All Around Us*, demonstrates that while the human face of seafaring may be out of sight, the same technology as used to track automobile parts to service the just-in-time production system, can also be used to track relationships. Raising awareness about global seafaring has also been the focus of other artists and creative projects. Australian based company BighART has a project on fair shipping called *Blue Angel* using performance, storytelling by seafarers and commissioning portraits of seafarers (http://blueangel.bighart.org). Container Artist Residency 01, a unique artist-in-residence program that takes place on board commercial cargo ships was also launched in 2015, inviting artists to spend 3 weeks aboard a cargo ship, working from a studio space at sea (http://www.containerartistresidency01.org/).

Contemporary Seafaring

> *"It's been a great journey since I left Australia...as a seafarer many things could happened to us due to our nature of works but thanks to HIM, he always keep us safe."*
>
> *(Comment from a seafarer left on project website http:// sensingtheremote.net/)*

In the remainder of this chapter I share some of the key concerns that emerged for me as a researcher over the duration of the project. As I'm now connected to many social media sites for seafarers I'm confronted by an unsettling sense of urgency, and sometimes emergency as I read stories with headlines such as:

> Mission to Seafarers Manila supports seafarer shot during piracy ordeal.
> Hackers, economics and extreme weather are biggest threats to ships.
> Last Aussie-Crewed Fuel Tanker, MT British Fidelity, Leaves Australian Coast.

In 2015, the Australia ABC television investigative journalism program Four Corners produced the episode *Ship of Death,* about suspicious deaths of three seafarers in six weeks on board the Panama registered bulk carrier, Sage Sagittarius en route to Newcastle, Australia. This brought to national attention the plight of seafarers:

> "These are the sailors we rely on to carry out the trade that underpins our national wealth. If you employ a foreigner to cheaply do what it is that you

> would like them to do because you don't want to pay Australian prices, there is a price to pay and it's somebody else paying." Maritime Investigator (http://www.abc.net.au/4corners/stories/2015/06/01/4244465.htm)

This tragedy also raised awareness of what is termed "flags of convenience" practices whereby ships are registered in a country or state different from that of the ship's owner. In this practice the genuine link between a ship's owner and the flag it flies is non-existent, (the genuine link is the central principle behind the UN Convention on the Law of the Sea). This also means for workers on board they are out of sight of regulators with very low wages, poor on-board conditions, inadequate food and clean drinking water and long periods of work without proper rest, leading to stress and fatigue. Flag of Convenience (FOC) practices take advantage of minimal regulation, cheap registration fees, low or no taxes and freedom to employ cheap labour from the global labour market. According to the International Transport Federation who are campaigning against FOCs, Panama has the highest number of FOC ships registered. They lay the blame on globalisation which "has helped to fuel this rush to the bottom. In a competitive shipping market, FOCs lower fees and minimise regulation, as ship owners look for the cheapest way to run their vessels" (http://www.itfglobal.org). This website lists countries to be campaigned against for their abusive poor industrial practices, many of which I recognised as the flags of the seafarer's ships who visited in Melbourne.

> *GLORY ATLANTIC, Singapore, ANTWERP BRIDGE, Panama MAERSK LAUNCESTON, Portugal, YM SINGAPORE, Liberia, TIJUCA, Norway, PAN EDELWEISS, Panama, ANL WYONG, UK, HARVEST LEADER, Bahamas, FORUM PACIFIC, Singapore, EASTERN HIGHWAY, Panama, HIGH PRESCENCE, Liberia, MAERSK VIRGINIA, Hong Kong, SUPREME ACE, Panama, ITAL MATTINA, Italy, ANL BINDAREE, Liberia, ELISABETH SCHULTE, UK, LUHE, China, PHILADELPHIA, Marshall Island, TASCO AMATA, Thailand, BENEDICT SCHULTE, Cyprus, LUCKY LIFE, Cyprus, SANTOS EXPRESS.*

Conclusion

The Sea is All Around Us investigates the potential for a designed artefact to activate social networks that cross geographic boundaries and borders of isolation. Returning to the concept of the "third space" as used in media arts theory (Packer, 2014), it is useful to recognise how this project is currently shaping a distinct form of third space. Packer's conception of third space is where it represents the fusion of the physical (first space) and the remote (second space) into a networked place that can be inhabited by multiple remote users simultaneously or asynchronously (third space) (www.randallpacker.com). *The Sea is All Around Us* fuses the first space, (the Dome Gallery drawing, drinking tea, talking, souvenir gift) with the remote second space of the sea and the ship, into a third networked space that is inhabited by multiple seafarers synchronously or asynchronously who are remaining engaged and connected with the project, through the small gesture of continuing to drink from their souvenir mug. Packer also argues that the hybrid notion of blurring the real and the virtual is expanded in the third space through distributed presence, in which the participants of the third space are networked in distributed physical spaces. The artwork has activated this third space, drinking from the mug, scanning the QR code, sending photos and emails, visiting the website to log the journey are all relational acts of connection, some synchronous, some virtual and asynchronous. It has collapsed the local and the global into a third, relational, inter-connected space. Those concerned for the welfare of seafarers form a global network of missions and seafarer's centres and they are joined by artists, designers, performers and creative workers. This chapter has presented a creative approach that blends technologies, including chalk, smart phones with easily downloadable apps, AIS systems and QR codes, allowing objects and vessels to be tracked remotely through technologies and processes of telemetry. This cocktail of technologies is freely available and accessible and can serve to enhance the visibility of the "the forgotten space" of the maritime work place of seafarers. These same technologies, I argue, have the capacity to facilitate connectedness where there is a desire to remain in touch, a "will to connect."

Although facilitated by technology, this project revolves around human enterprise. A tea urn marks the centre of the compass. Australian green tea is served in souvenir mugs and cakes are baked daily from the *Central Cookery Book*, a staple of Australian home cooking and rituals for welcoming guests. These sensorial gestures flavour the participant experience and infuse associated shipping data with an added human dimension. With each souvenir cup of tea, I issue an invitation. Journey. Scan. Map Journey. Scan. Map.

A year after its launch at the Mission to Seafarers Victoria, seafarers continue to feed this project with their journeys of lived experience. I follow their ships, checking in each day for a trace of their life at sea. I hover over the ports towards which they are heading, immersing myself in new geographies and destinations – islands, trade routes, coastlines. Geographies of body and mind. Imagined geographies I had never heard of. Uncannily, as I write this final paragraph, an email from one of the seafarers arrives, its Jonathan Pacifico and he is in the Port of Singapore, and sends me the following message and photos (see Figures: 2.1 and 2.9).

> *"Good day Miss Margaret, I am just sending you this pic taken this morning here at the port..."*

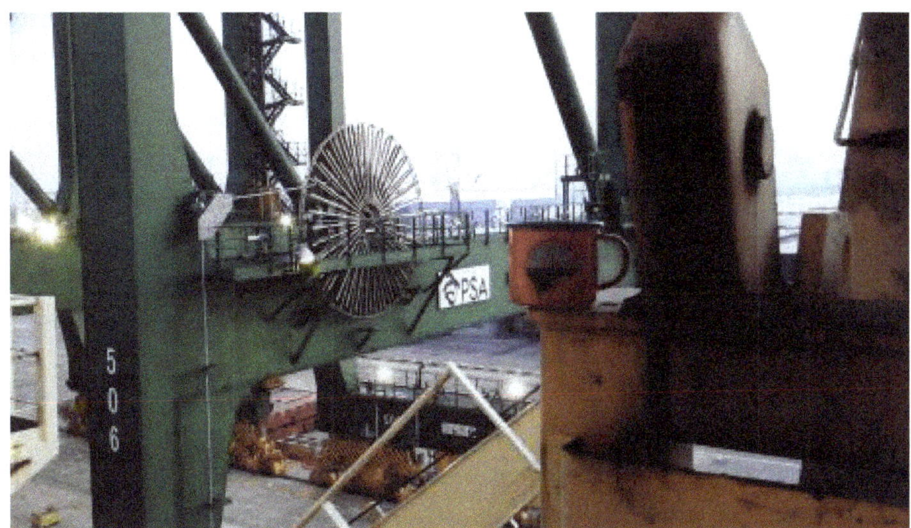

Figure: 2.9 - Jonathan Pacifico. *(2016). Port of Singapore.*
Image credit: Jonathan Pacifico.

The sea is all around us.

References

ABC Four Corners (2015). *Ship of Death. Retrieved from http://www.abc.net.au/4corners/stories/2015/06/01/4244465.htm*

Appadurai, A. (ed.) (1986). *The Social Life of Things: Commodities in Cultural Perspective*. Cambridge: Cambridge University Press.

BBC (2012). *The Box*. Retrieved from http://news.bbc.co.uk/2/hi/business/8314116.stm

Big hART (2016). *Blue Angel - Big hART website. Retrieved from* http://blueangel.bighart.org/

Container Artists Residency (2016). Container Artists Residency website. Retrieved from http://www.containerartistresidency01.org/

Cook, I. (2004). Follow the thing: papaya. *Antipode, 36,* 642–64.

———. (2006). Geographies of food: following. *Progress in Human Geography, 30,* 655–66.

Gibson, C. (2014). Souvenirs, materialities and animal encounters: Following Texas cowboy boots. *Tourist Studies, 14*(3), 286-301.

Gordon, B. (1986). The souvenir: messenger of the extraordinary. *Journal of Popular Culture, 20,*135–46.

International Shipping Federation (2016). ITF website. Retrieved from http://www.itfglobal.org/

Kiln (2014). *Ship map website*. Retrieved from http://www.shipmap.org.

MacCannell, D. (1976). *The Tourist: A New Theory of Leisure Class*. New York: Schocken Books.

Marine Traffic (2016). *Marine Traffic website*. Retrieved from: http://www.marinetraffic.com/

Packer, R. (2014). *The Third Space*. Retrieved from http://www.randallpacker.com/third-space/.

Peters, K. (2011). Negotiating the 'Place' and 'Placement' of Banal Tourist Souvenirs in the Home. *Tourism Geographies, 13*(2), 234–256.

Ramsay, N. (2009). Taking-place: refracted enchantment and the habitual spaces of the tourist souvenir. *Social & Cultural Geography*, *10*(2), 197–217.

Sekula, A. (2012). The Forgotten Space: Notes for a Film in *A Film About the Sea, Notes on Allan Sekula and Noël Burch's The Forgotten Space*. Canada: Centre for European Studies.

Sekula, A. & Burch, N. (2010). *The Forgotten Space, A film Essay by Allan Sekula and Noël Burch*. Doc.eye Film

Stewart, S. (1993). *On Longing. Narratives of the Miniature, the Gigantic, the Souvenir, the Collection*. Durham: Duke University Press.

Woodward, M. (2016). *Sensing the remote website*. Retrieved from *http://sensingtheremote.net/*

CHAPTER 3

#MuseumEdOz: Facilitating Socially Distributed Meaning Making through Twitter

Narelle Lemon

ABSTRACT

Social media has transformed how we can communicate, connect, and socially engage with one another. Platforms such as Twitter offer the opportunity for like-minded people with common interests within education (Carpenter & Krutka, 2014) and across the arts and cultural sectors to come together to participate in the sharing and curating of practices (Charitonos, et al., 2012; Kelly, 2014; Lemon, 2014; Russo, 2012; Russo et al., 2008). Underpinned by this use and engagement is a reciprocity that is supported by ongoing digital participation that is boundary-less in time and geographical location. This chapter shares the establishment of an ongoing digital ethnographic project called #MuseumEdOz, an online community facilitated on the platform of Twitter. The hashtag unites teachers, museum educators and cultural organisations from Australia through the contemporary social media practice of a tweet chat – a one-hour online conversation guided by specific advertised questions with a focused topic. The act of tweet chats and subsequent formation of a community demonstrates how social media supports a paradigmatic shift in communication practices that are underpinned by spontaneity, informality, and active participation (Trembacj & Deng, 2015). By building from the anytime, anywhere notions of social media, the findings indicate that rich dialogues between arts, cultural and education audiences can extend contacts, insights, and perspectives while contributing to the formation of a national community united by the topic of learning in and with the Galleries, Libraries, Archives and Museum (GLAM) sector. A discussion critically framing the notion of digital interaction through Ingold's lines, intersections and meshworks (2015) is presented. The data is explored through the entanglement of lines by digital becoming, visibility and connecting, and reciprocity. How social media enables meaning making to be socially distributed (Rowe, 2002) is illuminated whereby the emergent participatory culture offers abundant advantages for ongoing learning with like-minded individuals, new partnerships, collaborative problem solving, and the development of a more empowered sense of citizenship (Trembacj & Deng, 2015).

INTRODUCTION

Digital platforms and Web 2.0 applications are changing how the Galleries, Libraries, Archives and Museum (GLAM) sector engage with their audiences (Cathcart & Taylor, 2014; Charitonos et al., 2012; Giaccardi, 2012; Lemon, Molloy & Hocking, 2015). The ways in which GLAM organisations "communicate and interact with their audiences has undergone a rapid and profound transformation… [and] this has been especially noticeable over the past five years, due to the rise of the Internet and social media together with the explosion in mobile technologies" (Kelly, 2014, p.54). Consequently, there are various "ways in which audiences engage, participate, review and critique museum practices…in the realm of online media" (Russo, 2012, p.145). The use of social media to connect with audiences is paralleled with a paradigmatic shift in communication practices that are underpinned by spontaneity, informality, and active participation (Trembacj & Deng, 2015). The use of various social media platforms brings together GLAM organisations, brings the user (the visitor), and the content together, encourages visitors to curate their interest with cultural materials publicly and digitally, encourages critique, and establishes a steady social connection with one another (Simon, 2010). This is a remarkably different way of working that is primarily facilitated by and through the digital.

> [The] emergent participatory culture fostered by social media offers numerous benefits for peer-to-peer learning, collaborative problem solving, and the development of a more empowered sense of citizenship, as well as skills in modern academic settings and the workplace (Trembacj & Deng, 2015, p.101).

For the GLAM sector, from here on referred to as museums to refer to the collective of all types of cultural organisations, the user of, or integration of, social media enables possibilities to engage with ideas and with audiences who want to participate, who can generate content, and who would like to create a community (Boches, 2013). Social media platforms encourage and support participatory communication, which in turn transforms the relationships that museums have with their audiences (Charitonos, et al., 2012). This is particularly noticeable, as Kelly (2014, p.56) reports "in the educational sector, including schools, universities and museums" where opportunity exists for "discussion and shar[ing] subject knowledge outside of the museum" (Russo, 2012, p.153).

In this chapter I explore how social media can support museums to engage with audiences, specifically museum education audiences through the platform Twitter. I introduce the hashtag Museum Education Australia (written and known as #MuseumEdOz) and the contemporary practice of a tweet chat facilitated through this hashtag. The hashtag brings together audiences interested in a topic, in this case museum education, and provides a forum that focuses on conversations by like-minded audiences, for example teachers, museum educators, and cultural organisations. The hashtag can be added to a tweet and serves as a way to bring together the targeted audience. A hashtag also enables specific conversations to occur through the practice of a tweet chat, which is a one-hour online conversation guided by specific advertised questions underpinned by the focus of the hashtag at a particular moment in time. The tweet chat is facilitated by a host; usually the person who has generated the questions. Their role is to welcome participants, pose the questions, interact with others sharing, and encourage sharing of perspectives through the mediation of the conversation. In the creation of #MuseumEdOz and the hosting of a once a month tweet chat an opportunity is created to bring together and engage audiences of museum educators, teachers, curators, digital advisors, and cultural organisations with a united focus on museum education.

In this chapter I refer to Tim Ingold's notion of meshwork. This conceptualizes the practices in the Twitter community of #MuseumEdOz as movement and growth that consists of complex, layered spatial weavings. Ingold's conceptualization of meshwork, lines run through space as lines of movement and growth, as real lines of life, where they meet and sometimes are bound together is "re-imagined as sites of external contact or adjacency" (Ingold, 2011 p.63). This is a different conceptualisation of a network of drawn lines with intersections at point A and B, rather as an *inversion* (Ingold, 2011 p.63) of thinking about interaction as a simple meeting of lines of flights (Ingold, 2010). In this conceptualization of a meshwork Ingold is describing a complexity that is layered. It is both connecting and adjacent; external meeting and intersecting "behind the conventional image of a network of interacting entities" (Ingold, 2011 p.63). It is in this layered, complex space where a formalized notion of social media is extended with a conceptualization of a meshwork that layers the space, time and life with intersections of external meetings, connecting and adjacent, "a meshwork of interwoven lines" (Ingold, 2011, p.63), if you like, like a textile weave or as referred to in this chapter, as a spider's web.

Before moving into a discussion about #MuseumEdOz framed by the entanglement of lines and intersections, I will frame the context of social media and the formation of the hashtag and subsequent monthly tweet chat. This leads into a discussion of the #MuseumEdOz online community positioned on Twitter referring to Ingold's (2010, 2011) concept of meshwork. Then an unpacking of lines of entanglement follows referring to digital becoming, visibility and connecting, and reciprocity as demonstrated within this online community.

Literature Review: Social Media

Digital technologies are changing the way we engage with each other. They are also changing the way we learn. Social media is one such example that has shifted the ways in which we communicate, collaborate, and learn socially (Boyd, 2014; Boyd, et al., 2010; Junco et al., 2011; 2014; Prestridge, 2014; Rinaldo, et al., 2011). Profiles, friends and comments are common features of social media and are usually intuitive across platforms (Boyd, 2008). In addition, text, images and video can be shared and curated. There are opportunities to link with others giving opportunity for sharing content with each other within a community. Participation and interaction with social media allows for extended practices and activities that are "geographically unbounded" (Boyd, 2014, p.8) and that construct networked publics. Networked publics have different characteristics than traditional physical public spaces: 1) *persistence*: the durability of online expressions and content; 2) *visibility*: the potential audience who can bear witness; 3) *spreadability*: the ease with which content can be shared; and 4) *searchability*: the ability to find content (Boyd, 2014. p.11). Social media thus highlights *content*, *context*, *connectivity*, and *continuity* (Lemon, 2013).

While some debate still exists about social media value for learning (see for example Giaccardi, 2012; Kelly, 2012), Maloney (2007) makes the connection with sociocultural understandings of learning illustrating how these sites "mirror much of what we know to be good models of learning, in that they are collaborative and encourage an active participatory role" (p.26). Furthermore, Francis (2010) reiterates that the connections developed through online social networking can be seen as globally distributed funds of living knowledge, demonstrating how they can both convey knowledge and provide collaborative spaces in which knowledge can be developed. Social media enables meaning making to be socially distributed. As Rowe (2002), states "…the processes of meaning-making are generally distributed among members of the group who build up a store of "knowledge" or "cultural capital…family member [or others such as class mates, museum staff, public, or other experts] not only help share what each other experiences, but also together build up a fund of shared knowledge they use in later meaning-making" (p.19). Thus, by engaging in a variety of online practices (social networking, information searching, remixing and sharing content), Twitter participants are "becoming skilled at constructing their ecologies of learning in pursuit of identity formation and knowledge building" (Shaw & Krug, 2013, p.246).

In keeping these aspects in mind, this chapter focuses on Twitter, a microblogging platform that emerged in 2006 where small elements of content are shared such as short sentences with or without media (such as a photograph, video, or web link) in up to 140 characters. Users demonstrate reflective practice and concise articulation as they share tweets in the online forum. Short and sharp response with opportunity to post multiple tweets in response to the dialogue is considered normal practice. A participatory learning culture with active content generation (Davis et al., 2015) underpins Twitter.

For the museum space, this type of interaction via Twitter highlights the social nature of learning in and across different boundaries, that is face-to-face and in online spaces (Charitonos et al., 2012; Shaw & Krug, 2013; Lin, et al., 2014). Given the rapid change, and indeed pace, of new technologies, access to these tools for engagement of both teachers, students, and museum educators is required (Kelly, 2012). This aligns to what the research finds whereby synchronous tweet chats of one-hour duration with a moderator and based around a hashtag are popular among tweeting educators (Brown, 2012; Carpenter & Krutka, 2014b; Wesely, 2013).

INTRODUCING #MUSEUMEDOZ

A dedicated hashtag on museum learning for Australian teachers, museum educators, curators and cultural organisations emerged from my work as a Visiting Research Fellow at the Museum of Applied Arts and Sciences (MAAS), Sydney, in early 2015. The Education & Digital Learning Manager and I were discussing how we could integrate social media into museum education programming and in doing so realised that we needed to build museum educator and teacher capacity and voice before inviting students in school settings to participate in use formally through integration into the museum learning programs. In focusing on teachers who already use social media such as Twitter to "engage in professional development with colleagues by using popular hashtags related to subject area" (Carpenter & Krutka, 2014a, p.416) we were looking to build the possibility of extending the dialogue of what is possible in museum education and with students in the future. This approach sees Twitter as a medium that can bring together voices to deepen the conversation and thicken access to perspectives and knowledge. A key driver was the formation of a community, facilitated online, where multiple voices could be present (for example museums, museum educators, teachers, curators, and administrators), and that connected participants without the constraints of physically having to be in the same location.

The formation of #MuseumEdOz was guided by the need to target specific audience engagement, that is to support teachers and museum educators, as well as curators and cultural organisations themselves, to engage in a dialogue about museum learning across disciplines and key learning areas. The use of the hashtag supports the community to "share ideas, resources, and encouragement, and connect with other educators" (Carpenter & Krutka, 2014a, p.416). This was most important as there had been significant observations from both teachers and museum educators independently about the difficulty to make contact, consult, and discuss what is possible in regards to philosophy, value, access, curriculum development, inquiry, and specific discipline needs. The objective was to provide a voice for museum educators and for teachers, with opt in from curators and cultural organisations with a Twitter handle. The development of an Australian profile on social media to further strengthen international presence in this space via hashtags such as #MuseumEdChat or #museumed was a guiding factor in the highlighting of voice. This was seen as a way to demonstrate how social media can be a professional learning platform providing opportunity for connection in real time and across boundaries with fellow museum educators, curators, museums, and teachers. As the community of practice develops it is envisaged that support and the access to resources, pedagogical strategies, and ideas will become more fluid in the online environment with possibility to transfer to face-to-face interactions and partnerships. Most importantly #MuseumEdOz has been envisaged as one approach to extend experiences for teachers in schools as well as community settings, museum educators, and those working in museum public programs while providing a forum for posing questions, discussing best practice, and innovative educational approaches to engage learning for all in the museum setting with objects, exhibitions, and cultural assets. In hosting a once a month tweet chat, possibility was seen in building connections and the conversation with aims of contributing to the understanding of museum learning, museums as spaces for learning, and what the needs are from multiple perspectives.

Context of the Project

This chapter shares an ongoing project that is a digital ethnography; that is, a study of online communities and human-technology interactions through the use of qualitative research methods. Digital ethnography allows for "us to follow ethnographically the (dis)continuities between the experienced realities of face-to-face and social media movement and socialites" (Postill & Pink, 2012, p.2). This is as Pink (2009) calls a part of the process of making an 'ethnographic place' where there is an emergent understanding of relations between things and processes that are not bounded by territories. As Dannah boyd (2008; 2014) reiterates, participation and interaction with social media allows for extended practices and activities that are 'geographically unbounded.' Thus as the researcher I enacted what Boyd (2014) refers to as ethnographic practices whereby one undergoes 'participant observation' and 'deep hanging out' in the online space (monitoring the hashtag) alongside qualitative field notes.

Data collected included observations of hashtag activity monitored through tweets shared during the #MuseumEdOz hashtag and supported through analytics platforms of Tweet Archivist, Hashtracking, and KeyHole. Hashtag mapping of relationships between contributors was accessed through NodeXL and approaches to 'dashboarding.' Storify was also accessed to archive the tweet chat collated within 24 hours of the online conversations.

The method of analysis is both qualitative and quantitative. The statistics for participation in the tweet chat included an analysis of participants' roles and locations, while social media analytic platforms provide an insight into the analytics of engagement with the hashtag. Tweets were hand coded to capture the intricacies and context of online discussions between participants guided by emergent thematic analysis. Although discussed here, this data is not a part of this book chapter.

The Spider's Web: Lines, Intersections, and Meshworks of a Hashtag

Twitter is an entanglement of interwoven lines of movement. The handles, profiles, content, interactions, tweets, retweets and hashtags are all examples of different movements, or practices, that are representative of the common complexities, action and language of the platform. This way of seeing the social media platform is one way to understand the intricacies of the pathways along which practices unfold. Ingold refers to this as "improvisatory practice[s] [which] unfolds [and] are not connections, nor do they describe relations between one thing and another. They are rather lines *along* which things continually come into being…[an] *entanglement* of things...not a network of connections but a meshwork of interwoven lines of growth and movement" (Ingold, 2010, p. 3). In focusing specifically on #MuseumEdOz, I refer to Ingold's notion of meshworks, that is a layering of the practices that unfold in the online community such as how the hashtag emerged. The life of this hashtag has no defined end, it labels a discussion, brings together lines of being and understanding, links and cross overs with other hashtags and online discussions. People or organisations come in and out of conversations, and there is a constant interweaving of growth of understanding, relevance, and inquiry connected to where people or organisations are at with their thinking at any one time.

The space is fluid. There is an entanglement of interest in regards to museum education. However, how each participant is connected to the hashtag in the scheduled tweet chat conversations or through spontaneous sharing is organic. No one participant is linked in the same way. Some come from the perspective of being a teacher situated in a school, others come from being a museum educator, and then there can be organisations or individuals that hook up in the conversations but who may not have a specific formal education background, but offer a technology, engagement, or curatorial perspective. This is where Ingold (2010) invites us to "think of every participant as following a particular way of life, threading a line though the world, then perhaps we could define the thing…as a '*parliament of lines*'" and these can be bounded by threads, knots that can "become caught with other threads in other knots" (p. 4). A line is followed but not a straight line. Knots and threads can be present in regards to a variety of reasons that participants come to engage with #MuseumEdOz – personal, professional, networking, community, to test, to experience, to lurk, to see, to connect, to access information, to communicate, to ask questions, to broadcast, to observe, to be active, to share content, to learn, to inquire, etc. These lines, knots and threads of entanglement are what Deleuze and Guattari (2004) remind us are a "matter in movement, in flux, in variation" (p.451). Along thread lines, or 'lines of becoming' or 'lines of flight' as Deleuze and Guattari (2004) label them, fluidity of engagement and becoming:

> …is not defined by the points it connects, or by the points that compose it; on the contrary, it passes between points, it comes up through the middle…A becoming is nether one nor two, nor the relation of the two; it is the in-between, the…line of flight…running perpendicular to both (Deleuze & Guattari, 2004, p. 323).

For #MuseumEdOz this is akin to the movement of becoming in relation to the growth of the community, ability to connect in and out of tweet chats as a whole each month or indeed spontaneous sharing of content that may be of interest to others. It is a gathering of threads that can flow and counter-flow, "winding through or amidst without beginning or end, and not as connected entities bounded either from within or without" (Ingold, 2010, p.11) that form the entanglement of the meshwork. The metaphor of a spider's web is a beneficial visual that assists in defining and applying Ingold's notion of meshwork.

> The lines of spider's web. For example, unlike those of the communications network, do not connect points or join things up. They are rather spun from materials exuded from the spider's body and are laid down as it moves about. In that sense they are extensions of the spider's very being as it trails into the environment (Ingold, 2008, pp.210-211).

The lines are along which it lives. If a spider catches a fly, the line of the web does not link the spider to the fly, nor does the fly become linked to the spider. This is rather an unfolding of counterpoint. The web provides a possibility for the spider to run along lines to retrieve the prey or not. There is therefore a "condition of possibility" (Ingold, 2010, p.12) for the spider and fly to interact. They are themselves not the line of interaction, rather there is a line in which they move along, not between. If you like, for a moment in time, say a scheduled #MuseumEdOz tweet chat, could be a web, where lines unfold guided by pre advertised questions and the condition of possibility is established. The web is laid in announcing the tweet chat. Participants, or flies if you like, are caught by their interest in the community or the tweet chat theme. They are not linked specifically although the tweet chat itself guides them towards an attraction of some type. The lines of interaction in and between the questions emerge. The conditions are set for participants to interact, to follow lines of flight as the questions are posed. Participants can interact and extend along different lines posing counter questions and forming different threads and knots, or intersections, within the meshwork of the web.

As this chapter continues, Ingold's notions of lines, intersections, meshworks are explored in relation to #MuseumEdOz and through the entanglement of lines by digital becoming, visibility and connecting, and reciprocity. The digital space of Twitter enables meaning making to be socially distributed (Rowe, 2002) and illuminates how a tweet chat connected via a hashtag can support changing and emergent participatory culture in offering abundant advantages for ongoing learning with like-minded individuals that supports new relationships, partnerships, collaborative problem solving, and the development of a more empowered sense of citizenship (Trembacj & Deng, 2015). It is in this layered, complex space where a formalized notion of social media is extended with a conceptualization of a meshwork that layers the space, time and life with intersections of external meetings, connecting and adjacent, "a meshwork of interwoven lines" (Ingold, 2011, p.63).

Lines by Digital Becoming

New forms of content production and being social have been enabled by digital technologies such as social networking sites like Twitter. This has noticeably altered relationships between cultural institutions and public culture in terms of knowledge production and power relations (Kelly, 2014; Russo, 2012). Museum information, including that related to museum education,

> ...now operates within networks that transcend their immediate location, placing them in wider flows of interconnected cultural, political, economic and technological ideas, agendas and resources. Through these public spaces, collections are able to garner greater interest and cultivate meanings within wider cultural and social contexts. Social actors in various locations and contexts are acting on and modifying collections information according to their interests (Cameron, 2008).

It is from this approach and view that #MuseumEdOz was started. By engaging in the socially enacted space of Twitter, relationships can be formed that are underpinned by knowledge production in new ways that are not bounded by the physical, rather building on the benefits of the digital anytime, anywhere access. As Cameron & Kelly (2010) reiterate, "through these public spaces, museum information and collections, for example, are able to garner greater interest and cultivate meanings within wider cultural and social contexts" (p.3). #MuseumEdOz has facilitated new relationships nationally as a way of digital becoming. In thinking about digital becoming in this context, I refer to re-examining and being open to understanding and exploring new ways of doing things through the digital. Digital becoming requires a commitment to exploring identity, to engagement with audience, and to access and curate content.

The space of Twitter enables participants to be located anywhere in Australia, and indeed the world. The establishment of #MuseumEdOz in May 2015 came from an invitation to the museum, museum education and teacher community based on the need to explore new ways to professionally connect, as introduced earlier in this chapter. Observation has been made that the identified audience were using Twitter but links had not been made been different industries in a formal way in Australia. #MuseumEdOz establishment was a way to illuminate the digital becoming of participants and the importance of museum education in the conversations about GLAM while leveraging the social media sphere.

Digital becoming is illuminated through the new way to connect and extend the conversation about museum education for the participants. The lines of digital becoming are entangled for many of the #MuseumEdOz participants in terms of individual needs and analysis has produced themes of:

- Creating a professional digital presence;
- Tweet with focus;
- Moving towards a professional Twitter profile;
- First time tweet chat participation;
- Voice creation;
- Value of social media for museum education conversations;
- Curation of digital content relevant to museum education; and
- Ongoing development of skills.

Unpacking all these areas further is undertaken in Table: 3.1 to further explain the main aspects of digital becoming in relation to #MuseumEdOz as observed in the participants, both regular and one off participants, as well as those who volunteer to become hosts or cohosts of the discussions.

Table: 3.1- Lines of digital becoming demonstrated through the #MuseumEdOz online community facilitated through Twitter

Ways of digital becoming	**Description**
Creating a professional digital presence	By engaging with #MuseumEdOz participants are invited to engage with a professional dialogue about museum learning in a public space. This highlights a professional digital presence visible to both participants and those lurking (or observing in real time or later).
Tweet with focus	A Twitter handle can be present but not active with a museum education presence within an institution. The #MuseumEdOz existence supports dialogue within institutions. Leverage is possible for museums to allow museum educators to tweet from handle/or create a new handle to establish a link for why to tweet on the topic. Digital identity is open for discussion within the institution and is acted out online.
Moving towards a professional Twitter profile	Some of the participants specifically created a professional Twitter profile for engagement with #MuseumEdOz and subsequent conversations and curation of content related beyond the hashtag. They had previously been users of Twitter under a different Twitter handle personally.
First time tweet chat participation	Learning about a tweet chat, the purpose, expectations, and behaviour was new to some participants in #MuseumEdOz. The tweet chat each month focuses on welcoming each participant no matter how many times they have been present in the past or if they are joining for the first time. Everyone is welcomed and encouraged to participate with all contributions valued.
Voice creation	#MuseumEdOz has supported a voice for Australian museum educators, teachers and museums to discuss learning. The online space promotes the voice, and subsequent conversation both online and in person (with participants or with others professionally/personally within institutions/publicly) extends the voice, value, awareness, and cultural capital (where reciprocity, trust and cooperation are present to promote the social mobility and knowledge that extends participants access to information, strategies or approaches to museums education or engaging with museums as learning sites).
Value of social media for museum education conversations	In discussions within the GLAM and education sector, the place of social media for learning and creation of professional learning networks (PLNs) is ever present. #MuseumEdOz is an example of how the valuing of social media to support connections, curation of content, and professional discussions contributes to professional voice, meaning making, knowledge production, and ongoing learning. This is achieved through the monthly tweet chat questions posed, and subsequent directed conversations.
Curation of digital content relevant to museum education	Curation in this context focuses on the sharing of new content, engaging with others content, maintenance, collection and archiving of digital assets (tweets, web links shared, connections made online that can be transferred to face-to-face opportunities and captured in Storify for post real time conversation archiving). Learning to value contributions from others and how to share relevant content for the #MuseumEdOz community that is not predisposed by broadcasting or self-promotion of an institution is present and developed.
Ongoing development of skills	There is an ongoing development of skills within the #MuseumEdOz community in the use of Twitter for professional connections in areas such as professional profile development, tweet chat etiquette and protocol, hosting (both generation of questions relevant to the community and supporting a community of practice during a tweet chat), knowledge production, curation of content, archiving, networking, and the value of personal learning networks.

Using networks such as #MuseumEdOz is a way to keep in touch with streams of knowledge, finding similar and disparate voices and points of view which can then be retweeted, and engaged with discussion individually and collectively. This is no longer dependent on location or time as Twitter hashtags can converge the conversation with active participation of professional networks. This visible conversation is then also merged into other network structures, as the museum education network as a leaky dispersive model is tangled in other networks.

LINES BY VISIBILITY AND CONNECTING

"The contemporary museum is a media space" (Russo, 2012, p.145) in which audiences can and do engage with, participate in, and co-create their own knowledge through social media, and they are, thus, no longer a 'new technology', they just are. #MuseumEdOz discussion is located on Twitter and engages participants to create new cultural content and add to those that are presented by cultural organisations and the various education fields. In creating #MuseumEdOz opportunity is afforded for participants to extend conversations, become visible and connect with likeminded and interested people and organisations. #MuseumEdOz is public and thus gives an online space that promotes visibility. Many of the participants are museum educators and some use their personal profiles while others use their professional learning accounts connected to the organisation they are currently employed at. The public notion of #MuseumEdOz makes visible the conversation(s) and allows for a chance to connect to collections, others (individuals and institutions), and knowledge production. The tweet chats shift the work of museum educators to be more visible in the online space of social media and supports the development of a personal learning network (PLN) that allows for connecting with other museum educators, museums, and teachers nationally.

The lines of visibility and connecting associated to #MuseumEdOz have resulted in impact beyond just the tweet chat links made. Face-to-face relationships already established have been extended, as to the opportunity for online relationships to move to face-to-face connections. For example, from tweet chat discussions museum educators and teachers located in the same state of Australia have become aware of one another, the work that they do, and how they can work together in the physical sense to support the objects or the young people they work with. Site visits for schools have been booked and carried out, all instigated from meeting through the #MuseumEdOz tweet chats. An awareness of cultural benefits and learning opportunities have been highlighted. This has been evident in a relationship developed by the Australian National Maritime Museum in Sydney and a teacher in South West Sydney (Bowen, 2015) whereby it has been shared:

> connecting with teachers using Twitter has been a great success for us and we are looking forward to future connections with teachers, exploring ways to open up the museum, find opportunities for students and teachers to enhance their learning through a museum visit [and] delivering great excursion experiences (para 13).

This was all facilitated through a #MuseumEdOz tweet chat connection and illustrates the social, visible and connecting nature of social media (Charitonos et al., 2012; Shaw & Krug, 2013; Lin, et al., 2014).

Lines by Reciprocity

Reciprocity is an underpinning behaviour in social media participation. When considering this complex concept Pelaprat & Brown (2012) remind us that it is about complex interactions of giving and returning. In the online environment "reciprocal exchange is symbolic insofar as it produces and enacts many forms of social life by drawing individuals into a relation of recognition" (Pelaprat & Brown, 2012, para 1). Furthermore,

> …reciprocity is a gesture that enacts and produces a social institution with an individual who, by their initial gesture of giving … [it is] not [about] profit or benefit, as in a contract or economic exchange…it is the symbolic nature of the object gesture given and returned that is critical to forming social relations between partners (Pelaprat & Brown, 2012, para 2).

The social actions of reciprocity can be understood through four parts (Pelaprat & Brown, 2012, para 21):

> 1. Symbolic exchange through objects – reciprocity is not an action that belongs to an exchange market, but rather belongs to symbolic exchange;
> 2. Obligations - such as commonplace exchanges (such as in the online environment of sharing links, resources, ideas, time or continuing the conversation) that are intended to draw others into social life and institutions;
> 3. The ambiguity of the economic value of objects - reciprocal exchanges of a symbolic nature have nothing to do with gain, equivalence, or loss; and
> 4. The role of giving and reciprocating to facilitate social bonds - some kinds of exchange enact practices of reciprocal recognition. Giving and exchange in these cases exist outside the logic of self–interest or gain. Indeed, in those cases, our actions towards another *generously* offer recognition in order to have it reciprocated in return.

Reciprocity develops with ongoing repeating of action. Social actions and relations are strengthened as individuals keep reciprocating to each other in one form or another. In the online space of Twitter, the strongest links are made through reciprocal recognition. This is an underpinning action of #MuseumEdOz. That is through the monthly posting of a set of questions and through the act of responding to a question in the tweet chat there is not an isolated social action where the goal is simply having your question answered. "It is, rather, a first move of in a series of turn–taking exchanges that form social bonds of diverse kinds" (Pelaprat & Brown, 2012, para 40). The conversational nature of #MuseumEdOz is an expression of reciprocity.

In regards to #MuseumEdOz reciprocity is enacted in two major ways. Firstly, it is enacted through participation in the monthly tweet chats. Participants nominate if they wish to participate each month according to the topic being discussed. This choice is based on the broadcasting of the questions leading up to the scheduled tweet chat. This often occurs in the week leading up in two locations, on Twitter and on the blog page. Participation in the tweet chat then is built on the reciprocity of individuals who respond to questions openly and generously – that is, with openness to share own experiences, share links to projects that could help others, and share insights and perspectives to extend the conversation. Participants help one another access resources and information triggered through the questions and subsequent conversation. This is demonstrated through responses, and the reciprocity, trust and cooperation that underpins the sharing of experiences and when appropriate further sharing of resources or links to a blog, website, project or cultural organisation project that is relevant and extends the conversation or contribution of thinking. Secondly, reciprocity is displayed through the guest hosting of tweet chats. A call is made at various times, for example at the start of the year, whereby interested individuals or cultural organisations volunteer to host. As a host participants generate a theme and usually five questions to guide the conversation.

In both of these actions exchange and sharing is underpinned by mutual dependence, action, influence, mutual exchange or cooperation, perceived value, and presence in the online shared space (Lemmermeyer, 2013; Pelaprat & Brown, 2012; Przemyslaw et al., 2014). There is a feeling of being valued, making a contribution, kindness, and feeling compelled to return the favour to support the #MuseumEdOz community growing in the space of Twitter. This aligns to the 'theory of reciprocity' of when someone does something positive and helpful for you, and then one would like to return this favour (Lemmermeyer, 2013; Przemyslaw et al., 2014). This action contributes significantly to both the personal growth and professional growth of participants interested in museum education and learning with/through objects. There is a building up of relationships over each monthly tweet chat that sees repeat participants whereby the furthering of conversations and relationships is built on to exchange ideas and experiences.

A further way reciprocity is demonstrated with #MuseumEdOz is the archiving of both the tweet chat questions on a blog space and the tweet chat conversations on Storify. This allows for ongoing access and sharing for those who participated or who could not participate at the time. There is an opportunity presented to go back, re-read, reflect on the fast paced conversations, and access information and resources shared.

Conclusion

New relationships are facilitated by the virtual. #MuseumEdOz is one example of how the online space of Twitter supports the construction and development of a networked environment whereby "a shift from matters of fact, to matters of concern or matters of interest as the various agendas and opinions are brought together through networks" (Latour, 2005, p.5) are brought to the forefront. The role of the virtual in social and cognitive participatory behaviour to support discussion around pedagogies, new relationships between objects, event, display, exhibition, and knowledge production are evident. The entanglement of the #MuseumEdOz community supports the threads, links and knots of lines of digital becoming, visibility and connecting, and reciprocity. There is an ongoing growth of the community, as well as contribution to museum education.

Social media use is ever evolving as platforms evolve and how we interact with these platforms is both contextual and relational. In considering the #MuseumEdOz practices on Twitter I do not want to say that this is a single complete story. There are, however, multiple ways of being a museum educator or teacher and these come to bear in what role we consciously or unconsciously take up in the practice of engaging in Twitter. Hooper-Greenhill (2000) reminds us, that "reworking the idea of the museum has much to do with understanding the relationship between museums and their audiences, as well as the recognition and exploitation of the generative power of the cultural sphere" (p.6). Social media, and how this online space can contribute to conversations, networking, learning, and sharing of resources is one way that the museum, and specifically museum education, is being reworked. #MuseumEdOz is demonstrating how an online space facilitated on Twitter facilitates reciprocity, trust and cooperation. All aspects are essential as participants and community members find their digital identity and explore the social actions of reciprocity (symbols exchange, commonplace exchanges, ambiguity, reciprocal recognition). Audiences are engaged with and opportunity is afforded to extend how we consider distributing meaning making.

As social media becomes more prevalent with learning and the museum world, communities that come together through hashtags and their subsequent impact ignite further questions for exploration. *What social media platforms work best for educators in schools and museums? How can we extend conversations about learning in museums through the digital? How can we link together museums, educators and teachers to discuss learning through social media? What is the impact from online conversation to face-to-face engagement?* These questions are just the beginning, and I encourage others to explore and share how social media supports the emergent participatory culture offering abundant advantages for ongoing learning with like-minded individuals.

References

Boches, E. (2013). Getty Museum being social with ideas that engage. Retrieved from: http://edwardboches.com/getty-museum-being-social-with-ideas-that-engage

Bowen, A. (2015). Connecting with teachers using twitter @ANMMEDU. Retrieved from: https://musdigi.wordpress.com/2015/12/02/connecting-with-teachers-using-twitter-anmmedu/

Boyd, D. (2014). *It's complicated: The social lives of networked teens*. New Haven: Yale University Press.

———. (2008). Why youth heart social media: The role of networked publics in teenage social life. In Buckingham, D. (Ed.). *Youth, Identity and Digital Media*. (pp.119-142). Cambridge, MA.: The MIT Press.

Boyd, D. Golder, S., & Lotan, G. (2010). *Tweet, Tweet, Retweet: Conversational Aspects of Retweeting on Twitter.* HICSS-43. IEEE: Kauai, HI, January 6.

Brown, E. (2012, January 22). Teachers take to Twitter to improve craft and commiserate. *Washington Post*. Retrieved from: http://articles.washingtonpost.com/2012-01-21/local/35439858_1_twitter-chat-three-teachers-lesson-plans

Burr, S. (2015). The value of lurking. Retrieved from: https://blogs.jobs.ac.uk/the-digital-academic/2015/08/17/value-lurking/

Cameron, F. (2008). Object-Orientated Democracies: Contradictions, Challenges and Opportunities. Museums and the web, April 9-12, Montreal, Quebec, Canada. Retrieved from: http://www.museumsandtheweb.com/mw2008/papers/cameron/cameron.html#ixzz46JVdH3Kh

Cameron, F. & Kelly, L. (2010). *Hot Topics, Public Culture, Museums.* Newcastle, UK: Cambridge Scholars Publishing.

Carpenter, J.P., & Krutka, D.G. (2014). How and Why Educators Use Twitter: A Survey of the Field. *Journal of Research on Technology in Education*, *46*(4), 414-434.

Cathcart, M. & Taylor, A.F. (2014). Museums step into the future with digital presence. Retrieved from: http://www.abc.net.au/radionational/programs/booksandarts/museums-step-into-the-future-with-digital-presence/5884474

Charitonos, K., Blake, C., Scanlon, E., & Jones, A. (2012). Museum learning via social and mobile technologies: (How) can online interactions enhance the visitor experience? *British Journal of Educational Technology*, *43*(5), 802-819.

Davis, J. L., Compton, D., Farris, N.D., & Love, T.P. (2015). Implementing and Analyzing Social Media in Higher Education. *The Journal of Faculty Development, 29*(2), 9-16.

Deleuze, G., and Guattari, F. (2004). *A thousand plateaus*. London: Continuum.

Francis, R. (2010). *The Decentering of the Traditional University: The Future of (Self) Education in Virtually Figured Worlds.* Oxford: Routledge.

Giaccardi, E. (2012). *Heritage and social media: Understanding heritage in a participatory culture*. London: Routledge.

Hooper-Greenhill, E. (2000). *Museums and the Interpretation of Visual Culture.* London: Routledge.

Ingold, T. (2015). *The lines of life.* New York: Routledge.

———. (2011) *Being alive: Essays on movement, knowledge and description.* London: Routledge.

———. (2010). *Bringing things to life: Creative entanglements in a world of materials.* Manchester: ESRC National Centre for Research Methods.

———. (2008). When ANT met SPIDER; social theory for arthropods. In Knappertt, C., & Malafouris, L. (Eds.), *Material agency: Towards a non-anthropocentric approach.* (pp.209-215). New York: Springer.

Junco, R., Heiberger, G., & Loken, E. (2010). The effect of Twitter on college student engagement and grades. *Journal of Computer Assisted Learning, 27*(2), 119–132.

Kelly, L. (2014). The connected museum in the world of social media. In Drotner, K., & Schroder, K.C. (Eds.), *Museum communication and social media: The connected museum.* (pp.54-71). London: Routledge.

———. (2011). Learning in the 21st century museum Retrieved from http://australianmuseum.net.au/uploads/documents/22908/lem%20paper%2012%20oct%20kelly.pdf

Latour, B. (2005). From Realpolitik to Dingpolitik or How to Make Things Public. In B. Latour and P. Weibel (Eds). *Making Things Public: Atmospheres of Democracy.* (pp.14-43.) Cambridge Mass, The MIT Press,

Lemon, N. (2014). Twitter for arts community collaborations and networking: Social impact of fostering partnerships. In Lemon, N., Klopper, C., and Garvis, S. *Representations of working in the Arts: Deepening the Conversations.* (pp.29-50). London: Intellect.

———. (2013). @Twitter is Always wondering what's happening: Learning with and through Social Networks in higher education. In Patrut, B., Patrut, M., & Cmeciu, C. (Eds.). *Social Media in Higher Education: Teaching in Web 2.0.* (pp.237-261). Hershey, Pennsylvania, USA: IGI Global.

Lemon, N., Molloy, J., & Hocking, C. (2015). Musing, media, and mediation: Social media and museum learning. Refereed paper for Museums and the Web Asia, Melbourne, 5 to 8 October 2015. Published August 14, 2015. Consulted August 18, 2015. Retrieved from: http://mwa2015.museumsandtheweb.com/paper/musing-media-and-mediation-social-media-and-museum-learning/

Lemmermeyer, F. (2013). *Reciprocity Laws: From Euler to Eisenstein.* New York, Springer.

Lin, X., Hu, X., Hu, Q., & Liu, Z. (2014). A social network analysis of teaching and research collaboration in a teachers' virtual learning community. *British Journal of Educational Technology*, *46*(3), 1-18.

Maloney, E. J. (2007). What Web 2.0 Can Teach Us About Learning. *Chronicle of Higher Education 53*(18), 26.

Marwick, A.E., & boyd, D. (2011) I tweet honestly, I tweet passionately: Twitter users, context collapse, and the imagined audience. *New Media Society. 131*(14), 114-133.

Mazuro, C., & Rao, N. (2011) Online Discussion Forums in Higher Education: Is 'Lurking' Working? *International Journal for Cross-Disciplinary Subjects in Education (IJCDSE)*, *2*(2) 364-371.

Pelaprat, E., & Brown, B. (2012). Reciprocity: Understanding online social relations. Retrieved from: http://firstmonday.org/ojs/index.php/fm/article/view/3324/3330.

Pink, S. (2009). *Doing sensory ethnography.* London: Sage.

Postill, J., & Pink, S. (2012). Social media ethnography: the digital researcher in a messy web. *Media International Australia, 145*(1), 123-134.

Pestridge, S. (2014). A focus on students' use of Twitter – their interactions with each other, content and interface. *Active Learning in Higher Education*, *15*(2), 101-115.

Przemyslaw A. Grabowicz, P. A., Ramasco, J. J., Gonçalves, B., & Eguíluz, V. M. (2014). Entangling Mobility and Interactions in Social Media. *PLoS ONE*, 9(3). Retrieved from: http://journals.plos.org/plosone/article?id=10.1371/journal.pone.0092196

Rinaldo, S. B., Tapp, S., & Laverie, D. A. (2011). Learning by tweeting: using Twitter as a pedagogical tool. *Journal of Marketing Education, 33* (2), 193-203.

Rowe, S. (2002). The role of objects in active, distributed meaning-making. In Paris, S. (Ed.), *Perspectives on Object-Centered Learning in Museums*. (pp.19-37). Mahwah, NJ: Lawrence Erbaum Associates Inc.

Russo, A. (2012). The rise of the 'media museum': creating interactive cultural experiences through social media. In E. Giaccarddi. (Ed.). *Heritage and Social media: Understanding heritage in a participatory culture*. (pp. 145-158). New York: Routledge.

Russo, A., Watkins, J., Kelly, L., & Chan, S. (2008). Participatory communication with social media. *Curator: The Museum Journal*, *51*(1), 21-31.

Satchwell, C., Bartone, D., & Hamilton, M. (2013). Crossing boundaries: digital and on-digital literacy practices in formal and informal contexts in further and higher education. In Robin Goodfellow & Mary R. Lea (Eds.). *Literacy in the digital university: Critical perspectives on learning, scholarship, and technology.* (pp.42-55). London: Routledge.

Shaw, A., & Krug, D. (2013). Heritage Meets Social Media: Designing a Virtual Museum Space for Young People. *Journal of Museum Education, 38*(2), 239–252.

Simon, N. (2010). *The participatory museum*. Santa Cruz, CA: Museum 2.0.

Trembacj, S.A., & Deng, L. (2015). Social media and participatory culture: Opportunities and challenges for reforming the contemporary museum. In Hastings, A.K. (Ed.), *Annual Review of Cultural Heritage Informatics: 2014.* (pp.99-116). South Carolina, US: The University of South Carolina's School of Library and Information Science.

Wesely, P. M. (2013). Investigating the community of practice of world language educators on Twitter. *Journal of Teacher Education, 64*(4), 305–318.

CHAPTER 4

Windows and Frames on Young People's Artwork

Jayson Cooper and Maureen Ryan

ABSTRACT

How children communicate to their communities is significant. Likewise, how the public communicates to children is of equal importance in establishing interconnectedness. Understanding how "little publics" (Hickey-Moody, 2014) speak with, and to, larger public identities enables a shared dialogue. Embedded in the work of Gallery Sunshine Everywhere (GSE), primarily in its nine years of exhibitions in a cafe/gallery space in Melbourne's western suburbs, children, adolescents and adults, each mutually support lives—locally and globally—through intergenerational experiences. The agency and voice provided to young people by GSE extends learning beyond formal schooling experiences. Through art young people are given a venue to articulate their aesthetic being. As such GSE becomes a contact zone for members of local communities, schools, municipal councils, historians, community artists, cultural groups and more.

Juncker (2012) notes aesthetic reasoning is an everyday practice that involves everyday participation. In our everyday lives we (children and adults together) are practising, growing, dancing, singing and engaging with our aesthetic reasoning and articulations. Being inclusive of children's creativity and aesthetic communications enriches and maintains the cultural ecologies of our local places. In this way, little public pedagogues are leading adults as much as adults are guiding youth. Little and big publics meet at the intersection—the contact zone—of *little and big aesthetics*.

Exploring the little worlds and aesthetics of GSE, the everyday is celebrated through relational (youth<=>adult) interactions. Building upon the field of public pedagogy, public arts pedagogy, and community education the artistic re-presentations of young people shape and make Hickey-Moody's (2014) idea of "little publics" (p. 117). GSE provides the structures to frame little worlds in community contexts, maintaining authenticity for young people's voices. Together the glass and frame constitute the major transformative components of the visual arts experiences of GSE.

FRAMING THE WINDOW

The windows and frames that shape the actions of Gallery Sunshine Everywhere (GSE) (www.gallerysunshine.com) embrace relationality between schools, families, and communities. Through youth arts, the worldviews of children frame conversations around identity, place and community with adults beyond formal sites of learning: sparking conversations that are related to how we sense and know the places where we live and share. GSE's facilitation of holistic and complex forms of communication between children and adults, schools and communities, is integral and located in the western suburbs of Melbourne, Australia. Sunshine can be seen as a meeting place of cultures, languages, customs, beliefs and experiences. A highly ethnically diverse, and culturally rich suburb of Melbourne, Sunshine brings together lives: refugee, migrant and Australian born. With over 150 different languages spoken in Sunshine and over half the population speaking languages other than English (Brimbank City Council, 2014), Sunshine can be seen as a microcosm of the diversity, and intercultural interactions found across Australia. With recent and continuing urban development in the area the local demographic, while consistently divergent, is also changing through the processes of gentrification. Highly interesting for its cultural, social, economic and political life, Sunshine offers deep insights into the dynamic overlaps of contemporary Australia, and even further outwardly into the global locations whose languages are being uttered along Sunshine's main street, Hampshire Road, in real time.

Engaging in meaningful communications between adult's and children's visions of publicness GSE frames the art of young people and invites public interaction in public spaces. In every kindergarten, primary school and secondary college found in Sunshine, the paintings, sculptures, mixed media collages, photographs and music echo around the walls. Transcending the walls of traditional learning environments GSE invites larger audiences to hear the voices of youth. In this way, they see and hear young people's lived realities and aesthetics, encompassing communication, cognition, memory and imagination. Networked between schools (usually the art educator) and GSE, children create work specifically for exhibition—online and on-site. GSE then prepares photographs of the artwork, advertising material, and frames and hangs the work: glass on glass, wood and wood. Housed in a warm, inviting and accommodating café, the art of young people is a central feature of the overall ambience of the space. Sipping a coffee, flat white, cappuccino or hot chocolate the vibrant worlds of younger people quietly contribute to a sense of being, and belonging: quietly speaking the little truths. Exhibit after exhibit, the children's art paints moments in the everyday as part of the everyday. Painting perceptions of the public for the benefit of publicness (Biesta, 2014) is embedded in the actions of GSE, where the voices of children are positioned as valid contributors to the revitalisation of *the cultural commons* (Bertacchini, 2012; Bowers, 2006).

Artistic ways of valuing, being, knowing and doing are seen as powerful ways to stimulate and share the idiosyncratic articulations of a community's cultural identity. These articulations act as a form of aesthetic cognition emerging from everyday encounters. Through art, these everyday encounters communicate moments in time, connections to events, and the worlds around us as artists and as audiences. Following this idea, we see all figures in this chapter, taken from GSE online gallery, as holding the voices of those who created them. The images speak with our words: words and pictures make this text a vibrant confluence of ideas. We present the images in this text as a way to weave ideas, concepts and voices, existing with, and beside the words presented by us as the authors. GSE facilitates multifaceted arts-based forms of dialogue between youth and the larger communities (or publics) where children and adults live. These intergenerational and intercultural conversations, in both the text and the figures, help us to appreciate how children and adult worlds connect and communicate.

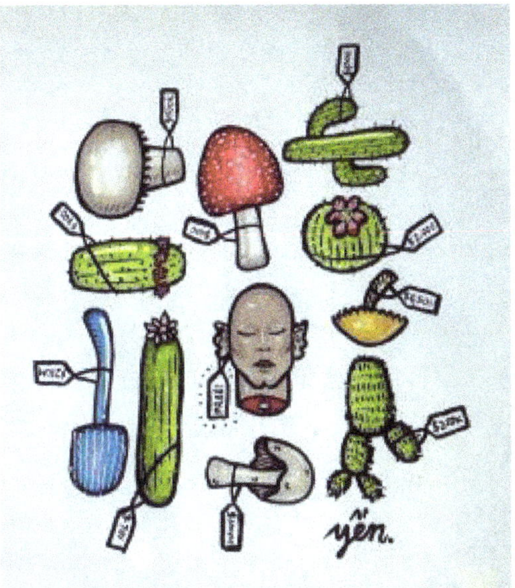

Figure: 4.1 - Connecting youth and adult worlds through artistic expression. (2016).
Source: Gallery Sunshine Everywhere ©

LITTLE PUBLICS

Being within, becoming, belonging to and defining the cultures of youth are essential when interacting and engaging with Hickey-Moody's (2014) conceptualisation of little public spheres. Understanding how "little publics" speak with, and to, larger public identities fosters a shared dialogue. Often a non-linear, and intertextual discourse moving between youth worldviews and interacting and mingling with the public spheres inhabited by adults these public spheres can be seen to echo each other in mysterious ways. Hickey-Moody (2014, 2015, 2016) extensively articulates the importance of including social, political and cultural practices of youth expressed through arts-based processes and practices to lessen the power struggles that can be found between young and old. Positioning the worlds of young people as valid contributors of our communities, shapes, speaks to, and performs a collective sense of place. Art is social, political, economic, environmental and cultural, and through arts-based practices the contributions of young people can engender alternatives in how adult worlds impact those of youth, and vice versa. The presentation of art work in public spaces, created by young people is a moment in time, an experience for the creators and viewers that echoes back into the past for some, and hints at the future for others.

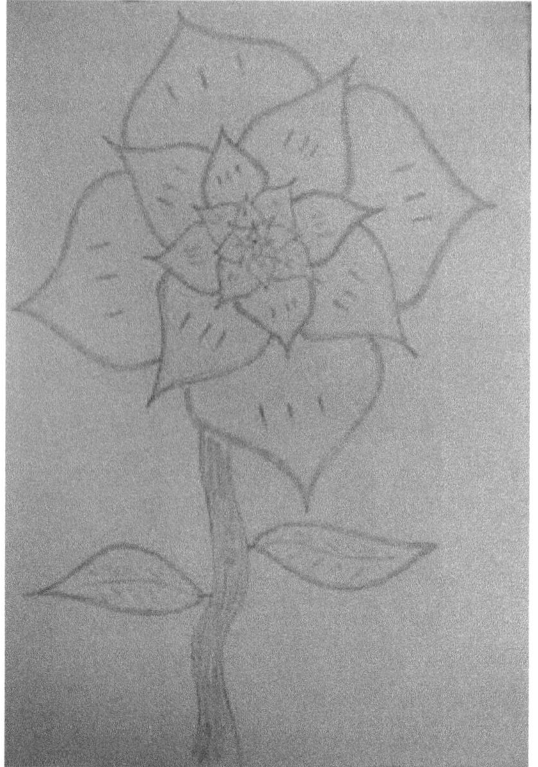

Figure: 4.2 - A moment in time holistically connected. (2016).
Source: Gallery Sunshine Everywhere ©

How "little publics" speak with, and to, larger public identities can enable collaborative communication. Such collaborative actions frame the work GSE does, offering windows of perception into these unique and often non-linear conversations. There lies a danger however, where adult perceptions can take on a position of power over the voices of the young: impacting what is being communicated, impacting relationality and what is spoken, what is heard, what is seen and sensed. Hickey-Moody (2014) reinforces little publics as the conveners of their roles within culture, which are pluralistic; embedded within civic responsibilities and visions, and carrying political outlooks that shift across social and cultural lives. Like adults, the lives of young people are constructed through rich webs of experiences that are informed by home life and through global connections, taking a diverse range of adult concepts and transforming these into their lived realities (Hickey-Moody, Savage, & Windle, 2010). Collaborative communication enables the disruption of power relationships and for even a moment the viewer may see at least a tiny fragment of life through different eyes and insights generated by experiencing art. At the same time, the young artist, with their work presented perhaps for the first time under glass may capture a hint of where their skills may carry them into the future.

ART WITH COMMUNITY

In larger projects like the Deer Park History Mosaic Mural (figure: 4.3), GSE moves beyond the confines of its cafe gallery space to a public laneway space between shops in the nearby suburban shopping strip. Coordinated for GSE by local artist Debbie Qadri this project drew together over 600 artists from schools and from the broader community, enabling research about and representation of history and currency in Deer Park. Engagement with the project was led by the local Indigenous community and extended through schools and community organisations with all contributing artists named on the final work which will adorn this public space for many years to come.

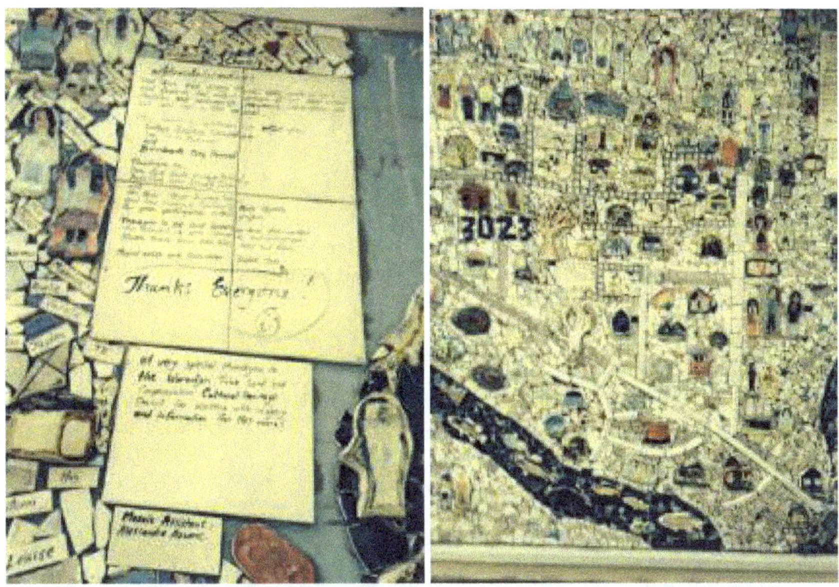

Figure: 4.3 - Deer Park History Mosaic Mural (communal art project). (2016).
Source: Gallery Sunshine Everywhere ©

Hickey-Moody et al. (2010) communicate how hip-hop culture impacts, defines, shapes and constructs social and cultural identities: in particular how hip-hip culture has taken on new definitions, and articulations in the global south. Building upon where hip-hop originated, youth have adopted and re-fashioned street culture in new ways that are relational and contextual to where young people live. Through cultural hybridisations new expressions and senses of self are constructed: merging global and local identities. This reconfigured way of being, extends and contributes to how cultural trends migrate. In their study, they talk about how children in Noble Park, Melbourne, have adapted, claimed and reinforced social and cultural behaviors from the United States to be contextual within an Australia landscape. Much like an Andy Warhol screen print of Marilyn Monroe cultural interpretations become emergent, generative and affective publics, where new behaviors disrupt, challenge, and contribute towards what came before, volunteering localised interpretations.

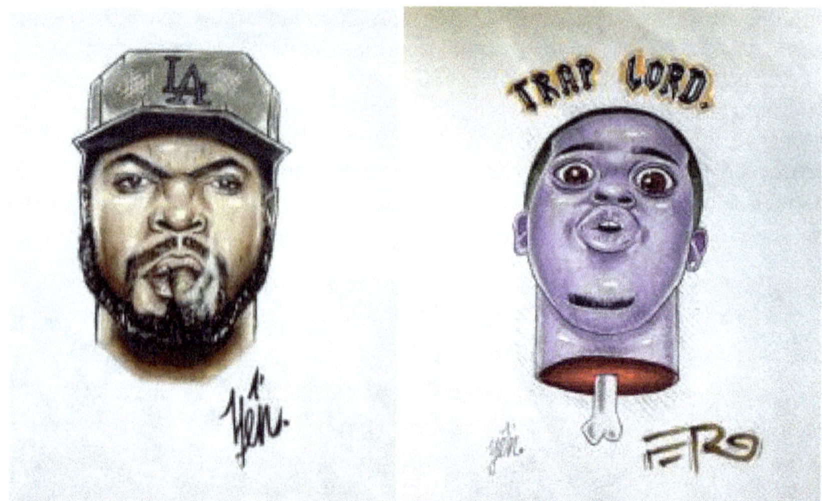

Figure: 4.4 - Engaging with popular culture. (2016).
Source: Gallery Sunshine Everywhere ©

In collaboration with Sudanese Australian Integrated Learning (SAIL)—http://www.sailprogram.org.au—GSE offers the volunteer program arts-based activities that extend young Sudanese-Australians learning, and connections with each other and the local communities. Run by volunteers SAIL provides a tutoring service for young people and their families who speak English as a second language. The arts-based learning is organic, fluid and dependent on the interests of the students. Enhancing and contributing to the larger context of learning, GSE bring materials, resources, local artists and educators to offer their knowledge to assist young people in creating and making works that express their interests and identities. Building strong social structures the young people are engaged on their level, which includes the connections youth have with popular culture. Firmly planted within community learning, in one iteration the collaboration between GSE, SAIL and a local circus group provided holistic learning experiences where young people created circus costumes with GSE for their circus performances.

Creating their own costumes, the children participating in this program drew inspirations from a wide range of stimuli found within popular culture: wrestling outfits and masks, hip-hop/pop music regalia, football, dance, basketball and film acted as starting points for the children's creations. Young people's perceptions of the world are intertwined within popular culture: establishing relatedness with community artists, popular culture became the middle ground, the place where connections were made. Asking questions like: Who is your football team? What music do you listen to? How can I put this image onto a tee-shirt? Have you see the Terminator? These lines of conversation and inquiry enabled the tastes of youth—*the little aesthetics*—to drive what was made and how it was made. Performing lives through the creation of art is powerful, never more so than when listening to the little aesthetics, hopes, dreams, fears, concerns and worldviews of children.

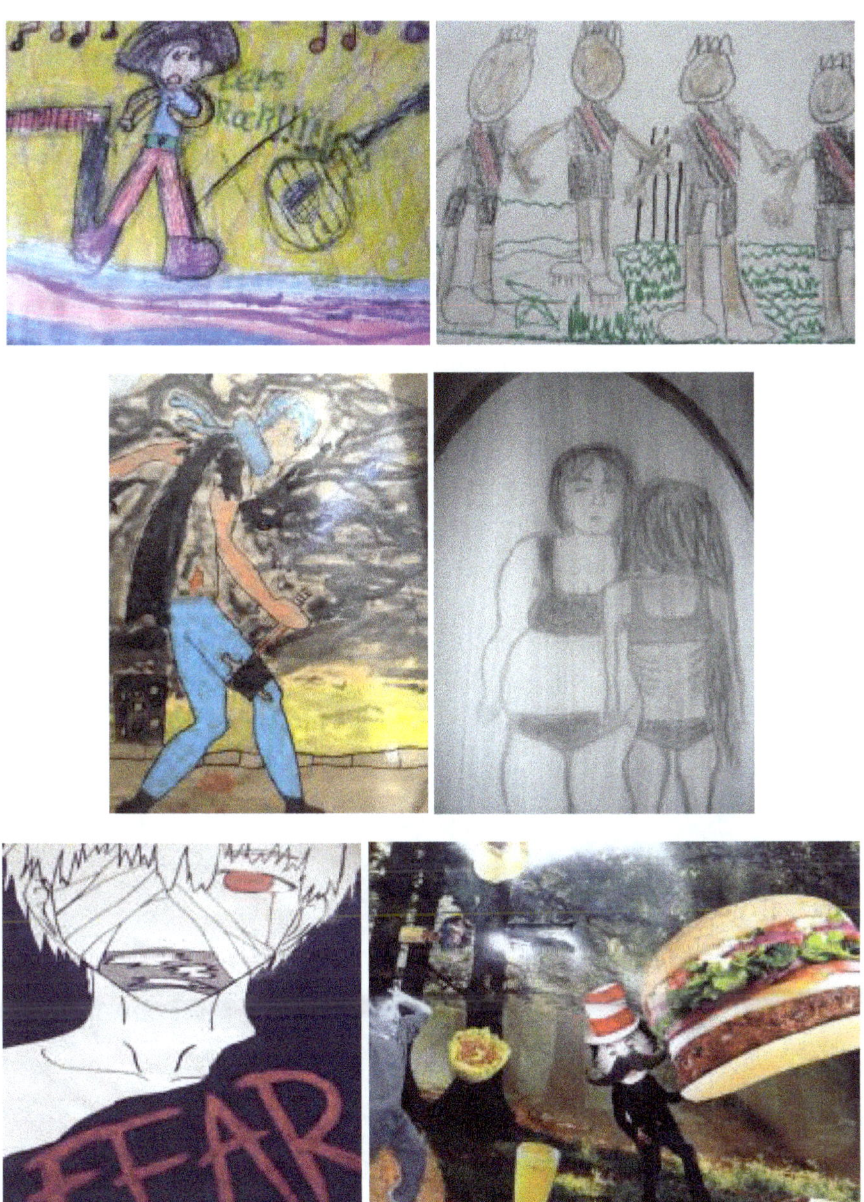

Figure: 4.5 - Little aesthetics. (2016).
Source: Gallery Sunshine Everywhere ©

Hopes and Dreams

In another project, *Hopes and Dreams*, comic strips and cartoons were the popular cultural vehicle to communicate the past experiences and aspirations, hopes and dreams for the future of young people. In collaboration with another community organisation that works with youth in the western suburbs of Melbourne, Adult Multicultural Education Services Youth Programs—the voices, experiences, and visions of recent refugee and immigrant youth were honoured. The impressions of young people about their lives are celebrated through the public exhibitions supported by GSE, and offer adults a deeper understanding about the lives of young people around us: building insights into how the adult worlds, including those found in popular culture impact, shape and communicate to the young. In this way, the voices of children speak back to adults, and are highly political, cultural, social and affective (Luttrell, 2013).

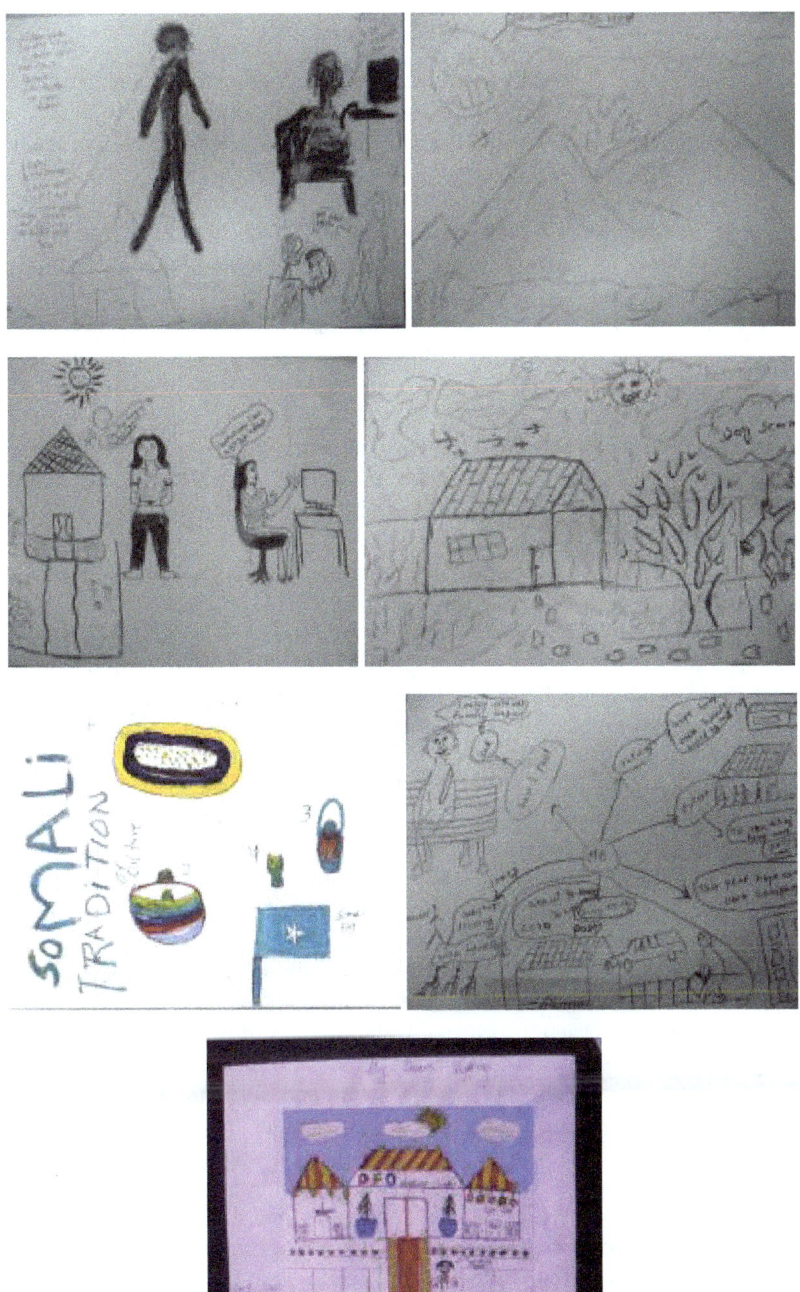

Figure: 4.6 - Young people's perspectives on their worlds. (2016).
Source: Gallery Sunshine Everywhere ©

THE PUBLIC PEDAGOGY

The cultural identities of youth are abstract and concrete, and can be articulated and normalised through popular culture. In this way, popular culture is seen as a form of grand education; where the transnational influence of media acts as the pedagogue, consisting of many and varied parts (Giroux, 2016; Maudlin & Sandlin, 2015). Savage (2014) refers to the pedagogical nature of popular culture as "popular public pedagogy" (distinct from the other two forms he identifies of public pedagogy: concrete and political). Concrete public pedagogy is spatially bound, existing within concrete locations, with a fixed geographic location. Political pedagogical discourse is inclusive of the political commentary, insights and understandings that exist on a large scale or through a specifically defined scope. Within all three forms of public pedagogy noted by Savage, there are overlaps found in the work of GSE. First, GSE is located within a spatially bound place (Sunshine), and secondly, politically as the voices of children are privileged, included and transformed through intercultural, communal and intergenerational experiences within Australia and internationally. Thirdly, the role popular culture plays in young people's lives is most applicable in understanding the work children bring to GSE.

Popular public pedagogy is public pedagogy located within the realm of popular culture. Savage highlights how cultural objects, artefacts and texts generate this form of public pedagogy: assemblages that are interdisciplinary, multimodal and can be interpreted in a diverse range of ways: splicing cultural, media, political, social and environmental borders and boundaries in new and amplified ways. Ways that are often non-linear and indeterminate but which impart knowledge, interact and teach, following our interests, aspirations, dreams and curiosities through popular culture.

Strong-Wilson and Ellis (2007) highlight three principal educators in a young person's life—parents/guardians, formal educators, and the learning environment. Building upon this idea many teachers (human and nonhuman) can be identified. Popular culture and media become active educators and informants to what young people connect with, and learn from. Generating a multiplicity of teachers, popular culture acts not only as a consumerable product, but also as a pedagogue and social driver. Internet, films, YouTube, Facebook, Instagram and many more communicate social, cultural and political fabrics for adults and children. Similarly to adults, these everyday threads are woven together by children as they express their aesthetic reasoning and identities. By contrast, at the heart of many children's artwork is the theme of family, a shared concept between young and old. The expressions of family are pivotal in shaping our identities and the communities around us. GSE contributes to this profiling of families in various ways, especially in the presentation of preschoolers' art, which so often represents family members, and for all age groups in the exhibition celebrations, which draw immediate, and extended families together. Further through its involvement in community activities including local festivals and other activities mentioned in this chapter GSE relates with school students within their broad family context.

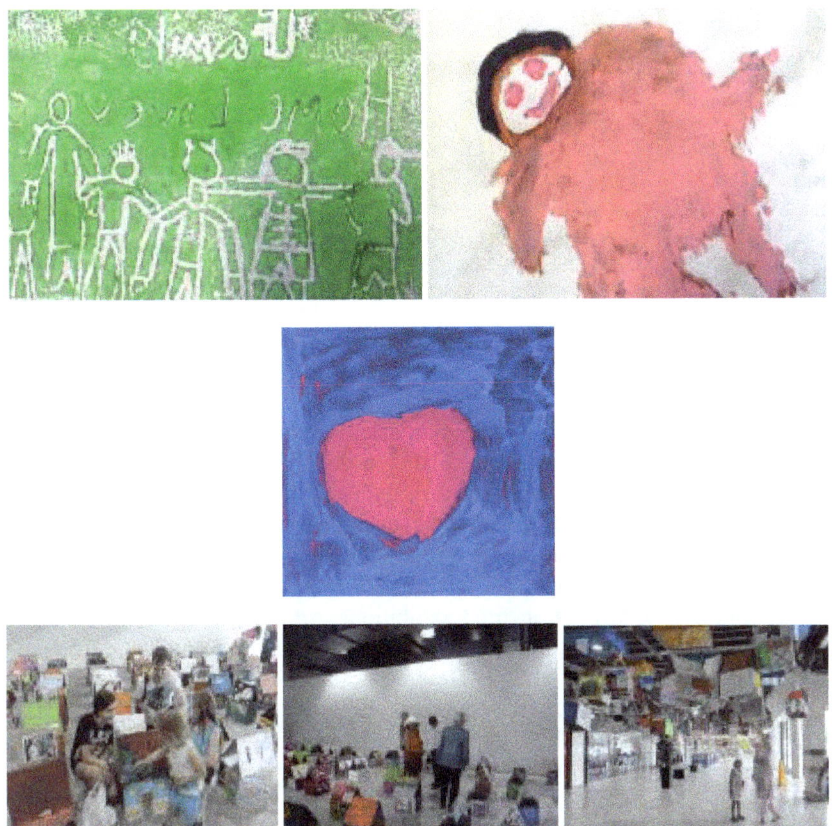

Figure: 4.7 - Self, family and home – children expressing themes of home, family and self across a range of GSE experiences. (2016).
Source: Gallery Sunshine Everywhere ©

Artistic knowing is relational to the interests, tastes, and knowledge of popular culture. Dance moves, graffiti, hip-hop, fashion, televised reality and advertisements all inform and contribute towards young people's identities as much as the adults who interact with them. There is a "leaning" in and/or away (Pelias, 2011) from what popular culture presents to us (adults and children), be it cute animals, how to make dumplings, selfie culture or videogames. What is found in popular culture can be adopted and/or critiqued in a young person's life, and interpreted back through their artistic expressions. Entwined in the dissemination of popular culture, arts practices become an engaging and powerful medium (for adults and children) to express with and through: expressions that aid in shaping opinions and communicating how we know and be in the present moment. Children communicate citizenship and being by blending the personal with the social, the social with the cultural, the cultural with the political, the political with the environmental, and everything in between in fluid ways. Mapping their everyday, children choose how, what, when, and who is entitled to their knowing, presenting vivid accounts of their places in the world around them.

Informed by many educators, and performed in many classrooms, within, outside and beyond learning institutions, young people's aesthetics are unique to youth worlds. We refer to this as *little aesthetics* (Cooper & Ryan, 2016). Embracing this multiplicity when engaging with youth worldviews requires flexibility in providing authentic avenues that communicate children's global and local communities, identities and growing perceptions of the world, in local contexts that maintain children's integrity.

Connected through Caring

Arts activities seek to celebrate children's imaginations, aesthetics, knowledge and realities, embracing versatility by prompting genuine youth-youth, youth-adult interactions as demonstrated in art work produce by children following the 2009 bushfires in Victoria. Although the children involved are not located in the vicinity of the 2009 bushfires the psychological impact on young people was a concern and art provided an ideal way for young people to express their responses to such disasters and a platform for them to talk about such concerns. Further as in the example of the bushfire art work, life within local communities fosters civic accountability and ethics of connection and care. GSE extends this ethic of care and connection to the worlds of young and old people through themed exhibitions: such as yearly exhibitions around neighbour day, families and local diversity: engaging a diverse range of participants—artists and community places, and people. In this way, GSE accommodates an ethic of care and connection (Noddings, 2015; Rose, 1999) by inviting children to be teachers and learners simultaneously, blurring the boundaries of knowledge transfer: mutually mending intergenerational gaps when perceiving lived realities—avoiding the potholes between generations. Reconfiguring the archaic saying *children are to be seen and not heard,* the notion of little publics and little aesthetics takes away the traditional stance of adults and refashions how children are heard and seen, how youth co-creates the publics we inhabit together.

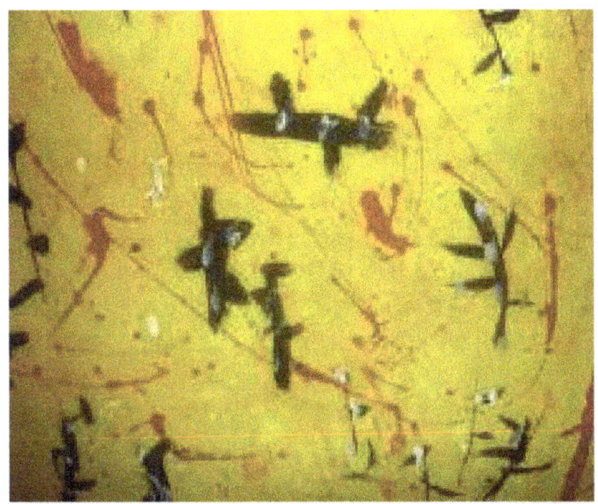

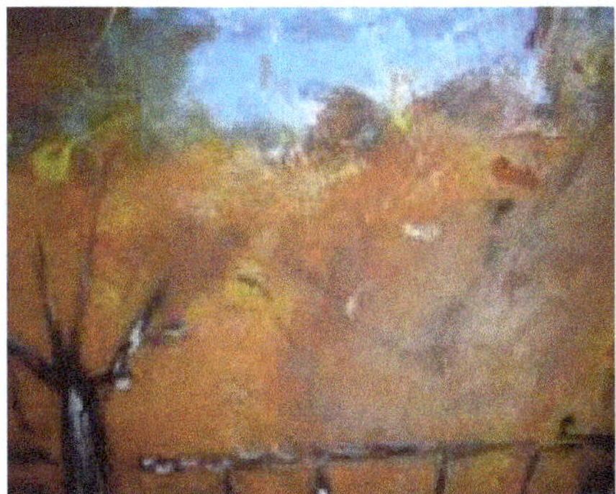

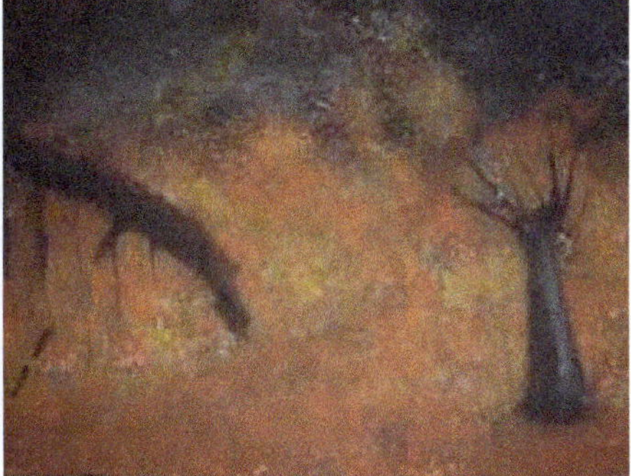

Figure: 4.8 - Responses to 2009 Victorian Bushfires. (2016).
Source: Gallery Sunshine Everywhere ©

Embedded in the worlds communicated through GSE is a deep ethic of care, an ethic of connection and one of caring with young people together. Aligned with Luttrell's (2013) expression of care, "the choreography of care work" dances with love, respect, identity and unity (p. 296). Through art and visual texts the roles and responsibilities of educators, within and beyond schooling, locate education perceptions with far more than scores, grades and budgets. Instead it seeks to find and listen to the knowledge and being of how people are growing and becoming, being and belonging, as adults and children: kindling alternative ways of knowing: multimodal forms of expression made with young people, adults and communities in GSE. As with Spivak (1988) the lines of "power, desire and interest" (p. 271) are blurred when it comes to authentic inclusion of children's voice and care and are merged into institutional ideology.

Ideas that position children into subject-object relations reinforce youth as being always reliant upon the guidance, instruction and modeled behavior of adults, where young people are seen lower in status and with less knowledge of adults. What is important to highlight through the exhibitions by GSE of art work prepared by pre-primary, primary and secondary school students, is the embodiment of a heightened sense of relatedness that shifts the power dynamics between object and subject relationships. Connecting students and educators in alternative ways, transforms the lines of desire to be about what young people see, feel, touch and do as the foci of communication: transferring the interest of working with children to be children driven, to be subject to subject, object to object; working and learning together between people (subject) and via the art work produced (object). In concert, young and old live and learn from each other in pluralistic forms and ways, marking new pathways of interaction: designing and travelling these roads in unison. These directions demonstrate caring beside and with young people, placing value upon the experiences and aesthetics of children and adults combined. Luttrell (2013) maintains that in addition to caring *for* and *about* children, educators need to care *with* students: collaboratively working in proactive ways to place value on young people's thoughts, visions, hopes, and ideas of social justice and listening to children's counter-narratives and relationships for, about and with education. This, as highlighted by Luttrell (2013), transfers the individual notions of care between educator and student, to be collective, to carry a sense of care that is constructed with children and adults together in order to celebrate the interrelated web of connections that can be co-constructed: authentically shaping each other's growing identities.

Community and place are major elements in how we construct identity. This formation of identity is constantly evolving, much like the development of places and communities, constantly changing with life's ebb and flow through the learning and teachings of life. Strong connections with the places we live and communities we belong to are as vital to adults as they are to children. The places and communities we inhabit also occupy us in a myriad of ways: held by memory, lived experiences, future goals and through dreams and aspirations. Central to our identities, places are major components of who we are, and where we are from. How we connect, share and co-create where we live is important for adults and children (Cooper, 2015).

Adult connections and collaborations are seen to be vital in establishing positive and authentic engagements with children. The United Nations Conventions on the Rights of the Child (CRC) (United Nations, 1990), plainly states that children have the right to express their self-efficacy and agency, to be active decision makers in their existence. In order to live these rights, youth are dependent on adult participation, yet adults can carry skepticism about children's capacity to fulfil their self-determination. Challenging adult authority and regulation within a non-standard art gallery format GSE works with young people in democratic ways. Celebrating autonomy, the community and civic participation(s) endorsed by GSE constructs bridges over these troubled waters. Crossing borders and boundaries GSE publically acknowledges the diversity of children's worlds and how they see, hear, sense, be and know where and how they live within dynamic local and global worlds, often simultaneously. Seeking the dynamic overlaps between young and old, school and community these powerful partnerships come together to generate possibilities for all involved. In examining Article 12 of the CRC, Lundy (2007) outlines four elements to consider when adults interact with youth. She highlights in order for adults to promote autonomy and agency in young people's lives there needs to be space that allows children to speak, so children can freely express their views. However, this is not enough in bypassing adult-youth power relations that position adults as the all knowing, all governing body. Youth perspectives need to be heard, witnessed and taken on their level, and given space to be heard. Doing so highlights children's worldviews and places value upon how young people are, in relation to those around them, including adults.

MUTUALLY SUPPORTING LIVES

The child-adult, school-community partnerships GSE creates, function as a cultural and social driver for change and development. Actively validating young people through community arts practices listens to, and privileges the views of young people, encouraging their imaginative and artistic ways of being and knowing, of belonging and becoming. By providing avenues and support for youth across a range of arts-based community activities GSE takes "little publics seriously" (Hickey-Moody, 2014, p. 118), by fostering authentic relationships with the communities where they are part, by inspiring kids to make, to interact, to communicate, to offer perspectives, to engage with their local places, schools, and neighborhoods in constructive and elaborate ways.

Embedded in the work of GSE, children, adolescents and adults, mutually support lives, locally and globally, through intergenerational experiences. The agency and voice provided to young people extends learning beyond formal schooling experiences. Through art young people are given an avenue to articulate their aesthetic beings: to reflect on what is important in their lives at a particular time and place. Providing a fluid communal gallery space GSE engages, exhibits, values, celebrates, extends, enables, increases, develops, and mentors children's creativity, imaginations, and designs. Further in maintaining an array of partnerships and pathways that promote youth connections, GSE brings families, members of the local community, local councils, teachers and schools together. This involves celebrating the diverse pathways and partnerships that engender re-presentations through artful inquiry and expression of what it means to be a young person in the western suburbs of Melbourne, Australia in 2016.

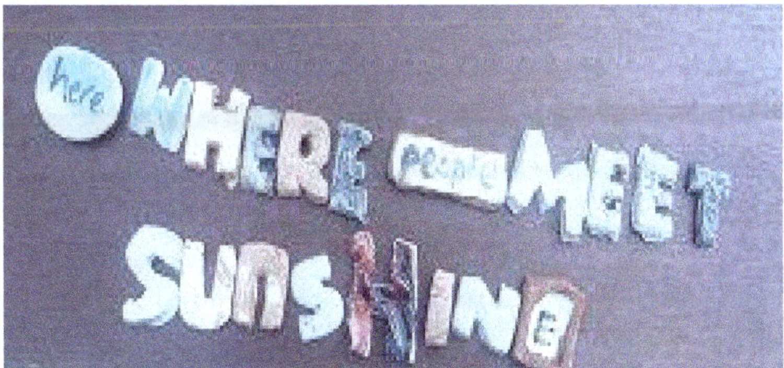

Figure: 4. 9 - Here where people meet sunshine (a collaborative installation where members of the community arrange ceramic words, letters and objects into meaning). (2016).
Source: Gallery Sunshine Everywhere ©

The purposes of GSE are to promote engagement with art-making and art education among pre-primary, primary and secondary school students and their schools and families and business and the broader community of the western suburbs of Melbourne through:

(a) Exhibiting and valuing the art of pre-primary, primary and secondary students
(b) Celebrating the talents of young artists and enabling community access to the art of pre-primary, primary and secondary school students
(c) Extending the involvement of families, schools, business and the broader community with youth oriented art activities
(d) Increasing community understanding of the art of pre-primary, primary and secondary school students
(e) Developing art focused partnerships with schools and other organisations
(f) Mentoring young and emerging artists
(g) Undertaking collaborative projects to raise the status and accessibility and visual arts for young people in the western suburbs of Melbourne.

Since its establishment in 2007 GSE has curated close to 100 exhibitions, most of which have been displayed at the Granary Café in Sunshine, a major suburb in the City of Brimbank in Melbourne's west. The exhibitions combine the formality of the work being framed and opening events being organised for each exhibition with the accessibility of their location in a local café. As well as the exhibitions, which are mainly of school students' work, GSE has worked closely with local artists and arranged exhibitions of their work in an area where there are no galleries. Also, GSE has been involved with various other local activities including the development of a history mosaic mural in the nearby suburb of Deer Park, an exhibition in the local shopping centre of 1,000 houseboxes (presented lantern like, telling home and family stories inside and community stories outside), arts activities at local festivals and annual celebrations of Neighbour Day. These are documented on the web site along with an art gallery section, which includes photographs of work submitted for exhibition since 2007. In many of these activities, including particularly the 2015 Sparkles weekend workshop, GSE has drawn together increasing numbers of local artists, who both shared their skills and exhibited their work. In a similar way, each year the Young Teachers' exhibition profiles the art work of recent graduates from the teacher education program at the local university.

The strong local base of GSE and its longevity is borne out in the partnerships established and sustained but importantly in the ways in which local stories can be told and shared locally and globally. There are exemplars of such layered aesthetic representations in the concrete poetry activities facilitated by a local artist, photographed and embedded in subsequent blog, web site and Facebook entries.

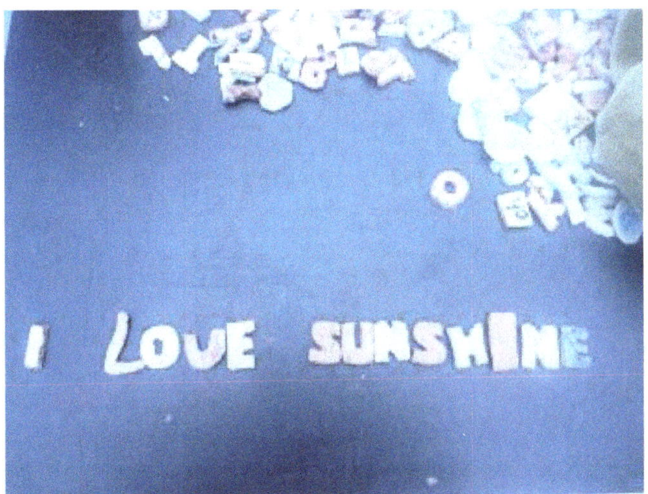

Figure: 4.10 - I love Sunshine. (2016).
Source: Gallery Sunshine Everywhere ©

FRAMING THE CREATIVE GARDENS WITH THE STUFF OF LIFE

In line with its broad purposes outlined above GSE is framing how young people interact with art within and beyond systems of conventional schooling. Through an intertextual engagement with place, personal narratives and arts-based activities GSE contributes towards and regenerates the little and big publics that construct local communities. In doing this GSE seeks authentic collaborations between little and big worlds, between child and adult perceptions of beauty and between the aesthetics of kids and adults (little and big aesthetics). Bringing together and navigating relationships found in the Weltanschauung of adults and children resonates well with how GSE operates: fostering the creative gardens children move through, plant, and care for, by enhancing young people's engagement with the parks children and adults toil, stroll through and play in together, our communities, within and outside schools. Schools and school culture are one part of the larger worlds adults and children frequent. In working with schools but not in schools, GSE becomes a contact zone for members of local communities, schools, municipal councils, historians, community artists, cultural groups and more. Deeply advocating for young people's participation and roles in communities aligns with concepts that emerge from public pedagogy. This is clear in the location of the exhibitions in a public (non school) space but more explicitly in examples like *the metaphor story*.

As part of the GSE's 1,000 Houseboxes Project workshops were conducted at the Brimbank Festival in 2010 and 2011 and at Funtasia Children's Festival in 2010. With the houseboxes hanging throughout Sunshine Plaza, GSE was allocated a shop along the busy shopping strip for further display and workshops. Lots of families came by during the day, including Braydon, his brother Tyler and his grandmother. Braydon said he was off to a party at 1pm so couldn't use paints. Tyler didn't have that constraint and painted away happily. Using texta pens, Braydon drew a figure, which he labeled 'Rey Mysterio', who he noted was 'a pretty good television wrestler' (depicted in figure 4.11). Braydon explained, 'He's small (like me), but very strong and beats the big guys.' Braydon wrote, Big things come in little packages' and asked, 'How do you spell metaphor?' Impressed, the GSE facilitator told him and asked, 'Why do you want to know?' Pointing to the picture. 'Big things come in little packages' he said, 'Because that's one.'

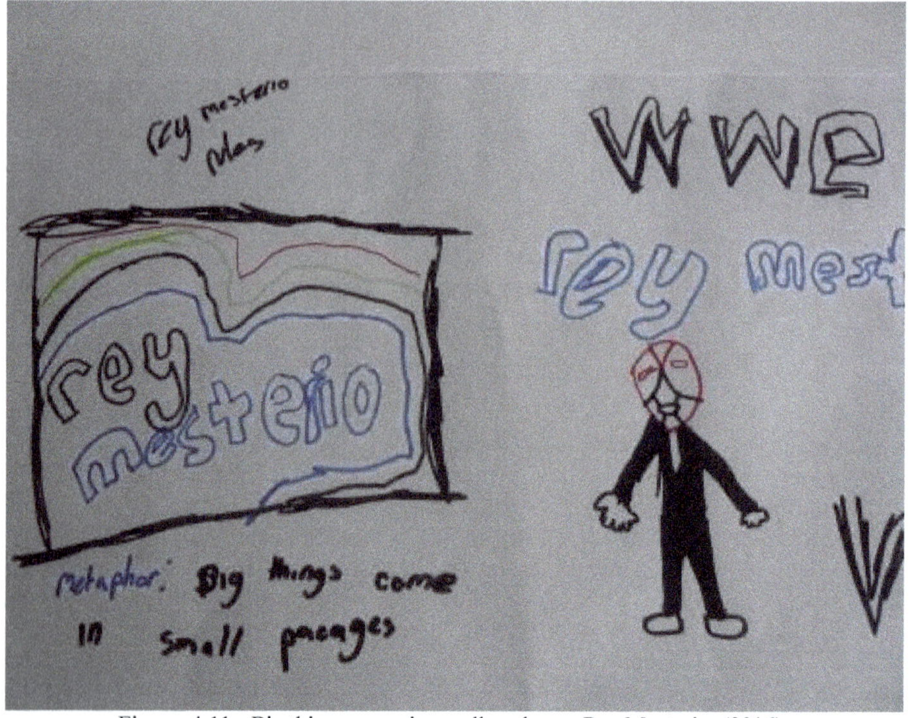

Figure: 4.11 - Big things come in small packages Rey Mysterio. (2016).
Source: Gallery Sunshine Everywhere ©

With this exchange still in my mind, GSE started to collect children's work from local kindergartens for the next exhibition at the Granary Café in Sunshine. When we visited one kindergarten to collect work for the exhibition, our attention was drawn to a tiny storybook, drawn in pen and ink, no bigger than a postage stamp, demonstrating excellent control by a four-year-old. This promoted memories of Braydon and his "small packages" drawing. Through its networks, GSE was able to bring together in the next exhibition, the two young artists, their families and the ways in which their drawings were linked.

This example weaves together school (meaning of metaphors/idioms) and non school/popular culture learning (television wrestling) brought together in a public arts space linked to two formal education sites. Further, it draws attention to the diverse influences on the two children that initiated the drawings they produced: one, the television wrestler, the other, the tiny book. The exhibition of the artworks in the public space of the gallery along with the story that brought them together, presented side by side with them on the gallery wall and on the GSE web site enabled reflection by viewers of the works on the themes noted above and more especially in relation to the meanings of public and of pedagogy.

GAZING THROUGH THE WINDOWS OF PUBLICNESS

Education in a general sense is most often aligned with progressing through formal schooling, moving from classroom to classroom, year to year, shifting through the progression points and levels of learning outlined by a standardised curriculum and located in a formal site of learning. Public pedagogy illustrates how learning and education are embedded within life-pursuits within and outside traditional school settings, and is inclusive of curricula content as well as of content found in life and the everyday. A broad idea, public pedagogy, has been ascribed many guises, masks and costumes as it is expressed in a range of ways (Sandlin, O'Malley, & Burdick, 2011). Noting in their review of literature from the late 19th century to early 21st century the term public pedagogy is seen within a range of definitions and intentions subsumed in the separate terms *public* and *pedagogy*. How the terms *public* and *pedagogy* have been framed, applied and theorised has generated frays and loose ends in the fabric of public pedagogy discourse over this period. In a more recent publication Burdick, Sandlin, and O'Malley (2014) suggest how public pedagogical discourse can be addressed within a 21st Century context. Savage (2014) argues that the work of public pedagogy needs to delineate how the pedagogical lives in the public; asking how is the public conceptualised. He also asks the same questions of how pedagogy is conceptualised, where pedagogy resides in the public, and how is the pedagogical public, through all this asking who is teacher and who is student. These discussions construct the glass that makes the windows GSE looks through with youth in the City of Brimbank where the suburbs Sunshine and Deer Park referred to earlier are located. Education is found dwelling within schools, colleges, kindergartens and universities, as well as being deeply rooted in local communities, and places: made from the stuff of life: supporting holistic perceptions about education consisting in lifelong, relational learning that crosses theoretical and physical borders found at the "intersections with culture, media, informal sites of learning, democratic education, and social activism" (Sandlin et al., 2011, p. 339). The publicness of GSE carries deep social and democratic ethics that are expressed, lived and performed through a range of events and experiences: from painting, music, fashion design, sculpture to hosting exhibitions and public speaking and communal conversations that are temporal and fleeting: activities that invite members of the public to create, make, explore and respond with and to each other. One way the pedagogical actions of GSE work is illustrated is through concrete street poetry (poetry made from ceramic words and letters), an innovative practice initiated by local artist Debbie Qadri.

Open ended and invitational, ceramic letters are scattered along a bare table like Scrabble or Lego pieces, awaiting the actions of a person to fashion words, statements, names into existence: generously becoming inspiration for the next person to play with. The community day stall of creativity interacts with the public: young and old. There are letters for those who can easily create words, words for those who prefer to make sentences and phrases as well. The words move, change forms and shift around the surface of the table like the moving of feet within the festival. Play-based interactions between adults and children, grandparents and grandchildren, siblings and friends cultures with cultures organically intersect: demonstrating the diversity found within little and big aesthetics. Passing over authentic space to what the public wish to say, wish to leave for another to read, to interact with, these experimental actions spark new ways of communicating our civic entanglements with each. Biesta (2014) highlights this approach as generating new ways of doing: new ways of doing learning and teaching, in new and different contexts that push, pull, give and take, co-constructed as a "pedagogy that is entirely public" (p. 23). Bringing places, people, nonhumans, epistemologies, ontologies, axiologies together, for the benefit of public interests and needs, these actions cause a point of rupture that challenges how we learn, how we teach, and how we interact at the intersections of public life. Facilitated by GSE, arts-based ways of doing hold a passionate concern for reclaiming "public ways of acting in concert" (p. 23). Passing the microphone to the audience, to transform the audiences of art (the public) into the creators. Dismantling the privileged and out-of-reach qualities of arts-practices by providing accessibility and engagement with art in local contexts, relevant to the everyday lives of those who breathe the same air. Engaging members of the public in this way reinforces Biesta's notion of a public pedagogy enacted in and with the interest of the public.

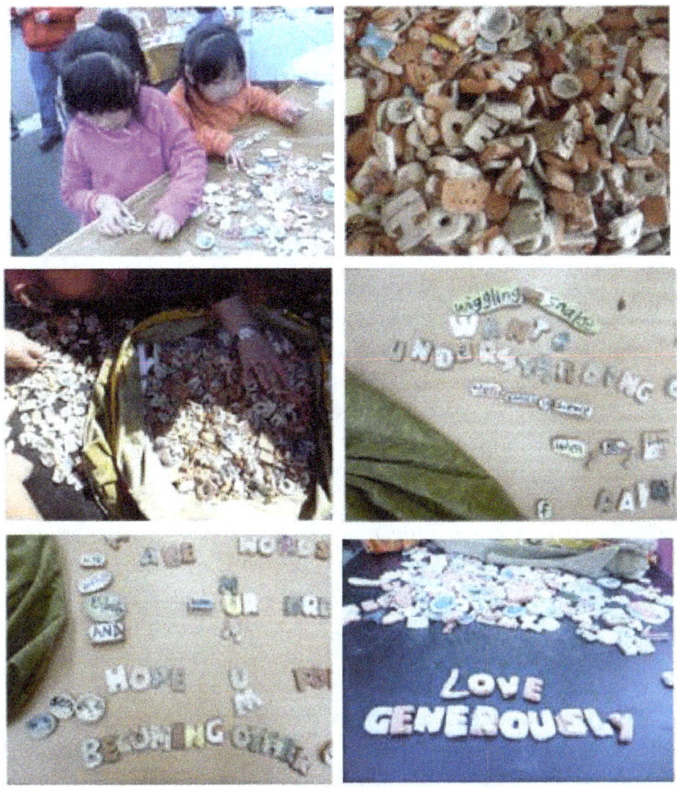

Figure: 4.12 - Concrete poetry in collaboration with local artist Debbie Qadri, Brimbank festival. (2016).
Source: Gallery Sunshine Everywhere ©

CONCLUSION

Glass on glass, wood on wood: the glass and the frames lift the art work of kindergarten and school children into a traditional form and enable community engagement with the art work in public spaces. Art work prepared on cheap butcher's paper and on the back of teachers' strike posters in poorly funded schools is transformed through formal framing. Similarly, the young artists are transformed in the opening events that carry them, their families and teachers from their usual classrooms to a public space where their work and that of their friends covers the walls for all who visit the cafe gallery space to share.

Glass on glass, wood on wood: so many skills, so many rules to support the inherent creativity in the art work displayed. So many enablers to lift the work into the public realm: allen keys, screw drivers, wire and screws, spirit levels, hanging systems: lining frame tops or bottoms, curating according to colour, form, theme: considerations around fairness: opportunities for all young people in the group.

Double frame, double hang, wood on wood, glass on glass: "*we need to problematize the critical public pedagogical work that takes place between artists and their participants, but also question how the work circulates as a work of art*" (Springgay & The Torontonians, 2014, p. 144). Double frame, double hang, double states of being, double ontology. Youth art and the wider communal connections compose various states of being within youth and adult worlds and can be communicated through artistic products and processes: following artful pedagogies. Springgay and The Torontonians (2014) urge us to think about how "*pedagogy-as-art*" works in intimate ways, but also across "*the larger art field*" (p. 144). Likewise, Savage (2014) urges us to think about how public pedagogy works in intimate ways but also across the larger public and pedagogical fields. In this way wood on wood, glass on glass becomes a powerful metaphor for the work done by GSE, as they frame the double ontologies found in and between youth and adult art encounters, between schools and communities, children and adults, families and neighbourhoods, cultures and cultures. "*The two audiences...know the work differently*" (Springgay & The Torontonians, 2014, p. 144), yet, are equally celebrated in collaboration, and are accountable through their degree of relationality and connections of care.

Noddings (2015) urges educators to think about how we are accountable to caring, how we communicate caring in the work we do. Focusing on school accountability and the homogenous perceptions of care in a system of standardisation, the work of teachers is complex and highly political. Within these adult teacher visions of learning and teaching the need to foster authentic dialogue with children is vital: dialogue that does not centre itself on the topic of testing, but rather actively listens and finds connections. There is a danger of relying solely upon political thinking that is laid over the top of education as it can negate the voices of children. Bringing the educators' work to sit alongside and with the perspectives of children in spaces other than schools counters the political one-sidedness of education, enabling it to be holistically created with youth, teachers, families and community organisations. Valuing the expressions and visions of the young people within a locality through art incites a relational artistic public pedagogy.

Children and youth are in a temporal, liminal state of becoming, opening ways for adults to be relationally dynamic with them and their worldviews. In such moments of youth-adult coalition, the social, cultural, and ethical perspectives of little and big worlds meet (Hickey-Moody, 2014). At the contact zone between internal and external realities adults can reach into their childhood and reflect back, having a diverse, multiplicative array of experiences to bring into the contact zone of aesthetic awareness. As seen in the work of GSE, the splendid array of children's expression, voice, imagination and designs are exhibited within adult and youth aesthetics.

Children are shaping and growing their identities. Juncker (2012) notes aesthetic reasoning is an everyday practice that involves everyday participation. In our everyday lives we (children and adults together) are practising, growing, dancing, singing and engaging with our aesthetic reasoning and articulations. Pelias (2011) refers to this aesthetic cognition as a form of leaning, moving in and away from everyday encounters, teaching us about ourselves as adults, and about the children we interact with as educators. GSE exercises the little and big aesthetics of the everyday, providing rich encounters between young and old, schools and communities, through positive and inclusive partnerships. Being inclusive of children's creativity and aesthetic communications enriches and maintains the cultural ecologies and commons of our local places. In this way, little public pedagogues are leading adults as much as adults are guiding youth.

Little and big publics meet at the intersection—the contact zone—of *little and big aesthetics*. Exploring the little worlds and aesthetics of GSE, the everyday is celebrated through relational (youth<=>adult) interactions. Building upon the field of public pedagogy, public arts pedagogy, and community education the artistic re-presentations of young people shape and make Hickey-Moody's (2014) idea of "*little publics*" (p. 117). Taking the civic, social, economic, cultural, and political worlds of young people seriously celebrates and provides supportive ways for little publics to teach, mirror, become and contribute to the maintenance of our local communities. The rich opportunities GSE offers little and big worlds encourage people to look through the windows generated by young people as artistic expression. GSE provides the structures to frame little worlds in community contexts, maintaining authenticity for young people's voices. Together the glass and frame constitute the major transformative components of the visual arts experiences of GSE.

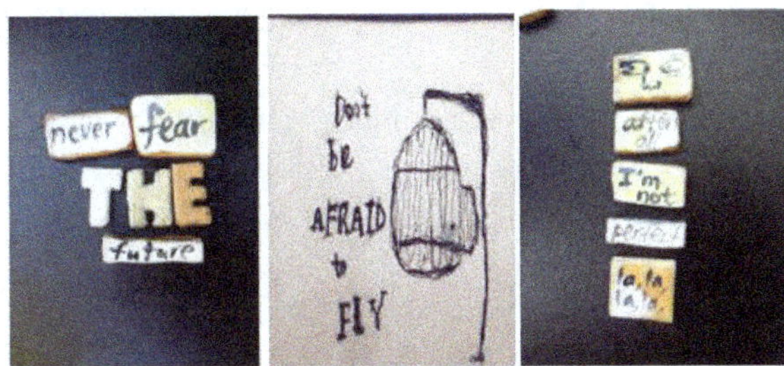

Figure: 4.13 - Never fear the future and don't be afraid to fly and see after all I'm not perfect, la, la, la, la. (2016).
Source: Gallery Sunshine Everywhere ©

References

Bertacchini, E. E. (2012). *Cultural commons: a new perspective on the production and evolution of cultures*: Edward Elgar Publishing.

Biesta, G. (2014). Making pedagogy public: for the public, of the public, or in the interest of publisness? In J. Burdick, J. A. Sandlin & M. P. O'Malley (Eds.), *Problematizing public pedagogy* (pp. 15-25).

Bowers, C. A. (2006). *Revitalizing the commons: Cultural and educational sites of resistance and affirmation*: Lexington Books.

Burdick, J.,, Sandlin, J.A., & O'Malley, M. P. (2014). *Problematizing public pedagogy*: Routledge.

Brimbank City Council. (2014). *Mapping Bimbank's Diversity*. Brimbank City Council, Retrieved from: http://www.brimbank.vic.gov.au/files/1873c408-bbb9-40ed-9832-a42e00ef5b8b/Mapping_Brimbanks_Diversity_2015.pdf.

Cooper, J. (2015). *Co-Creating With, and In, a Southern Landscape.* (PhD), Victoria University. Retrieved from http://vuir.vu.edu.au/30165/

Cooper, J., & Ryan, M. (2016). Little Learning in Big Worlds. Manuscript submitted for publication.

Gallery Sunshine Everywhere. (2016). Online Gallery. Retrieved 15 April 2016, from http://www.gallerysunshine.com/

Giroux, H. (2016). Cultural Studies as Public Pedagogy. *Making the Pedagogical More Political. Penn State Univ.*

Hickey-Moody, A. (2014). Little Public Spheres. In J. Burdick, J. A. Sandlin & M. P. O'Malley (Eds.), *Problematizing public pedagogy* (pp. 117-129): Routledge.

———. (2015). Little publics and youth arts as cultural pedagogy. In M. Watkins, G. Noble & C. Driscoll (Eds.), *Cultural Pedagogies and Human Conduct* (pp. 78): Routledge.

———. (2016). Youth agency and adult influence: A critical revision of little publics. *Review of Education, Pedagogy, and Cultural Studies, 38*(1), 58-72.

Hickey-Moody, A., Savage, G. C., & Windle, J. (2010). Pedagogy writ large: Public, popular and cultural pedagogies in motion. *Critical Studies in Education, 51*(3), 227-236.

Juncker, B. (2012). What's the meaning? The Relations between Professional Theatre Performances and Children's Cultural Life. In M. van de Water (Ed.), *TYA, Culture, Society: International Essays on Theatre for Young Audiences*: Peter Lang.

Lundy, L. (2007). 'Voice' is not enough: conceptualising Article 12 of the United Nations Convention on the Rights of the Child. *British Educational Research Journal, 33*(6), 927-942.

Luttrell, W. (2013). Children's Counter-narratives of Care: Towards Educational Justice. *Children & Society, 27*(4), 295-308.

Maudlin, J. G., & Sandlin, J. A. (2015). Pop Culture Pedagogies: Process and Praxis. *Educational Studies, 51*(5), 368-384.

Noddings, N. (2015). *The Challenge to Care in Schools, 2nd Edition*: Teachers College Press.

Pelias, R, J. (2011). *Leaning: A poetics of personal relations*: Left Coast Press.

Rose, D, B. (1999). Indigenous ecologies and an ethic of connection. In N. Low (Ed.), *Global ethics and environment* (pp. 175). London: Routledge.

Sandlin, J. A., O'Malley, M. P., & Burdick, J. (2011). Mapping the complexity of public pedagogy scholarship 1894–2010. *Review of Educational Research, 81*(3), 338-375.

Savage, G. (2014). Chasing the Phantoms of Public Pedagogy. In J. Burdick, J. A. Sandlin & M. P. O'Malley (Eds.), *Problematizing public pedagogy*: Routledge.

Spivak, G. C. (1988). Can the subaltern speak? Basingstoke: Macmillan.

Springgay, S., & The Torontonians. (2014). How to be an artist by night: critical public pedagogy and double ontology. In J. Burdick, J. A. Sandlin & M. P. O'Malley (Eds.), *Problematizing public pedagogy*: Routledge.

Strong-Wilson, T., & Ellis, J. (2007). Children and Place: Reggio Emilia's Environment As Third Teacher. *Theory Into Practice, 46*(1), 40 - 47.

United Nations. (1990). *Convention on the Rights of the Child: Information kit*. Geneva: United Nations Centre for Human Rights.

CHAPTER 5

Communal Luxury and the Universal Republic of the Arts: Transcultural Flows of Art Pedagogy

Angela Giovanangeli

ABSTRACT

In France, the relationship between art, education and community has been a longstanding topic of discussion amongst artists, particularly in 1871 during the Paris working class uprising known as the Commune. These ideals have included the belief that art responds to the needs of the community and the valorisation of pedagogy. Whilst scholarly work exists on the transformative visions of artists' role in France with regard to art pedagogy and national interest, little is known about the transcultural flows of these ideologies and the potential for these cultural transfers to influence and transform community understandings of art and art pedagogy.

This paper examines the case study of Lucien Henry, a French artist, who was convicted of treason during the Paris uprising and banished to a penal colony in New Caledonia. Upon his release, rather than return to France, he settled in Australia from 1879 to 1891, and was appointed the first Instructor in the Department of Art at Sydney Technical College. Henry's teachings and decorative work mirrored the revolutionary ideas taking place in France in the second half of the 19th century, yet transposed these ideals into an Australian model that championed the urban landscape and validated a local sense of belonging and engagement. Moreover, Henry's work introduced visionary ways of understanding community that included Australian republican values, topics that remain relevant in contemporary Australian public discourse.

Using a transcultural framework, this paper suggests that the relationship between community engagement, art and education can be associated with cultural flows of ideas that connect with and transform the local. It will do this by examining Henry's ideology and designs that are found in letters and articles written by the artist during his period in Australia.

INTRODUCTION

In 1873, French revolutionary and artist Lucien Henry was tried for acts of treason against the French government during the 1871 Paris uprising known as the Commune. He was condemned to life imprisonment and transported to a prison in

New Caledonia. Following an amnesty in 1879, instead of returning to France with fellow pardoned prisoners, he settled in Australia and was appointed the first Instructor in the Department of Art at Sydney Technical College. Henry's teaching represents the ontology of transculturation in his overlapping identities. On the one hand, he is the French revolutionary caught up in late 19th century French republican debates on the democratic responsibilities of artists and their pedagogical role in society. On the other hand, he is the Australian artist who believed that Australia had a responsibility of providing a technical art education that would be accessible to all students in Australian schools and technical colleges (Henry, 1883). Indeed, Henry's teaching and decorative work reflect communard ideals of community inspired art that has the potential to shape society by placing aesthetic expression at the forefront of everyday life, yet transpose these ideals into an Australian context that champion the urban landscape and validate a local sense of belonging and importance. Moreover, Henry's work introduces visionary ways of understanding community that include republican values, an aspect that remains relevant in contemporary Australian public discourse.

A transcultural perspective is concerned with the fluidity of ideas and the way these notions adapt to specific political and cultural concepts which may differ from those in which they began. It underscores the entanglement and co-presence of trajectories and people previously separated by geographical and historical factors. If a transcultural perspective can be broadly understood as "the process of transition from one culture to another" (Ortiz, 1947, p. 6) as well as the complex processes that go into shaping this perspective (Codell, 2012; Flüchter & Schöttli, 2015; Welsch, 1999), then Henry is a reminder of the cultural trajectories influencing the relation between art, education and community.

Recent studies on art and community refer to the relation between pedagogy and art, with teachers as participants in a community of artists who teach (Pearse, Snider & Taylor, 2011) or to the arts' potential to transform the relationships between students and teachers (Vettraiano, Linds & Goulet, 2013). Little analytic attention has been paid to the transcultural trajectories in the relation between pedagogy, art and community and the potential for these cultural transfers to influence and transform community understandings of art and art pedagogy. This chapter addresses this issue by using the lens of transculturation and a case study of Lucien Henry to suggest that the relation between art, education and community may be shaped by ideas that have crossed cultural borders. It will do this by examining specifically some of the ideology and designs of Henry, notably the letters and articles written by the artist in art journals as well as in letters sent to government officials during Henry's period in Australia. These documents are currently archived in the State Library of New South Wales (NSW) and State Records of NSW. The objective of this analysis is to explore the capacity of Henry's vision on art and art education to mediate cultural borders as well as the attempt by Henry to develop, through this vision, a sense of local belonging and community through art education.

Communal Luxury

During the 1871 popular uprising in France known as the Paris Commune, artists seized upon the political and social turmoil affecting much of the working class people in Paris to fight for a more democratic vision of the artist's role in public life. Indeed, this struggle between artists and the broader social order for greater autonomy dates back to the founding of the French Academies in 1648 and reflects a continuity in French republican culture, notably that of the French Revolution of 1789 (Sánchez, 1997, p. 5). The artistic republicanism of the French Revolution stressed the pedagogical and utilitarian aspects of the fine arts, viewing the arts as representing an "effective way of communicating social and political meanings" as well as part of the "essential branches of public education" (Sánchez, p.18).

During the uprising, an assembly of artists was formed and named the *Fédération des artistes*. This artists' assembly met to voice a program for radical change in artistic independence and education. Though only short-lived (7 April - 9 May 1871) the *Fédération* drew up a manifesto dated 15 April 1871 calling for the "régénération de l'avenir par l'enseignement" [the regeneration of the future through education] (*Journal Officiel*, 1871). The manifesto's closing sentence refers specifically to the "régénération à l'inauguration du luxe communal et aux splendeurs de l'avenir et à la République universelle" [cultural regeneration, the building of a communal luxury and future development of art and the Universal Republic] (*Journal Officiel,* 1871). This document identifies the artist as an educator serving the needs of the community, that is, the wider public. For the community, this also translates into the democratisation of arts training and the removal of hierarchy amongst various art forms with the aim of developing a national aesthetic in republican allegory, public sculpture, architecture and civic decoration (Adamson, 2001, p. 27). In the context of the Commune, communal luxury refers to the way art could be used to create alternate aesthetic expressions that convey meaning to a community as a whole rather than to elite social groups. In such a way, art is understood to be common to all people through the extension of aesthetic dimensions "into everyday life" (Ross, 2015, p. 64). While these notions reiterate many concepts linked to French revolutionary communard ideals, they also underscore the artists' democratic responsibilities and role in organising arts education and creating art works that include the decorative arts. Indeed, one of the innovations of the Commune was the recognition of the decorative arts within the ranks of the fine arts, liberating the decorative arts from the confinement of its lower status as an industrial art (Sánchez, 1997, p. 65). Likewise, the artists of the *Fédération* believed that all of the arts were "artisanal in procedure and socialization" in an attempt to dismantle the tight control of the French authorities on the styles and subjects dictated to artists (p. 66). Generally, these artists believed that contemporaneity was a key aspect of this pedagogy and many favoured aspects of daily life that would validate a community's sense of belonging and importance.

In terms of legacy, the ideas of the *Fédération* were characterised in the values of subsequent French governments following the end of the Paris Commune. These governments supported the idea of placing politically and civically moralising imagery in French public spaces (Sánchez, 1997, p. 67). However, immediately after the Commune, the government during the Paris uprising of 1871 was hostile to the views of the Commune. After numerous violent confrontations between the two, the Commune was overthrown and Communards were condemned for treason and punished by execution or deportation to New Caledonia.

One deportee was the artist Lucien Henry. This artist's language was acquired as a student in the late 19th century beaux arts traditions and as a commanding general for the Commune. Henry was sentenced to death for his active role in the Paris uprising, his sentence later overturned to deportation to New Caledonia alongside other political exiles. Pardoned by the French authorities in 1879, Henry settled in Australia from 1879 to 1891, and during this period was appointed the first Instructor in the Department of Art at Sydney Technical College.

Described as "the most productive and influential artist during his time in Sydney" (Stephen, 2001b, p.10), Henry was regarded as both an educator and an artist in the area of reform "to construct a more democratic and urbane city for its citizens", fighting against "the imperial dependency of a colonial culture" (p.11). Henry's teaching paralleled the revolutionary ideas taking place in France in the 1870s, reflecting the democratic responsibilities of artists and their pedagogical role in society, while situating art education in an Australian context that was leading up to Australian Federation in 1901 and the building of nationhood. Henry believed that the state had a responsibility to provide technical art education to everyone through state schools and technical colleges (Henry, 1883) and in this way art education would generate a "communal luxury" that would foster an aesthetic style relevant to Australian society.

AUSTRALIAN ICONOGRAPHY

When Henry arrived in Sydney in 1879, Australia was constituted of British colonies that were debating the question of whether to break away from or remain a part of the British Empire. Historian Mark McKenna describes this period in Australia as a time "when the fundamental bases of institutional and social practice were open to question" (1996, p. 131) and when discussions on Australian patriotism were flourishing. In the 1880s and 1890s, the issue of an "Australian republic" and a call for a "unique cultural and national identity" were raised (p. 151). Indeed, official images of Australia did not exist and many Australian journals of the time acknowledged "the need for new symbols of national life, new anthems, flags, histories and art" (p. 168).

During the years when Henry was based in Sydney, an Australian patriotism pushing to establish an Australian national interest was developing. Meanwhile, technical education, while still in its infancy, was also emerging and placed a particular focus on the relation between technical and manual education, art and nation. A report on Technical Education and Manual Training published in 1891 by Edward Combes linked technical instruction to a shared national destiny. For instance Combes' first recommendation in this report on future courses outlined "the necessity that the valuable subjects of instruction included in the term manual training should be universally taught and believing them to be absolutely essential to the national interests of this country..." (Combes, 1891, p. 173). The definition of technical instruction provided in this report reveals how art is an integral part of this education and refers to the "careful and practical instruction of our youth in the scientific and artistic knowledge demanded by any branch of industry" (p. 2) with drawing "one of the most powerful agencies in the education of the child…" (p. 168).

Meanwhile, by 1891, Henry was considered a key figure in the establishment of a "special school of Australian decorative arts" (SMH, 1891, p. 5). One of the local newspapers, the Sydney Morning Herald, describes a banquet held in 1891 in honour of "the art lecturer at the Sydney Technical College" and refers to the "disciples who have caught his inspiration and who now form the nucleus of the school which is to develop and foster the growth of this new form of Australian nationality" (p. 5). Brought up in the generation of French art students who called for the democratisation of arts training in the mid to late 1880s, Henry's art education principles were intrinsically connected with the notion of community. For instance, in a letter written to the Minister of Public Education, Henry makes suggestions relative to technical art education, expressing that the state should "provide a technical Art Education as will really benefit the community as a whole" (1883). In another document, he proposes the publication of some of his designs and addresses this publication to "the youth of Australia in order that induced by example, they may bring their quota of efforts, and formulate ultimately a National expression" (1890a). In a subsequent letter intended as a prospectus for this publication, a page with the heading "INTRODUCTION" indicates that it will be the opening page of the book and it is dedicated "TO THE PUBLIC" (see Figure: 5.1). In the final version of the book proposal which appears in a publication edited by Ann Stephen and titled *Visions of a Republic*, Henry's dedication has been modified and states using the following typography: "this work is earnestly dedicated to the YOUTH of Australasia" (2001, p. 132). Both these dedications show Henry's engagement with local community and in particular, as indicated in the final version highlighting the word "youth" in slightly larger and varied font, with the young students of Australia who will benefit from designs that Henry was hoping would be used as a source of reference by institutions such as schools, technical colleges, libraries and museums. For Henry, the relation between art education and the wider public represents, therefore, the transmission of knowledge within society.

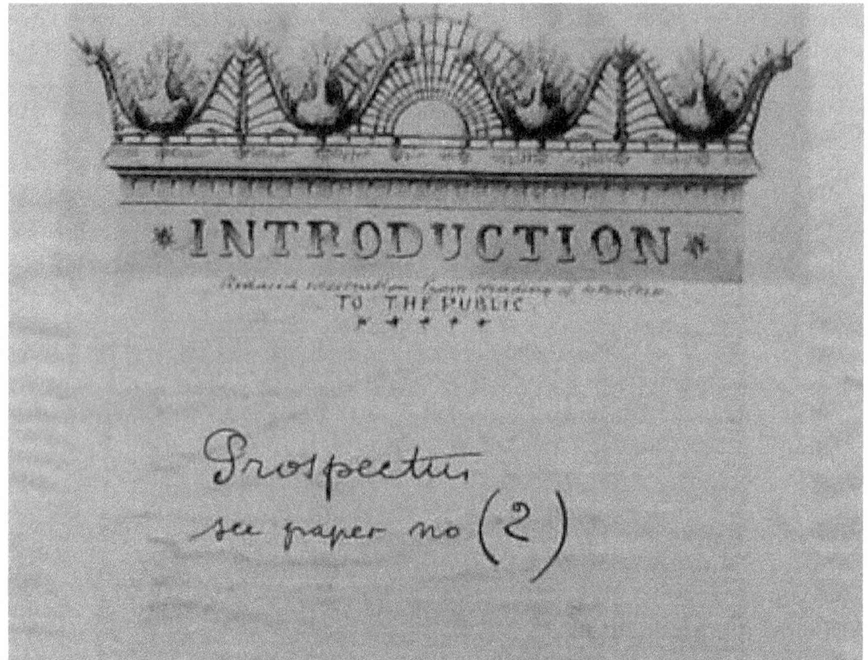

Figure: 5. 1 - This engraving describing an introductory page appears in the letter addressed to the Minister for Public Instruction and was part of the prospectus for the book *Australian Decorative Arts* (Henry, 1890b).

Meanwhile Henry's teaching objectives characterised by the transmission of knowledge also reflect the need for social equity, criticising any art instruction that is elitist. Henry stipulates that technical training in Art should be of "a practical and commercial value to students (…) "and not merely (…) a pleasant pastime" or "in the hands of gentlemen who have been more desirous to use them [the Fine Arts] as a means of making their fortunes" (1883). Indeed, for Henry, the notion of art and community is equally associated with education that provides "a thorough acquaintance with the styles, and therefore an opportunity of creating a style of Australian Art" that can be applied to a broad range of trades whether it be skills in drawing and perspective to be used by "a miner, a geologist (…) or in fact any technical engagement with the range of the Plastic Arts" (1883). Consequently, community refers to the development of an Australian style that is transmitted to people with the goal of building a shared sense of space. For Henry, Australian art did not necessarily mean just the painting of landscapes or figures but "Architecture, Sculpture, Modelling, Terra-cotta work, design of every description" (Aurousseau, 1912, p. 34).

If community signifies accessibility and the creation of an Australian Art, then art education is considered a key vector in this process. Henry's art pedagogy draws on his training as an art student in Paris to suggest that Australian technical training in art should refer to the "most important authorities on Art principles" (1883) namely

Frenchmen such as Charles Blanc, Jean–Léon Gérôme, Viollet-le-Duc, De Brie and Diderot whose work on art theory and principles were used and recognised in 19th century France in the mid to late 1800s. This European inspired method of teaching is for Henry, a stepping-stone leading to the development of a distinct Australian style. In the colonies, art education is limited and Henry calls for the establishment of an Art College because through this "there would be a respectable show of Australian Arts having originality and elements of their own to stamp them" (1883). To complement the emergence of this unique style, Henry proposes developing a reference book with his designs on architectural subjects and settings originally titled *Elementary Course of Ornamentation* for the benefit of students. In a subsequent letter to the Minister for Public Instruction, Henry mentions this book again but refers to it this time as the *Australian Decorative Arts* (1890a). This later title highlights the distinct national intent of the work and its relation to education, a notion further underscored by Henry when he describes this undertaking as "both distinctly national and Educational in character" (1890a). While Henry's writings display some modesty with regard to his contribution to Australian style, stating that he did not "want to be credited with having invented a new Art" (1890a), art historian Bernard Smith's work on *Art and Taste in Australia* during the colonial period suggests, rather, that Henry "was one of the first practising artists in Australia to advocate a national art" through the use of the motifs, symbols and patterns found in the local fauna and flora (1975, p. 230).

While national in character, this model of art education is also part of what Henry refers to as "an admirable testimony of the Universal order" (1890a). This "Universal order" refers to the development of a national style alongside those of other nations. In Henry's scheme of things, "the wealth of nations and their prosperity reside in the intelligence displayed in the working out of national industries" (1890a). Consequently, this interest in a national style is embedded within a global framework and is associated with the idea of progress and civilisation. For Henry technical education in art represents "a powerful agency of progress" (1890a). Not only that, the "young colonies have an immense natural supply of material in the way of form and color (…) to work out of such elements a style of ornamentation which may play its part in the development of civilisation under the Southern Cross" or as Henry goes further in stating: "with decorative elements second to none under the Sun" (1890b).

Colour and Style, Flora and Fauna

For Henry, the "advancement of Australian civilization" is achieved through the decorative arts (1888b, p. 9). By dedicating an article in the journal of *Australian Art* in 1888 in defense of ornamentation, he brings a transcultural perspective to his ideology and mirrors the fight of the Paris Commune a few years earlier to raise the decorative arts into the ranks of the fine arts (Sánchez, 1997, p. 64). Henry's article is quick to defend ornamentation and addresses the "sceptic persons (…) who are disposed to laugh at the importance" of the decorative arts and who consider them "superfluous and insignificant adjuncts of civilized life" (1888b, p. 10). Furthermore, Henry defends the social condition of the decorative artist and refers to the "improved social condition of the Artisan class" as a result of technical art education (1883). For him the decorative arts "constitute the substrata of civilization, the rich soil from which the other arts draw their sap" (1888b, p. 11). In this privileged position, the decorative arts precede all arts and foster specific traits associated with a national character.

While Henry's article is a synthesis of some of the ideology that existed in France at the end of the 19th century in defense of the decorative arts, it also shifts its focus to refer to the creation of an Australian style in ornamentation that does not yet exist and can be found in nature. Henry insists on the need "to branch off from the barren circle of imitation" and "to go straight to nature, the inexhaustible fountain of plenty and beauty" (1888b, p. 11). For him, the distinct features of Australian animals and plants in the decorative arts are key to the emergence of a national identity, relating that:

> there are in the Australian Flora and Fauna elements of Decoration which either for form or color, and in some instances for both, are as beautiful and as original as any which have ever been employed in Decorative Art and that to offer them to Industry by introducing them into Technical Schools, Libraries and Museums most undoubtedly give to all industrial production a distinctive national character (1890a).

It is precisely in the form and colour of Australian flora and fauna that the "wants" and the "ideals" of a national spirit are derived (1888b, p. 12), with the artist leading the community in this endeavour. Henry's ongoing belief in the opportunities offered by Australian nature is further documented in his letter to the minister for Public Instruction referring to specific plants and animals of Australia:

> What real or imaginary Bird of any Art or of any period can compete for Beauty and nobleness of form with the Lyre-Bird? What can equal in form or color the flowers and foliage of the Waratah and Stenocarpus? They are undoubtedly the richest of all flowers known for constructive ornamentation and seem to have been designed to teach man what is conventionalism in Art (1890a).

This description demonstrates not only Henry's wonderment and awe of species that were distinctly different to those in his native France, it also identifies an Australian style that belongs to a higher order. In general terms, what this shows is that, on the one hand, Henry feels a deep concern for the lack of training and art style in Australia while, on the other, he champions the decorative possibilities of animals such as the lyre-bird or flowers such as the waratah that characterise for him the fundamental principles of design.

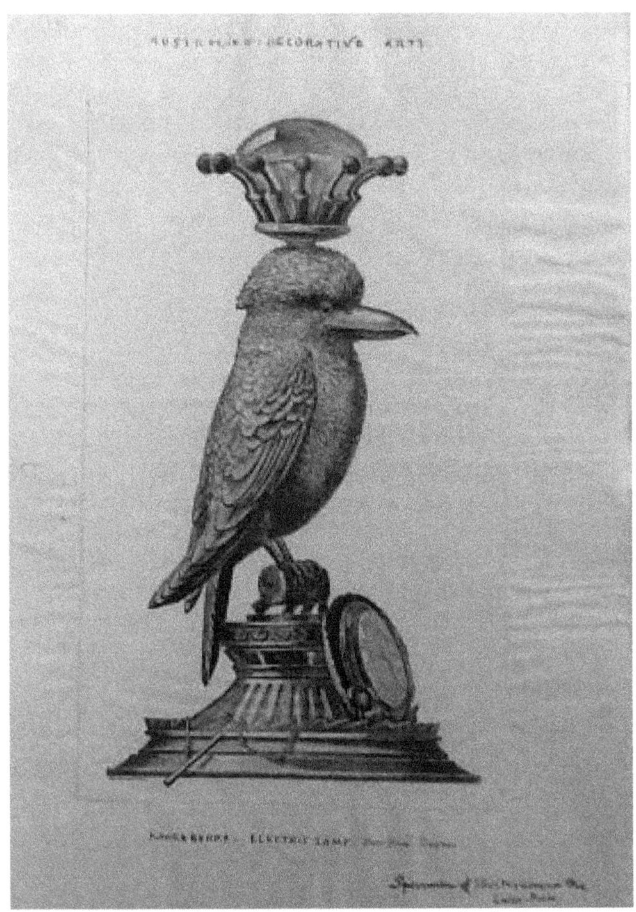

Figure: 5.2 - This engraving titled *Kookaburra electric lamp for bedroom* appears in the letter addressed to the Minister for Public Instruction and is part of the prospectus for the book *Australian Decorative Arts* (Henry, 1890b).

Figure: 5.2 shows how Henry incorporated Australian characteristics into local design for everyday use around the home. The engraving titled *Kookaburra electric lamp for bedroom* is a lamp in the form of the kookaburra with the crown reminiscent of the stenocarpus that Henry used repeatedly in other designs. This flower in the shape of a crown could be a playful pun on the bird's association with the kingfisher family or perhaps a tongue in cheek allusion to decorative designs elaborated in France over the centuries under various monarchies. Historically in France artisans and artists were expected to include allegories of regal figures in their work. Henry as a former member of the Paris Commune would have held deep anti-royalist feelings, supporting strong republican ideals and would have been aware of the republican fervor taking place in the colonies at the time of this engraving. Meanwhile, Smith's work on Australian art highlights the extent of Henry's innovation, stating that for designers of this period "the idea of incorporating parrots and kangaroos, wattle and waratah into their designs was as embarrassing as asking them to cultivate a broad Australian accent. It was safer, less culturally déclassé, to follow European modes of design…" (1975, p. 231). Despite what seems to be, according to Smith, the peculiarity at the time of Henry's vision, hand written comments that appear in the margin of the artist's October 1890 letter to the Ministry for Public Instruction requesting support for his work, also dated 1890, describe Henry's work as "very beautiful", the subjects "distinctly Australian" and the designs to be "used with great advantage in promoting National Art Education" (1890b).

Shaping Cultural Flows

While for Henry, art and community were synonymous with the establishment of a national style fostered by technical art education, the notions of art and community were also associated with the creation of designs that communicated social and political meanings between the artist and the public. Henry's art training in Paris coincided with social political change that raised questions about the role of art within society. Art was not only seen to provide students with technical skills, it also problematised political and cultural issues taking place.

France in the 19th century had inherited a fine arts system that dated back to monarchies favouring selective art patronage, hierarchies in artistic genres and references to religion. Meanwhile, the French Revolution of 1789 had introduced alternate visions of the nation that centred on a republicanism that was anti-clerical and anti-authority. What this meant by the 19th century was a deep social divide between those that supported the ancient system under the monarchy and those in support of the new ideals of the republicans. Artists in France were faced with the iconographical problem of the period that questioned how to represent through allegories the ideal to be honoured (Agulhon, 1981, p.27). The end of the Paris Commune had sparked lengthy debates on the kind of republican ideology that should be established in France.

Similarly, during this same period Australia was caught up on "the issue of a republic" (McKenna, 1996, p.121), which up until Federation in 1901 consisted of numerous discussions concerning the colonies' relationship with Britain. The issue of an independent Australian republic was a significant aspect of political culture and in the period between 1887 and 1893 republican sentiment surfaced in the colonies in a way that McKenna describes as "not to be seen again until the late twentieth century" (p.131).

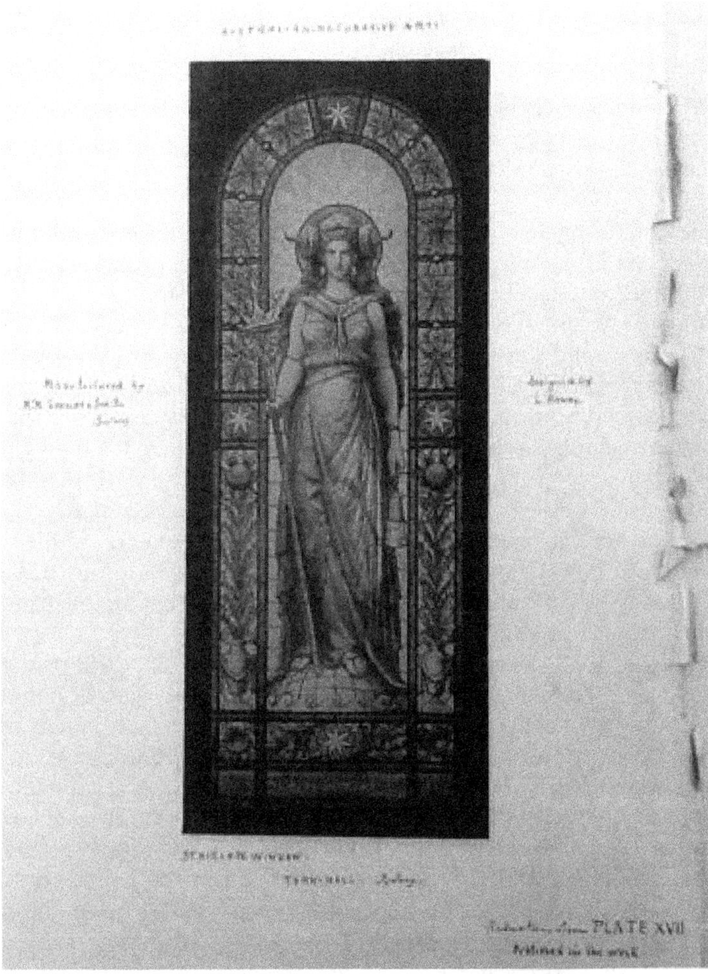

Figure: 5. 3 - This engraving titled *Stained Glass Window, Town Hall, Sydney* appears in the letter addressed to the Minister for Public Instruction and is part of the prospectus for the book *Australian Decorative Arts* (Henry, 1890b).

The designs Henry completed while in Sydney suggest a parallel with French ideology with regard to the relation between national values and visual representations of the nation. In 19th century France, visual displays of imagery were a form of civic and political education and communicated meaning and values to the public through the fine arts. Henry seems to have transferred some of this French ideology into the work he undertook in Australia. By way of example, Henry designed two stained glass windows for Sydney Town Hall in 1888: the Captain Cook window and the Centennial window (also referred to as the Australia window by Henry's former student George Hippolyte Aurousseau). The latter provides us with a glimpse of how ideas in imagery cross over cultural borders, particularly with regard to the democratic responsibilities and pedagogical role of the artist (see Figure: 5.3). This work provides us with an example of the way Henry draws on local imagery in his work but also hints at the influence of 19th century iconographical representations developed in France where Henry was an art student.

A homage to Henry by Aurousseau, who assisted the artist with the preparation of this stained glass window (Figure: 5.3), describes the symbolism in the work:

> the female figure signifying Australia, draped in the red and blue ensigns, symbolic of our allegiance to Great Britain, the ram's head and fleece, for a most graceful head dress typifying the wool industry; the miner's lamp, the mining industry; Neptune's trident, for maritime power, then the four stars in the frame and the one on her forehead showing that we live under the Southern Cross. With conventional designs from the waratah, stenocarpus, and lambertia round the outer border, the full sun's rays above the head, the figure standing on the globe below, with Oceania and the rolling sea (1912, p.35).

This description not only explains the meaning behind the imagery in the window, it also demonstrates how Henry put into practice his principles of art pedagogy that focuses on the use of Australian form and colour inspired from local nature to convey a message of national importance.

Research on 19th century imagery in France (Agulhon, 1981; Ozouf, 1976) reveals that some of the imagery evoked in the Centennial window mirrors similar iconographical representations used in France around the time of the debates on French republicanism. For instance, after the fall of the last French king in 1848 and the French Empire in 1870, female images replaced those of monarchs and were commonly used to represent the Republic in paintings, statues and busts. These female images were allegories of liberty – the Republic – and usually placed in public places such as town halls. The five pointed star was commonly used on the head of busts to replace any signs of the monarch and suggested the "idea of political progress and that of the enlightenment of reason" (Agulhon, 1981, p.86). In the republican spirit, the star was also considered "an anti-religious, rationalist symbol." Indeed, religion was replaced in public imagery in France by the cult of nature. Subsequently, Republican imagery favoured visual representations associated with nature and freedom such as flowers, olive branches, laurel leaves, oak leaves as well as the Gallic cock to symbolise the motherland and the plough to represent work on the land (Agulhon, 1981, pp.86-87). As an art student in France Henry was surrounded by the history of political art in France which is to "some extent a history of political symbolism" (p.87).

While the Centennial window bears similarities with the political republican imagery used in France (despite Aurousseau's reference to the allegiance of Britain), the designs also reinvent the way nature is used to refer to a local sense of belonging anchored in Australia. This borrowing from a European context hints at the republican vision Henry had in mind for an Australia that was still debating its ties with the British monarchy and was still very much a part of the British Empire. The design also presents a social understanding of Australia's future associated with the work, knowledge and material emanating from its local wealth while placing this perspective within a global context.

CONCLUSION

Henry did not live to see the publication of his book on Australian decorative arts. He died in France in 1896 from ill health following several unsuccessful attempts to publish his work in France and England, despite the support he received by the Ministry for Public Instruction in Australia. His unpublished designs remained in the archives of the Sydney Powerhouse Museum up until a 2001 retrospective of his work at this museum, accompanied by the publication of Henry's decorative arts designs in a book titled *Visions of a Republic* (Stephen, 2001a).

Henry's belief in social equity and national destiny through the opportunity of education and art remain, nevertheless, distinct characteristics of his time in Australia and reflect clear transcultural flows. Louise Pratt's *Imperial Eyes* (1992) on transculturation introduces the notion of the contact zone. Pratt associates this notion of contact with transculturation in order to identify the ways by which "subjects are constituted in and by their relations to each other" in terms of "mutually transformative, but hierarchized, historical encounters, intersections, and power struggles" (Allatson, 2007, p.231). If transculturation can be understood as a crossing of cultural borders "where identities are inflected by multiple contact points and agendas between different populations" (Ray, 2012, p.21) then Henry is a transcultural figure who mediated cultural borders in art education and artistic creation. The transcultural encounter of Lucien Henry's ideas within Australian society reflects more than a simple mix of national cultures but rather complex and unresolved possible meanings on a local level. The artist not only reflected national ways of understanding the relation between art and community, he also invented and constituted a specific way of understanding art education with the aim of transforming the way aesthetic expressions should be understood within Australia. It is the fluidity of Henry's concepts and ideas as well his ability to adapt to specific political and cultural concepts, different to those in which they began, that underscore the entanglement and co-presence of trajectories within art pedagogy and community. Henry's vision of art education, artistic creation and their relation to the wider public is enmeshed in his concern for the democratisation of the arts and the role art plays in establishing a national style through local colour and form.

In 1975, Smith wrote that few Australian designers paid any attention to Henry's work and that his work "remains little known even today" (p.231). In 2001, however, Stephen's work revises this view and refers to Henry's continuing relevance, stating that his designs and ideals for "social equity and national destiny" have inspired subsequent artists and teachers in Australia "through the opportunity of education" (2001a, p.124).

ACKNOWLEDGEMENT

The source of Materials for this chapter is State Records NSW.
State Records NSW:NRS 3834, Correspondence files concerning technical education [Correspondence Branch], 1880-1940, Images enclosed with the Letter from Lucien Henry to Carruthers, Minister for Public Instruction dated October 1890, [10/14285].

REFERENCES

Adamson, N. (2001). Lucien Henry in Paris: Artist and communard. In A. Stephen (Ed.), *Visions of a republic. The work of Lucien Henry* (pp. 13-31). Sydney: Powerhouse Publishing.

Agulhon, M. (1981). *Marianne into battle. Republican imagery and symbolism in France, 1789-1880.* Translated by Janet Lloyd. Cambridge: Cambridge University Press.

Allatson, P. (2007). *Key terms in Latino/a cultural and literary studies.* Malden: Blackwell Publishing.

Aurousseau, G. H. (1912). Lucien Henry first lecturer in art at Sydney Technical College. *The Technical Gazette*, *3*(3), 33-35.

Combes, C. (1891). *Report on technical education and manual training at the Paris universal exhibition of 1889, and in Great Britain, France, and the United States of America.* Sydney: Government Printing Office.

Codell, J. F. (2012). The art of transculturation. In Julie F. Codell (Ed.), *Transculturation in British art, 1770-1930* (pp.1-20). Surrey and Burlington: Ashgate.

Flüchter, A. & Schöttli, J. (2015). Introduction. In Antje Flüchter & Jivanta Schöttli (Eds.), *The dynamics of transculturality concepts and institutions in motion* (pp.1-26). Cham, Heidelberg, New York, Dordrecht, London: Springer International Publishing.

Henry, L. (1883, May 21). Letter to the minister of public education making suggestions relative to technical art education in New South Wales. State Records NSW [10/14282].

———. (1888a). Color. *Australian Art*, February, 24-27.

———. (1888b). Australian decorative arts. An essay. *Australian Art*, March, 9-12.

———. (1890a, Sept. 25). Letter to the honourable Carruthers minister for public instruction asking for support in production of work on 'Australian decorative arts' including prospectus for the book. State Records NSW [10/14285].

———. (1890b, Oct. 2). Letter to the honourable Carruthers minister for public instruction asking for support to publish Australian decorative art. State Records NSW [10/14285].

———. (1891, May 21). Instructions to Mr. L. Dechaineux, Mr Henry's substitute teacher in design class. State Records NSW [10/14033]. *Journal Officiel de la Commune* (1871, 15 April). Retrieved from http://archivesautonomies.org/IMG/pdf/communedeparis/JOS/jos-n105.pdf

McKenna, M. (1996). *The captive republic. A history of republicanism in Australia 1788-1996*. Cambridge: Cambridge University Press.

Ortiz, F. (1947). *Cuban counterpoint: Tobacco and sugar.* New York: Knopf.

Ozouf, M. (1976). *La fête révolutionnaire (1789-1799*). Paris: Folio.

Pearse, H., Brook Snider, A. B. & Taylor, C. (2011) The lost art of pedagogy: An exploration in three parts, *The Canadian Review of Art Education 38*, 5-16.

Pratt. M. L. (1992). *Imperial eyes. Travel writing and transculturation.* London and New York: Routledge.

Ray, R. (2012). Baron of Bengal: Robert Clive and the birth of an imperial image. In Julie F. Codell (Ed.), *Transculturation in British art, 1770-1930* (pp. 21-38), Surrey and Burlington: Ashgate.

Ross, K. (2015). *Communal luxury. The political imaginary of the Paris Commune.* London, New York: Verso. .

Sánchez, G. J. (1997). *Organizing independence. The artists federation of the Paris Commune and its legacy, 1871-1889.* Lincoln, University of Nebraska Press.

SMH *The Sydney Morning Herald,* Monday (1891, 18 May), pp.1-10.

Smith, B. (1975). Documents on art and taste in Australia. The colonial period 1770-1914. Melbourne: Oxford University Press.

Stephen, A. (Ed.). (2001a). *Visions of a republic. The work of Lucien Henry.* Sydney: Powerhouse Publishing.

———. (2001b). Introduction. In Anne Stephen (Ed.), *Visions of a republic. The work of Lucien Henry* (pp. 10-11). Sydney: Powerhouse Publishing.

Vettraino, E, Linds, W. & Goulet, L. (2013). Click, Clack, Move: Facilitation of the Arts as Transformative Pedagogy. *Journal of Transformative Education, 11*(3), 190-208.

Welsch, W. (1999). Transculturality: The puzzling form of cultures today. In Mike Featherstone and Scott Lash (Eds.), *Spaces of cultures* (pp.194-213). London: Sage.

CHAPTER 6

The Company It Keeps: Arts-based Research as Assemblage

John Rae

ABSTRACT

In this chapter I investigate the notion of 'assemblage' and illustrate the work that assemblage-informed arts-based research can do. Taking the view that an assemblage represents a complex of material – that is, more than technique – I explore how connections between artist/researcher, artwork, and other material aspects of the research context are established as assemblages. This is discussed in relation to two cases, one relating to academic leadership and scholarship, and the other to rural health. In both cases, a research participant was interviewed and an artwork made. These artworks were then shown back to the respective participants as a way of furthering our conversations. The ways in which the artworks gave free rein to deep thinking by the research participants and me as researcher are discussed. Highlighted is the manner in which this arts-based approach, conceptualised as assemblage, created connections, generated insight and transformed ways of knowing and acting in relation to the research topic. This discussion crosses the disciplinary boundaries of art, research, higher education and health care. In doing this, knowledge of assemblage and its application to arts-based research is extended.

INTRODUCTION

The way in which researchers understand their positions in relation to their research context influences how they conduct their research. Researchers from a positivist paradigm purposefully locate themselves at a distance, if not external to their research, claiming 'independence.' Qualitative researchers prefer to locate themselves *in* their research, as an 'instrument' of research. The centrality of the researcher affects how knowledge is generated, if not what knowledge is generated. Questions of centrality in arts-based research are just as important if the potential of arts-based research is to be realised – to take us "to where we've never been, to see what we've never seen" (Sullivan, 2009, p.62). How best, then, to conceptualise these relationships between artist-researcher, artwork, research participants and all other elements of the material research context? A useful approach comes from what is often referred to as the 'new materialism', which "abandons the idea [that] matter [is] inert and subject to predictable forces" (Springgay & Rotas, 2015, p.552), and in particular, the notion of 'assemblage.'

Drawing from Deleuzian theory and a lineage going back to Spinoza and Nietzsche, Ninni Sandvik (2012, p.203) defines assemblages as "compositions of heterogeneous elements – for instance, physical elements, happenings, events, signs, utterances and so on – that enter into relations with one another." Phillip Mar and Kay Anderson (2010, p.37) summarising the work of various scholars, including DeLanda (2006) and Olds and Thrift (2005), add that assemblages have symbiotic connections, retain the singularity of their participating elements, co-evolve, mutate, and are temporary and provisional. They are structure-like surrogates, a contradiction between the ephemeral and the structural, rhizomes that undermine traditional ideas about structure (Marcus & Saka, 2006, pp.101-102). According to Giles Deleuze and Felix Guattari (1987, p.22), assemblages "act on" flows of desire – on semiotic, material and social impulses and drives (Smith, 2011, p.132). Thus, assemblages are agential. They are not merely convenient groupings around which action may take place: assemblages do work. Here, that work is research. Sandvik (2010, p. 31) explains that "particles, intensities, forces and flows of components meet with and link with the forces and flows of the other components" as a quality passes from one assemblage to another (Deleuze & Guattari, 1987, p.306). Assemblages establish connections (Deleuze & Guattari, 1987, p. 23) bring passions into play (Deleuze & Guattari, 1987, p. 399) and are "a source of emergent properties" (Marcus & Saka, 2006, p.103), including knowledge.

In this chapter, I apply the notion of 'assemblage' to arts-based research. In doing so, my ideas fall in line with – or re-assemble with – the work of scholars such as Lisa Mazzei (2013) as well as a range of discursive and material practices that work together to offer a post-humanist perspective on qualitative research more generally. What follows are two case presentations that are taken from a larger study (Rae, 2015) based on the methodology of 'postmodern emergence' (Somerville, 2007). In using postmodern emergence, I sought "new knowledge ... rather than old knowledge being re-told" (Somerville, 2008, p.6) about organisational creativity. One case relates to academic leadership and scholarship, and the other to rural health. In both cases, a research participant was interviewed and an artwork made. These artworks were then shown back to the respective research participants to further our conversations. The artworks gave the research participants (and me as researcher) free rein to think deeply about creativity in their organisation. This arts-based approach, conceptualised as assemblage, created connections, insight, and new ways of knowing, and offers researchers and practitioners a transformed view of organisational creativity.

Case 1: Richard, the Academic Leader

Richard is a digital learning scholar who has received national awards for his use of and research into technologies for teaching, and also for leadership at the university where he works. He said that he had spent many years "skirting between a technology focus and an education focus." Richard's history is that he was a computer programmer, and then managed the professional development arm of an IT company before completing his PhD. He lectured in IT but did his research in education. Of this, he said:

> So I've sort of got those constant back and forth between those 2 threads – I do think that sometimes I can see maybe affordances of technology for learning that other people don't see because I'm probably maybe slightly more empowered in my relationship with technology – I can make technology do things differently to what it actually currently is. So I can imagine possibilities, I guess, that maybe other people aren't seeing.

I had two conversations with Richard, preferring a conversational interview style because of the way it "offers maximum flexibility to pursue information in whatever direction appears to be appropriate, depending on what emerges" (Patton, 2002, p.342). Thus, more emphasis was placed on Richard than me, and any pre-constructed notions I had regarding organisational creativity would have been reduced. Between these conversations I made a painting (Figure: 6. 1) in order to begin knowing more about Richard's work. This painting was to do more than serve as a prompt for our ongoing conversation; it was, as will be discussed, to assume a 'position' at our next meeting, an element of our assemblage. I hoped that the painting would work in a way similar to how Paul Carter (2007, pp.15-16) described invention, that is, as "a double movement of… decontextualisation in which the found elements are rendered strange, and of recontextualisation, in which new families of association and structures of meaning are established", or allowed to emerge.

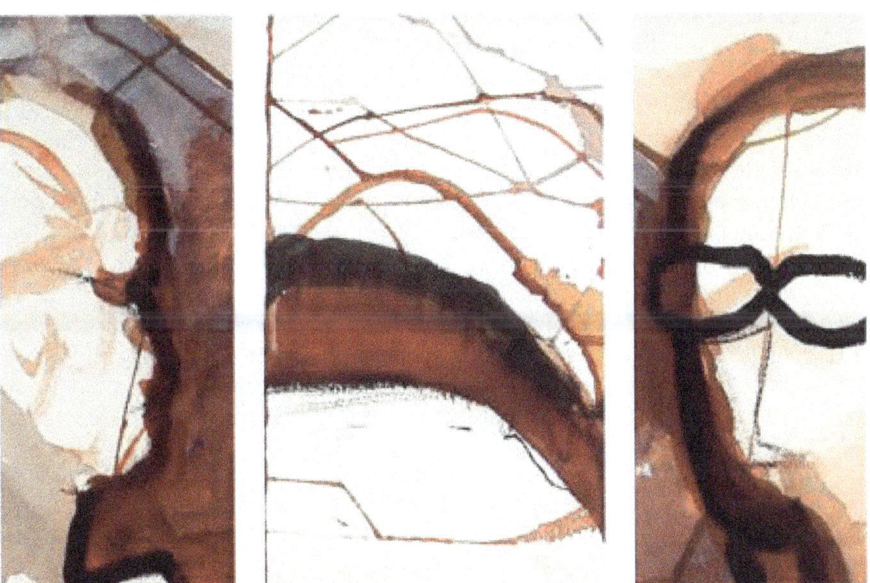

Figure: 6. 1 - Connections (2010). John Rae.

The painting I made for Richard emerged as a "conditional representation" (Somerville, 2007, p. 240) of something that he said to me the first time we met. He used the phrase, "a few beers with a colleague", to express his relaxed and contemplative relationship with his research peers. This was an enduring image for me, but my first attempt at representing it in acrylic paint was unsuccessful. As I explained to Richard: "I got the Stanley knife to it and cut it up." I then reconstructed the remnants to create a triptych measuring 330cm by 510 cm. What I was searching for was balance in the painting – a balanced composition and a 'steadying' of ideas about creativity held within the painting.

With the completed painting leaning against the wall of Richard's office, Richard and all that was assembled with him, including me, 'met.' Once we three (Richard, I and artwork) had connected, Richard clarified his role: "you're asking me to try and identify meaning in it", which, of course, is exactly what I wanted. Then, of the painting, he said:

> the left hand side [of the painting] looks like a side profile of a person's face. The right hand side looks like a person's face wearing some glasses. The middle could be a river – landscape with hills. The colours are sort of reds and so they sort of imply a – I don't know, probably an Australian summer kind of impression to me. But that middle certainly, every time I look at it, it looks like a landscape – a rural sort of landscape.

During the course of the conversation, Richard continued to build this metaphor based on a rural landscape, which he acknowledged was something he was deeply familiar with: "Aerial views of a paddock keep coming to mind ... I spend a fair bit of time in that sort of paddock type of terrain", he said. The metaphor provided a context for how Richard saw his role as leader, and how he balanced listening to his colleagues with taking the lead: "obviously you try and sort of sow the seeds of challenges and thinking." My (aesthetic) ideas about balance seemed to link with Richard's (leadership) ideas about balance.

Looking thoughtfully at the painting, Richard spoke about what he saw as connections in his practice as an academic:

> it kind of is like you're sitting on a veranda looking out at something, chatting in that kind of a way rather than the sort of more intense way you might if you were sitting facing each other – there's a relationship between the 2 figures of either sides. And so maybe there's something in that landscape in the middle that's connecting 2 people together – could be a shared experience too.

In terms of Richard's leadership, he saw:

> that's very definitely a process of being part of an organisation and part of groups and working with other people. It's very much a collaborative thing.

> So there's a lot of those conversations – you could see the picture as an example of one of those conversations.

However, what the painting did not show, according to Richard, was:

> the network of multiple projects in terms of the research and different combinations of people. And then sort of the even more complex network is involved in the leadership stuff because it's often leadership through working collectively with others on change

These assemblages and the relatedness of these assemblages can be thought of as acting on social flows. Richard explained that if there is, for example, a shared vision in a university, it emerges through conversation rather than exists in advance. This is supported, he said, by building on relationships and building rapport.

> So I see it as a real building block kind of thing – that the relationship development is a really important prerequisite to collectively working on improvement – these things are often a convergence of different conversations around different tables. Each time you have a conversation with someone who's in a position of influence, they're influencing you, you're influencing them. And collectively you are contributing to that sort of messy discourse that leads to the outcome.

Case 2: Heather, the Rural Health Manager

I used a similar interview style for Heather, a manager of a rural primary health service. The conversation started by Heather acquainting me with the community that her organisation served, describing it as "small" and "rural" and explaining that:

> people identify with their local community more strongly – people are really interested – they see what's going on out there and they're really interested in collaborating to try and find solutions to engage people to be healthier, to have access to higher level services when they need it.

Heather also spoke about trust being an important ingredient in the health service's relationship with the community. Further, and not surprisingly for such communities: "there's a real culture of connecting up with other organisations and other services to get the resources you need." For her, the bedrock of her community was trust, not just of the health service, but all that the health service is connected to.

Working with Heather's phrase, "connecting up", I began her painting with a single line that I imagined represented the beginning of a network or a link. Abstract shapes came forth out of lines that I made in yellow and white acrylic paint. I applied a glaze to a section, working and re-working the paper with brushes and my hands. I then created the panels – panels of lines and shapes – wondering about other relationships, including the relationship between 'health' and 'community', and also between 'urban' and 'rural.' As I did this, I tried to show respect for Heather who had been so generous with her time and conversation. That is, I strove to balance art-making as a generative process – to generate new knowledge – with art-making as a means of responding to and connecting with Heather.

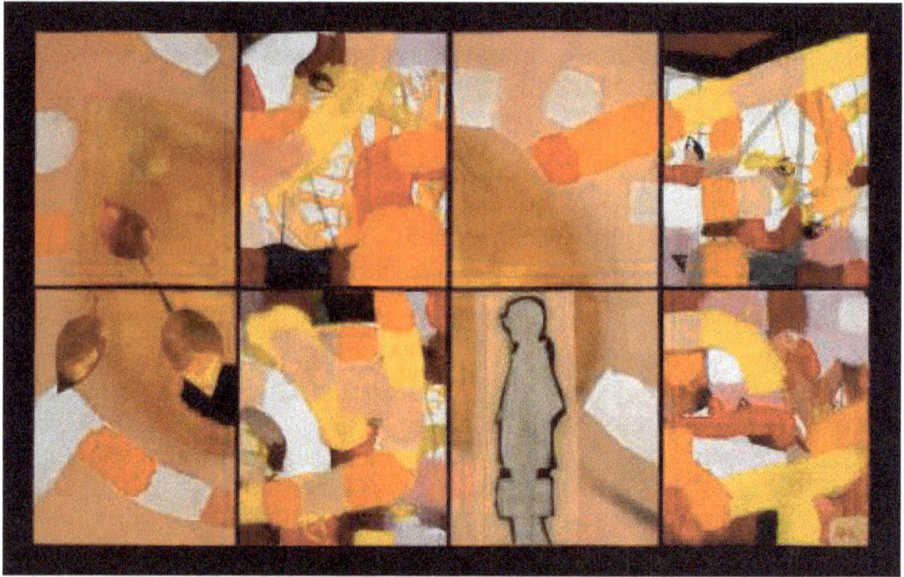

Figure: 6. 2 - Immersion, John Rae

Heather mentioned that she preferred improvised over formal and planned health promotional interventions, and I was particularly mindful of this as I painted *Immersion* (Figure:6. 2), made up of eight small panels painted in acrylic and measuring 62 cm by 94 cm. I knew my painting needed to be loose and organic, and Heather seemed to pick up on that when she saw it:

> There's a different kind of energy, a different kind of activity or vibe within each panel and yet that's how I feel, I feel it's integrated. I can see there's some calmer panels actually now that I look a bit closer one with the human figure in it that seems to be a little more passive and contemplative and there are people – it feels like there's leaves and its sort of autumny in a way but then I feel there are people getting their heads together – that bottom left hand panel really seems like the people are sort of getting together and thinking about where they're going.

Heather responded to *Immersion* thus:

> My eyes are drawn to that second [panel] from the left and I'm thinking it's complex, it isn't easy, doesn't come easily and in order to move into that

> complexity and almost immerse yourself in it – I want to be embedded in the community.

This theme of complexity was taken a step further as Heather continued to survey the other panels of *Immersion*: “it's quite vibrant but there's also calmness in it and I think that’s a good analogy or good description of how we are with the community; it is dynamic but it's also there's an ongoing foundation of trust and that we all manage complexity in a calm and rational and supportive way.” Although Heather’s words “complexity” and “rational” seem to clash, loudly even, her suggestion about how to respond to complexity is useful. Connecting panels of the painting with ideas about her community, as if the painting and her community were one, Heather continued:

> I'd see them immersing in the complexity there and feeling a bit lost and valuing moving across that left [panel] which is more contemplative and having space to actually get into that space and understand where they're at but it's up to us to venture out into the complexity and to engage with them to be engaged but to be engaged in a culturally appropriate [way] and in a context where they feel that they're being understood that what they believe is valid.

Immersion is indeed complex, yet hopefully not in a burdensome way; it reflects how Heather’s health service becomes integrated, productively, with the community that it serves. The place of that community is what informed *Immersion.* I painted preliminary sketches in that place as a way of understanding its rurality, and to experience its relationship with other larger places as I drove to and from it.

For Heather, to embed oneself in the community with all these complexities was necessary. It is “about people feeling that they are being listened to – thinking of their best interests”, she said. Encouraged by one of the panels in the panting, Heather spoke about people with mental health illness who were “really disconnected.” The health service’s response was to facilitate weekly meetings with them:

> We went to the community and said look you know they're a really fringe sort of group but the community rallied around and they’ve donated quite a significant amount of money and goods and they wanted that group to be supported.

As Heather said later: “there's a high level of empathic caring and so what they do also and because it is connected.”

Heather was a very perceptive and engaged collaborator, and accepting, I thought, of the agential qualities of art: “I like art, I enjoy art, but I’m pretty impressed how it’s been able to elicit just feelings and thoughts about the organisation, yeah”, she said.

Cases 1 and 2 as Assemblages

The paintings *Connections* and *Immersion* were not made out of a response to some predetermined mental image of what was to be painted, then executed through, say, neuromuscular activity orchestrated by cognition, as Cartesian thought may suggest. Rather, they emerged out of me working with materials and practices that I performed in the context of earlier conversations with Richard and Heather, which hung over me as I painted. I was remembering too my affective responses to those conversations. The artwork came from paint, paper, brushes, varnish, wood that had been fashioned into something I also used called 'table', and something else known as 'chair', and my electronic tablet that allowed me to view the developing artworks from different perspectives (two-dimensional, upside-down, and flipped from one side to another). It came as I painted, as my body moved, swayed, and rocked in rhythmic pace with the constantly changing colours, lines and form, as if reflecting the movement of the research assemblage that I belonged to at that time. That, assembled in my studio, Sandvik (2010) would call "thinking machine"; the machine that includes the researcher's mind, and body, and all the other materials of research (p.30). In Sandvik's case, and also in the cases of Richard and Heather, art was brought to the assemblage. Put differently, art assumed its position and potential for action within the research assemblage, with a relatedness to other human and non-human elements of the assemblage (p.30). As Sandvik (2010, p.30) suggests, my role was to relate *in* the field of materials, instead of *to* it.

The agency of art is often acknowledged in discussions about arts-based research. In *Visual methodologies: An introduction to researching with visual materials*, Gillian Rose (2007) writes that "the image has its own effects" (p.35) and "power" to "catch the gaze of spectators and affect them" (p.35), which is exactly how Heather responded, her eyes drawn to a certain panel of the painting. Of course, not every form of arts-based research takes this line. Methodologies such as compositional interpretation and content analysis tend to "thingify" (Barad, 2003, p.812) images, holding them at a distance to the research flow as analytical techniques are applied *to* them. An assemblage-informed approach is different; it insists on recasting art as both "data generating" (Titchen & Horsfall, 2007, p.216) and "knowledge-generating."

John Dewey "sought to overcome rigid dichotomies [between] creative process and creative product" (Leddy, 2012, p.126), which is not unlike Carter's (2004, p.11) concern that; "[t]he process of making the work becomes inseparable from what is produced", and similarly the artist becomes inseparable from the audience (Leddy, 2012, p.126). Thinking materially disrupts "the gulf that exists generally between producer and consumer in modern society" (Dewey, 1934, p.8) so that the experience of art becomes a complex, larger and pleasurable whole (Leddy, 2012, p.130). Here, that whole is taken to be a research assemblage, established, in Richard's case, out of my recollections of our first conversation, my first unsuccessful painting attempt, and so forth, as we sat *with* the final artwork in Richard's office. In Heather's case, more than Richard's, the assemblage included the place of research – a rural landscape, its autumnal colours and the sounds of a nearby cattle-yard that helped me ponder rural life. In such assemblages, one is less concerned with parts and more with the relatedness of its various human and non-human elements (as they move, sway and rock). These interactions create sensations (or registrations of affect) and thought (Sandvik, 2010, p. 31-32). Recall, here, Heather's reference to "energy or vibe" in response to *Immersion* and how that made her feel. These sensations (and thoughts):

> claim priority on the cost of consciousness and academic reflections and work in favour of a capacity to let go of discursive and habitual stratification of thought' – paintings work as powerful flows and ruptures in the creation of thoughts, providing the assembled research machinery with even more fuel so to speak' (Sandvik, 2010, p. 32).

Decentering and Connecting

Sandvik (2010, p. 29) suggests that the concept "research assemblage" provides a way of decentring the researcher as subject. Did I, as artist and researcher, and so called 'chief investigator', have primacy over Richard and Heather, and the material elements of our arts-based research assemblage? Given the choice of interview style, and from the perspective of the new materialism, the answer would have to be 'no.' Continuing this line of questioning, as Sandvik (2010, p. 31) does: "How does a researcher become decentred and start engaging in the flows, intensities and speed' of research assemblages?" Karen Barad (2003) offers some assistance here by referring to the interactivity between discursive and other matter, where these "are not reducible to one another – [n]either can be explained in terms of the other – [n]either has privileged status in determining the other" (p. 822). This is a point that Mazzei (2013, p. 739) notes also: "they exist simultaneously and continuously collide to produce new becomings." The discursive practices of Richard, Heather and I therefore existed in our assemblages equally, along with the non-human material with which we were also knotted. Mazzei (2013, p.737) writes of no longer thinking of participants' voices "as separate and individual but only within the entanglement it immediately becomes and continues to become as it joins other enactments, other assemblages." Thus, researchers do not *become* decentred, they are *always already* decentred. Acknowledging this and troubling the dominant anthropocentric view of research is a first step in engaging with the movement, swaying and rocking of research assemblages.

The assembled thinking machine operates across the research context as "researcher-data-participants-theory-analysis" (Mazzei, 2013, p. 734). For Richard, this involved me steadying my ideas (represented in and as paint), which Richard connected with a familiar environment (paddocks) and valued practices (conversation). Added to this assemblage were emergent knowings about "connecting people" and new conceptualisations about the critical role of "messy discourse." Heather responded to my improvisation and the way I moved around paint, and panels of paint, which seemed to work alongside her enjoyment of art and appreciation of the work that art can do. What emerged from this was Heather's view that her community could be vibrant and dynamic and that this was related to its connectivity and the trust held within it. Entwined with this was Heather's conclusion about the need, as a health professional, to work and engage with the complexity of social life.

In the two cases presented, the thinking machine may be considered to have operated across artist-ideas-participants-ideas-knowing. It may also be considered to operate at different stages of research, including, for example, the interview stage. If research is an assemblage:

> There can no longer be a division between a field of reality (what we ask, what our participants tell us, and the places we inhabit), a field of representation (research narratives constructed after the interview), and a field of subjectivity (participants and researcher). Instead, these are to be thought as acting on one another simultaneously (Mazzei, 2013, p. 735-736).

In qualitative research, the field of representation often includes the interview transcript. In humanist terms, this serves as a representation of the research participant, their experiences, ideas, beliefs, and so forth. Much emphasis is placed on this when it comes to 'data analysis.' From the perspective of the new materialism, however, the transcript is not privileged in the same way; it is part of the research assemblage, connecting with other human and non-human elements and practices of that assemblage. With the "de-privileging of the interview" (Mazzei, 2013, p. 738) in post-humanism, the transcript also becomes de-privileged, and decentred. In arts-based research, then, art's agency in the "collision of forces" (Mazzei, 2013, p. 737), flows and entanglement of the assemblage, is better accounted for, curtailing to some extent "an over-reliance on words as the primary source of meaning" (Mazzei, 2013, p.739).

I was grateful that Richard was able to schedule time to meet for our second interview, moving, as he did, from one set of assemblages to form this new one; from the assemblages of people and materials that made up, for instance, a learning and teaching committee, a performance management review, seminar or classroom, and the assemblages that were his history. Like many of my research participants, he came to this second interview with a sense of anticipation, especially regarding the artwork that he knew I would be bringing with me. Heather also graciously allowed me to become entangled in her assemblages, as she brought in memories of her community and its culture. I too entered these relationships assembled from past interviews, transcripts, meetings with colleagues, relationships with texts, journals, notes, and the paintings that I held under my arm. The temporary and provisional nature of these assemblages I had formed with Richard and Heather did not, and could not, work towards closure. Rather, a transformational process had begun and a conceptual advance made – organisational creativity was re-conceptualised (Rae, 2015) – and this had been mediated materially (Carter, 2007, p. 16).

Giving Free Rein to Deep Thinking

Art is generative, and its work is heightened through the company that it keeps. Referring to the human qualities of arts-based assemblages, Silvia Bettez writes:

> new possibilities might arise when we critically reflect upon our assemblage in relation to those associated with our research (participants, co-researchers,

> readers, etc) ... this framing of reflexive assemblage can minimize potential tendencies to essentialize others and ourselves and maximise our awareness of multiplicities of difference, particularly as they relate to structures of oppression (Bettez, 2015, p. 935-936).

The anthropocentric perspective typical of much research is further challenged when one considers, again, that art has its own agential qualities, alongside other material often associated with arts-based research (paint, paper, brushes, varnish, tables, chairs, tablets, the researcher's body, and so forth). Opening up the research context in this way and producing these multiplicities of difference leads to new possibilities and "passions" (Deleuze & Guattari, 1987, p. 399), which, as was noted earlier, is "a source of emergent properties" (Marcus & Saka, 2006, p. 103). As an apparatus for emergence, the mark of assemblages includes novelty, an association with a new set of relations, new laws or principles (Kontopoulos, 1993, p. 22-23). Jeffrey Goldstein (1999, p. 49) adds that this occurs at the macro level during a process of self-organisation, over time, and is not pre-given. Chad Barnett (2009) proposes that in some contexts (for him, social networking amongst adolescents), assemblage is a more useful concept than emergence, which for him is a reference to Margaret Somerville's (2007) article *Postmodern Emergence.* Barnett (2009, p.205) suggests the term "methodology of postmodern assemblage." Notwithstanding, Somerville also connects assemblage with emergence in qualitative research and writes of "coming to know in research" (2007, p. 235) where "meaning is created from an assemblage of representations" (2007, p. 239), and where writing (in research) itself is a form of assemblage" (2007, p. 241).

For Richard, art worked to generate a view about universities that may have otherwise been hidden, even subverted, in the research. One comment that he made was:

> It's just that idea that there isn't a grand vision and that organisations don't operate through a grand vision. And even if somebody thinks they do, actually they don't because not everyone buys into the grand vision. Not everyone interprets the grand vision the same way. And it's the nitty-gritty things going on in all the different parts of the organisation. It is those sorts of conversations playing out that results in change rather than the grand vision.

Such a comment would be out of step with many higher education practices. Take for example strategic planning; this widespread activity is often based on visioning and indeed frequently directs the allocation of valuable resources. The (grand) vision, therefore, is a powerful concept in universities. Richard expressed his opposition to this as we assembled in his office, amidst an assortment of university materials of different textures, colours, meanings and agential qualities, as well as recollections of successful (and probably unsuccessful) interactions he had experienced that morning. Further, his comments were made to me whom arrived at our meeting in a vehicle emblazoned with the university logo and name, carrying thoughts from prior university-based assemblages that I had just been part of. How did these materials impact on Richard's thoughts and words? Did other material factors serve to support thinking differently? Our conversation was, to some extent, isolated from university life and many of its material qualities. Heavy brick walls formed the office in which we met, and the well-varnished wooden door gave a sense it had secured many private conversations in its time. Our bodies, mature, tall and bespectacled, seemed to give support to an intellectual connection. Of course, the painting *Connections* was present. What part had these materials, and especially the artwork, played in Richard's thinking, such that he was able to resist convention thought? Had the painting's qualities, reminiscent of Australian summers, rural landscapes and paddocks, which Richard spoke about just minutes' prior, managed to reverberate against those lacquered doors, fuelling Richard's passion and work on his thinking about vision? Of course, this apparatus for emergence could not and refused to be thingified. One might imagine that there were forces and flows at play, and that these assembled with ideas from all the other people Richard had spoken to about vision, and all the other people I had interviewed as part of the same project, and the materiality of all those contexts. Assembled and decentred, I could only wonder, as I do now. What emerged from this broad assemblage (or cluster of assemblages) was a 'knowing' about the importance of conversation and relationship in higher education. This linked, sometime later, with other ideas about liminality and authentic leadership to create a transformed view – what others may call a 'model' – of creativity in higher education.

Emerging from the assemblage that Heather and I were part of, after it had co-evolved and mutated and come in contact with other assemblages, other conversations, paintings and material of numerous forms, was a different way of thinking about the creativity of health services. Bringing Heather's thinking and also the extant literature on complexity theory to this broader assemblage highlighted the relevance of complex adaptive systems to creativity. This connected with other research assemblages made up of other health professionals (and all they were assembled with) to eventually advance the concept of a practice-theoretic approach to creativity (Rae, 2015).

CONCLUSION

Knowing how to understand the work that art does is a central concern for artists and arts-based researchers. The new materialism is providing a useful platform for exploring this task and for re-imagining the agency of art, and post-humanists such as Sandvik make this point well in relation to arts-based research. It is useful to also draw from comments made by Elizabeth Grosz – actually a comment that she made during a 'round table' interview about art and Deleuze (McDonald, Grosz & Rothfield, 2015). Grosz said that art is "the place where we contest the possibilities of the future" (2015, p.11). This, of course, is no surprise to many artists or arts-based researchers. However, Grosz takes us further by adding: "[W]hat Deleuze promises is the possibility of looking at those underlying invisible forces that art is always trying to capture" (2015, p.12). These invisible forces, what here have been referred to as forces, flows, energy, connections, emergence and passions, get closer to an answer about how to understand the 'work' of art. The dynamic relationships between the elements of assemblages, including, of course, artworks, transform researchers' sensations and knowing. This is only possible through the decentring of the researcher, and even the decentring of the research participant, interview and transcript. It is only possible too if the whole research context is acknowledged, and that includes non-human material. Otherwise, there would be only limited space for the materiality of art to create possibilities for the future.

Arts-based researchers should move away from boundaries – the boundaries between human and non-human, artwork and other material, and the boundaries that separate disciplinary groups. Here, there has been little difference between 'artist' and 'researcher', apart from name, and when the broader material contexts of higher education and health care are included in the debate, what are considered to be separate disciplines move into closer alignment. At the very least, the differences between disciplinary practices, and no doubt a variety of social practices, are counteracted by what they have in common – the company they keep.

Acknowledgement

I am grateful to Emeritus Professor Bill Green for our conversations about many of the concepts covered in this chapter, especially the new materialism, and for his advice in the preparation of this manuscript.

References

Barad, K. (2003). Posthumanist performativity: Toward an understanding of how matter comes to matter. *Signs, 28*(3), 801-831.

Barnett, C. (2009). Towards a methodology of postmodern assemblage: Adolescent identity in the age of social networking. *Philosophical Studies in Education, 40*, 200-210.

Bettez, S. C. (2015). Navigating the complexity of qualitative research in postmodern contexts: Assemblage, critical reflexivity, and communion as guides. *International Journal of Qualitative Studies in Education, 28*(8), 932-954.

Carter, P. (2004). *Material thinking: The theory and practice of creative research.* Melbourne: Melbourne University Press.

———. (2007). Interest: The ethics of invention. In E. Barrett & B. Bolt [Eds.,] *Practice as research: Approaches to creative arts enquiry* (pp.15-25). London: I. B. Tauris.

DeLanda, M. (2006). *A new philosophy of society: Assemblage theory and social complexity*. Continuum, London and New York.

Deleuze, G., & Guattari, F. (1987). *A thousand plateaus: Capitalism and schizophrenia*. Minneapolis: University of Minnesota.

Dewey, J. (1934). *Art as experience*. NY: Penguin Group.

Goldstein, J. (1999). Emergence as a construct: History and issues. *Emergence, 1*(1), 49-72.

Kontopoulos, K. (1993). *The logics of social structure*. Cambridge: Cambridge University Press.

Leddy, T. (2012). John Dewey. In A. Giovannelli (Ed.), *Aesthetics: The key thinkers* (pp.126-138). London: Continuum.

Mar, P., & Anderson, K. (2010). The creative assemblage: Theorizing contemporary forms of arts-based collaboration. *Journal of Cultural Economy*, *3*(1), 35-51.

Marcus, G., & Saka, E. (2006). Assemblage. *Theory, Culture & Society, 23*(2-3), 101-106.

Mazzei, L. (2013). A voice without organs: Interviewing in posthumanist research. *International Journal of Qualitative Studies in Education*, *26*(6), 732-740.

McDonald, H., Grosz, E., & Rothfield, P. (2006). Art and Deleuze: A round table interview with Elizabeth Grosz. *Australian and New Zealand Journal of Art*, *7*(2), 4-22.

Olds, K., & Thrift, N. (2005). Cultures on the brink: Reengineering the soul of capitalism—on a global scale. *Global assemblages: Technology, politics, and ethics as anthropological problems*, 270-290.

Patton, M. (2002). *Qualitative research and evaluation methods*. Thousand Oaks: SAGE.

Rae, J. (2015). *Practising creativity: An arts-based investigation of creativity in professional practice, with specific reference to public health services*. Unpublished PhD dissertation, Charles Sturt University.

Rose, G. (2007). *Visual methodologies: An introduction to the interpretation of visual methods*. London, UK. SAGE.

Sandvik, N. (2010). The art of/in educational research: Assemblages at work. *Reconceptualizing Educational Research Methodology*, 1(1).

———. (2012). Rethinking the idea/ideal of pedagogical control: Assemblages of de/stabilisation. *Contemporary Issues in Early Childhood, 13*(3), 200-209.

Smith, D. (2011). Deleuze and the question of desire: Towards an immanent theory of ethics. In N. Jun & D. Smith [Eds.], *Deleuze and ethics* (pp.123-141). Edinburgh: Edinburgh University Press.

Smith, H., & Dean, R. (2009). [Eds.], *Practice-led research, research-led practice in the creative arts* (pp.41-66). Edinburgh: Edinburgh University Press.

Somerville, M. (2007). Postmodern emergence. *International Journal of Qualitative Studies in Education, 20*(2), 225-243.

———. (2008). Bubbles on the surface: A methodology of water, Retrieved 20 January 2010 from: http://www.aare.edu.au/data/publications/2008/som08701.pdf

Springgay, S., & Rotas, N. (2015). How do you make a classroom operate like a work of art? Deleuzeguattarian methodologies of research-creation. *International Journal of Qualitative Studies in Education, 28*(5), 552–72.

Sullivan, G. (2009). Making space: The purpose and place of practice-led research. In H. Smith & R. Dean [Eds.], *Practice-led research, research-led practice in the creative arts* (pp. 41-66). Edinburgh: Edinburgh University Press.

Titchen, A., & Horsfell, D. (2007). Re-imaging research using creative imagination and expression. In J. Higgs, A. Titchen & H. Armstrong [Eds.], *Being critical and creative in qualitative research* (pp.215-229). Sydney: Hampden Press.

CHAPTER 7

Medical Imaging, Modern Clinical Practice, and the Art of Exploration

Gregory Turner-Rahman

ABSTRACT

In this chapter, I am describing how the use of project work - primarily the production of visual images - can be an effective type of abductive visual reasoning that facilitates student-directed investigations of interwoven themes and theoretical contrivances. A good visual studies course should be an analysis, evaluation, and critique of visual practices, technologies, and epistemological structures at the intersection of the sciences, medicine, technology, art and design. The visual studies class I describe here was an examination of the beginnings of modern clinical medical practice and the advancement of visualisation technologies. Students were tasked with mapping the domain of the visual medical technologies from the late 1700s to the late 1900s alongside the conceptual and artistic representations of the body. Discussions about the patient experience circumscribed the clinical practice and the constituent visualisation technologies. In the end, the creative projects revealed that students had thoughtful critiques and, sometimes, personal connections to the conceptual aspects underpinning the contemporary clinical approach. Ultimately, through project-driven abductive reasoning and critical content analysis, a deeper discourse about the treatment of disease and death provided what I feel is strong evidence of higher-order critical thinking.

INTRODUCTION: ABDUCTIVE VISUAL REASONING

It is often assumed the production of imagery must serve the purpose of communicating something. Image making as an exploratory act of visual reasoning is therefore commonly overlooked. This chapter outlines how project work - primarily the production of images - in visual studies and other art history and theory courses can engage students in the exploration of topics seemingly well outside of the art and design disciplines and their proverbial comfort zone. I argue image making, supplemented with image collecting and critical analysis, can foster a type of abductive visual reasoning wherein the producer is in dialogue with abstract ideas through the act of making. I will synthesise a model of engagement wherein students' exploration and creation of multiple types of imagery ultimately fosters a richer understanding of course topics.

The concept of abductive visual reasoning is not new. C.S. Peirce (Peirce, Hartshorne, Weiss & Burks, 1958) outlined how abductive reasoning is an act of inferring a hypothesis from observational data therefore, abductive reasoning stands in contrast to deductive and inductive reasoning as an inference that depends on the most logical explanation. It makes sense that abduction was originally described by Peirce as 'hypothesis'. To abduce, then, is to best use the data available and to come to a conclusion. For instance, medical diagnoses are abductively derived. What is important about Peirce's pragmatism is that it maintains learning is inherent in the process of perception and science as the extension of "perception into new forms" (Nesher, 2001). I've always taken this to include technological developments that support scientific discovery and reasoning. Nesher goes further to tie this type of inference to any act of discovery and tells us that:

> These new cognitions evolve from perception with our instinctively controlled operation of discovery, whose logic Peirce calls Abduction. All other emotionally and rationally controlled artistic, creativity, and scientific discoveries are based on and analogous to [Abduction] (Nesher, 2001, p. 24).

Abductive reasoning is simply a creative act of discovery (Nesher, 2001; Lu and Liu, 2012) shared by all disciplines. David Gooding, in his description of Michael Faraday's creative process, outlines a dynamic interplay of "concrete objects, visual images, abstract, theoretically-informed visual models and metaphysical precepts" (2006, p. 40). Faraday, as Gooding tells us, manipulates both material artifacts and representations as cognitive strategy. Gooding explains:

> This work produced representations, artefacts and procedures whose cognitive (generative) and social (communicative and critical) functions combine to produce knowledge that can be networked. New empirical evidence emerges from the interaction of visual, tactile, kinaesthetic and auditory modes of perception together with existing interpretive concepts that integrate different types of knowledge and experience (2006, p.45).

In the 1930s Rudolf Arnheim similarly argued that visual thinking was a powerful aspect of human intelligence (Arnheim, 1969). About the same time, Gyorges Kepes and others at MIT's Center for Advanced Visual Studies explored visual methods of problem solving across disciplines and the interconnectedness of art and science (Kepes, 1965). Arnheim and Kepes outline a common language of visual learning that can be applied to any discipline. More recently, Cameron Shelley (1996) similarly describes how visual abductive reasoning is used in Archeology and classifies the various modes of abduction:

- Abductions that constitute the recognition of objects of theoretical significance

- Abductions that concern the shape of objects
- Abductions that address the structure of objects
- Abductions that are produced by analogical inference (1996, p. 280).

Shelley discusses the application of these abductions within the archeological context. For instance, the abductions of recognition and the shape or structure of objects are key aspects of recognizing bone fragments. Archeologists explore and learn from a dialogue between image, mental representation and artefact. Gooding describes something similar when discussing Whittington's models of extinct organisms from fossils embedded in rock. Whittington had to use only partial information and through sketches was able to infer the three-dimensional structure from the fossil evidence (Gooding, 2005, p.183). Sketching is a method of exploring not only complex forms from partial information from inference but also constructing new combinations of existing elements.

Gabriela Goldschmidt explains how architects use sketching in a reiterative method of "visual design thinking" wherein the designer ultimately fails to reproduce an accurate version of a mental representation but the result is ultimately something new. A dialogue emerges between the designer and the sketch (Goldschimdt, 2003). Magnani's *manipulative abduction* also refers to an "extra-theoretical behavior that seeks to create communicable accounts of new experiences to integrate them into previously existing systems of experimental and linguistic (theoretical) practices" (Magnani, 2013, p. 304). Magnani describes this type of visual abduction for creative discovery in mathematics where constructing diagrams is an important act of visualisation. Magnani and Goldschmidt are addressing the same fundamental notion: working through sketches and diagrams provides for the dialectical interaction of mental representation and externalised extension of imagery. From a feedback loop of sketch making emerges new, unintended results (Goldschimdt, 2003).

Artists and designers often work between sketches, physical models, and mental representations as well as augment project briefs with ample discussion, note taking, and even doodling. It seems reasonable then that an art history or theory course could introduce concepts in a manner native to the type of problem solving undertaken by art students. In the following section I will describe how I created a challenge for students in a Visual Studies course: to construct an intricate sort of matrix that combined historical events, overarching theoretical concepts, artwork, technologies, and a set of narratives about medical practices. All the while, I worked to maintain a more student-centered and self-directed, exploratory style of class. What follows is a description of the various ways that I incorporated the use of imagery for analysis and the production of images as integral part of the learning. Later in the discussion of outcomes, I will use Shelley's abductions and these constituent aspects of visual reasoning: *recognition*, *functional explication (or shape and structure)*, and *analogical inference*. Using these various visual abductions as a guide, I intend to provide a blueprint of sorts for others teaching art history and theory who wish to better serve artists and designers. The use of abductive reasoning, I maintain, can be a transformative way to connect students to complex, interconnected themes, ideas, and even communities such as health care providers.

MAPPING A VISUAL STUDIES DOMAIN

There are many ways to use imagery in the classroom. I will later describe how the creative products of abductive visual reasoning serve the purpose of not only being a record of one's thinking but can also, at times, reveal deeper critical engagement and render surprisingly aesthetically pleasing results as well. Most importantly, however, the production of visual images can open new means of critical analysis.

I am describing a Visual Studies class, at the University of Idaho, that is an examination, evaluation, and critique of visual practices, technologies, communicative and epistemological models and structures. Students - primarily from the College of Art and Architecture, English, and Political Science - were asked to explore the historical, theoretical, and aesthetic provocations of visualisation in fields such as biology, medicine, genetics, and information technologies. In the Spring 2015 iteration of the course, I asked students to investigate the development of modern medical practices and the constituent visualising technologies. This effort better aligned the course to STEM (Science, Technology, Engineering, and Math) initiatives and could potentially foster interdisciplinary connectivity across programs on campus and with external communities. For instance, one research track within the College of Art and Architecture spearheaded by the Interior Design program explores quality healthcare environments. The visual studies course was intended to augment, explore, and leverage that research to also support a new experience design emphasis. Regardless, the medical focus was daunting to some students who initially approached the topic with some trepidation. To allay their fears, they were first asked to collectively create visual mind maps of broad topics, ideas, concerns, and issues regarding contemporary medicine. These diagrams circumscribed subsequent class discussions by identifying key themes. For instance, a keystone issue was the term *diagnosis* (see Figure: 7. 1). The word - described by students as the use of an examination to determine the nature or circumstances of a patient's condition - was set in contrast to the term *prognosis* (a forecasting of a probable outcome of a disease) and highlighted how doctors need to categorise illness in order to problem solve.

This led to a much more substantial discussion about what students classified as "clipboard culture" or the legal and bureaucratic dimensions of contemporary American medicine. Students expressed a desire to understand the conditions that have led to the more problematic aspects of contemporary medicine such as cost, poor treatment of patients, and access to newer preventative treatments and technologies. Ultimately students focused on the patient's quality of life and the experience of dying. These are weighty topics but fundamental to understanding the changes in medical practices in our era.

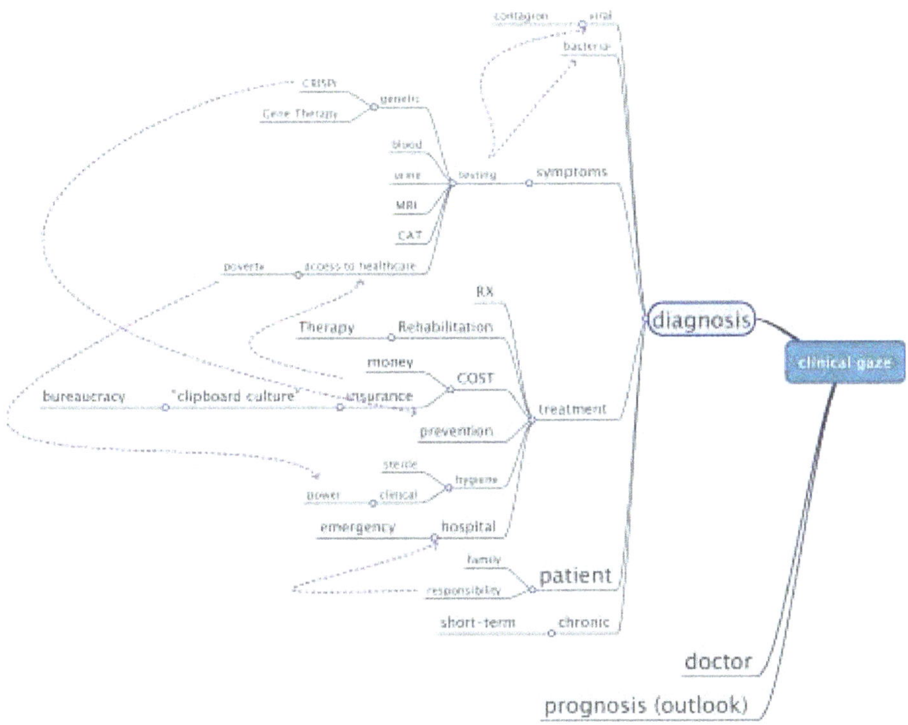

Figure: 7.1 - Student-defined conceptual map regarding the clinical gaze (2015).

Centering the discussion on diagnosis was fortuitous as it was a natural segue to the first text, Michel Foucault's *Birth of the Clinic.* Foucault's post-Structuralist critique attempts to extract the structures of power and knowledge implicit in modern medicine (Foucault, 1973). Foucault looks at factors including the French revolution and changes in scientific and medical knowledge that led to a different type of conceptual model at the core of physician-patient experience. As they read the book, students began to overlay the tools and technologies of late 18th to mid-19th century with prior discussions of contemporary medical practices. Foucault provided some context but I asked students to explore some other aspects of technological progress and other historical eras. For instance, I wanted students to collect images relating to the themes:

- Renaissance and Enlightenment Era Medical Images
- Modern Medical Technologies
- The 19th Century Body
- The Visual Turn and Modern Medicine
- Contemporary Medical Artifacts and Visualisation Devices

Each of these topics could easily have been the basis of a semester-long class and our review was not thorough. Every discussion was student-directed and centered on the collection of imagery. We used an online learning environment (BBLearn) to store and share our images as well as to house subsequent online discussion. The class collectively contextualised the findings within a framework laid out in earlier in-class conversation and in regards to the readings. For instance, there was ample discussion about changes in art and science during the Renaissance that allowed for a different kind of relationship with the human body. Students were keen to find visual evidence that made connections between scientific discovery and artistic representation. The result was a visual record of medical instrumentation, visualisation technologies and significant artwork but also of the various ideas brought about in the text.

Giving visual form to ideas is fundamental to production of imagery and texts can provide much inspiration. For example, a fourth year art student created illustrations for Foucault's text (see Figure: 7.2). She remarked that her drawings were literal translations of the readings meant to comment on the sterility of the clinical practice. Additionally, she described how she placed the images into the library's copy of the text before returning it. That subsequent and intentional act was meant to be a statement about exposing what this student felt was problematic in both the modern clinical practice and Foucault's logocentric analysis. She had made a connection between the clinical practices and the conditions of her own education. This student felt that both modern medical practice and education were dehumanizing. Her response – the hand drawn sketch – is a personal indexical trace and placing the image in the book is a way to connect with other humans.

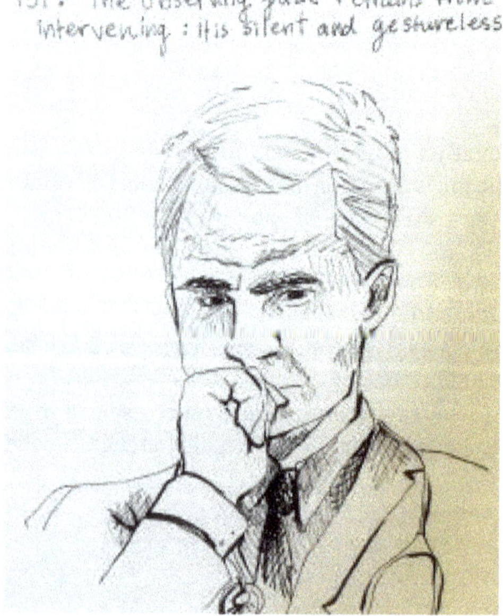

Figure: 7. 2 - Sketch complementing Foucault's text (2015).
Image credit: Gregory Turner-Rahman

MEDICAL IMAGING AND THE BIRTH OF THE CLINIC

The challenge of creating a matrix of concepts, events and artefacts mandates that there also is some sort of historical foundation. The theoretical cornerstone for the course was the rise of contemporary medical practices. Michel Foucault's *Birth of the Clinic* outlines the changes in medical practice from the late 1700s to the early 1800s. Foucault probes the changes in language and conceptual models to examine a shift in the relationship of medical practices to the body. For instance, the first chapter of the book outlines a specific geometric localization of disease in late 18th century medicine. Disease is mapped onto the body and a resulting cognitive model requires a two-dimensional spatial representation. The physician would primarily investigate illness through a patient's narrative.

After the revolution, Foucault tells us, there is a restructuring of practices in the effort of making medicine more rational - including opening dead bodies. Foucault argues that the evolution of the modern clinic comes from an amalgamation of political and economic factors as well as philosophical demands. The result of these changes is the emergence of a medical gaze based on empirical approaches fostering a type of analysis that sees disease as a symptom or sign of illness and eschews the earlier nosological or classification system (Foucault, 1973). This conceptual change shifts the dynamic of the medical dialogue away from the patient narrative. In discussions of the text, we constantly referred back to the collection of images of late 19th and early 20th century medical visualising technologies: microscopes, otoscopes, x-rays, tomography, ultrasounds. I asked students to describe how the conditions of the era outlined by Foucault relate to and establish the clinical approaches of our era and the constituent technologies.

The in-class conversations bled into online discussions as students began to explore this shift towards the clinical gaze. BBLearn proved to be an excellent warehouse to store our collections of imagery. Early on, several students focused on the work of Andreas Vesalius. Vesalius was a physician and anatomist who, in 1543, published *De humani corporis fabrica,* a pioneering work of human anatomy. Students remarked that the engravings indicated that the work was intended for printing - a new technology at the time. Printing provided the means to a mass audience (albeit one that was of a particular socio-economic situation) and the transmission of knowledge is significant because there is a conceptual revisioning of the body that becomes shared and distributed. Beyond the dissemination of the work, Vesalius' drawings provide evidence of a shift in how the body is visualised: the beginnings of more studied anatomical approach.

Others found Li Shizhens' *Compendium of Materia Medica* and Govard Bidloo's *Anatomia humani corporis* as equally valuable studies showing changes brought about by the systematic study of nature and the body. Students investigated the conditions leading to and resulting from these visual treatises. In a discussion someone remarked that the anatomy illustrations of the Renaissance provide a statement about the treatment of prisoners whose corpses were provided for dissection. The exquisite engravings of someone like Bidloo are both works of art and compelling visual atlases of the body as well as indications of power and political or legal structures. Students commented on the medical instrumentation from the same time period that they felt were primarily for treating the wounded on the battlefield.

The discussions then shifted to focus on death and how the body is presented in various contexts: casualty of war, object of inspection, property, or artistic representation. The clinical gaze - a separation of person from the physical body in order to hone in on the causes and treatment of disease - also requires a shift in power relations. The students then began to explore patient empowerment through written accounts of clinical experiences.

A third year printmaking student produced a print that takes the clinical gaze to an extreme (Figure: 7.3). Using imagery that references Bidloo or Vesalius's work, this student produced a print of a dissected body. Below the corpse is a cost of the parts contained within. The piece makes the connection between a disinterested clinical gaze and the value of human organs on the black market. She is making connections between the modern clinic and the body as commodity.

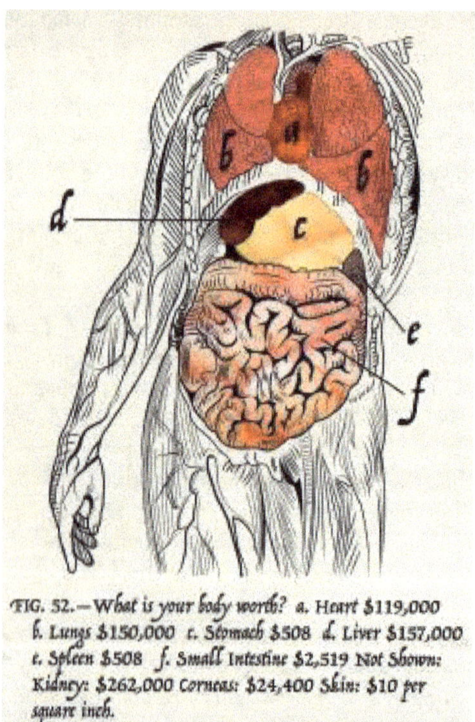

Figure: 7. 3 - Student's project listing the value of body parts on the black market (2015).
Image credit: Gregory Turner-Rahman.

About this time, an English major in the class visited my office with a book called *L'Image Obscene (The Obscene Image): Parisian Hospital Breakroom Graffiti* by Bouchon and Tondini (Bouchon and Tondini, 2010). The book documents the breakrooms of Parisian hospitals whose walls are covered in vivid, sometimes lewd imagery created by the medical staff. These rooms and their decoration are a tradition that begins in the middle ages that continues through to the 18th century and into our time creating a dichotomy between the external world of the rest of the hospital and this private domain of the doctors and nurses. The graffiti is grotesque, often humorous, and ultimately a stress-relief for physicians. The student rightly pinpointed that in the medical gaze we neglect the narratives of the caregivers as well as those of the patient. In an email, he remarks:

> Apart from the overt connection between a document of French medical history specifically and Foucault's medical history of the French Enlightenment generally, I feel the theses of both works correlate. Both works are critical of the trend in modern medicine to institutionalize the practice of medicine at the expense of human experience.

A RETURN TO PATIENT NARRATIVES

The second text for the class, *The Wounded Storyteller: Body, Illness, and Ethics* by Arthur W. Frank, centers on the use of storytelling as a method of understanding and coping with illness. Frank outlines a number of narratives that writers with chronic health problems use to describe and make sense of their illnesses. The three narratives are: *restitution*, *chaos*, and *quest*. In the restitution narrative, the writer foresees a time when they overcome the illness and the quality of life is restored. The chaos narrative "presupposes lack of control" (Frank, 1997, p. 100) and reveals "vulnerability, futility, and impotence" as the disease is understood to be unconquerable (Frank, 1997, p.97). The quest narrative describes a particular type of writing wherein the writer and sufferer directly confronts and engages her illness.

The narratives outlined by Frank are written texts but students felt that there was something inherently universal that could apply to visual imagery. The written accounts mirror expressions in visual art that underline the patients' engagement with their illnesses. For instance, students associated artists Frida Kahlo and Vincent Van Gogh with the quest and chaos narratives. Kahlo's work shows an engagement with, if not control of, her illness whereas Van Gogh's work seems to perhaps indicate an all-consuming mental illness that would not get better. Students then began to compare individual modes of expression with developments in medical imaging. In class discussions we outlined how visualisation technologies alter the relationship between doctor and the patient's body. If Foucault's thesis maintains a separation of body and patient as result of certain techniques and technologies that allow for a direct observation and interaction with disease, as Frank tells us:

> The story of illness that trumps all others in the modern period is the medical narrative. The story told by the physician becomes the one against which others are ultimately judged true or false, useful or not (Frank, 1997, p.5).

Frank champions a shift in the physician-patient dynamic when he describes a thoroughly postmodern patient experience where "the capacity for telling one's own story is reclaimed" (1997, p.7). The shift in focus towards patients re-exerting their power through narrative was also reflected in classroom discussion. In class and online, students opened up and there was a significant shift from apprehensive discourse to intense debate punctuated by many personal stories. Postmodern illness, as Frank reminds us, is a "reflection on body, self, and the destination that life's map leads to" (1997, p.7). It became much easier for people to understand the varying narratives because they had, at one point or another, experienced aspects of each. It was surprising how many students had, at some time in their life, dealt with chronic pain or serious health issues.

It was a challenge to bring the conversations back to the interconnectedness of more recent visualising technologies. Visual studies demand that students explore the development of conceptual frameworks and power relationships with varying modes of visuality and visualisation technologies. For this purpose, I've followed narratives outlined in Johnathan Crary's *Technique of the Observer* and other texts that discuss the evolution of technology and certain types of visuality (Crary, 1990; Foster, 1987). The last of the in-class, student-led discussions explored the role of technologies such as ultrasound, PET and CAT scans, MRIs and electron microscopy. We ascribed these tools to a lineage of visualising technologies that make the invisible visible. The import of these tools is that they maintain the body as whole, provide evidence of internal conditions without requiring the invasive opening of the body thus, for the most part, favoring the comfort of the patient. As one student described, these visualising tools are open windows into hidden worlds. Students also drew parallels between these tools and photography's influence on art. We had abundant conversations about how photography changed pictorial representation and allowed the artists to begin to more directly represent things, for example, states of consciousness which were previously deemed non-representable. A student remarked: "expression champions the sufferer, the artist."

VISUALISING THE PRACTICE/PRACTICING THE VISUAL

The challenge of visual studies is to facilitate exploration of interconnected themes not isolated moments in a timeline or individual pieces of artwork or technology. The goal is to have the experience be, for the most part, student-directed and allow for the synthesis of disparate ideas. This is a creative act to which I alluded in the introduction. It is important to note that images offer only a partial glimpse into a more complex set of socio-cultural, political, and technological factors influencing a historical moment. My role as facilitator required creating opportunities for students to use the imagery to make conceptual connections. As outlined so far, I have suggested using the following: diagrammatic mind-maps of broad themes and interrelated terms, collections of images to define technological progress, and discussion centered on modes of representation including historical examples from various artists.

These activities and the collection of images are fairly common in many history and theory classes. For many students, however, the act of creating something provides a unique method of 'playing' with a topic. The mid-term project brief asked students to do just that: design a device that could help patients recovering from an illness or in dealing with a long-term medical condition. The device did not need to be functional and could be completely fantastic. However, our review of visualisation technologies and historical devices should, in some way, inform the design in some manner.

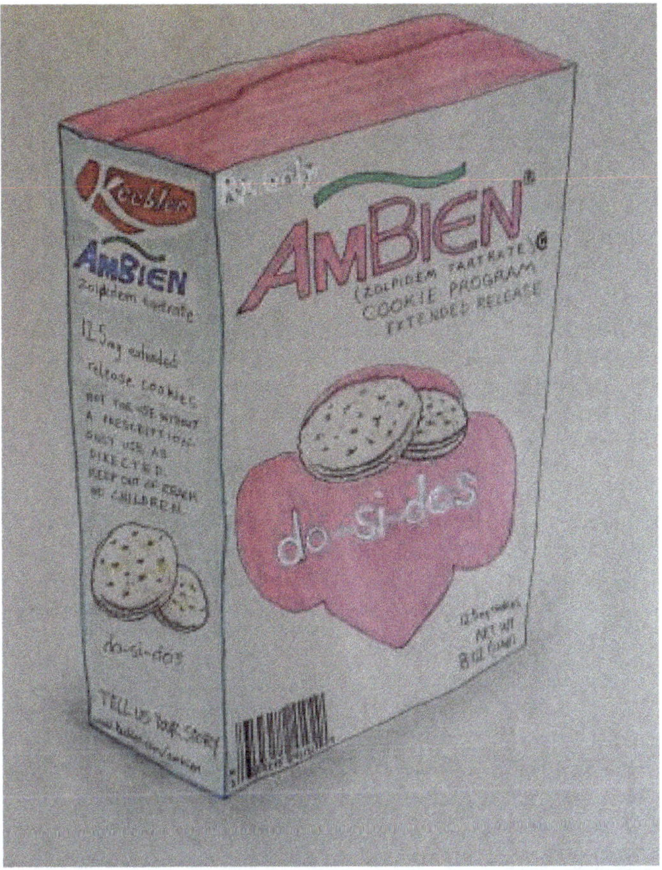

Figure: 7. 4 - A mid-term project: Girl Scout cookies as drug delivery system (2015).
Image credit: Gregory Turner-Rahman

The solutions varied widely from a cookie drug delivery system (Figure: 7. 4), designer emergency ID bracelets, therapeutic armor, echolocation eyeglasses, to a paper-based (read: disposable) hospital monitor. Students were asked to present their work and to contextualise their device within the historical trajectory outlined throughout the first part of the semester. The final projects were similar in that the brief was loosely defined and required engagement with the texts and discussions. The project brief asked students to:

> ...create a work that focuses on some aspect of the history and theory we've explored throughout the semester. There are no limits as to what the project can be. The final result can be a film, visual story, design (object, space, experience), or whatever suits the solution of whatever you've explored.
>
> The project however must relate to course topics. Use the knowledge that you've garnered from class discussions and the readings along with your research to produce something that will undoubtedly make your classmates question the interactions of technology, medical practices, and even the arts.

Mid-term and final projects allowed students to take the catalog of imagery gathered throughout the semester and expand class themes of contemporary medicine, newer technologies and more subtly, the role of the designer/artist/critic. Students were asked to help define a design brief for the final project and to provide a summary of their intended project once they had conferred with their classmates and myself. Each week a portion of class time on Friday was reserved for project review. Project updates also happened online and provided a constant record of their work. Sketches, notes, photographs, web links, and student-moderated discussions within BBLearn provided a rich collection of resources back to which students could refer.

Outcomes and Assessment

It may seem a daunting task assessing project work for an art history or theory course. Throughout this course, I made it explicit that the work should relate back to themes discussed throughout the semester and most importantly, students should be able to defend their creative efforts. We reserved several days at the end of the semester for student presentations of the final projects. The collection of work was compelling:

- Portraits of disease (portraits with faces replaced with the sufferer's disease)
- A hospital experience redesign project
- A carnival game that used actuary chart and death statistics
- Advertisements for drugs with side effects as the prominent feature
- A self-portrait poster made of images of student's struggle with anxiety and other medical conditions
- A collection of medical instruments made from industrial re-bar
- An illustrated book describing one young woman's first and horrific hospital visit
- Motion graphics describing epidemiological principles
- Composited images of an operating theater as metaphor for the clinical gaze

Students were asked to make a formal presentation wherein they would need to contextualise their projects within the larger matrix we had developed throughout the semester. Other members of the class, along with myself, provided an oral critique of each student's work. While most projects were images there were a few more sculptural pieces. For instance, a student constructed a set of medical instruments using industrial rebar. Rebar is reinforced steel bar embedded in cast concrete to add strength by keeping it in tension. Included in this student's collection were a scalpel, forceps, and a spreader (Figure: 7. 5). This political science and pre-law student had found the form of the instruments compelling and had learned to weld and fashion the rebar specifically for this project. The resulting tools are rough, industrial, strange, out-of-scale, and oddly beautiful. The student felt that the modern clinical practice had mirrored other industrial processes thus the use of a heavy industrial material seemed appropriate.

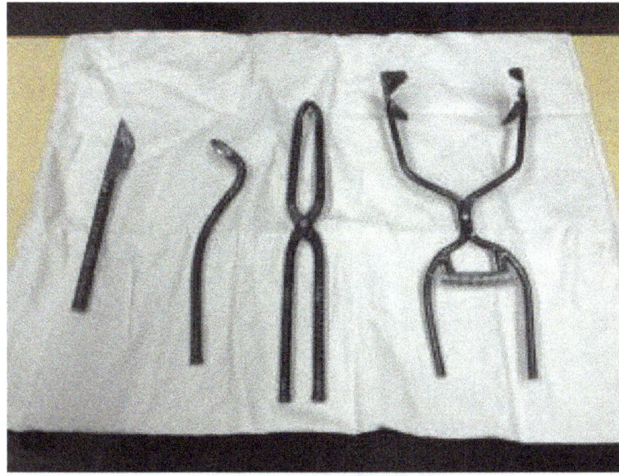

Figure: 7.5 - A final project: medical instruments made from industrial re-bar (2015).
Image credit: Gregory Turner-Rahman

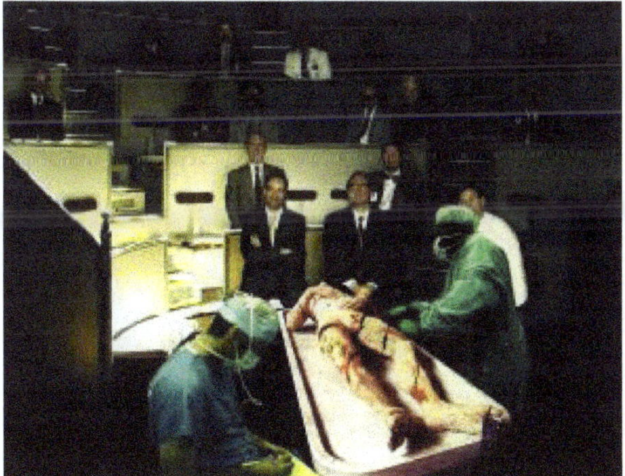

Figure: 7.6 - A student's final project: Composited images describing the evolution of the clinical gaze (2015).
Image credit: Gregory Turner-Rahman

Other students found that imagery was effective as a method of similarly describing the theory we had explored. A Virtual Technology and Design student wanting to explore the disinterested clinical gaze used digital models along with found imagery to composite scenes (Figure: 7. 6). This student chose the operating theater as the nexus of the clinical experience as it marks the rational, communicative aspects of modern medicine. The body, in this instance, is carved and probed but ultimately not of interest to the doctors and administrators who share the scene.

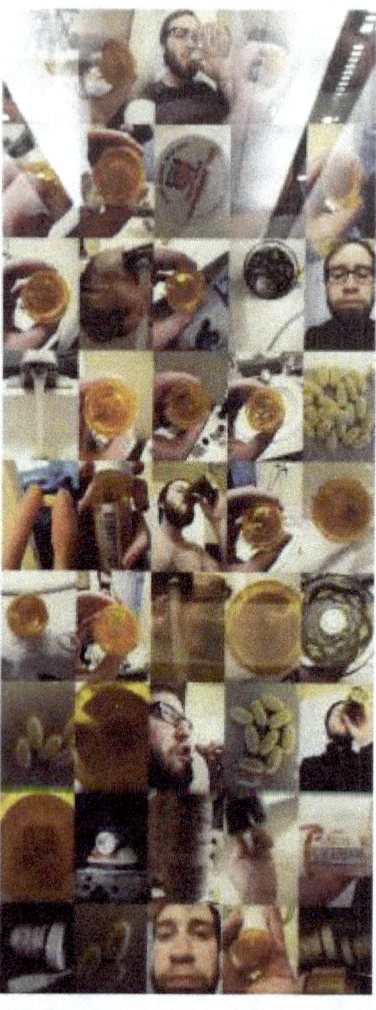

Figure: 7.7 - A student's final project: A static documentary on the challenges of dealing with a health issue (2015).
Image credit: Gregory Turner-Rahman

Another student provided a touching visual documentary about the various medications he must take to combat a number of health and anxiety issues (Figure: 7. 7). The images are displayed in a grid that represents one week of classes and shows how frequent and demanding his treatment is.

Some projects strictly adhered to a design brief and involved a particular sort of problem solving. The notion underlying many of these efforts was a sense that something was not quite working in the American healthcare system. One student explored the representations of the female figure in ergonomic data (Figure: 7. 8). Data regarding the 'average' woman was overlaid with other medical data and statistics (average heart rate, blood pressure, etc.). Words pulled from some the readings were then affixed to magnetic strips and placed on the metal backing. The resulting composition is dependent on the viewer who can obfuscate and hide with the words or, in another manner, the words can support and explain the visuals of the body. The project brings together the two primary texts and overlays the personal narrative over a quantified, studied body.

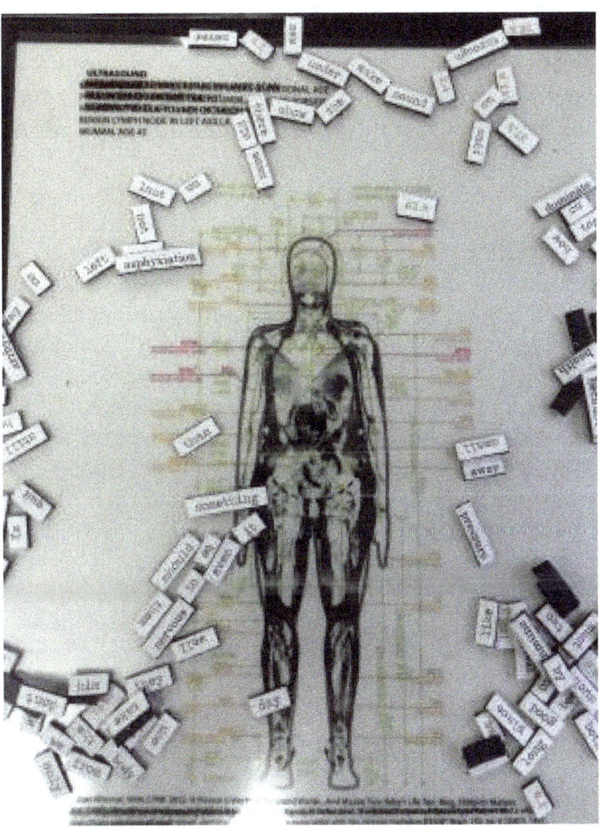

Figure: 7.8 - A student's final project: Data about the average woman is overlaid upon one another (2015).
Image credit: Gregory Turner-Rahman

In the final critique, many of the discussions about the final projects returned to quality of healthcare in this country. The more expressive products tended to center on the patient narratives with the artists and designers recounting their experiences. The focus of the class was brought back to the idea of medicine as method to stave off disease and death. Death and end-of-life issues, the students concluded are woefully not addressed well in contemporary medical practice. Regardless, each student gleaned something of value from the readings and exploration.

Discussion: A Visual Reasoning Emphasis

In art history and theory courses we often train art students to study images in ways that are tantamount to reading. The result of say, critical or content analysis is an understanding of the various motivations and structures that supported the construction of that particular image. This is an important and essential aspect of analysis. But what is missing perhaps is a type of hands-on visual production that stimulates a student's ability to make connections between disparate themes, historical periods, and even technologies. Our students often lack the ability to synthesise concepts. I maintain by using methods akin to studio or design practices students – through the production of imagery – are able to view theory and history in unique and sometimes surprising ways. This can be a transformative creative act of visual reasoning.

There are many parts to the abductive visual component of the course which I have adapted from Shelley (*recognition, functional explication, and analogical inference*). As I've outlined in the previous sections, students were asked to engage with course materials, including the readings and discussion, in a number of ways that required the use of some sort of visual reasoning: conceptual mapping, thematic exploration and organization, image-based historical contextualisation, visual storytelling, design fiction making, playful, artistic investigations:

Conceptual Mapping (mind-mapping) provides an introduction to a broad but shallow understanding of a range of concepts and terminology. This is usually the first exercise as it allows students to get start forming an understanding of the connections without necessarily knowing much about each. Following Shelley, this process encourages the *recognition* of various concepts and terms. It also allows the student to begin making inferences. The visualisation of the connectivity of words and ideas is important. The challenge of using mind maps is to not have words be abstracted and unconnected but instead to provide a framework for subsequent discussion and project work. To not have the students to attempt, early on, to make connections between concepts amounts to a sort of mindless exploration of merely words that can be affirm stereotypical views or misunderstandings. The simple act of asking students to draw connections and, more importantly, explain their thinking provides for more complex *inference*.

Thematic exploration and organization requires students to collect images of pertinent technologies, artwork, historical imagery, and even ephemera. The act of organising the material asks students to consider relationships between each and the broader themes outlined: (Renaissance and Enlightenment era medical images, modern medical technologies, 19th century body, the visual turn and modern medicine, contemporary medical artefacts and visualization devices). This is also a type of *recognition* and subsequent *inference*. Students are able to understand how visual materials relate to themes from specific periods of time. It is important to get some additional understanding of topics through quick research. This can be online but should also include other trusted resources. Often I will have a reference librarian attend a class session and explain how to do high-quality library searches including finding visual resources. It is essential that the research and collection of resources happen near to the beginning of the course thus giving students the skills and opportunity to apply those skills throughout the semester.

Image-based historical contextualisation is perhaps a more focused version of thematic exploration. Students are responsible for collecting imagery from a particular period of time. This may or may not be directly related to the topics at hand and can be tangential. However, ultimately the collection of images must serve the purpose of describing or giving some sense of that period of time. This is important because it is at these moments when students get a "feeling" for an era. Often film can provide this contextualisation quickly and effectively.

Visual storytelling tasks ask students to take their knowledge and synthesise a cogent story. This aspect of visual reasoning, as Shelley outlines, is a more productive *functional explication* and *inference*. In order to tell the story well, students must have an understanding of the tacit components such as place, history, and motivation. The challenge for students is to explain something within a narrative with attention paid to accurate details or appropriate theoretical underpinnings. Usually shorter narratives (minute long films or static images) work best as they force the student to condense and focus ideas. Another method of engaging storytelling is to provide a theme related to readings or group discussions.

Design fiction making allows students to project into the future using trends from the past. This project requires not only recognition of prior trends but also *functional explication* and *analogical inference* (what exist now vs. what could exist and why). I often ask that the design of something maintains some sort of connection to a historical technological development. Design fiction often requires an understanding of the conditions that have led to the development of a product. Students, in a roundabout way, must consider the many factors - socio-cultural, political, economic - that have to coalesce for some technological product to come to fruition. The exploration is also beneficial to students as it allows them ample freedom to play and, inadvertently, start building a more sophisticated understanding of interrelated themes.

Playful, artistic investigations need to be very open-ended as they include all aspects of visual reasoning (*recognition, functional explication, and analogical inference*). If the other methods described above enable abduction across the various aspects of the course (moments in time, key concepts, technological innovations), artistic investigations require students to synthesise their knowledge. Student-defined project briefs require that there be some evidence of contextualization (*recognition*) but, as the student begins to produce the artwork or designs, it is essential that it be dynamic in order to accommodate the changes or maturation of one's ideas throughout a semester. At each step of the project's development, students must be able to explain how the ideas relate to course themes (*inference*). The creation of new visual material is similar to design fiction making in that it requires the artist or designer have an understanding (*functional explication*) of how systems work. Regardless, it is important to give students time to explore a topic through the artwork in a re-iterative manner, to make those inferences, to really understand connections, and I carve out time each week in class to review and discuss project work.

Conclusion

A student-directed, exploratory and project-oriented class may seem like a significant addition to a traditional art history or visual studies course but the results are surprising. During the final review of work, students in this Visual Studies course could, for the most part, speak competently about how their work probed the course topics. The semester-long development provided students ample time to explore connections between topics and concepts through the production of imagery. Students were able to 'go deep' by having to investigate more thoroughly some aspect of the course content. For instance, one of the students from the course, an experience design student, decided that for his final project he would redesign the waiting room experience at our local hospital. The student had, prior to the beginning of the term, been on a skiing trip when his companion was injured. He accompanied his friend to a hospital and the experience was such that this student decided our regional hospital was not welcoming and should better serve patients. This student's discussions about his impressions of the patient experience were informed by the readings regarding the clinical practice and patient narratives. Towards the end of term, the student went to interview hospital staff for his final project. He spent time and learned about the myriad of factors influencing hospital design decisions. His interactions with the heath care community were positive and, as a result, he was subsequently hired as student assistant on a wayfinding redesign project.

Abductive visual reasoning is a type of inference that requires working back from data to a hypothesis of sorts. It requires that we study, recognize, and understand how multiple factors might contribute to a complex collection of interconnected theoretical contrivances, visual products and technologies. We encourage our students to do critical thinking but often neglect to model how that can be done for art history and theory using methods that mirror their practices in the studio. Abduction is a process of discovery shared by the sciences, the arts, and humanities and is therefore no less rigorous than other forms of engagement and assessment. In fact, abductive visual reasoning projects can effectively link theory to studio production and creative scholarship in an organic manner. Through the act of making or drawing, students learn to recognize the systems contributing to the construction of something. They must then mimic or understand the processes in order to synthesize something new. Finally, they must infer whole systems from their interconnected parts. The caveat is that the instructor must shift their role slightly to become a facilitator of sorts and to provide many different opportunities for students to collect, analyse, critique, and ultimately create images.

REFERENCES

Arnheim, R. (1969). *Visual thinking*. Berkeley: University of California Press.

Bouchon, M. L., & Tondini, G. (2010). *L'image obscène = Obscene image*. New York: Mark Batty.

Crary, J. (1990). *Techniques of the observer: On vision and modernity in the nineteenth century*. Cambridge, MA: MIT Press.

Foster, H. (1987). *Discussions in contemporary culture*. Seattle: Bay Press.

Foucault, M. (1973). *The birth of the clinic; an archaeology of medical perception*. New York: Pantheon Books.

Frank, A. W. (1997). *The wounded storyteller: Body, illness, and ethics*. Chicago: University of Chicago Press.

Frappier, M., Meynell, L., & Brown, J. R. (2013). Special issue on visual representations and reasoning. *The Knowledge Engineering Review, 28*(03), 231-236. doi:10.1017/s0269888913000301

Goldschmidt, G. (2003). The Backtalk of Self-Generated Sketches. *Design Issues, 19*(1), 72-88. doi:10.1162/074793603762667728

Gooding, D. C. (2006). From Phenomenology to Field Theory: Faraday's Visual Reasoning. *Perspectives on Science, 14*(1), 40-65. doi:10.1162/posc.2006.14.1.40

———. (2005). Seeing the Forest for the Trees: Visualization, Cognition, and Scientific Inference. In M. Gorman, D. Gooding, R. Tweeney, & A. Kincannon (Eds.), *Scientific and Technological Thinking.* Matwah, N.J.: Lawrence Erlbaum.

Historical Anatomies on the Web: Bidloo. (n.d.). Retrieved June 05, 2016, from: https://www.nlm.nih.gov/exhibition/historicalanatomies/bidloo_home.html

Kepes, G. (1965). *Education of vision*. New York: G. Braziller.

Lu, S. C., & Liu, A. (2012). Abductive reasoning for design synthesis. *CIRP Annals - Manufacturing Technology*, 61(1), 143-146. doi:10.1016/j.cirp.2012.03.062

Magnani, L. (2013). Thinking through drawing. *The Knowledge Engineering Review, 28*(03), 303-326. doi:10.1017/s026988891300026x

Nesher, D. (2001). Peircean Epistemology of Learning and the Function of Abduction as the Logic of Discovery. *Transactions of the Charles S. Peirce Society, 37*(1), 23-57.

Peirce, C. S., Hartshorne, C., Weiss, P., & Burks, A. W. (1958). *Collected papers of Charles Sanders Peirce*. Cambridge, MA: Harvard University Press.

Shelley, C. (1996). Visual Abductive Reasoning in Archaeology. *Philosophy of Science, 63*(2), 278-301. doi:10.1086/289913

CHAPTER 8

Connective Understanding: Traditional Materiality and Contemporary Installations

Jamie-Lea Hodges and Eleanor Venables

ABSTRACT

This chapter will illuminate the transformative role of the arts worker and public exhibitions including those which present alternate realities of human experience and the landscape. The discussion will also present the underlying value of artistic collaboration and contemporary installation art, focusing on the creation of artistic form from raw material inherent within the processes of traditional Australian Aboriginal string making. The artwork and its materiality, includes experiences and knowledge of those involved in the project: *Connective Understanding*. Furthermore, theoretical contexts will introduce the concept of materialism and apply this theory to unpacking culturally rich works which celebrate a sense of place.

INTRODUCTION

When a group of Australian Aboriginal artists came together in 2014 to create a contemporary piece titled *Connective Understanding*, the work highlighted the materiality often overlooked in contemporary cultural production. *Connective Understanding* uses ancient string making methods to create a collaborative weaving, emphasising the potential of artists who work directly with communities and arts organisations. The cultural knowledge inherent to the processes behind this work might also be understood by investigating 'haptic' knowledge preservation. The ancient methods of string making reveals an ecological embeddedness requiring sophisticated kinaesthetic sensitivities, as well as a broad range of ethnobotanical understanding. The co-created installation, curated by Aboriginal Australian artist, co-author of this chapter and Regional Arts Development Officer (RADO) of *Outback Arts* Jamie-Lea Hodges, was exhibited in conjunction with the 2015 Venice Biennale in a collateral exhibition titled *Country*. The Venice Biennale is recognised as a key visual arts event on the international calendar, offering a global snapshot of the most current and insightful ideas and practices in the contemporary arts sector.

This chapter investigates how an artwork can constitute important ecological, material and cultural research. Specifically how opportunities for artists to be directly connected to communities, suggests that arts facilitators and artists working in community arts contexts may also become art theorists, supporting community endeavours, reconnecting knowledge ecologies and enriching individual creative potential, is also illuminated. Harnessing the power of the artefact, knowledge, production and habitation, exhibitions such as this, provide culturally and geographically diverse audiences with innovative understandings of materiality.

Community and Connection

Artists across time and space have infused materials not only with ritual and symbolic significance but also social, political, and economic functions. As artworks move between cultures, their materials are given new meanings, thereby accumulating additional interpretive layers. Knight and Schwarzman (2009) working from a functional perspective have outlined five key steps to follow in order to create successful community art based projects.

- Contact – cultivate trust, mutual understanding and commitment as a foundation for your creative partnership;
- Research - Gather information about the people, places and issues you are working with;
- Action - Produce a new work of art that benefits the community;
- Feedback – Spark community reflection, dialogue and organising to spread the impact of the new work;
- Teaching – Pass on new community building skills to others to sustain the impact.

This simple approach, referred to by the acronym CRAFT, sets up a working model by which community arts practitioners might begin the process of cultural collaboration. The contexts for contemporary art are expanding and providing community minded artists with new opportunities and sites for artistic production. In this ecology of knowledge, theory and practice can exist as potential sites for making art and supporting research. This investigative model also moves the artist as facilitator beyond boundaries that divide disciplines, cultures and technologically diverse audiences, individuals and communities.

The Penguin Dictionary of Sociology (Abercrombie, Hill & Turne, 2006) describes community as one of the most elusive and vague terms in sociology and by now largely without specific meaning. The concept of community has such a variety of references; nations, states, regions, neighbourhoods, cultural groups, ethnic groups, online gateways and any sort of group may be defined as a community. The diversity and consequent ambiguity around the term becomes most important when practical decisions must be made; for example - who should represent a community? Despite this complexity, we make use of the term to describe groups of people with a relationship built from common interest with each other and the world.

When investigating the benefits of community engagement, social capital plays an important role. Cox (1995) defines social capital as an imaginary form of shared human wealth that grows with development of trust, mutuality and reciprocity. Social capital is enhanced through collaboration and in the case of community arts practice, a vehicle capable of transformative powers at the pinnacle of participation typologies, by which artist and audience can engage with one another. In this cultural interface a genuine dialogue can arise effectively enriching the global community at large. In a community arts context Cornwall's typologies of participation offer the careful analysis and specificity of key agents and collaborators (2008). Facilitators working across multiple community groups engage artists and participants in deep connection with the work, stepping back and allowing emergent outcomes to develop in the process of creation. In this chapter community relates to a group of artists whose work, ideas, skills and knowledge are curated and shared. The neighbouring Aboriginal communities are involved through artistic inclusion, facilitated by a roaming arts professional (the Aboriginal artist and co-author of this chapter - Hodges) who physically transports the work in progress across various geographical sites and simultaneously acts as advisor, curator and custodian of the artwork: *Connective Understanding.*

The communicative function of practice has the capacity to inform contemporary art. In this sense what might have been local knowledge moves across geographical divides and is shared as building new global knowledge systems, fostering environmentally responsible and ecologically literate cultures sitting inside the last phases of community practice as "feedback" and "teaching" (Knight and Schwarzman, 2009). This project nurtures understanding of the past and present, traditional and contemporary, which in this project are rarely disconnected as histories and traditions continually inform group identity. New models of art are needed in contemporary Australian community arts, whereby institutional practice validates participation, engagement and cohesion – the reconnection of artist and community within shared spaces (McGonagle, 2007).

Community art, oral traditions and cultural education revolves around the centrality of the artistic collaborators, a key component of community work, not just in terms of the processes and methods, but also in terms of meaning, experience, and responsiveness. One might also question what constitutes 'participation'; does it function as a means and an end, or a continuing dynamic? If we apply a typology of community participation to the artistic project *Connective Understanding,* we could position the level of engagement somewhere within interactive participation. According to Pretty's typology *interactive participation* (cited in Cornwall, 2008) is that which an individual can participate in joint analysis, and whereby the development of shared activity and ideas also strengthens local institutions. In this interactive category, participation is related to the artistic production of the work and is maintained as a power of ownership of cultural knowledge in which multiple perspectives make use of learning experiences. Groups of artists and collaborators determine how available resources are used in interactive participation, therefore maintaining authorship of local knowledge. In this context participants retain a stake in the continuation of key cultural practices.

Sarah White's typology of interests (cited in Cornwall, 2008, p. 273) can be applied to an analysis predominately as a way of working out how people make use of participation, and ranges from nominal to transformative. The process in this case of community arts practice involves interactive involvement, underpinning interdisciplinary methodologies that seek multiple perspectives and make use of systemic and structured learning processes. Over a long period of working with a community, arts professionals might begin to see slow transformations and increased levels of social capital whereby inclusion in a celebrated project, exhibition or outcome becomes only a small part of a much larger process of transformation (Kay, 2000). As groups take control over local decisions and determine how available resources are used, so they have a stake in maintaining structures or practices (Cornwall, 2008). A community arts project such as this has the capacity for bringing people together from around the region and showcasing a community that has respect for itself. People are present, they are living in this area and Aboriginal Australia is a living culture that is connected right through the region.

The sense of community is widened by the inclusion of an international stakeholder. The Italian artist in residence for this project within the Venice Biennale, Georgia Severi, visited Australian artists and communities prior to the 2015 exhibition. Severi's residency occurs across different regions of Australia culminates in the group exhibition *Country* presented in Venice, showcasing Indigenous practice and a collection of works which are steeped in ancient methods of artistic production. These important and initial stages of community practice of "contact" and "research" set out by Knight and Schwarzman (2009) are important foundations to building the creative partnership imperative to the culmination of the *Country* exhibition. The exhibition itself may be included in the "feedback" stage as the curated art works included in the exhibition selection, encourage dialogue and engagement beyond a local community context (Knight and Schwarzman, 2009).

> At a time when globalization and technological advances rupture national and cultural boundaries, artists are increasingly called upon to work in different sites across the world. The artist as ethnographer model may be more than a recent trend, given these changes. It is therefore necessary to remember, given the differential access to power in our society and the world, that experiences can only be understood relationally (Desai in Sullivan, 2010, p. 166-7).

The quote above by Desai positions the community artist within postmodern discourse and subverts the power mechanisms inherent within the art world. This theoretical framework positions Severi as ethnographer and art works created as a result of her Australian residency may be understood by audiences relationally. One might also be reminded of the misconceived position that community arts usually occupies in high culture which is essentially a marginal position (McGonagle, 2007). However, despite the prevalence of activity in community arts, little distribution of the creative outcomes is usually evident beyond the contexts of production. Exhibitions of community art and dissemination of communal art to the wider public are slowly emerging. The research undertaken to produce *Connective Understanding* illustrates that situated and contextual knowledge is nurtured through communication, embodied haptic knowledge, conceptions of place, artistic collaboration and theories of materiality.

COMMUNICATION

Dialogue and communication in itself is a co-operative activity involving respect and reciprocity. The communication process is important and can be seen as enhancing community and building social capital, leading individuals to act in ways that increase an awareness of the "other" (Cox, 1995). Communication between cultures in our digital age is increasing. *Connective Understanding* highlights the power of cultural communication in two ways. Firstly, through the continuation of ancient traditions and Australian Aboriginal string making skills which are transmitted orally from one individual in a local community to another. This kind of cultural dialogue is imperative to the living oral culture of Australian Aborigines. Australian colonial history reveals repeated mistreatment of the Australian Aborigines; a narrative fraught with denial, trauma, dislocation and disconnection of first peoples from their cultural origins, language and expression. As a result, much of the work of contemporary Australian Indigenous artistic practice involves cultural research, fostering a reawakening of 'sleeping' arts, languages and cultural expression. Secondly communication between cultures, in this instance between an Italian and several Australian artists. This second form of creative dialogue is evident in the culmination of works including in the exhibition *Country*, highlighting how geographically disparate societies might shed new light on concepts of hybridity and artistic cultural exchange.

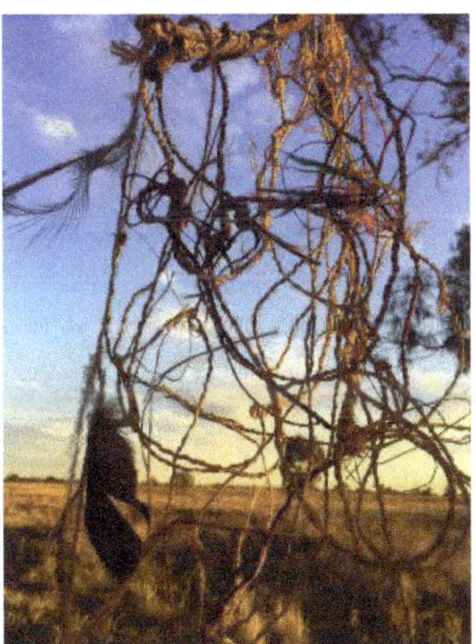

Figure: 8. 1 - Connective Understanding (2014). Aboriginal artists from Outback Arts, various materials, 15m long. *Connective understanding: a focus on String through contemporary Aboriginal art* - Collateral event at 56th Venice Biennale 2015 Outback Arts, Boolarng Nangamai and Galamban.
Image credit: Courtesy of the artists and Outback Arts.

Connective Understanding involved the following artists: Jamie-Lea Hodges, Clive Freeman, Sam Turnbull, Lorraine King, Kevin Welsh, John McBride, Helen McBride, Rhianna McBride, Lola Roberts, Jenny Trindall, Wendy Ashby, Barbara Ashby, Patricia Weatherall, Stella Sands, Jenadel Lane, Barbara Stanley, Mary Kennedy, Minnie Riley, Karrin Thurston, Monica Summers, Una Bibby, Rozzi Smith, Maree Bolton. Artists were from Artists from New South Wales including Bourke, Cobar, Coonamble, Walgett and Warren Project facilitator and curator was Jamie – Lea Hodges. Workshop and cultural liaison was conducted by Clive Freeman. The cultural exchange artist was Giorgia Severi. Project partners were Boolarng Nangamai and Together Dreaming.

Community Engagement: How Long is a Piece of String?

In *Connective Understanding*, there is an intentionality in the length of the piece of string, the ends were joined together, woven together as a continuous loop of fibre. In the collaborative production methods (facilitated by the co-author Hodges: Aboriginal artist & Regional Arts Development Officer (RADO)), the art work travelled around communities, and each piece was connected together. All the joins had to be completed in order for the work to show respect for each piece and when curating the work it was important to ensure the audience could look along the piece and see the changes where each individual had collaborated in each section of string. Contemporary arts practice is important to define to audiences as work which has been created in the "now" or the near past, no matter the methods of production. When the piece was exhibited in the *Country* exhibition it was able to present the unique traditions of arts practice which took place right across the landscape across all of the community groups of collaborators.

The artistic collaborators agreed that the single piece string would be facilitated by the RADO, constructed by participants with ongoing input and exchange of skills and ideas along the way. The RADO's role was to assist with coordination, transportation and communication within and across the Indigenous communities. With the community partnership formed between the RADO and the artists in the remote NSW regions, the crafting of the artwork could begin. This part of the community arts process constitutes the stage of "action" according to Knight and Schwarzman (2009), however due to the restorative nature of the skill preservation involved can also be considered as being relevant to the "teaching" stage, imperative to community building skills.

Connective Understanding is a contemporary artefact, audiences will take from it what they will, bringing their own individual stories and knowledge. An important aspect of this work is the consideration of connection and diversity of culture. When viewing the work, the audience may notice that there are different individual pieces of string connected together from each region. In the photograph (Figure: 8.1) it is important to show the piece on country and to view the piece in the environment in which it was created. Knowing that the work might be shown in many different contemporary arts spaces especially when exhibited internationally, it was important for participating artists to document the piece in the place from which it originates. In Venice, the work was installed and configured differently (see Figure: 8. 2) to that shown in the photo (Figure: 8. 1), as it was suspended from the roof within the gallery space. Within this contemporary curated space, audiences could walk right around the piece. The installation was positioned in a corner with some sections looped over to assist in the depiction of a sense of movement. Sections which featured feathers would dangle down to the viewer from above and other areas where Quandong seeds were woven into the piece a natural sense of gravity and 'earthedness' was evident. The textural and structural intricacies of the work were most apparent when standing in front of the work and the audience could easily perceive these qualities and the various fibres and objects that constituted the work. The lightness, weight and movement varies depending on the inclusion of the feathers and length of the fibres used.

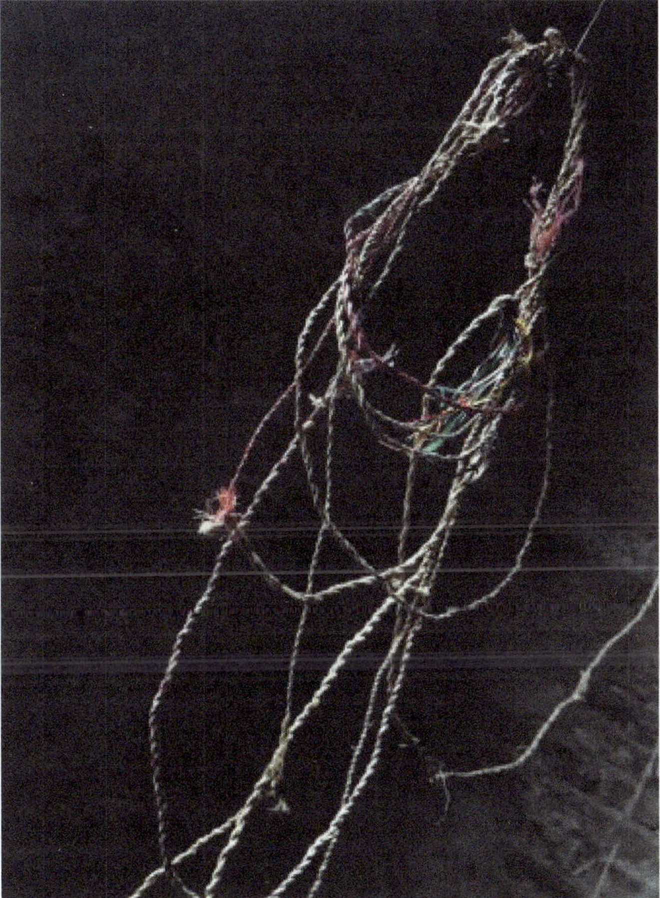

Figure: 8. 2 - Country: Installation view (detail), Connective *understanding: a focus on String through contemporary Aboriginal art* - Collateral event at 56th Venice Biennale 2015.
Image credit: Courtesy of the artists and Outback Arts

Engaged or participatory art practice presents new models of creative community practice that has the emancipatory power to reposition traditional art forms from previously marginalised art and restrictions inherent to the realm of consumerism and commodity. For Aboriginal Australian artists working on country it is interesting to identify a shift in international audiences and previous widely accepted values within the art world of what constitutes differences between fine arts or 'high arts' versus 'community arts' practice (McGonagle, 2007). The 2015 *Country* exhibition may have been viewed by some as 'gate crashing' the Biennale (within the context of Venice during the 2015 Biennale event). However interesting opportunities were fostered as a precursor to the Venice exhibition event, creating a cross cultural community partnership resulting in Aboriginal Australian artists being invited to showcase works on a global scale. Giorgia Severi's international artistic exchange to the Coonamble region in Australia was facilitated by *Outback Arts*, and as a result enabled her Italian works to be shown alongside Australian artists' works in the Venice exhibition. Giorgia Severi whose works were exhibited alongside Australian Aboriginal works in the Venice exhibition *Country* are concerned with traditional human tool making and mark making technologies.

Severi works across different media including printmaking, carving and drawings, and her works were placed alongside various Australian Aboriginal artworks in the *Country* exhibition. Additional collaborative works were also included by Indigenous artists from different parts of Australia including works from the Northern Territory, Western Australia and New South Wales. Australian artworks were selected for their use of traditional materials and included hand woven utilitarian forms such as baby carriers and cradles. Severi's works included in *Country* reference her Italian ancestral past, as well as ceremonies, naturally sourced materials and artefacts observed during her Australian residency. In a series titled *Ancestors*, Severi engraves sandstone forms with geometrical mark making and pattern. In many works included in the exhibition *Country*, Severi responds to the Australian Aboriginal art forms through observational drawings and prints created directly from the bush grasses and fibres used by traditional artists. The 2015 exhibition *Country* made parallels between the two cultural locales, highlighting common themes and spiritual significance between ancient Italian practices and those used by contemporary Aboriginal artists working through traditionally informed practices. For Severi the interest in ancestors or "one who was born first", relates to historically significant objects found in mountainous parts of Italy such as Val Camonica. Severi's practice creates links between European spiritual rituals which celebrate the earth, primordial beings, water, constellations and fertility (*Country: Artworks and Artists*, http://project-australia.blogspot.com.au/p/blog-page.htm).

The events that foregrounded the 2015 Venice exhibition *Country*, involved an artist in residence program, which was significant in assisting the Italian exhibition opportunity through the *Gervasuti Foundation*. Severi's international exchange opportunities prior to the exhibition, were crucial to the exhibition project, supporting a partnership with *Outback Arts*, developed through a mutually beneficial international exchange, reciprocity and relationship fostering. Developed in 1999, *Outback Arts* is a not-for-profit arts and cultural development organisation working in the five local government areas of Bourke, Coonamble, Cobar, Walgett and Warren. This regional arts development organisation services the Far West New South Wales region of Australia. *Outback Arts* receives core funding from *ARTS New South Wales* (formerly known as NSW Ministry for the Arts) on an annual basis as well as an annual contribution from the contributing local government areas. *Outback Arts* works with individuals, organisations and government to generate, promote and advocate for the arts and creative industries in the Far West region of NSW. Through new experience and engagement, contemporary arts exchange programs can offer diverse audiences alternative windows into the world of local, national and international art practices.

Connective Understanding explores the ancient ways of Aboriginal Australian art making through connections between traditional and contemporary practices of string making. This installation, engaging an innovative approach to contemporary fibre art, was just one among several artworks in the exhibition *Country* which transformed the interior of a disused Venetian industrial house into a contemporary international gallery space. The exhibition highlighted the collaborative practices of contemporary Aboriginal Australian artists, responding and participating in conversations that carry out the connective understanding of community across physical and cultural divides. Sharing knowledge and exchanging stories to reflect a collective voice. The exhibition project and installation of *Country*, highlighted the power of cultural exchange, curated spaces and participatory practice engaging thirty Australian Indigenous artists in production of the exhibition at the Gervasuti Foundation. This exhibition project was multifaceted and presented collaborations between the Indigenous Italian artist Giorgia Severi and Aboriginal artists from different parts of Australia working between communities, across generations and lands.

COUNTRY: THE WORK IN CONTEXT

Building an 'in' bridge or entry into the contemporary art world is the challenge of artists, arts workers, exhibitions, arts educators and institutions. In an era where almost all global consumables are mass produced, using advanced technologies of production, the concept of fibre art utilising string made by hand, using native grasses and barks found within the natural landscape, seems far from everyday experience.

Highlighting the relationship between traditional and contemporary arts practice is not one of causal influence but a form of "continuous exchange" (Gilmore cited in Carmen & Hansen, 2005). While much contemporary art from the western world is focused on new media such as film and complex digital technologies, there continues to be a resurgence of contemporary practice steeped in tradition, utilising ancient production methods binding natural materials. Nonetheless the materiality of form in *Connective Understanding* forces the viewer to look closely at the art object, focusing on the singularity and seeming simplicity of the material agents in the work. Inviting the viewer instead to share in a reverence for materiality and consideration of the cultural significance.

"Art does not exist in isolation from life and culture as it plays a crucial role in cultural life, extending its relationship with country" (Martin in Barret & Bolt 2013, p.196). In this quote one is reminded of the interconnection of art and culture. In Australian Aboriginal culture, art and country are inherent to life and spiritual connection. The work *Connective Understanding* represented *Country* by revealing an example of Indigenous practice from one Australian state. New South Wales is a south-eastern state of Australia approximately eight hundred and ten thousand square kilometres. To put this into perspective geographically, the entire United Kingdom would fit inside of this large Australian state three times with room to spare. Regional New South Wales (NSW), Australia is serviced by a network of cultural facilities including regional galleries, regional conservatoriums, performing arts centres and museums. These venues offer a mix of locally produced and touring arts activity. *Regional Arts NSW* is the state advocacy body which receives core program funding from *Arts NSW*, providing a range of services to fourteen state wide Regional Arts Development Organisations. *Regional Arts NSW* works within the key areas of advocacy, capacity building, communications and support. Regional Arts Development Officers (RADOs) are employed by Regional Arts Development Organisations, (also funded by ART NSW) such as *Outback Arts,* to facilitate arts opportunities within diverse and remote communities. The first RADOs were employed in the 1980s by the Head Office of the Arts Council of NSW to work in the Central West, South Coast, Far West and South West NSW Regions. The vast region from which this artwork was produced spans across five council areas, located approximately five hundred and sixty kilometres west from the mid north coast of the Eastern state. Workshops, discourse, residencies, exhibitions, collection and publishing of information are coordinated by RADOs to reflect the possibility to reconnect art's ethical responsibilities to its aesthetic responsibilities.

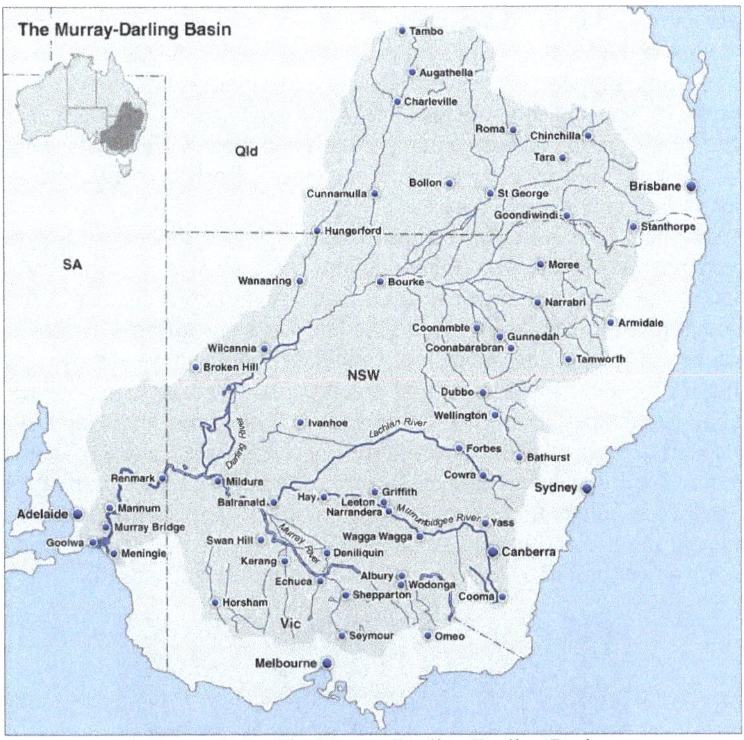

Figure: 8. 3 - The Murray-Darling Darling Basin
Image credit: Ben Spraggon ABC, http://www.abc.net.au/news/rural/specials/murray-darling-basin-plan/

A significantly large council area in central-western New South Wales, Coonamble is the major town in the shire which covers almost ten thousand square kilometres and reaches to the western slopes of the Warrumbungle Range and the alluvial plains of the Castlereagh constituting part of the country's 'food bowl', situated within the Murray-Darling Basin. Lying along the Castlereagh River, at the western edge of the Warrumbungle National Park, the region is surrounded on the right by the Macquarie Marshes. Apart from heritage listed and nationally protected pockets of wilderness, contemporary Australian landscapes such as this one remain ecologically vulnerable and present evidence of colonial agricultural activities and western natural resource land management such as mining. The town's name derives from an Aboriginal Australian term 'gunambil', thought by some to mean - 'place of dirt.' In these dry and remote inland farming regions, land clearing risks the preservation of native vegetation and introduced plant species often thrive at the expense of the native flora. In semi-arid areas of the country Aboriginal fibre artists sourcing locally growing native flora materials must work with what they can find in these landscapes.

The *Outback Arts* community weaving and string making project: *Connective Understanding* would not have been possible without the RADO fostering relationships around the region with all different communities and artists. Therefore, the project and the completed artwork become a collective learning site and sharing experience that provides a sense of camaraderie and support for each of the embedded spaces. Providing support for cultural sharing and collaboration, artists bring along unique narratives and subjective experience (Snepvangers & Allas, 2013). This in turn fosters community relationships, binding creative groups continuously, encouraging individual projects by providing tangible outcomes of practice and support for the production of further creative works.

For Australian Aborigines the English word 'country' refers to culture, nature and land which are all linked. Aboriginal communities have a cultural and spiritual connection to the land, which is based on each community's distinct traditions and laws. Country takes in everything within the landscape - landforms, waters, air, trees, rocks, plants, animals, foods, medicines, minerals, stories and sites of significance. Community connections include cultural practices, knowledge, songs, stories and art, as well as all people: past, present and future. People have custodial responsibilities to care for country, to ensure that it continues in proper order and provides physical sustenance and spiritual nourishment. These custodial relationships may determine who can share and hold cultural knowledge. Aboriginal communities associate natural resources with the use and benefit of traditional foods and medicines, caring for the land, passing on cultural knowledge and strengthening social bonds.

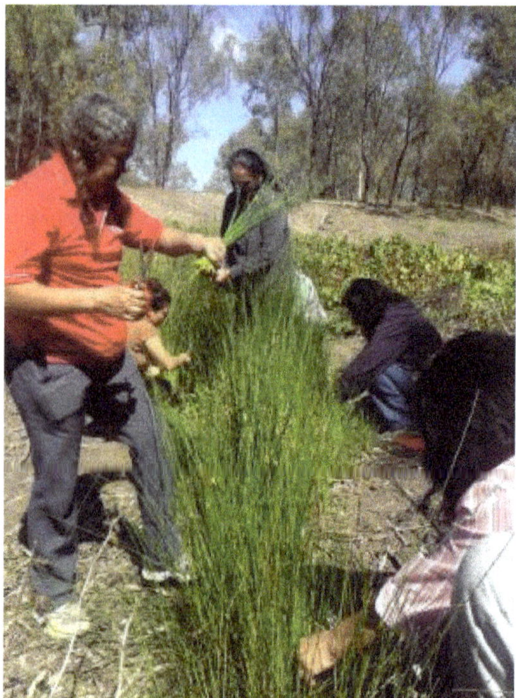

Figure: 8. 4 - Artists harvesting Emu Foot Sedge grass on the banks of the Namoi River, Walgett.
Image credit: Jamie-Lea Hodges and Outback Arts

In many traditional Aboriginal societies making objects from plant fibres is an important activity. Utilitarian items required for hunting, carrying and collecting food can be resourcefully handcrafted. In addition to these food-related design objects, fibres are used to create body adorning ritual items which can be worn in religious ceremonies. These days many contemporary Australian Aborigines have little need for string making or traditional objects hand made from natural fibre, however in some communities, artists are reviving and preserving Indigenous fibre arts skills constructing large scale hand woven string objects. Contemporary Aboriginal Australian artists such as Yvonne Koolamatrie and Ellen Treverrow's cleverly constructed sculptural weavings move beyond the utilitarian premise of materiality and creative production. Contemporary Aboriginal Australian artistic practice engages conceptual aesthetics and tradition, and builds new bridges between past and present, material and temporal, physical and spiritual. Significance of contemporary fibre arts also lies in the preservation of knowledge ecologies unique to these practices such as associated plant uses and cultural knowledge. Through making lengths of string in the work *Connective Understanding*, participating artists and neighbouring communities are able to increase social capital, share local and cultural knowledge, embedding narratives across time and place. In the process of collaboration and dialogue important transactions feed into the collaboration of significant environmental awareness through a stocktake of what is readily available to use in the landscape.

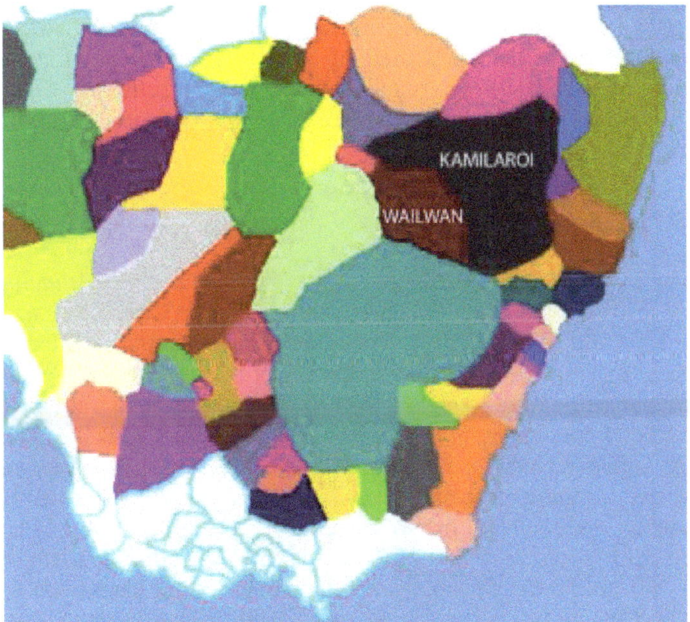

Figure: 8. 5 - Aboriginal NSW (detail) - Map of the Aboriginal nations of NSW.
Image credit: http://www.curriculumsupport.education.nsw.gov.au/shared/abmaps/nsw.htm#

The artwork *Connective Understanding* was created across six communities and five local government areas of far north western NSW where approximately thirty percent of the population is Indigenous. Some of the original custodians of the area were the Wailwan, Kawambarai, Gamilaraay/ Kamilaroi and Ngemba groups. The landscape in this region is flat, usually very dry and in a good season it is a beautiful place. In the dry season the area is dusty and it is difficult to source traditional materials. The landscape affects the community completely by surrounding individuals with a flat horizon giving one the feeling of being in the middle of nowhere. For many, the vastness can resonate internally as a feeling of being 'lost.' Isolation is also a good recipe for the loss of social capital. Therefore, it is important for people to feel connected to community.

Connective Understanding is made of various materials relating to the landscape through the application of locally sourced native grasses. In other parts of the artwork manmade contemporary found materials were also sourced. Touring around communities the string making workshops and artistic collaborations would be held in a different geographical community for days at a time. Collaborators and artists would be creating string and then the work would be facilitated by the RADO to move on to the next community. The act of bringing, for example, the Walgett material to Bourke, (another important role of the RADO) would provide a conversation across the landscape, building a dynamic and fluid map from one community to the next. An important part of this project was linking, relating and following one place after the next. Each collaborating artist would bring their own meaning and materials to the piece of string, ensuring the work remained very landscape focused. Through a western perspective the land is something akin to the concept of the wilderness needing to be tamed to be controlled and defined by authority. Simultaneously Australian Aboriginal ideology presents the ecology of all aspects of culture which do not and cannot stand alone.

Materiality and Liminality

The ecology of the artistic practice behind *Connective Understanding* includes relationships between materials and the environment. A variety of materials were sourced in the production stages of *Connective Understanding* including found and locally sourced native vegetation such as Emu Foot Sedge grass and Lomandra grass. Cotton twine and raffia were also included to support the artwork's structural integrity and accessibility to contemporary materials. In some places embellishments such as emu feathers and seed pods were entwined into the string. The sophisticated and labour intensive technical processes within Aboriginal traditions around harvesting, drying, soaking and reusing materials provide access to preserving ecological significance and application of intuitive scientific methods. Members of the community who are wise to the applications and traditions of plant life are imperative to projects such as this, and provide other members of the community with crucial support to keep that information alive. So for example, being able to educate the community about bush tucker, tool making and traditional uses of native vegetation is vital to retaining ecologies of knowledge and practice. Aboriginal Australian artists who are still making traditional pieces, either for tool making, baskets or string, are extremely important cultural assets to facilitate this kind of work, sustaining and preserving knowledge associated with a previously endangered or sleeping art.

Perhaps what makes us uniquely human is our ability to modify our environment to suit our needs. "In creative practice, matter, artist and world are engaged and co-emerge through the work of art" (McCosh in Barrett & Bolt, 2013, p. 131). Human knowledge is complex and intertwined in ecologies of practice, individuals throughout various communities can only know by understanding what the self has attempted to share, explain, present or negotiate. By understanding the collaborative artwork or community artefact and the production processes, key agents are required to communicate or represent to others working alongside the self not just what is 'known', but also what is 'intended', together with what has been 'done.' It is what transforms the conceptual in contemporary art, beyond the cerebral, exploring the two conditions that rarely correspond exactly; intention and realisation. Within the context of current efforts to respond to environmental degradation, art in this sense acts as a vehicle through which a community can express common creative goals through skill sharing and collaborative exchange. During the art making, emergent conversations act as an important part of the artistic process constituting research and action, providing artists with support to go out into the environment and look at what is available. So for example, identifying a useful plant may not be enough as a limited supply may be evident. This is due to activity on the land and some of these native plants need to be cut right back to regenerate. Evidence of dwindling flora, where once there was an abundance of native vegetation, can result in traditional artists experiencing issues around access, availability or material limitations. Until individuals and communities are working with traditionally sourced materials such as those used in *Connective Understanding*, the awareness of ecology and native plant species may not happen. The maintenance of native vegetation is very much dismissed in contemporary society and artists can initiate important environmental conversations about these neglected and disregarded plants. These dialogues create waves of ecological awareness across the region's communities which can result in regeneration programs such as those which reintroduce Indigenous vegetation back into landscapes, schoolyards and community gardens so that artists can begin to use these traditional materials once again in an arts-based practice.

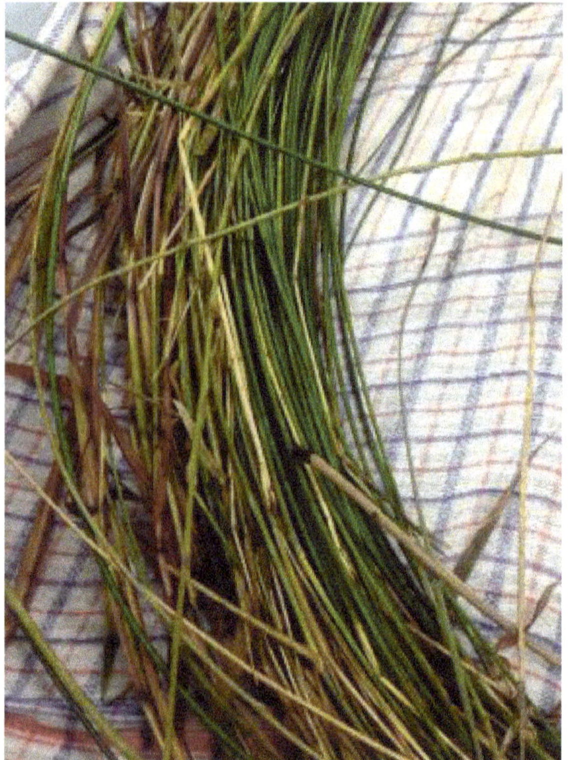

Figure: 8. 6 - Detail: freshly harvested Emu Foot Sedge grass
Image credit: Jamie-Lea Hodges and Outback Arts

As artists or creative practitioners, the 'doing' or the act of creative practice becomes vital to the active process. In this instance the community artist/facilitator negotiates the 'liminality' between intention and realisation; deliberately positioning themselves in the spaces between key individuals, across generations, linking the network of communities within a council district by supporting knowledge preservation and facilitating artistic practice. In order to assist the work of another artist (or in an educative sense to nurture for the artistic production of the student) the community arts facilitator begins the process of sharing knowledge, bridging spaces in between; the person and the communal, the individual and the social. The notion of the term liminality, meaning 'betwixt and between', was initially developed by social anthropologist Turner, (1967) however the term may also be understood as a dramatic tying together of thought and experience.

According to theorist Merleau-Ponty levels of experience and the primacy of perception analyses the power of communication and its important role in the human's ability to understand and learn from another, therefore constructing lived and shared knowledge (Merleau-Ponty & Edie, 1964). Merleau-Ponty presents perception as a creative practice. Merleau-Ponty offers the concept that physical space is both perceived and imagined as we construct space and our movement through it in our own minds by investing it with symbolic significance. Kupers (2011) maintains the phenomenological approach of space and perception of Merleau-Ponty by elucidating that spaces and places have always been basic conditions for all transitions of human beings. Kupers also argues that the process of movement through open, ambiguous and liminal spaces, is essentially transformative for human beings. In this context, liminal space can be understood as holding ambiguous potential as movement through space is a fundamental principle of human existence. Liminal potential is harnessed by the community arts worker acting as a traveller, extending creative engagement across distance and communities, linking different spaces and enriching cultural experiences while simultaneously binding human relationships with the landscape.

The liminality of the community arts worker is experienced by physical movement through country, negotiating the threshold between spaces, linking places and people. Occupying a position on both sides of the boundary of community and place. However, the use of liminal space can also be determined by the exhibition *Country* which positions local and global frameworks of knowledge by contrasting Australian Indigenous artists work with the work of Italian artist Giorgia Severi. In postmodern artistic practice and international intercultural exchange, communication of meaning and thematic significance focuses on the interaction between cultural elements and artistic forms. The coexistence, negotiation and transformation of natural raw materials is crucial to the understanding of meaning. Turner's (1967) conceptual framework becomes a useful analytic tool for the study of different kinds of spaces which enable communication, especially for spaces where cultures meet. These spaces of intercultural contact are characterized by a state of liminality.

These spaces of liminality are important sites for cultural interactions between images, symbols, ideas, ideologies and powers. Exhibitions therefore may become spaces of intercultural communication allowing flux between; here and there, past and present, global and local. These intercultural liminal spaces of communication incorporate aspects of more than one cultural identity, and encourage viewers to consider the spaces in between. The sharing involved in artistic collaboration sets up a reciprocity which becomes integral to the production of skill, awareness and preservation of wisdom. In this experience rich context, learning from another person while in their presence involves emulation, something the human body is remarkably good at. In the same way one might learn a dance movement by following the moves of another, the hand works with a spatial sensory perception constructing an extensive 'haptic' body of knowledge (O'Neill, 2001). The hand concentrates for the mind and will develop a 'feel' for the materials. Multiple perspectives are needed to locate something in our cognitive process of artistic production. The hand has complex and hierarchical degrees of freedom, providing multiple perspectives through the sense of touch.

String Making: Materiality & Haptic Knowledge

Materialism determines that human form and matter is not distinct from the objective world and that thought and mind are strengthened from physical activity. Boundaries between the senses, such as sight and touch are broken down and as a result mind, body, activity and environment intertwine becoming shared perceptions of experience. The term 'haptic' refers to a multi-sensory perceptual system through which we comprehend spatial, tactile, and kinaesthetic elements of our environment in relation to our body's position and condition (O'Neill, 2001, p. 3-4). The haptic is considered to be multi-sensory in nature because it includes spatial, tactile, and kinaesthetic perceptions. For example, spatial sensations are likely to be intertwined with the kinaesthetic and visual perception of a space. Touch commonly involves optic and kinaesthetic perception as one simultaneously feels the texture of an object by looking and moving over the material with the hands. This special kind of 'bodily intelligence' is often referred to as kinaesthetic knowledge is sometimes associated with the knowledge concept of 'metis' (Detienne & Vernant, 1978).

'Metis' a type of cunning intelligence involving a unique way of knowing and thought, can be observed in the deft movements of hands of a skilled craftsperson at work (Detienne & Vernant, 1978). The creator's sleight of hand seems to move of its own volition, perhaps without even needing the maker to look at the art object while working. Broadening ecologies of creative practice and increasing metis between participants, community art is rarely invited to share the international stage of high art within the art world. It is refreshing to reflect on creative and community arts opportunities which showcase collaborative exchanges and consider how artistic interchange programs can facilitate reawakening of ancient methods of production. Through the curatorial selection of *Country* we can begin to forge conceptual links of global contemporary artistic practice which reflect upon relationships between raw materials, haptic intelligence, innovation, ecological embeddedness and ancient human traditions.

A key component for the artists involved in *Connective Understanding* was the experience of being in the landscape, seeing the work being woven in a group. The phenomenological perspective accepts that is that the human body which is considered to be "a source of consciousness, perception, and reason" (Peters, 2004, p. 14) which we are mostly not consciously aware of until it is needed or is drawn upon. Demonstration and the opportunity to discuss and experience the method of string making in an almost meditative way becomes a celebrated opportunity. Artist's hands become automated in construction of the string piece. An ancient scientific and technological tradition becomes a haptic skill imbued with capacity for a heightened state of relaxation for the maker, transference of skill for the group and transformed state of creative automation for the artist's fingers.

Materiality, Landscape and Embeddedness

The community arts field has included thoughtful and provocative examples of theoretical and practical approaches that promote art research into environmental concerns. The artistic conversations in community arts production such as those outlined in this chapter begin to highlight important links back to culture, knowledge, place, location and the landscape that the artists are living in. Traditions that have been lost, traditions that can be seen now, these are all important to understanding the ecological systems in a community. Looking at surrounding materials artists can begin to study nature and the inspiration that comes from that. Substance, according to new-materialists (Cool & Frost, 2010; Connolly, 2013), is imbued with vibrant qualities which contain energy and the latent ability to metamorphose. All physical matter is complex and in constant flux. Matter, and henceforth the art object, is not seen as inanimate, instead it is imbued with an innate complexity which highlights the overlapping and inter-connected character of human and non-human forms. New-materialists would also argue that there is a tendency for more complex constructions of matter and artistic forms to appear (Cudworth & Hobden, 2015). The materials used in the methods of production are selected deliberately to signify precision and nuances (Carmen & Hansen, 2005).

'Sustainability' and 'sustainable development' are often used interchangeably in academic and public discourse in discussion about the natural environment. From an anthropological perspective, research into land "management practices of Indigenous peoples rely on a personal and cultural storehouse of traditional ecological knowledge, which is gained through firsthand interaction with the surrounding ecosystems" (Whiteman & Cooper, 2000, p.1267). A culture's social embeddedness in many Indigenous societies is closely tied with ecological embeddedness. The ecologic place and ecologies of knowledge become part of reconnecting with living culture, imperative to the remembering of "being a place" (Livingstone in Whiteman & Cooper, 2000, p.1267). Post-colonial dislocation of Aboriginal connection with 'being a place' can be slowly reinstated by practicing traditional skills. Here the cultural amnesia that underpins the colonisation of Australia may be treated by the careful reintroduction of exchange relationships that reinstate the ancient wisdom of traditional knowledge ecologies (Horton & Berlo, 2013). Embeddedness of human beings within nature as well as the ecological imperatives of community arts initiatives help to develop a culture of belonging and connectivity. This theory can be aligned with a transpersonal ecology; a type of ecological philosophy that is centred around the idea of dissolving perceptions of boundaries between self and nature in an effort to move toward a realisation that humans are a part of the environment, rather than separate from it (Blandy and Fenn, 2012).

The human interaction with the landscape and environment can provide knowledge, arousing senses, signifying values and posing material limits. Therefore, the materiality of the work *Connective Understanding* informs the conceptual potential. As an artistic collaboration the string work signifies conversations, embeddedness and landscape experiences. This experience of 'being a place' is a view which corresponds with Merleau Ponty's writings on the reciprocity of artist and subject. When the world of the artist is experienced through the primacy of perception, senses are heightened, the material world is transformed to the limitless through the methods of production.

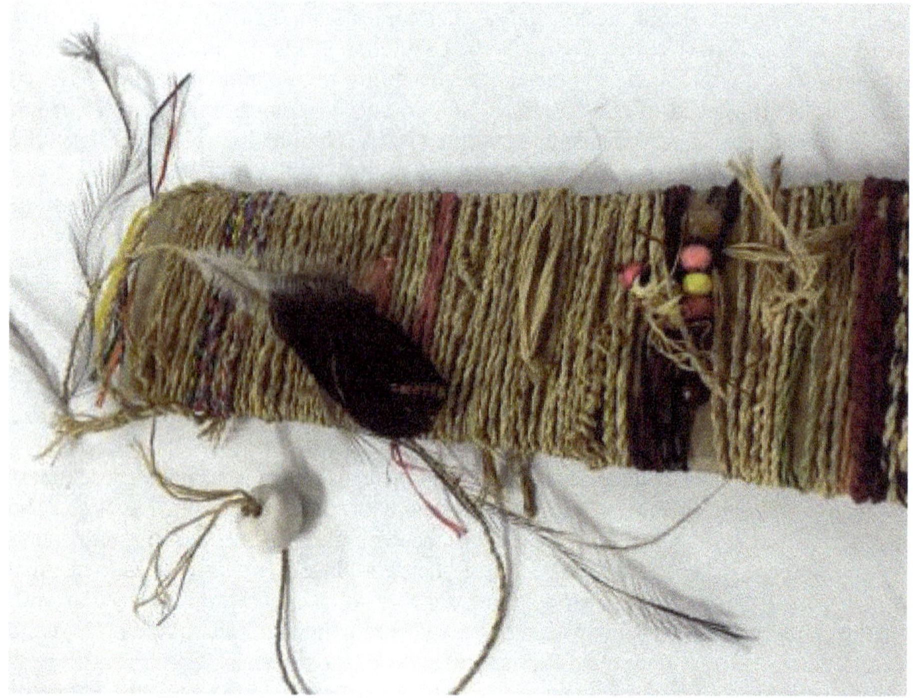

Figure: 8. 7 - String piece packed for transportation and storage.
Image credit: Jamie-Lea Hodges and Outback Arts.

Conclusion

Art of the present activates previously marginalised methods of the past, while materiality informs and inaugurates tradition. The artist's role is to express a way of existing in the world that is not just their own but is that of the collective group or milieu to which he belongs. A collaborative piece such as *Connective Understanding* also speaks of a way for a culture to express a way of existing within nature, environment and materiality. Community arts projects and exhibitions which highlight collaborative exchange have an authentic potential to engage community knowledge, increase social capital, and reposition a large group of geographically diverse participants into an ecology of practice. Such activities broaden opportunities to revisit a shared understanding of ecological embeddedness and sustain cultural knowledge.

Contemporary arts practice is imperative to keeping and supporting skills in arts practices which are haptic, skilled and technical. Without Indigenous contemporary arts practice or the oral tradition of sharing stories including ecological knowledge, contemporary arts audiences would only be able to view traditional Aboriginal and Torres Strait Islanders artefacts through historical museum collections. Shared knowledge and artistic notions of materiality may be understood in relation to the practice of community arts projects, by unravelling the continuing role of ancient and traditional methods of contemporary artistic production.

Participatory interventions may result in effects that were never envisaged at the outset. Community art projects at *Outback Arts, NSW* support new experiences and connect places where inspiration can be facilitated in unexpected ways. There is always a way for history and lost or sleeping history to find a way back into contemporary creative practice. Being inspired by place, family, community and informed landscape traditions, Australian Aboriginal contemporary art has the capacity to present a unique ancient history that exists in Australia. When travelling to a European city like Venice, where much of the architecture, classical art and culture is hailed as being 'old', one is reminded that Australia's cultural history is much older indeed.

REFERENCES

Abercrombie, N., Hill, S. & Turne, B. S. (2006). *The Penguin Dictionary of Sociology*. 5th ed. Penguin.

Barratt, E. & Bolt, B. (2013). *Carnal Knowledge: Towards a 'New Materialism' Through the Arts*. I.B Taurus & Co. Great Britain.

Blandy, D. & Fenn, J. (2012). Sustainability: Sustaining Cities and Community Cultural Development, *University of Oregon Studies in Art Education,* Summer.

Carmen, T. & Hansen, M. B. N. (2005). *The Cambridge Companion to Merleau-Ponty*, Cambridge University Press: UK.

Connolly, W. E. (2013). *The Fragility of Things. Self-Organizing Processes, Neoliberal Fantasies, and Democratic Activism.* Duke University Press: USA.

Coole, D. & Frost, S. (Eds). (2010). Introducing the New Materialism, in Diana Coole and Samantha Frost; editors, *New Materialisms: Ontology, Agency, and Politics*, Duke University Press: Durham and London.

Cornwall, A. (2008). Unpacking 'Participation': Models, meanings and practices in *Community Development Journal, 43*(3), 269-283. Oxford University Press.

Country: Artworks and Artists, http://project-australia.blogspot.com.au/p/blog-page.htm. Retrieved 30/04/16.

Cox, E. (1995). *A Truly Civil Society*. 1995 Boyer Lectures, ABC: Sydney.

Cudworth, E., & Hobden, S. (2015). Liberation for Straw Dogs? Old Materialism, New Materialism, and the Challenge of an Emancipatory Posthumanism, *Globalizations*, *12*(1), 134-148.

Detienne, M., & Vernant, J. P. (1978). *Cunning Intelligence in Greek Culture and Society,* Harvester Press: Sussex.

Horton, J. L., & Berlo, J. C. (2013). *Beyond the Mirror*, Third Text, *27* (1) pp. 17-28.

Kay, A. (2000). Art and community development: the role the arts have in regenerating communities, *Community Development Journal*, *35*(4), 414 – 424. Oxford University Press.

Knight, K., & Schwarzman, M. (2009). *Beginners Guide to Community-Based Arts,* New Village Press: Canada.

Küpers, W. 2011. Dancing on the līmen - Embodied and Creative Inter-Places as Thresholds of Be(com)ing: Phenomenological Perspectives on Liminality and Transitional Spaces in *Organisation and Leadership*, Tamara - *Journal for Critical Organization Inquiry Special Issue on Liminality, 9*(3-4), 45-59.

McGonagle, D. (2007). 'A New Deal': art, museums and communities – re-imagining relations in *Community Development Journal*, *42*(4), 425–434, Oxford University Press.

Merleau-Ponty, M., & Edie, J. M. (1964). *The primacy of perception: And other essays on phenomenological psychology, the philosophy of art, history and politics*. Northwestern University Press.

O'Neill, M. E. (2001). Corporeal experience: A haptic way of knowing. *Journal of Architectural Education*, *55* (1), 3-12.

Peters, M. (2004). *Education and the philosophy of the body: Bodies of knowledge and knowledge of the body*. Chapter 2 in L. Bresler (Ed.), Knowing bodies, moving minds: Towards embodied teaching and learning (pp. 13-27). Norwell, MA: Kluwer Academic Publishers.

Snepvangers, K., & Allas, T. (2013). Bending the Twig – Indigenous Learning Ecologies Video Series. UNSW Australia: Art & Design. www.youtube.com Retrieved 30/04/16.

- Jessica Bulger – Wiradjuri, Tumut, NSW http://www.youtube.com/watch?v=SDk9U9J1QLQ
- Jamie-Lea Hodges – Wiradjuri, Cowra-Coonamble, NSW http://www.youtube.com/watch?v=IyBZhtbtVVU
- Brady Prescott – Ngiyampaa Wangaaypuan, Broken Hill, NSW http://www.youtube.com/watch?v=h6NTxcfErQY
- Lowanna Moran – Gamillaroi, Mudawarray, Walgett, NSW http://www.youtube.com/watch?v=c8Yx47Y2nvY

• Jesse Ingrey Arndell – Yuin, Port Macquarie, NSW http://www.youtube.com/watch?v=A-41qifywog
• Wesley Shaw – Yuin, Wreck Bay (Jervis Bay), NSW http://www.youtube.com/watch?v=iR_vmNaGMwc

Sullivan, G. (2010). *Art Practice as Research: Inquiry in Visual Arts,* 2nd Edition, SAGE Publications: Los Angeles, London, New Delhi, Singapore, Washington DC.

Turner, V.W. (1969). The Ritual Process: Structure and Anti-Structure, Aldine: Chicago.

Whiteman, G., & Cooper W. H., (2000) Ecological Embeddedness, *Academy of Management Journal, 43*(6), 1265-1282.

CHAPTER 9

Collaboration or Cooperation: Peer-led Learning and Institutional Partnerships through Two Case Studies

Jo Higgins and Sarah Coffils

ABSTRACT

This chapter explores from a practitioner-based perspective, two recent arts projects, that employed peer-led and project based models of learning to engage with a specific audience of young people aged 13-25. While distinct in their organisational structure, duration and delivery, both projects were conceived as part of unique institutional partnerships that engaged artists, creative industry practitioners and curatorial and educational peers as central to each projects' realisation. The two case studies include a UK project called the Louis Vuitton Young Arts Project (LVYAP) that was conceived by the South London Gallery and ran from September 2009 – March 2013 in partnership with the TATE (across both Tate Modern and Tate Britain), Whitechapel Gallery, the Hayward Gallery and the Royal Academy of Arts. Both authors worked on this project. The second case study is from Australia and is the Kaldor Public Art Projects Pilot Regional Engagement Project, which in contrast with the LVYAP, ran for a shorter period of just 12 weeks, from May to July 2015. The project was part of the educational program for Project 30 – *Marina Abramović: In Residence.* It was delivered in partnership with the Western Plains Cultural Centre in Dubbo in central western NSW with support from regional arts board Orana Arts. One of the authors, Jo Higgins, worked on this project. Using a dialogic conversational format to reflect on what worked and what didn't in these two projects, the authors' explore the institutional nature of collaboration, as something distinct from cooperation, and considers the role of agency and outcomes for both facilitators and participants in understanding what may constitute success. The relative successes of each project are considered in light of Australian and International evaluative reports on peer-led learning and shifting cultural agendas as well as key academic texts on collaboration and models of museum-based learning. Ultimately, we attempt to draw some conclusions about best practice models of working in regards to institutional partnership projects and innovative engagement programs that target a specific audience of young people; an audience that necessarily needs to be nurtured if cultural institutions are to have vital and engaged future audiences.

INTRODUCTION

In September 2009 an ambitious education partnership project was announced in London. Funded by the French luxury brand Louis Vuitton, this innovative three and a half-year project brought together five of the city's most recognisable institutions: Tate, Whitechapel Gallery, the Hayward Gallery, the Royal Academy of Arts and the South London Gallery, as lead partner.

The Louis Vuitton Young Arts Project, or LVYAP, gave young Londoners aged 13-25 unprecedented access to those curators, artists and museum directors currently shaping the London contemporary art world. Led by the South London Gallery (SLG), the project was conceived by SLG Director Margot Heller and Sarah Coffils, then Young People's Program Manager and now Head of Education, who oversaw the development of the project. While each gallery had distinct individual programs for young people, the LVYAP brought the institution's youth groups together across a series of dedicated programs that included peer-led, cross-site visits and events; an annual week-long 'Summer Academy'; and the creation of www.REcreativeUK.com, an open access, online community and platform for young people anywhere to share their own work and learn about the contemporary art world. Critically, the LVYAP also brought together the education teams at each institution, who met collectively each month to discuss the project's on-going deliverables and their own professional development.

By the time the project ended in March 2013, hundreds of young people had engaged in the project. Crucially this engagement was over a long-term period and offered young people a chance to programme professional events across the five institutions. Alongside this unusual level of participant engagement there was arguably an increased understanding of the value of peer-led models of learning for the partner institutions, but also of the potential for productive inter-institutional collaboration.

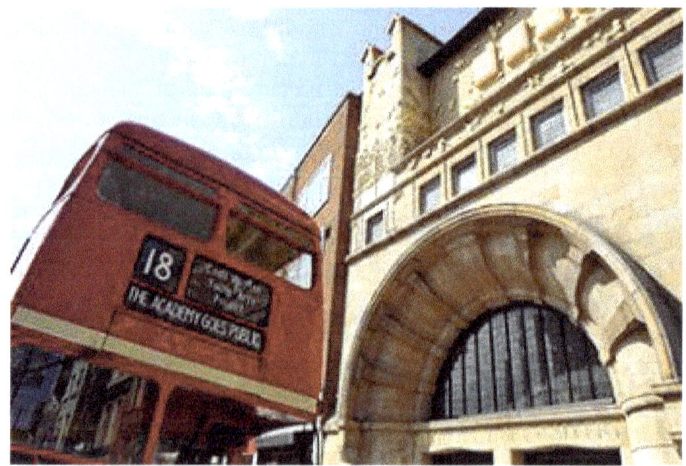

Figure: 9.1 - The Academy Goes Public, 2012. Louis Vuitton Young Arts Project.
Image credit: Richard Eaton. Courtesy: REcreativeUK.com/South London Gallery

Several years later in 2015, literally on the other side of the world, another unique education partnership project was launched. Kaldor Public Art Projects (KPAP), as part of their wider public program for Project 30: *Marina Abramović: In Residence*, announced their Regional Youth Engagement Program. This pilot project ran for just 12 weeks, from May to July, in partnership with the Western Plains Cultural Centre (WPCC) in Dubbo, in Central West NSW.

Over five weekends eight local teenagers, recruited through the Cultural Centre's network of local art and drama teachers, interrogated and developed an understanding of performance art and created their own works of performance inspired by their own interests and experiences. KPAP's Regional Engagement Co-ordinator Jo Higgins and theatre director Imara Savage guided participants through each weekend and at key stages, artists including Lottie Consalvo and Abramović (who met with the group in Sydney) and WPCC Curator Kent Buchanan were brought in to mentor the participants; to develop their learning and support them in the creation of a final exhibition of their work.

Overseen and supported by Sue Saxon, KPAP's Education and Public Programs Manager, the project was developed by Higgins, who from 2011-2013 worked at the South London Gallery on the LVYAP and REcreativeUK.com as the Young People's Online Editor. Jo Higgins and Sarah Coffils author this chapter and the conversations within it reflect their on-going interest in the nature of collaborative work and the impact of young people's peer-led learning on both the participants themselves and on the institutions that facilitate it.

These two projects are in many respects very different. The LVYAP was built on existing relationships between established art organisations with a history of youth programming; the Dubbo project was the first time that KPAP, an organisation that has brought international artists to Australia to develop short-term projects since 1969, had ever worked in this way, in terms of delivering a dedicated educational program for teenagers and one with a peer-led focus, but also in partnership with a regional gallery. Similarly, the Cultural Centre had no existing youth group and no experience working with young people in this peer-led, informal manner. Additionally, the Dubbo project, while nearly 12 months in the planning, was only 12 weeks long, and clearly outcome-oriented. The LVYAP by comparison, ran for three and a half-years and so had time to experiment with different models of working.

What these two projects have in common, and what makes them interesting to compare, is not just their working with young people and focus on informal learning methodologies, but also their approaches to institutional collaboration and the challenges of developing meaningful partnerships. In discussing the nature of partnership work, the subtle but significant semantics of these related terms – collaboration, cooperation, co-production – become important because they necessarily raise issues around ideas of agency, authenticity, leadership, risk, ego and the role of outcomes.

The inherent challenges of working together (both between institutions and between institutions and young people) are considered in this chapter, as is the role of peer-led learning programs within arts organisations. While peer-led youth practice is not widely undertaken in Australia, it has been comfortably part of the cultural landscape of the UK for two decades now. In her 2010 report 'Youth-led Practice in Galleries, Museums and Archives' for engage, the UK's National Association for Gallery Education, Norma Rosso identified 106 museums and galleries in England that program youth-led activities, which had been running on average for 3-8 years. She argues that this rise in activity can be partially attributed to an increase in funding but that overwhelmingly it has flourished because of the dedication of educators to "offering [young people] a voice and space within their organisations" (Rosso, 2010, 5-6).

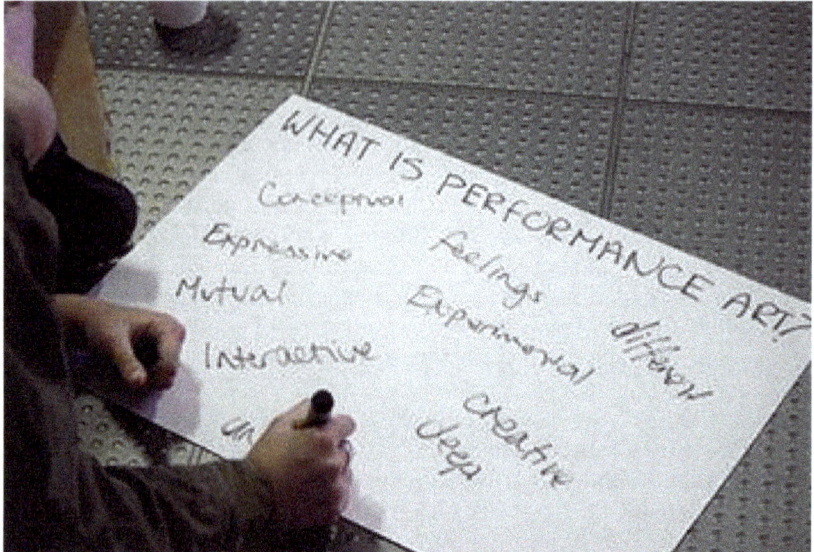

Figure: 9.2 - Kaldor Public Art Projects Pilot Regional Engagement Project, weekend workshop, May 2015.
Image credit: Paige Williams / Orana Arts. Courtesy: Kaldor Public Art Projects

Fast-forward to today and many educators are now critically re-appraising this widely successful work and examining those relationships between institutions and young people to ensure a creative autonomy. This re-appraisal must necessarily also involve a closer examination of some of the key terms that define it. Nicola Sim, a Doctoral researcher at Tate and the University of Nottingham, has found 'collaboration' to be a much-overused concept in gallery education, alongside other affiliate terms like 'partnership.' She observed to the authors:

> These terms are enthusiastically applied to various different types of association between institutions and young people and many projects and programmes claim to work collaboratively. I would argue that practitioners could benefit from critically reflecting upon the nature of their engagements and from bringing greater definition to the naming of their relationship. In programmes involving galleries and young people, there is often minimal interrogation of the terms used to describe co-working practices, and there is

much to gain from acknowledging the value of cooperation, if (as is sometimes the case) institutions, artists and young people have different agendas for working together (Sim, 2016, Email correspondence with Authors).

The terms collaboration, cooperation and agency are referenced throughout the chapter and are understood by the authors from an arts-based practitioner perspective within the cultural sphere. Agency is taken here as having capacity or confidence to enact change, whether as a partner or participant, while the seemingly interchangeable nature of the terms collaboration and cooperation is discussed throughout the chapter. For the authors, in the context of these case studies, the distinction ultimately lies in an understanding of collaboration as something inherently mutual between partners in the planning, decision-making and delivery of work while cooperation acknowledges a willingness to work together despite the reality of different agendas, ways of working or relative senses of agency.

In reflecting on these two projects, and understanding collaboration as something distinct from cooperation, this chapter takes a particular focus on the organisational partnerships and the relationships that were fostered between those running the projects and the young people participating in them. In particular, it focuses on the importance of agency and how, for young people, this sense of agency can be enabled by effective peer-led, informal learning.

The Director of Learning at Tate, Anna Cutler, in "attempting to unpick the differences between the formal and informal defines learning and education as two distinct entities. She writes, "Educational psychologists often describe learning as change through experience… Education, on the other hand, might be defined as the structures and system established to manage and guide learning" (Cutler, 2010, 7-8). In this same article for *Tate Papers,* Cutler examines the necessity of creative cultural learning to develop vital critical thinking and emotional skills and argues that it is the responsibility of cultural institutions to continue to lead this change. She asks, "Why do we place such high value on the kind of knowledge that trains us for [television quiz show] *University Challenge* but that does not enable us to ask better questions?" (Cutler, 2010, 8).

Creating a peer-led learning environment is certainly one way of doing this. While it is important that critical questions continue to be asked by institutions about the role of youth groups within them, the long-term benefits of participation in these programs for young people are being increasingly quantified, as the Whitney's recent report, *Room to Rise* demonstrates (Linzer & Munley, 2015). It supports Cutler's claim that "(this particular kind of) learning that is taking place affects attitudes and behaviours… generating critical, reflective thinking and transferable skills (and) sustained engagement and application across disciplines… (It is) helping to form habits of mind, potentially for a lifetime" (Cutler, 2010, 12). She extends this argument to partnerships and while in the context of the article she refers to those between cultural and educational institutions, it is widely true that, "Partnerships, dialogue and cultural and educational collegiality need to be extended to generate new ideas and learning opportunities together" (Cutler, 2010, 21).

In attempting to establish some parameters in what is already an expansive field of discussion, this chapter is shaped by three questions or concerns: the nature of collaboration versus cooperation; the importance of agency for participants and partners; and the role of outcomes in young people's learning programs. Both projects are reconsidered within these lines of enquiry and their successes and failures – as partnerships and as projects for young people – are reflected upon with the view to establishing some best practice strategies for the future of these valuable models of working. Methodologically, the chapter draws from a recorded conversation between the authors that took place in April 2016. Each section of conversation is supported by first-hand reflections from partners on both projects, and by additional conversations with selected academics including Dr Esther Sayers, Goldsmiths College and Doctoral Researcher Nicola Sim, Tate/University of Nottingham, to ensure a broader and more critical context for both projects has been accounted for. Cited projects partners and participants include Kent Buchanan, Curator, Western Plains Cultural Centre, Dubbo, Australia; Ann Gilmore, Young People and Teachers Programmer at the Royal Academy of Arts, UK; Mark Miller, Circuit Programme National Lead, Convenor: Young People's Programs at Tate Britain and Modern, UK; Leyla Tahir, Assistant Curator, Young People's Programs, Tate, UK; Daniel Wallis, Educator, formerly Southbank Centre, UK; and Ashley Whitfield, Educator, formerly Young People's Coordinator, South London Gallery, UK.

The chapter is organised under a series of headings, the first of which is: Collaboration or Cooperation: An Opening Conversation. This dialogic conversation between the authors introduces the two case studies and establishes some of the key concerns of the chapter. The following headings, Collaboration of Cooperation: Wider Context & Reflections; The Importance of Agency; and On the Role of Outcomes situate the authors' conversation and project-based experiences in the wider context of the projects, with reflections from partner participants and references to key writings on peer-led learning and partnership work. The chapter's final heading, On Reflection: A Conversation Concludes, returns to the authors' dialogic conversations to draw some conclusions about the success of the projects and what lessons there might be for future partnership and peer-led learning projects.

Collaboration or Cooperation: An Opening Conversation

Mirroring the premise of co-presence, co-authoring and co-development as a beginning theme in this chapter, the two authors utilise a critically reflective conversation to highlight key terms: collaboration and cooperation. Jo Higgins is referred to throughout as JH and Sarah Coffils as SC. Each author has the opportunity to question and respond in the following dialogic transcript.

> **JH**: Did you have any initial sense about how you would approach collaborating – or cooperating maybe - with all these stakeholders in the LVYAP?

SC: It was quite intimidating at first, being the smallest organisation with the least amount of resources. If I think about it in terms of collaboration or cooperation, I feel that initially our agenda for building the partnership was collaborative but through the course of the project it became clear how important the autonomy of each of the partner's programs were, and we became more cooperative than collaborative, which perhaps feels inherently thinner than a collaboration.

JH: Cooperation has a sense of acquiescing to somebody else's vision-

SC: Yes, and one of the things we first discussed was that all of the partners felt it was important to retain their own ways of working with young people. The project was an umbrella, which brought together these projects that already existed and knitted them together across the five institutions. It was clear from the start that the project shouldn't direct programming. The initial concept came from observing the momentum that was developing around peer-led practise, more organisations were starting their own youth forums, and we thought this was a good moment to try and bring that work together.
So I think we were collaborating in the sense of wanting to be more critical of what we were doing, wanting to be more reflective in response to each other's programs but we were probably less collaborative across those programs with each other. We all ran our own programs and even the cross-site visits, which happened once a month at each institution, were individually programmed by each host gallery. The Academies were the only part that we truly collaboratively programmed across multiple organisations and across the youth groups.
How do you understand collaboration and cooperation?

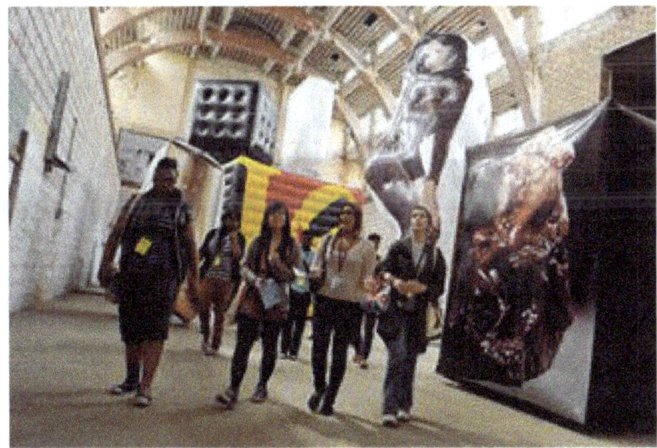

Figure: 9.3 - A visit to Frieze Projects, part of The Academy Goes Public, 2012. Louis Vuitton Young Arts Project.
Image credit: Richard Eaton. Courtesy: REcreativeUK.com/South London Gallery

JH: I think there's a strange sense that if you're cooperating with somebody, you're ceding to their vision. Whereas, collaboration suggests a mutual investment or creation of an idea during LVYAP I was very aware of the dynamics of the SLG being the lead partner, but I think that any project with that many stakeholders does need somebody to lead it or it risks not moving forward. I don't think you can have collaboration without cooperation.

I think too, cooperation raises a lot of ideas around ego and I think that can be challenging at times. With the Dubbo project, because it was a pilot and the first time KPAP had worked in this particular way, I was very mindful of speaking about the project as a collaboration because it was important to me that the team at Dubbo had a genuine sense of agency. But it absolutely relied on their cooperation - they allowed us to work in their space, they assisted us to recruit participants, they really gave over to our ideas and supported us logistically in the planning and delivery. The intellectual framework for the project was ours, something Sue and Imara and I developed, but we also relied on them for certain skills and knowledge that we didn't have in developing the final exhibition. So I certainly saw it as a true collaboration in that sense. But I was very aware of ego. And I think ego is a funny thing, especially when you're dealing with the machinations of enormous institutions like we were with the LVYAP.

SC: I think ego can't be discounted, especially from a Project Manager perspective because whoever takes on that role is usually putting all their energy into it and their ego somewhere too. Which is tricky because it's really important to have space to be reflective and I think at times, being the project lead meant the other partners probably didn't feel able to be as critical of us, because we were the ones offering up the space to make it happen.

It's difficult trying to create enough opportunities for criticality and reflection and it's always a challenge when you've got people who are incredibly engaged in what they're doing. For me the difference between collaboration and cooperation isn't about different levels of partnership. To co-operate you are lending yourself to someone or you're lending your skills and your resources to another group of people.

JH: There's a generosity to cooperation.

SC: There is a generosity and I think that was one of the things that I felt really keenly, the generosity of spirit, yes towards this idea of collaboration, but actually more towards the sharing of ideas and problems. Which is why the monthly meetings, with at least one member of staff from every organisation, were so important. Almost half of every meeting was spent sharing current programs and becoming more aware of how each institution worked.

JH: There was so much transparency and trust and advice seeking. That space did feel very equal, irrespective of the size of the institution or the issues. It enabled a lot of friendships.

SC: That felt truly collaborative I think.

JH: I agree.

SC: But then how truly collaborative can something can really be when the terms of a project are defined from the start? Working with Louis Vuitton, we knew from the beginning what form the project would take and this wasn't planned with input from the partners. So really, I don't think a project can be truly collaborative unless that knitting together part at the beginning happens with everyone involved. Dr Bernadette Lynch has spoken about this in her text *Whose Cake Is It Anyway?* which was commissioned by the Paul Hamlyn Foundation, a major funder of gallery education in the UK. For her, it's crucial for the funder to be in the room whilst the proposal is being put together, so that they become less silent partner and more able to respond by offering funding support in the right framework to enable organisations to take risks. For LVYAP the partner institutions were really involved in the process of developing each strand of the project, but they weren't involved in the initial project planning, which could have potentially created more collaborative programming opportunities, instead of projects that simply worked in parallel with each other.
It's very difficult to strike a balance between getting enough done and moving something forward and truly collaborating on it, with enough voices in the conversation from the beginning. Funding for the planning process of knitting together ideas is rarely available, so often it's a case of starting from a place of experience and then experimenting once a program is established.

JH: Given that everybody had their own way of working and each youth group had its own particular identity and sense of purpose, why do you think everybody agreed to collaborate on this project?

SC: I think youth programming is really hard and expensive. I think at that time particularly it was really difficult to advocate for it internally; to really show why it was important, because most of us work with quite small groups of young people, and the focus from funders is often on numbers rather than depth of engagement. The idea of a youth panel that would reflect on you as an organisation and how you engage with younger audiences is a hard concept for a lot of organisations. So the LVYAP offered visibility and credibility. I remember Mark Miller from Tate saying that because Louis Vuitton were funding this program, he could get people in the room, like Penelope Curtis (Director of Tate Britain from 2010-15) and Nick Serota

(Director of Tate since 1988), to actually see what he was doing. The project did offer those big moments.

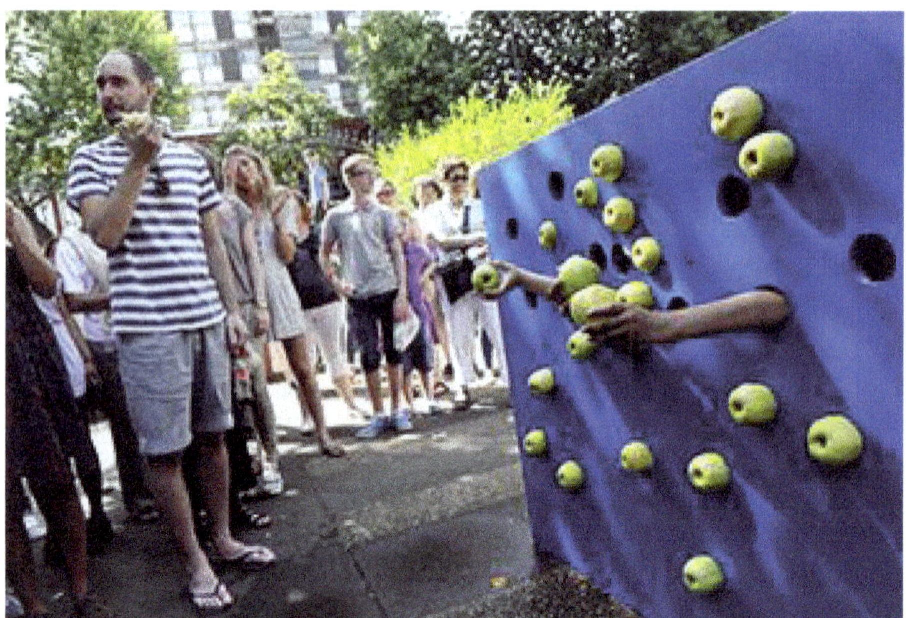

Figure: 9.4 - The Academy Goes Public, 2012. Various venues. Louis Vuitton Young Arts Project.
Image credit: Richard Eaton. Courtesy: REcreativeUK.com/South London Gallery.

But I think in the beginning it really just came from a sense of wanting to share, to make sure that their ways of working with young people were the most up to date. I think a lot of people really do want to collaborate, but it's just such a hard thing to make happen unless you have someone pushing to make it happen and funding that allows for the time it takes to develop the communication around it.

JH: Do you think there were instances where the project felt truly collaborative? Whether through the partnership or with young people?

SC: I think the annual Academies were often collaborative through their very design. It was easier to see them as distinct projects that we worked on together and they were spread across different venues over the three years. The first was at the Royal Academy, the second at the Hayward Gallery and the last across the Whitechapel and the SLG. They were so varied but incredibly ambitious in what we tried to achieve in a week. The final academy in particular, working with artists Elmgreen & Dragset to create four temporary public works across London, was perhaps the most balanced in that it offered a very public, pressure-filled, moment of success, as well as time and space for playful ideas sharing and relationship building.

JH: I think by the final academy we had developed a lot of confidence in our capacity to program these kinds of events

SC: The pressure on the first year was immense in terms of an outcome and the scale of possibilities. It felt like uncharted territory for everyone involved. Once we'd created a successful model of working with both artists and young people the academies became a fantastic opportunity for both the institutions and young people involved. It took that first year to test out the possibilities and realise what everyone's measures of success were. Including Louis Vuitton's. The Academy format though was still challenging, as it was so outcome focused and so short, which created a lot of pressure. It was the only time that all the youth groups came together quite intensively over a dedicated period of time. If I could go back, I would do it over a slightly longer period of time. It was incredibly intense working towards that final public outcome.

JH: It's interesting to reflect on the LVYAP project and partnerships in the context of Australian gallery education practices. When I came back to Sydney having spent three years at the SLG, I came home really agitating for this sort of work and collaboration to happen here. I met with gallery directors and education teams who all were really interested in the project and the SLG; but with the exception of the MCA, no other institution, certainly in Sydney works with young people in a dedicated or on-going way.

There was a real sense of not being able to afford it time-wise, but also because obviously it's very expensive. But if I'm honest, I also really felt that there wasn't an interest or institutional appetite for it. And it was the same with institutional collaborative practice. There was a sense of suspicion or reticence maybe. I do think that's changing, especially with regard to curatorial projects – the Biennale of Sydney has always brought all the major Sydney institutions together under their umbrella organisation and a new Biennale has just been announced in a partnership between Carriageworks, the MCA and the AGNSW. But it meant that when I was offered the opportunity to develop the project for KPAP in Dubbo, I made it a central part of my approach to be really consultative and collaborative with the Cultural Centre team because I wanted and needed them to have a stake in it and to feel proud of it.

The project really was like an Academy in the sense that it was incredibly intense; five weekends over 12 weeks; but also because it was developed with what I took to be best practice in collaborative work and working with young people.

It's interesting, a year after Dubbo, to be sitting back and reflecting on where I think things are at in Australia in terms of partnership work and peer-led learning and to compare the two cultural landscapes. I don't think there's enough risk-taking here but there's never been a better time to be collaborative. Setting aside the institutional benefits, with the current funding situation as it is, now is absolutely the time to starting thinking innovatively and collectively.

SC: In terms of how you worked with the organisation in Dubbo and how you worked with young people there as well - do you feel that was more collaborative than cooperative?

JH: Well KPAP hadn't ever worked with the Cultural Centre before and we approached them with a very specific idea of what we wanted to do, developed from my experiences with peer-led learning in London, Sue's experience running past educational programs and inspired by the project we were delivering in Sydney with Marina Abramović at the time. So while we really led on the development and delivery of the project, the fact is that we absolutely couldn't have done it without the Cultural Centre. Yes, they co-operated with us but really, what's extraordinary is that they took a risk and said yes to working with us, with all the unknowns. And that risk felt like a genuine collaboration. We were taking a risk in piloting this project and they absolutely met that risk by backing us.

SC: That's very true; the risk is all on the side of the people that aren't leading.

JH: I was very mindful of going out to Dubbo and not being "that Sydney organisation." Not in terms of KPAP specifically but I didn't want to be seen as thinking I knew the best or only way of doing things. I did have a very clear idea of what I wanted to do, but I knew, when it looked like we were going to be holding an exhibition of performance art, that it was going to need the Cultural Centre's buy-in and understanding of the process we'd undertaken to get there.

When you're working with teenagers, despite having a very certain idea of what you want to do, ultimately you just have to give over to the process and trust that you've set the framework and whatever happens from there is what was meant to happen. I would have liked it to be peer-led but given the time demands, it became more of a project-based learning methodology. We just didn't have the time to extend those relationships. It was a tight program but it still felt like there was enough space to explore, to get to know each other and to establish trust. And this trust was essential; it enabled the group to create some really powerful work exploring vulnerability, empathy, mental health.

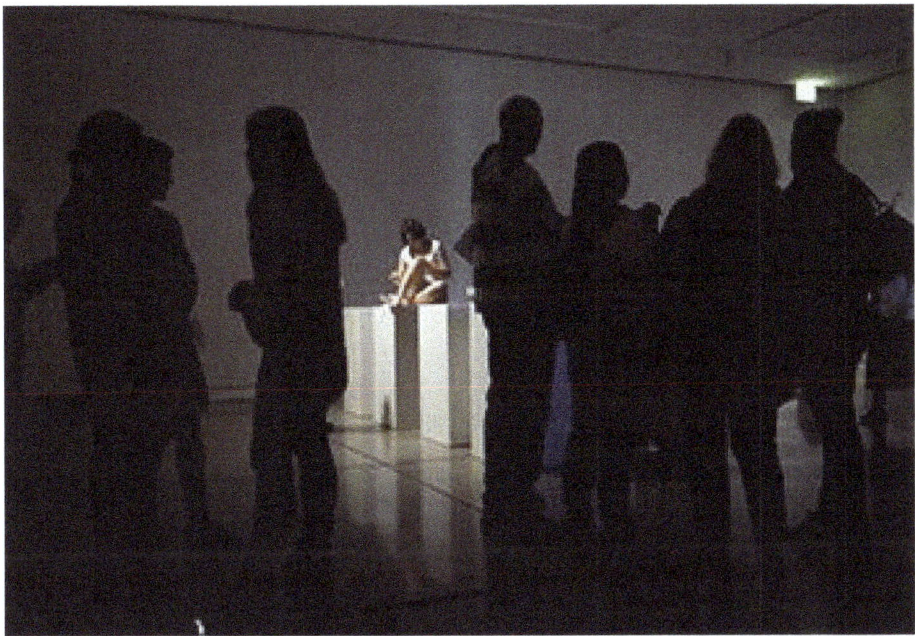

Figure: 9.5 - Caitlyn Coman-Sargent, Pruning Time - A collection of private and public rituals, 2015. Presented as part of "What It Means To Be Me", Saturday 26 July 2015, Western Plains Cultural Centre, Dubbo.
Image credit: Alex Wisser. Courtesy: Kaldor Public Art Projects

SC: In terms of talking about collaboration and young people, I think that certainly for the LVYAP, each venue collaborated with young people in the way they chose, which was very much peer-led for four of the venues and then there was the Royal Academy's structured, more formal education position. Although having said that, they worked in a very peer-led way for quite a lot of the project and took a huge risk experimenting with it, a level of risk that no one else took.

While I think each organisation had their own way of collaborating with their youth groups, the cross-site visits were great opportunities for all the groups to experience how the other institutions worked. I only really reflected on this later, but it was another way of helping us to discuss our own ways of working but also helping the young people themselves to be a bit more critical about the way that they work and in turn be critical of the institution they were working with. I think that criticality was incredibly powerful, and often produced difficult discussions about whether a young person should be paid to be programming events, (which happened in some venues and not others) and the differences between unpaid internships and youth panels, which in some institutions would parallel each other in age range and experience, which brings us to the issue of agency.

COLLABORATION OR COOPERATION: WIDER CONTEXT AND REFLECTIONS

Before moving to a discussion on the importance of agency, Higgins and Coffils reflect on some of the issues raised in their discussion on collaboration and the following text includes invited contributions from colleagues involved in the project and academics exploring peer-led programming.

There are many ways in which to understand collaboration and cooperation as subtle but nonetheless distinct ways of working together. Collaboration as a generic term refers simply to a group of people working together but as these projects demonstrate, it is the relationships between stakeholders that determines the nature of this work in regards to methods of creation and delivery. Cooperation as collaboration (Collaboration, 2016, tranzit.org/curatorialdictionary) is distinct from cooperation as participation (Participation, 2016, tranzit.org/curatorialdictionary) and as the authors' discuss, the relationships and organisational structure of each project played a significant role in how the collaboration was understood.

In a 2015 article for Tate's Circuit website, Nicola Sim discusses a presentation by Dr Richard Davies from Aberystwyth University titled *Partnership: a philosophical consideration*, as part of her investigation into models of partnership between arts and youth organisations. According to Sim's article, a small section of which is summarised below, it is suggested by Davies that partnership work requires collective agreement on partnership design when it comes to collaboration versus cooperation. Further, that co-operative alliances depend on agents working together to achieve one another's goals, even though they ultimately have *different* goals, whereas in collaborative relationships, different agents are said to share the same goals. Either of these approaches is valid, as long as each agent is aware of the configuration of that relationship (Sim, 2015).

For the partners and participants on the LVYAP, these ideas of collaboration were most successfully explored in the work that occurred with and amongst the young participants. From a partnership perspective, maintaining institutional independence was deemed as important as the value of the opportunity to learn from each other. Often partnerships occur as a result of wanting to advocate and make concrete the necessity of a new way of working, as in peer-led practice, but the need for tangible measures of success and the maintenance of organisational differences, as happened with LVYAP, means these relationships are fundamentally more co-operative, working towards a shared knowledge but with different organisational objectives.

Daniel Wallis, a freelance educator who worked with the youth program at the Southbank Centre during LVYAP, agrees that collaboration and cooperation are two different ways of working and says he would never describe his education work as cooperation – "When I use the term 'collaborate with young people,' it's on projects where the outcome is something I would equally put all our names to" (Wallis, 2016, Email correspondence with Authors). And on reflecting on the challenges of the LVYAP, Wallis is one of several to acknowledge the problematics of bringing together youth groups from such different places, a challenge that was also true for staff.

Ann Gilmore, Young People and Teachers Programmer at the Royal Academy of Arts and Mark Miller, Convenor of Young People's Programs at Tate Britain and Modern, both acknowledge that the "LVYAP was a perfect opportunity to observe and learn how other arts educators worked with young people, introducing ideas and content into the development of various projects" (Gilmore, 2016, Email correspondence with Authors). But, as she also observes, "You were not always aware of how [the other partners] worked, or the inner workings of the organisation itself and goals and outcomes seemed to be pre-determined, usually by the organisation that was the budget-holder (not surprisingly)" (ibid). During LVYAP the SLG was the primary organisation reporting to the funder, and this communication and pressure for outcomes, made the partnership unbalanced at times.

For Tate's Miller, the success of the LVYAP from a collaborative perspective was its "enabling of Tate's young people's programme to consider various methods of collaboration and co–production on a city wide level [and that] it enabled these multiple organisations to consider rationales for varied forms of collaboration such as, format or range of working with young people" (Miller, 2016, Email correspondence with Authors).

Leyla Tahir is currently Assistant Curator, Young People's Programs at Tate but she is also a former LVYAP participant. For her, the opportunity to collaborate with young people from outside her own youth group, from different backgrounds across London was invaluable for her "to be able to draw upon a really wide set of viewpoints to programme with and for other young people" (Tahir, 2016, Email correspondence with Authors). Tahir observed:

> For me, defining collaboration, cooperation and the difference between the two, both as a young person and now as an 'adult' working with young people, it's about who holds the power in the process of decision-making. Collaboration sees decisions being shared between young people and facilitators/adults, each regarded as peers. In contrast, cooperation feels more like a consultation process, where adults lead on decisions with input from young people who are informed as to how their contributions are used as part of adult-led outcomes. From my personal experience, peer-led practice goes one step further; it is a process facilitated by 'adults' where young people shape activity and make all the decisions (ibid).

Kent Buchanan is Curator at WPCC and a frequent collaborator with other regional institutions on the development of exhibition programs. The Kaldor project was his first educational partnership project. Buchanan told the authors he believes that working with any major stakeholder "involves collaboration with their processes and philosophies to ensure outcomes are achievable and unanimous" (Buchanan, 2016, Email correspondence with Authors). For Buchanan, successful collaboration should "see all stakeholders providing input and ideas to a project to add to its potential. Collaboration acknowledges pre-existing skills and utilises them to enable the best possible outcome" (ibid). Cooperation, by contrast, "allows individual stakeholders to take the lead on aspects of the project that may be required. This allows for a learning process for all involved" (ibid) and collaboration as a learning process only serves to highlight the value of difference and independence, terms that might otherwise be considered negative in a collaborative space.

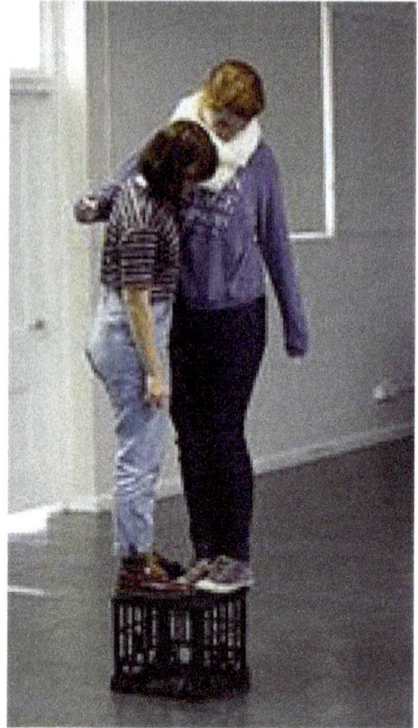

Figure: 9.6 - Kaldor Public Art Projects Pilot Regional Engagement Project, weekend workshop, May 2015.
Image credit: Paige Williams / Orana Arts. Courtesy: Kaldor Public Art Projects

In reflecting on the nature of the partnership between Kaldor Public Art Projects and the Cultural Centre, Buchanan believes that at the heart of project was an open notion of collaboration, one with "The collaborative notion of the project was its strength and lead to an enormously successful outcome. The project acknowledged the strengths and connections of each stakeholder and how each could support the young people who participated in the project" (ibid.)

For Ashley Whitfield, who worked with the SLG's youth forum as the Young People's Program Coordinator at the SLG, working collaboratively is a process of constantly letting go. She explained; "It is experimenting together, taking action together, relying on one another. Collaboration calls for trust in intention and skill, and to let go of commitments to an imagined result. Cooperation requires compliance, and conformity. Cooperating is about holding on to a defined way of being together. Effective collaborations emerge from relationships, not necessarily longstanding, or intimate, but planted in trust" (Whitfield, 2016, Email correspondence with Authors). This sense of letting go of a predetermined outcome or result is often where collaborative projects are undermined by organisations that are driven by outcomes and funders that want to see results. In order to successfully negotiate these relationships and expectations, stakeholders must have a sense of their agency within the project.

The Importance of Agency

The issue of agency can be surprisingly complicated and there is currently not a great deal of research into the role of agency in partnership work. Philosophers such as Michael Bratman have written extensively about shared agency (2013) but these discussions, in the context of education work remain firmly focused, not incorrectly, on the agency of young people as participants and authors of their own experiences.

For the authors here, it does appear that education staff regularly abrogate any desire or claim for their own agency, focusing instead on the agency of their young people. While developing and supporting this agency is critical, at a broader institutional level, and within a project framework such as the LVYAP, this forgoing or lack of agency as a stakeholder can be problematic. As the Royal Academy's Ann Gilmore observed, "I think it is important that staff and facilitators have agency when working in partnerships but how do you achieve that when the lead organisation has the vision and holds the budget? It tends to be skewed to whatever their aims and objectives are" (Gilmore, 2016, Email correspondence with Authors). The development of an understanding of agency for LVYAP participants was shown through their involvement in the creation and eventual direction of website REcreativeUK.com. This core strand of the project, which began in mid-2010, happened to occur in the context of wider conversations amongst the participants about their involvement in the project. At one point there was discussion amongst several Tate Collective members about building a 'super-group' of independent young people not connected to any one organisation. Coffils reflected:

> As an idea, as a way of thinking, it was really interesting to watch the participants becoming more aware of their own position within the project: "Why are we doing this? What is this about? I'm a young person. I'm part of this. Am I just towing a line? Why am I here? What am I here to do? What are *they* here to do? Why are they doing it that way and we're doing it this way? (Coffils, 2016, Authors in Conversation).

This criticality could not have occurred without a sense of confidence, which came from their early sense of agency and ownership over the project, something that was positively – but inadvertently – created by bringing a mix of groups of young people together and challenging them and their own assumptions about themselves and their organisations. For the authors, there is a sense, retrospectively, that it was the participants who best came together, who started to make authentic relationships, to collaborate and co-operate with a genuine sense of agency. Something Leyla Tahir also noted to the authors:

As a young person I certainly felt a strong sense of agency when devising and delivering Tate's contributions to the project, something that was heightened by working on programmes for the other partners as opposed to a general public (Tahir, 2016, Email correspondence with Authors).

The role of outcomes in peer-led and project-based learning is addressed later in the chapter but it is worth observing that for many young people, working towards and delivering an outcome is an easily identifiable means of establishing agency. For education staff, this is not always uncomplicated. Because, as Tate's Mark Miller observed:

> While staff should facilitate to enable young people's agency and authorship it's often hard for staff not to steer decision-making, or make 'suggestions', which can take away the agency and authorship of young people. The temptation to suggest or steer is often very strong, especially with deadline, delivery and outcomes to consider… Instead of the set ideals of production, tangible outcomes or meeting press, marketing or event deadlines, young people's agency in the collective context of group working is often achieved if the processes of transferable skills development and cognitive and social learning are instead valued and prioritised (Miller, 2016, Email correspondence with Authors).

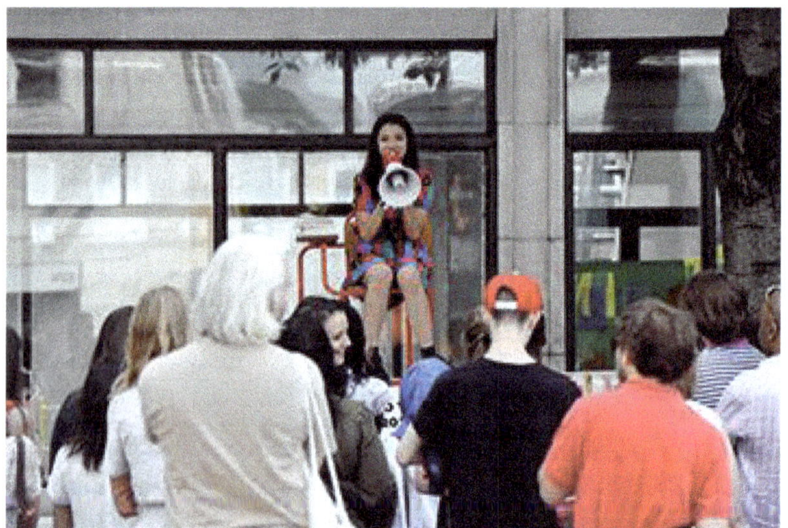

Figure: 9.7 - The Academy Goes Public, 2012. Various venues. Louis Vuitton Young Arts Project.
Image credit: Richard Eaton. Courtesy: REcreativeUK.com/South London Gallery

This was certainly the case with REcreativeUK.com. The process of creating the site involved the recruitment of a group of young people, from each of the partner organisations youth groups, who spent a year working with education staff, developers and designers on the development of the site from ideation to design and early content creation stages. The participants identified very early on in the process that they wanted it to be an online community for them and for other young people interested in art. It would not be a platform for the project, or the partner organisations - an early decision by the group that was ultimately respected by lead LVYAP staff.

As well as participation in the early development stage, a young people's editorial board was established 12 months after the launch, which returned the authorship and direction of the site to the participants after a much criticised gap while the technical development of the site was refined and staff struggled to determine how best to develop and maintain its content. The editorial board is still running today and remains a driving force behind the site is and how it is run. REcreativeUK.com continues to attract participants, with more than 2,500 people signed up to the site and it is widely considered to be successful. However, it's independence in identity from any major institution has meant that at times it has struggled to be recognised and has had to develop its own brand, without relying on the brands of the five institutions. Had the site been securely tied into the LVYAP partnership it arguably would not exist today as an independent, successful project that encourages editorial risks and allows the editorial board to guide it in the way they do.

For Mark Miller, in the context of the LVYAP, it was REcreative that "demonstrated how significant, empowering and progressive co-production, collaboration and real decision-making by young people and respected institutions can create quality and sustainable resources" (Miller, 2016, Email correspondence with Authors). Within the broader conversation around agency, Miller's further point about how best to achieve this for young people is also worth noting. He argues that agency and autonomy for young people is hugely important, especially in his own work, but that in order to achieve this an understanding of "the transparency of organisational aims and objectives; the framework we operate within; values; limitations; potential and possibilities are all extremely important" (ibid).

Nicola Sim also acknowledges the need for transparency by facilitators if young people are to be given a realistic experience of programming for and with galleries and not a false sense of agency. But for Sim, this transparency and the need for staff agency is also important for education teams, as she reflected to the authors: "Peer-led youth programmes in galleries are frequently so occupied with profiling the agency of young people that the agency and contribution of the staff member is overlooked or underplayed… This is problematic because if the programmer's curatorial investment is not properly recognised, then the status of that professional role will always be marginalised, and the facilitation skills required for the job may not be fully understood by the institution and the wider public" (Sim, 2016, Email correspondence with Authors).

As project lead, Coffils' experience was that when the partners were directly involved in the planning of an event, such as an Academy, the annual week-long focused program, there was a tangible sense of investment and clear moments of connection and collaboration but that often there was only a vague sense of agency amongst those working on the project across the organisations. She observed of her experience: "I think the idea of agency can be tricky when it comes to partnership work. I often found, as the project manager, that I wanted to ensure that I wasn't asking too much of the project partners which I think in turn meant we moved things forward without always having everyone's individual investment. Communication is so important in projects of this size, particularly as each partner had a number of staff involved at any one time" (Coffils, 2016, Authors in Conversation).

The decision to make REcreativeUK.com independent from the LVYAP raised similar issues around leadership and ownership. In taking the direction of the website away from the five partners and giving it to the young people, it disabled the possibility of using the site to help the partners connect with their own audiences and to make their own work visible. Coffils found that she "couldn't quite translate that idea to the group, as to why we'd done that [and so] there wasn't enough for them to be as excited by and that sense of ownership was lost. It was lost by the partners but gained perhaps by the group of young people that were working with it" (ibid).

The importance of staff agency – on partnership projects and otherwise – is a subject for ongoing enquiry but certainly the success of the LVYAP can be evidenced through the ongoing existence of REcreative three years after the project's completion, and in the collegial working relationships that still exist today. The issue of establishing a sense of agency and ownership for staff and participants of KPAP's regional pilot project was as important as in the LVYAP, though it came with a different set of challenges. Participants were recruited through the Cultural Centre's network of art and drama teachers and for Higgins it was important to collaborate with an organisation like the WPCC, who were confident enough to take a risk and say yes to the project and support it logistically and intellectually. The success of the project also relied on participants who were eager for the opportunity and would commit to it.

Because the project was structured to run for just 12 weeks and anticipated a specific set of outcomes, creating a sense of agency amongst the participants in guiding the direction of the project was not practical or possible. Instead, the focus was on encouraging their enthusiasm and a sense of creative authorship and risk-taking within their individual works. For Higgins, Savage and Consalvo, who ran the weekend workshops, the participants' enthusiasm in fact, became something else to have to manage. As Higgins observed: "We ended up with eight local teenagers who were really switched on but also very disconnected as regional young people. At the start of only the second day, two participants approached me saying, 'I've already got an idea for my performance piece' – before we'd even clarified what the outcomes of the project would be. It was challenging to manage their expectations - to want to encourage and nurture that sense of excitement and that creative journey but at the same time, really wanting for it to be an authentic, challenging, thoughtful process for them. It actually felt a bit risky, forcing them to slow them down and asking them to trust the process" (Higgins, 2016, Authors in Conversation).

Staff actively created space for the participants to listen and respond and to create impulsively and after every piece of work that was shown to them and after every creative exercise they were asked for their feedback. From the first weekend, the participants were asked to consider some of the terms of performance art – the role of the body, the role of the audience, what makes a successful performance piece? The workshops were devised around the expectation that the group would have to think and actively participate and that those responses and experiences would inform what happens next.

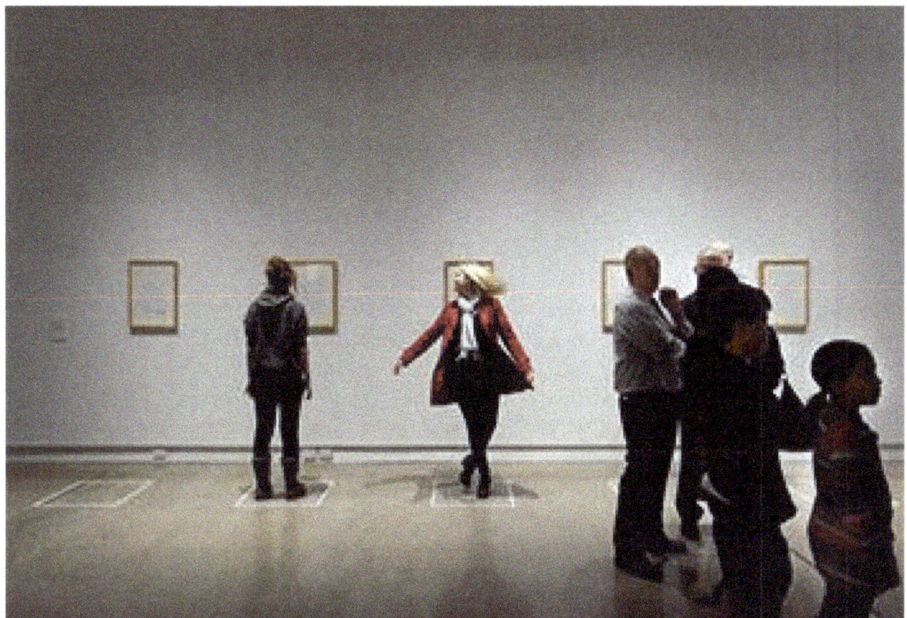

Figure: 9.8 - Kate Hagan, Five Performances for Imagination, 2015. Presented as part of "What It Means To Be Me", Saturday 26 July 2015, Western Plains Cultural Centre, Dubbo. *Image credit: Alex Wisser. Courtesy: Kaldor Public Art Projects*

When it became clear that the project would manifest in a final, public exhibition and that the participants had pushed themselves into quite exposing territory, in terms of some of the ideas they were exploring, Higgins and Savage realised that another level of support was going to be required. Until this stage, the involvement of WPCC staff had been largely logistical but it was an opportunity to invite the expertise of curator Kent Buchanan and to give visibility and a level of authorship to WPCC as one of the partners on project. Higgins recalled: "We went to Kent and made our case: "These participants need a legitimate exhibition; they can't be in the cafe or the garden or in a workshop space. They need the infrastructure and the framework of an exhibition space; they need wall text, an opening, the whole thing. They need that support" (Higgins, 2016, Authors in Conversation).

To Buchanan and the WPCC's immense credit, because they understood what was at stake for both the participants and the project, Buchanan de-installed a large painting show for just the day and spent several sessions with the participants helping them curate the space as a group exhibition. This ask of the Cultural Centre was a valuable thing, not least because they were absolutely relied upon to deliver it, which they did, but because it enabled a genuine sense of contribution and mutuality that enabled both partners to speak authoritatively about the project and the collaboration.

For the participants, while they were arguably without a sense of agency within the wider framework of the project, their ideas and experiences were taken seriously and they were given space and trust to present their work. In late July, only twelve weeks after they had begun, they presented a series of very beautiful performance art pieces for three uninterrupted hours in the Regional Gallery within WPCC. Their sense of confidence and achievement afterwards was palpable and in the evaluation undertaken by Higgins, Savage and Sue Saxon, much of the conversation was about future agency and how they might leverage this experience to develop their own projects going forward.

On the Role of Outcomes

Ensuring that the work towards outcomes is authentic, and that the process itself is recognised as valuable, is an on-going challenge for many educators. This is because, as Dr Esther Sayers argues, an "outcome focus limits the opportunity for creative, open-ended wondering, curiosity and not knowing" (Sayers, 2016, Email correspondence with Authors). Having researched the youth programmes at Tate, Southbank Centre, the Wellcome Collection and Camden Arts Centre, Sayers is aware that most youth programmes do focus on outcomes and that they are hugely important for young people. She acknowledges, "[Outcomes] have a high profile which is appealing and they are beneficial to future careers because there is something visible/tangible" (ibid). This was certainly the case for the Kaldor project. Almost all the participants acknowledged, as part of the evaluative process, that working towards a tangible outcome was a crucial motivating factor. This was perhaps not surprising but Higgins is aware that the intensity of the project's timeframe did make working towards a hard outcome almost inevitable. Had the project had a less specific focus there could have been greater scope to encourage an awareness in the participants of other less tangible outcomes – self-confidence, increased creativity and risk-taking – which were observed by Higgins, Savage and Saxon but arguably not immediately recognised by the participants themselves given their focus on presenting a finished work. Higgins remains aware though that in the instance of the KPAP regional project, the partners also needed a tangible outcome. She reflected:

> Had we not had the exhibition outcome, I still think the participants would have been very positive about the experience but it was important for us too. That visibility was essential given this was a pilot project, one that ultimately demonstrated that we could deliver something both meaningful and exciting. The NSW Arts Minister and John Kaldor both attended the exhibition and that visibility was very important for things going forward, so yes, that outcome was really important. But it did put a lot of pressure on us to deliver it successfully while also having to be vigilant in ensuring that the participants weren't ever pushed towards something that wasn't of their own choice or making (Higgins, 2016, Authors in Conversation).

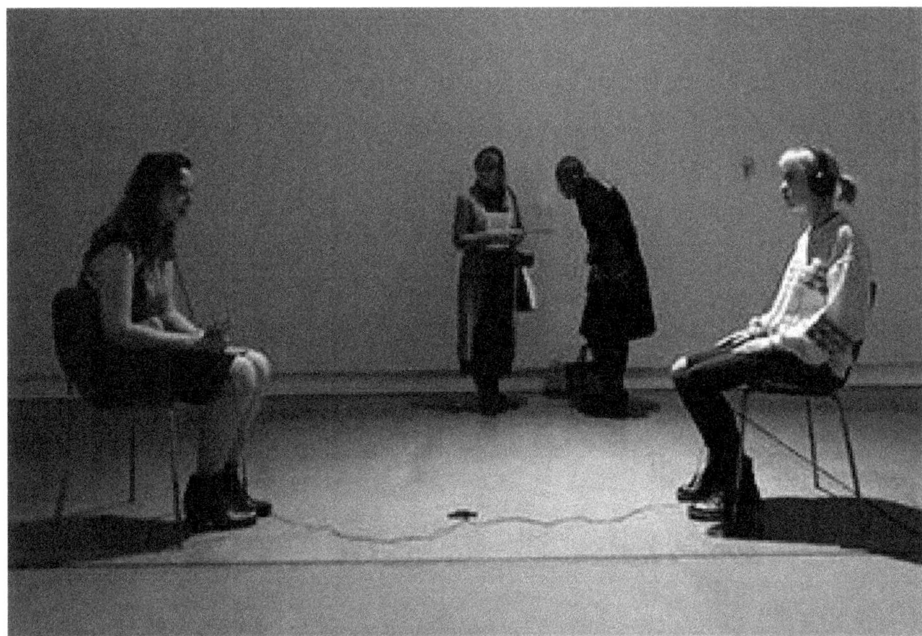

Figure: 9.9 - Grace Farmilo, Grace, 2015. Presented as part of "What It Means To Be Me", Saturday 26 July 2015, Western Plains Cultural Centre, Dubbo.
Image credit: Alex Wisser. Courtesy: Kaldor Public Art Projects

Ann Gilmore believes it is extremely important for young people to know that the process and outcome has been authentic. She commented, "They need to feel that the project or event has been largely developed through their input, that they have been really listened to and that the outcome reflects their work and practice" (Gilmore, 2016, Email correspondence with Authors). In Leyla Tahir's experience as a young participant, and now education facilitator, she is aware that when working towards 'public' outcomes, professional considerations and pressures are often more apparent to the staff facilitating than the young people being collaborated with. "Such considerations may not occur to young people who, in focusing on devising and delivering program, aren't exposed to all facets of an institution. Here, the onus is on the facilitator to be honest and transparent with the young people to enable a clear understanding of the complexities and intricacies that come with working professionally in public spaces" (Tahir, 2016, Email correspondence with Authors). For Sayers, an outcome focus – however construed – risks preventing opportunities for truly empowered learning and, as often false outcomes driven by ego, they "can be less generative of empowerment through personal development and crucially less about the content of the gallery" (Sayers, 2016, Email correspondence with Authors).

For Coffils, finding that balance can be difficult and she acknowledges that in her work with the SLG's youth group the Art Assassins, the participants are often unable to see the benefits of their conversations or excursions "unless it's packaged in a way that says 'This is worthwhile'" (Coffils, 2016, Authors in Conversation). In Coffils' experience, a large part of the role of a youth program facilitator is keeping up with the risk-taking and different directions projects might move in, but then being able to professionalise that process or experience, whether through a publication or an event, to enable the participants to recognise their learning and see it as something they have accomplished.

The LVYAP, like the KPAP regional project, was developed with an expectation of public-facing outcomes and at the start of the LVYAP, Louis Vuitton were quite nervous about how it might develop and had a very front-facing, outcome-oriented expectation, as the authors acknowledge is the case with many education funders. Trying to find those outcome moments at times felt very counterproductive, particularly in the case of the annual Academy. Coffils observed: "The pressure of that was unlike any I've ever had in any other project. The structure of the project didn't offer us the freedom to work the way we would normally with our youth groups; to build up to something and then decide what that final outcomes was going to be. Often, funding proposals that are rigid from the start don't offer enough flexibility for risk-taking" (ibid).

The nature of arts education funding is not the subject of this chapter but it warrants some discussion in the context of outcomes, given the inherent (and arguably increasing) challenges of fundraising for education projects in both the UK and Australia and the amount of money it does cost to work with young people in what is typically a low-key and unobtrusive manner. Outcomes do have to be anticipated and planned for - events where bigger, more diverse audiences and different groups of young people are encouraged to come to something. But this does create pressure. Coffils observed: "The cost per head is high, so there's pressure for public moments that open it out, quite rightly, to a wider range of young people. That can be a real challenge, but then I still agree that it's so important for them to have those moments too. What we often find difficult, is making sure that the young people we're working with are valuing the *process* involved in making those things happen, and valuing their contribution to that process and understanding that they're learning and developing along the way. I think highlighting the value of process is important, for the funders as well as the participants, because at the moment I feel there's a breakdown with funder's wanting to see the outcomes and being less scrupulous about how you get there" (ibid).

The importance of process and balancing that with the need for outcomes and happy partners and funders is something that requires future research and discussion but the Whitney Museum of American Art's recent report *Room to Rise* (Linzer & Munley, 2015) presents an extraordinarily in-depth, quantitative look at the long-term impacts of peer-led gallery youth groups in terms of creative and critical thinking skills, self-awareness, confidence and creativity. It will hopefully be the first of many to substantially acknowledge the value and long-term investment of the significant cost per head of these sorts of programs.

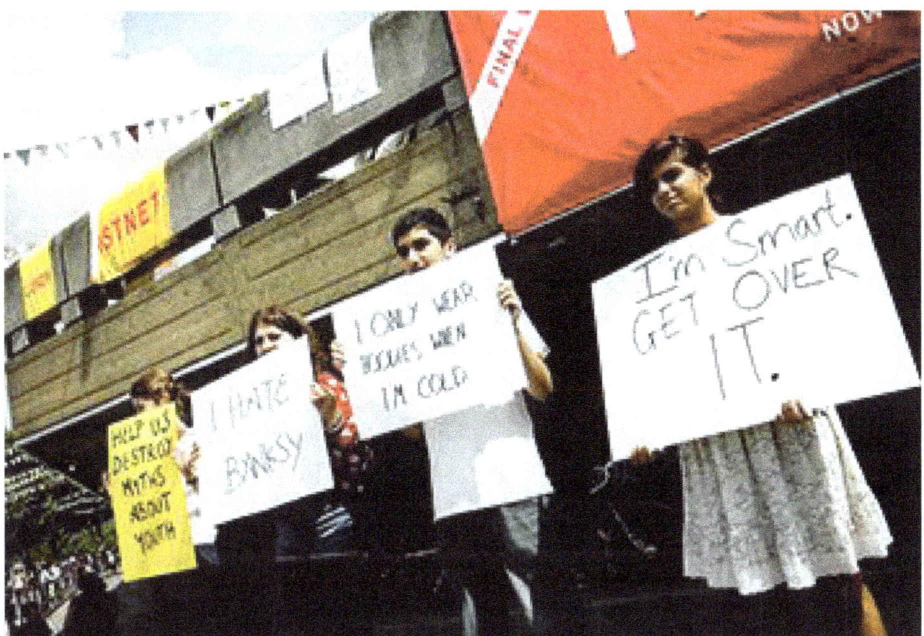

Figure: 9.10 - The Academy of Youth Mythology, Southbank, 2011. Louis Vuitton Young Arts Project.
Image credit: Richard Eaton. Courtesy: REcreativeUK.com/South London Gallery

In discussing the significant but intangible outcomes of this kind of work, including increased emotional intelligence, resilience, creative and critical thinking and negotiation skills, both authors acknowledge that today's school curriculums typically fail to recognise the importance of these skills, and so it falls to education projects and programs such as those discussed to develop them with and for the young people involved. But there is also something interesting about this way of thinking for organisations too, in learning how to cope with criticism of how things are done. Says Coffils, "The more critical or reflective you can be of yourself and your processes, the more agile you become. The more you change, the more you develop" (Coffils, 2016, Authors in Conversation).

In reflecting on the role of outcomes in youth-led practice, Mark Miller acknowledges the very real pressure and expectation of visible outcomes and the fact that institutional and public outcomes can often hinder in-depth collaborative, autonomous and agency-driven work. But, he also believes there is opportunity for organisations to learn from the process and outcomes of youth programming. Miller says:

> It can be beneficial and important for young people to understand the structures, expectation, strategies and the opportunities that exist within our organisations. Organisational change through diversity of artists, audience, programme, digital media, curators, learning staff may begin to happen when

process, knowledge, structure and culture of the galleries and museums are shared and understood (Miller, 2016, Email correspondence with Authors).

On Reflection: A Conversation Concludes

We now return to the reflective dialogue recorded in 2016 between the authors to make some concluding remarks about collaboration and cooperation using a conversational format. The authors take it in turns to ask and respond to questions and remarks. In conclusion the authors contend that cooperation was observed alongside keeping independence for each of the organisations. In terms of the co-presence and premise of collaboration the following issues are discussed as they emerged from the reflective dialogue: asking more of partners aims; responding to difficult questions; collaboration as collision, invisible hours; asking why?; balancing work with both individual participants and stakeholders; unexpected agency; necessity of impacting the whole organisation; time to establish; sustainability and tangible legacies. The next section presents the authors in reflective conversation from the perspective of working collaboratively after completing two peer-led youth projects, one long project from 2009-2013 (LVYAP) involving both authors: Jo Higgins (JH) and Sarah Coffils (SC) and a shorter instance in 2015 (KPAP), involving one author, Jo Higgins.

> **JH**: Given that some time has now passed since LVYAP ended, what have been your biggest takeaways, in terms of the way you work as the head of education, how you program peer-led learning and approach future partnerships?
>
> **SC**: I think I would ask more of partners and offer more in terms of the transparency of aims and difficulties. It comes back to the agency question and re-considering the project's problems. If I had my time again I'd ask a lot more of each of those people and those organisations. I would also have been less afraid of potential conflict. I think that I wasn't really able to open up enough space for us to be critical of each other. We co-operated well I think, we kept our independence, our own separate programs, and I would still say that's a good thing. But I think it would have been useful to have a few more moments where we were able to really ask difficult questions or to sit and debate and discuss - to ask questions of the project that we didn't entirely know the answers to. At the time it seemed difficult to open up those questions as the lead partner, as we felt the need to demonstrate where we were heading and what we could offer. But again, to be more transparent might have opened up opportunities for collaboration sooner.
>
> I think this idea of celebrating difference is an important part of partnership work. Collaboration as collision, or a space to knock us all off the course we're expecting to take. Convergence of ideas and ways of thinking is always a risk in such a small arts sector, and I think that to collaborate or cooperate shouldn't make for less varied practice, but instead offer a space for

advocating for a particular way of working, as was the case with the LVYAP.
What would you take away from these projects in terms of partnership work or working with young people?

JH: Dubbo was a very different entity to LVYAP in terms of the framework and length of the project and so I don't think there was ever really an opportunity for sustained, on-the-ground critical reflection in terms of the partnership there because the focus really was on the participants and working towards their particular outcomes.
I certainly have a real understanding, having worked on both of these projects, of the incredible amount of invisible hours that go into successful cooperation and collaborations. I think for any kind of partnership to really work, or any kind of creative idea, particularly when it comes to working with young people, the things that I have come to value most are empathy, trust and risk taking.
Off the back of these two quite different projects I'm not sure I could propose any singular working model for future partnerships because they're always going to be shaped by the politics and personalities of the stakeholders, aren't they? I think the critical question to ask though must always be: *Why* do we want to do this? - before you go anywhere near the how or when or what – *why* is this important to you, me, us as an organisation? Establishing that common ground and a sense of mutuality about what it is you want to accomplish together enables an honest space where genuine collaboration and risk-taking can occur. That's also going to inform how you work as a project manager.
In Dubbo I was very mindful that I was representing Kaldor Public Art Projects in the region, that it wasn't just me working with out there with a group of teenagers; there were all these other stakeholders. I think when partnership work is developed with the best of intentions, it can be really meaningful but at the same time it's fraught because as the manager of that project you are having to balance so many financial, political, intellectual, pastoral care issues and it can become quite fraught to carve a path through that while constantly questioning whose best interests are at heart. Is it the success of the project? Is it the wellbeing of the participants? Is it the future partnerships? How do all those things get weighed up? I appreciate that knottiness.

SC: I agree, that balance is always difficult to strike, but it often leads to some additional and unanticipated outcomes. One of the biggest takeaways for me was the unexpected agency that came from introducing the five youth panels to each other. Their supergroup idea, to build a new youth group that was entirely independent of all of us - this rebellion gave us something to think about in terms of what we were offering to them and how much we were gaining from having them work with us. Each of the youth groups seemed to have their own language of ideas and expectations that definitely came from the institutions they were working with - the participants were starting to reflect each organisation and its values. The original premise of a youth panel was to bring change to an organisation through the perspective of a young person but instead of agitating who we are, young people start to parrot the way we speak and learn; to become a part of us to ensure they're listened to. I think it's important to acknowledge this problem and ask whether we're allowing young people to challenge us enough? Often young people are given power to programme their own events and activities, but these activities sit outside the main exhibitions programme and within 'education.' Until this work starts to impact the organisation as a whole, the risks it takes will be minimal.

JH: I think if people are prepared to take risks and have difficult conversations but be generous to the process, then really important things can be accomplished and I'd like to see more of it happen here in Australia. The Dubbo project was just a drop in the ocean in terms of testing these models of working here but my biggest takeaway is that it is possible - I'd even go so far as to say it's imperative. Creating partnerships and offering funding for organisations to partner is vital in the current funding climates we're facing. The reality is that this kind of collaborative work does take time to establish, it takes time to build trust and to develop transparent environments and clear communication.

SC: And as we mentioned before, it's almost impossible to do this without someone taking the lead and pushing the partnership forward - and this needs to be a funded position in order to be sustainable. For us the legacy of the LVYAP is the continuing development of REcreativeUK.com as an independent online space for young creatives. Again, this was probably the most unexpected outcome of the project, given the site was made independent very early on in response to the young people who helped design it. Listening to this group and trusting their instinct has meant that the project has continued beyond Louis Vuitton funding and is still developing six years later.

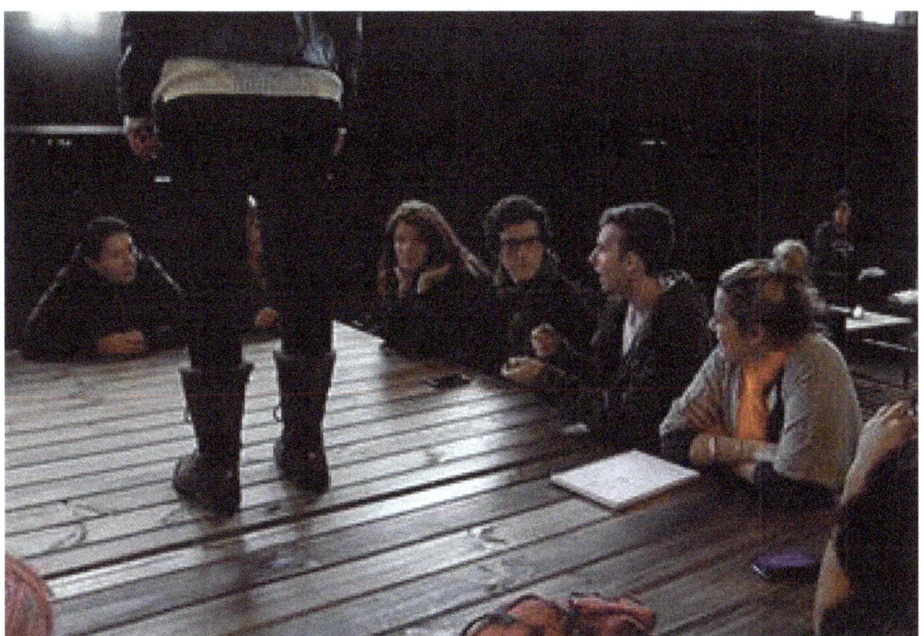

Figure: 9.11 - Workshop with Marina Abramović, Saturday 4 July, Pier 2/3 Walsh Bay. *Image credit: Kaldor Public Art Projects*

JH: The legacy of the KPAP regional project remains to be seen but I like to think that beyond any tangible legacy, there remains a sense of confidence for both the partner organisations and the participants in their tremendous capacity as future agitators for these kinds of projects. I think actually Marina Abramović herself said it best, when she said to the KPAP Regional Project group: "Those ideas that you're scared of - that seem too difficult or even impossible - those are always the best ones" (Abramović, 2015, KPAP Regional Project).

Acknowledgements

Kent Buchanan, Curator, Western Plains Cultural Centre, Dubbo, Australia; Lottie Consalvo, Artist; Ann Gilmore, Young People and Teachers Programmer at the Royal Academy of Arts, UK; Margot Heller, Director, South London Gallery, UK; Mark Miller, Circuit Programme National Lead, Convenor: Young People's Programs at Tate Britain and Modern, UK; Dr Esther Sayers, Lecturer, Centre for Arts and Learning, Goldsmiths' College, University of the Arts London, UK; Imara Savage, Theatre Director; Sue Saxon, Education & Public Programs Manager, Kaldor Public Art Projects, Australia; Nicola Sim, Doctoral Researcher, Tate and the University of Nottingham, UK; Leyla Tahir, Assistant Curator, Young People's Programs, Tate,

UK; Daniel Wallis, Educator, formerly Southbank Centre, UK; Ashley Whitfield, Educator, formerly Young People's Coordinator, South London Gallery, UK.

REFERENCES

Allen, F. ed. (2011). *Education, Documents of Contemporary Art*, Whitechapel Gallery: London.

Abramović, M. (2015). Talk with KPAP Regional Project Group.

Bishop, C. (2006). The Social Turn: Collaboration and Its Discontents, *Artforum,* February, 178-183.

Bishop, C. ed. (2006). *Participation, Documents of Contemporary Art*, Whitechapel Gallery: London.

Bratman, M. (2013). *Shared Agency: A Planning Theory of Acting Together*. Oxford University Press.

Buchanan, K. (2016). Email correspondence with Authors, 26 April.

Butler, D., & Reiss, V. (2007). *Art of Negotiation*, Arts Council England. UK.

Coffils, S. (2016). Authors in Conversation. April.

Curatorial Dictionary (2016). Collaboration. Participation. Retrieved 20 April 2016 from:http://tranzit.org/curatorialdictionary/index.php/dictionary/collaboration/

Cutler, A. (2010). What Is To Be Done, Sandra? Learning in Cultural Institutions of the Twenty-First Century, *Tate Papers,* no.13, Spring. Retrieved 15 April 2016 from: http://www.tate.org.uk/research/publications/tate-papers/13/what-is-to-be-done-sandra-learning-in-cultural-institutions-of-the-twenty-first-century/

Gilmore, A. (2016). Email correspondence with Authors 22 April.

Harding, A. ed. (2005). *Magic Moments, Collaboration between artists and young people*, Black Dog Publishing: London.

Higgins, J. (2016). Authors in Conversation. April.

———. (2015). A live blog of Kaldor Public Art Project's pilot regional engagement program with Dubbo Regional Gallery. Retrieved from http://kaldorpublicartprojects.tumblr.com/ 19 April 2016.

———. (2015). Kaldor Pilots Regional Education Project, Museums & Galleries NSW, 2 May. Retrieved from http://mgnsw.org.au/sector/news/kaldor-pilots-regional-education-project/

———. (2015). Lessons Learned, Museums & Galleries NSW, 23 June - Retrieved from http://mgnsw.org.au/sector/news/lessons-learnt-kaldor-progress-report/

———. (2015). More Marina Magic, Museums & Galleries NSW, 11 July - Retrieved from http://mgnsw.org.au/articles/more-marina-magic/

Higgins, J., & Coffils, S. (2016). Authors in Conversation, April.

Lind, M. (2007). The Collaborative Turn. In: Billing, J., Nilsson, L. and Lind, M. *Taking the Matter into Common Hands: On Contemporary Art and Collaborative Practices*, Black Dog Publishing: London, pp. 15-31.

Linzer, D., & Munley, M. E. (2015). *Room to Rise: The Lasting Impact of Intensive Teen Programs in Art Museums,* Whitney Museum of American Art, New York. Retrieved 10 April 2016 from: http://whitney.org/Education/Teens/RoomToRise

Lynch, B. (2011). *Whose Cake is it anyway? A collaborative investigation into engagement and participation in 12 museums and galleries in the UK*, Paul Hamlyn Foundation, London. Retrieved from http://www.phf.org.uk/publications/whose-cake-anyway/

Miller, M. (2016). Email correspondence with Authors, 30 April.

REcreativeUK.com. (2016). Retrieved 20 April 2016 from: http://www.REcreativeUK.com

Rosso, N. (2010). Youth-led Practice in Galleries, Museums and Archives, *engage.* Retrieved 10 April, 2016 from: http://www.engage.org/downloads/ylp_2010.pdf

Sayers, E. (2016). Email correspondence with Authors, 19 April.

Sim, N. (2015). Retrieved 10 April 2016 from: https://circuit.tate.org.uk/2015/09/in-a-relationship-its-complicated/.

Sim, N. (2016). Email correspondence with Authors, 23 April.

Steedman, M. ed. (2012). *Gallery as Community, Art, Education, Politics,* Bloomsbury Academic: London.

Tahir, L. (2016). Email correspondence with Authors, 23 April.

Wallis, D. (2016). Email correspondence with Authors, 23 April.

Whitfield, A. (2016). Email correspondence with Authors, 23 April.

CHAPTER 10

Digital Storytelling and Organic Theater: Pedagogies in 21st Century Learning

Marty Otañez and James Walsh

ABSTRACT

21st century learning is experiencing a dramatic change with instructors and students in roles as co-teachers to promote culturally appropriate and community driven learning strategies. Digital storytelling is a process of producing first-person narratives about three minutes long with audio narration, personal photographs and background music. In digital storytelling, the process of students' making videos about course topics in a group setting where collective solidarity is achieved is just as important as the final video. Similarly, organic theater is a collective process where individuals working in a non-hierarchical manner (e.g. without a director) and building on multiple experiences explore history and social justice through the art of theater. Our case study on contemplative (self-reflective) pedagogies compares digital storytelling and organic theater in the classroom for the first time, contributing a culture of trans-disciplinary scholarship and standards setting for instructors with a desire to promote peer-to-peer teaching through arts-based approaches. We applied digital storytelling (Otañez) and organic theater (Walsh) in our separate university courses, using data collection strategies such as brief survey questionnaires, videography and participant observation on students' engagement. In the spirit of transdisciplinary and collaborative research, we present our work in a diverse manner. Otañez showcases one student and her digital story and Walsh illuminates patterns associated with group-based, student theater performances. The juxtaposition of the two approaches and our research partnerships reveal a positive impact on learning outcomes and an emerging approach to contemplative pedagogies that is responsive to instructors who love teaching and doing ethical educational research.

INTRODUCTION

A theme in our teaching university-level courses is a shift from reliance on lectures and prescriptive teaching to student-led teaching and cooperative learning to encourage mindfulness and encourage peer-to-peer and arts-based learning. Marty Otañez, Associate Professor in the Anthropology Department at the University of Colorado Denver (UCD) and instructor for the course "Cannabis Cultures," and James

Walsh, Clinical Assistant Professor in the Political Science Department at UCD and instructor for the course Immigration Politics, also believe that community engagement is vital to encouraging students to see their education as something more than a utilitarian exercise in gathering knowledge. Together, we have 25 years of social science teaching experience with diverse students in ten institutions of higher learning in the U.S. Separately we have more than fourteen years of integrating politically engaged and arts-based pedagogy in the classroom, placing us in an excellent position to examine participatory practice in classrooms and engage in transdisciplinary research on teaching strategies.

This chapter is organized in two sections: digital storytelling and organic theater teaching approaches, and the influence of the approaches on students' learning outcomes. The project was designed to promote innovative practices to engage students directly with compelling social issues and with disenfranchised communities. Our research question was How can digital storytelling and organic theater approaches to teaching improve peer-to-peer learning for university students and transform teaching and engagement strategies for faculty? We applied digital storytelling and organic theater in under-graduate level university courses in cultural anthropology and political science, using data collection strategies such as brief survey questionnaires, videography and participant observation on students' engagement. Our findings demonstrate a positive impact on learning outcomes and an emerging approach to contemplative pedagogies that is responsive to the needs and priorities of instructors who love teaching and doing ethical educational research.

Our approach to 21st century learning is to view the classroom as a creative workshop setting where students and instructors engage in diverse learning strategies. Digital storytelling is a method and process of producing first-person narratives about three minutes long with audio narration, personal photographs and background music. In digital storytelling, the process of students' making videos about course topics in a group setting where collective solidarity is achieved is just as important as the final video. Similarly, organic theater is a collective process where individuals working in a non-hierarchical manner (e.g. without a director) and building on multiple experiences, explore history, political science, or some other social justice-related discipline through the art of theater. Otañez with expertise in digital storytelling and Walsh with expertise in organic theater, worked together for the first time to contribute a culture of transdisciplinary scholarship and develop standards of teaching for instructors with a desire to promote peer-to-peer teaching through arts-based approaches. The principles creating a safe, humanizing classroom space for students to engage in peer-to-peer learning, and building innovative community partnerships and expanding the classroom into the community through arts-based forms of student learning and assessment (Nasir 2013, p. 131) provide the basis of our pedagogies and teaching strategies.

Organic Theater is an exercise in empowering students to create their own narratives around themes and ideas directly related to the course. In small groups, the students turn a topic into a story-based presentation that is performed in the classroom, usually at the end of the semester. The only parameters that students are presented with are that the presentation must be theatrical and that it should be between ten and twenty minutes in length. Students are encouraged to simply tell a story and to tell it without a script or rigid structure. They are encouraged to use poetry, music, movement, and visuals to enhance their presentation. This open process invites students to share their most creative ideas, to translate sometimes dense and scholarly material into a language and format that speaks to their peers. This creativity in turn invites other groups to match the intensity and ingenuity of the performances, raising the level of the classroom entirely and building a new kind of teacher-student relationship and interaction, one that is more akin to the visions of Paulo Freire (1970) and Augusto Boal (2000). Through our pilot study of digital storytelling and organic theater, we contribute to new dialogue among social scientists and other educators who are exploring transformative pedagogy and co-authorship in arts-based research.

Literature Review

Digital storytelling is a field of classroom-based inquiry and practice among scholars who conduct image-driven, ethnographic, and public projects. Individuals apply digital storytelling to gender justice (Hill, 2010), pedagogy (Fletcher & Cambre 2009), visual-based theory (Benmayor, 2009), and new media technology (Biella, 2008). Digital storytelling overlaps with and is historically linked to photovoice approaches (Castleden, 2008), telenovelas (Tufte, 2000), video diaries (Roberts, 2011), 'tabletop videos' (Maier & Fisher 2006) and therapeutic films (Johnson 2008). Digital storytelling is presented as a compelling method and intervention in community based participatory research (Gubrium & Turner 2011) with implications for the decolonization of research (Salazar, 2005; Willox, 2012) and the politics of representation (Rony, 1996). Recently, the field of digital storytelling as a process has been associated with an increase in social wellness (Otañez & Lakota 2015) and collaborative story sharing where individuals narrate experiences in a visual format to promote social and political action (Gubrium, 2015). Educators who rely on didactic and written-word teaching approaches are challenged by the digital storytelling process that requires parity in terms of classroom time devoted to traditional text and visual image production (Otañez & Guerrero 2015, Otañez & Lakota, 2015).

The use of organic theater in the classroom is rooted in the work of Paulo Freire (1970) and Augusto Boal (2000). Freire wrote Pedagogy of the Oppressed in the 1970s, based upon his experiences in teaching literacy to campesinos in Brazil. Freire wrote about the traditional banking method of education, in which students are viewed as empty vessels to be filled with data, as a form of oppression. Boal in Theater of the Oppressed examines tactics and strategies for the use of theater for direct political engagement. For Freire and Boal, education is effective when students are engaging in dialogue and wrestling with social issues through creative and open expression. Students are considered as subjects instead of objects in the classroom. Organic theater turns the classroom upside down, empowering students to teach each other and engaging with marginalized and quiet students whose creative potential is not realized through traditional teaching methods. Walsh, also borrows from the methods of Denver's Romero Theater Troupe, which Walsh founded ten years ago, utilizing community-based and consensus-driven approaches (Kilman, 2014a, 2014b).

METHODOLOGY

The study design features digital storytelling, organic theater and ethnographic digital media analysis. The authors in their separate courses at UCD in August-December 2015 applied a multi-method, qualitative framework. Participant observation, or watching cultural activities with a critical eye, the authors conducted with students in each of the authors' courses with note taking (e.g. descriptive and preliminary analysis) was conducted in digital storytelling and organic theater activities. Periodic field notes written by the authors that included descriptions of production activities and students' experiences and preliminary analysis of cultural information about students' creative work routines and group activities collected by the authors were created after each class period on laptop computers. Methods included pre- and post-surveys with about ten questions on each survey administered to students involved in Otañez' course "Cannabis Cultures" and Walsh's course "Immigration Politics." Post-surveys were administered in the last week of classes. Student evaluations administered by the university after each course are data that informed the analysis. In addition, paper assignments related to course activities in the study informed the analysis. Walsh used archives of student evaluations and paper assignments from past courses. Individuals in Otañez' course were presented with the option to attend and present their videos in a public screening in a community (off-campus) venue. Two study participants in Otañez' course attended and presented their videos at the event, and an additional six students agreed to screen their videos publicly but not attend the event. The public event was videotaped for research, archival and dissemination purposes. Selected excerpts such as a semi-structured audience discussion with storytellers were transcribed and informed analysis and write-up.

Eight out of 14 students in Otañez' course participated in the study. All of the 21 students in Walsh's class participated in the organic theater exercise at El Centro Humanitario, and 11 out of 21 students participated in the study. Data such as student information and materials pertaining to digital storytelling and organic theater from non-participating students were excluded from analysis and research. Each study participant signed a consent form and media release form. Our institution's human subject research committee approved the study.

Each of the authors and their students met separately during regular class times during the term and performed video creation and organic theater performance processes as routine class activities (Table: 10.1). The digital storytelling process included students creating a narrative about a course topic (about 300 words long) and each student producing one, 3-minute digital story. Students received a tutorial in video editing to develop basic proficiency in media-making. The organic theater production process included students in groups assigned by the instructor creating short plays (15 minutes in length) that explored stories directly related to the central themes and politics of immigration.

Digital Storytelling	Organic Theater
• Recording students' voices with students reading their scripts • Storyboarding by writing a rough paper sketch of the student's video • Selecting source material and digitizing personal photographs • Choosing music and sound effects • Using video editing software such as Adobe Premiere Pro • Applying transitions and other effects in the video editing program • Watching the digital stories with other study participants or alone with the instructor	• Selecting specific themes around immigration politics and exploring the pertinent and defining research and literature surrounding that theme • Choosing a fiction or nonfiction story to build a play around. • Shaping the story as a team using the organic theater process, which combines a series of practice runs with dialogue, using a consensus model to shape the play and the values underlying the play • Rehearsing with feedback from instructor • Integrating other art forms into the play, such as music, spoken word, and photos

Table: 10.1 - Key Activities in Courses Designed to Promote Contemplative Pedagogies.

It is worth nothing that traditional university cultures, from our experiences, perceive the production of videos or performance of group skits in course assignments as less rigorous than writing papers or taking exams. Partly as a response to this limited understanding of arts-based pedagogies and partly as an effort to promote educational development among students, Otañez in his courses requires students to write a project plan, visit in-person a university librarian for steps in guided research, produce an annotated bibliography with ten or more sources that directly link to themes raised in student narratives, and write a companion paper with critical reflection on the topic and explicit links to five or more course concepts or issues.

In Otañez's course, students had the option to attend and show their videos in tandem with short theater performances of students in Walsh's course at a public screening in a day laborer's community center located three kilometers from the university on 16 November 2015. The timing of the event corresponded with the actual meeting time and day of Walsh's class (6-8pm Monday) and a different time of Otañez's class (9-11am Monday). Walsh required his students to attend and present at the event, which is consistent with Walsh's group-based approach to organic theater in the classroom. Otañez made attendance and screening of videos for his students optional, following the digital storytelling process where individuals are not compelled to publicly share their stories if they choose to keep the story private. This is done to avoid any potential re-traumatization of an individual reliving an experience during public story sharing. These details partly explain why eight out of fourteen students in Otañez's course agreed to publicly show their videos and only two students attended the event. All of Walsh's students attended and participated in the group theater performances at the event. Overall about 40 individuals participated in the event. Four performances by Walsh's students were conducted and digital stories created by Otañez's students were screened in between every skit. After each digital story and skit, audience members, skit performers and storytellers engaged in a semi-structured discussion. All the activities, including audience discussion with student presenters, were videotaped for research and dissemination purposes.

PARTICIPANTS

Participants included university students (ages 18-65) enrolled in Otañez's "Cannabis Cultures" course and Walsh's "Immigration Politics" course at UCD in August-December 2015. The courses were lower-division and elective courses, open to students from different academic disciplines and in different stages of their university training. Details on age, gender, socio-economic status and academic course of study were not collected in the study. No experience with digital storytelling or organic theater was required to participate in the courses. Audience members at the public screening of student work included students from other courses and the general public with an interest in project themes. Forty individuals participated in the screening as audience members, 21 students from Walsh's course, and two from Otañez's course. The day laborer's center El Centro Humanitario located two miles from UCD was selected as the venue to enhance the experiential learning aspect of the project and due to location nearby the university.

PROCEDURES

We applied ethnographic content analysis (ECA) to data collected in the study. ECA is a version of the classic content analysis defined as a "technique for making replicable and valid inferences from texts (and other meaningful matter) to the contexts of their use" (Krippendorff 2004). Classic content analysis focuses on fairly rigid predefined categories and numeric data (Merriam 1998). ECA is guided by predefined categories and other categories that are expected to emerge throughout the study. This method is based on an orientation toward constant discovery, and uses descriptive information to highlight the contexts in which the data were created and in which the data are currently being reread and analyzed. Since the data set was relatively small and we are presenting in this analysis one aspect of our study, we used selective, non-probability (e.g. purposive) sampling to identify data that corresponded to key themes to help us answer our research question. For instance, purposive sampling was used to select Pam's (pseudonym) digital storytelling case for the analysis. Other students and their videos were not selected for this analysis and are featured in a different publication. The selection was made based on knowledge of the participants in the digital storytelling portion of the study (N=8) and the research purpose- to apply and interrogate digital storytelling and organic theater teaching approaches and their influence on students' learning outcomes. Rigor of analysis was obtained by triangulating data by crosschecking patterns and emergent themes with each other as well as by returning to the lived experiences and health narratives of project participants to determine how well data reflects the field. Health narratives in this context refer to students' oral stories about their wellness experiences associated with cannabis and other forms of healing such as synthetic drugs. Otañez checked in with students on a daily basis through informal conversations about their narratives and challenges students may have had or overcame with the story sharing process. Input from students was documented in field notes and contrasted with themes in literature on cannabis and other wellness practices. This was done to ensure internal coherence of the analysis and validity with relevant narratives and personal experiences discovered through other research.

Study data are students' responses to the pre- and post-surveys about their experiences with digital storytelling and organic theater, responses to self-assessment on their own levels of engagement in the creative processes, narratives such as digital storytelling scripts and organic theater scripts, companion and reflection papers produced by students as part of the course assignments, and transcripts from discussions among audience members and students in the public event. Analysis was conducted in a purposive manner with selection criteria based on data that represented in a holistic manner the project focus on learning outcomes and transformational pedagogies. We acknowledge our interpretive schemes comprised of our political and pedagogical biases that undergird our study, viewing them as strengths in the project. This approach helps to advance the kind of deliberate research designs needed to implement transformational pedagogies and promote diverse interpretive frames among students.

Results and Data Analysis

Digital Storytelling

Videos created by students in Otañez' course "Cannabis Cultures" were about individual's experiences with cannabis or their views about the legalization of cannabis in Colorado. Course readings as well as an annotated bibliography created by each student after an in-person meeting with a university librarian were resources used by students to think more deeply about their emerging narratives and inform story writing. Out of thirteen students in the course, eight agreed to participate in the study. The students completed consent and media forms and a pre-survey in the second week of the course. Students completed post-surveys in the last week of the term. Two videos were about cannabis as medicine to address anxiety, two addressed personal cannabis use, and other videos were about cannabis decriminalization, cannabis tourism, employment issues, and industry representations of gender.

Eight students completed pre- and post-surveys. Responses to the question about previous experience with digital storytelling were "Yes" (4) and "No" (4). Data on level of student understanding of digital storytelling in the pre-test are "Above average" (1), "Average" (5), and "Below average" (2). The question about preparedness to use digital storytelling in the classroom yielded the responses "Very" (1), "Somewhat" (2), "Not very" (2), and "Not at all" (2), with one student writing "Somewhere between "Somewhat" and "Very." Students were asked in the post-survey "Would you recommend this class to your friends and colleagues?" One student said, "Yes! I've learned so much about myself but I've also refined my research skills" (emphasis in the original text). Another student responded, "Yes! This class taught me so many skills (writing, editing, and creative design) other than the information on cannabis and faces I as a 'stoner' did not know. Not to mention the public speakers were not all forced but took their time. I feel like this class is the first of many kinds, I feel like I should have paid more for this class! Awesome!" Other students' responded in the positive and with the same enthusiasm for the course.

Pam (age 20) was one of two students in the course who attended the optional screening of videos in a public setting and outside of regular class time. Her involvement in the screening, including discussion with audience members, and in all other project activities, makes her case representative of the key elements in the digital storytelling process. Pam's case is a prototypical example of a digital storyteller in a university setting, demonstrating the nuances of personal narratives and the subjective nature of arts-based coursework. In "Knowledge is Power" Pam narrates an incident when she experienced a severe allergic reaction to Percocet prescribed to her by her doctor for pain after throat surgery due to enlarged tonsils at age 10. The experience influenced her outlook as a young adult that physicians in the U.S. over-prescribe Percocet and other narcotics for pain relief. The sub-text of her story is that cannabis, if it is associated with fewer allergic reactions by its users, is a suitable alternative for individuals who are allergic to certain synthetic drugs. Pam said in her final companion paper that focused on themes of her digital cannabis story:

> I want other people to do research on what an actual allergic reaction looks like compared to a simple side effect and to know how dangerous the substance can be. I want people to understand that there are better alternatives than using synthetic chemicals that are created in a lab. If the allergic reactions in cannabis are not harmful, then they should be used instead life-threatening narcotics. It is important for people to know what they are putting in their body and narcotics are highly addictive where cannabis is not (Pam, 2 December 2015, Final Companion Paper).

Her final video included audio-narration based on a written script, photos, words on screen (title and closing credits), transitions between photographs, image movement (e.g. zooms and pans), and background music. All students in the course were required to record audio narration with the instructor using his professional audio recording devices to ensure optimal sound quality. Relative to her peers, Pam worked independently editing her video and did not seek additional help from the instructor, except prior to screening for some last minute adjustments to prepare the video for public presentation. She worked with two musician friends to compose an instrumental song for the video. Therefore, Pam's video included over two-dozen photographs that corresponded with her narrative. She received excellent marks in the class and on all assignments, including the research proposal submitted as her final project based on themes of her video.

Pam considers herself as an engaged learner. In the pre-test, she said, "I love learning about things I have never heard of digital storytelling." She is interested to develop her skill set to have an impact with her academic training beyond the classroom. "I would love to find new tools to better explain a topic especially that would reach a larger audience." She indicated that she had never heard of digital storytelling before enrolling in the course and that she was unprepared to use the digital storytelling process in the classroom or community. According to Pam, at the beginning of the semester she described her level of understanding of digital storytelling as average. In the post-test, Pam was asked again about her level of understanding of the digital storytelling process. She responded to the question with 'average,' indicating no change of understanding from the beginning and end of the semester. Pam's response may reflect the student's genuine view that she experienced little or no change in understanding. Alternatively, it may suggest that the student under-estimated her own learning or that she under-valued the quality of her visual work. Pam was one of the only students who worked virtually alone on her project and its quality especially along audio lines was inferior to the other students' videos created in the course.

When asked about what the digital story meant to her, Pam said, "It's a personal story that I hope people can start to educate themselves before consumption" of cannabis. The instructor on several occasions in class encouraged students to use existing friends and colleagues to collaborate on the digital story. Pam followed the suggestion and identified musicians to work with and create background music for her video. When asked in the self-assessment about one compelling memory of the overall digital storytelling creative process, Pam said, "I enjoyed working with the two males who helped create the music. I was not happy with the amount of pictures I put in. I wish I could have polished it more." Although Pam shared that she put too many photographs in her video, she stated that to her the most compelling picture was the one "with my mouth open sleeping is the whole point of the project. It's personal and important." She was proud of her piece and willing to share the video to broader audiences, including individuals who are opposed to legal adult use of cannabis. When asked, Is there one person or community group that you wish to show your digital story? She replied, "I would like to show this at my work [at the health care center] to inform them of the opposite side they aren't used to." In her companion reflection paper, Pam discussed the dissemination of creative work using non-traditional approaches and said, "My digital story demonstrates my ability to communicate ideas about anthropology verbally and aesthetically[…]I do not know many people who just read papers, but I do know a lot of people who search the Internet for hours looking at various videos."

Three weeks after Pam completed the digital storytelling assignment, she presented "Knowledge is Power" at the public screening event. At the end of video, Pam engaged in discussion for seven minutes with audience members. One of the students in Walsh's course performed a group skit during the event, asked Pam to discuss in more detail the issue of cannabis and its ability to alleviate symptoms of mental illness. The audience member indicated that Pam's video and other one screened by the second student in Otañez' course, addressed the idea that cannabis may partly promote wellness and alleviate mental health problems. The transcript from the discussion with audience members after the screening of her digital story shows Pam's response.

> That's actually what my next project is going to be. In my final project I want to try to write a research proposal in order [...] to further the advancement of cannabis as medicine. I am really allergic to Percocet and I know that when I was ten years old and if I got the option of taking cannabinoid extract or oil that maybe the worst side effect you get is a rash on your skin. It is so much better than having to go to the hospital to keep you alive. I think that is why a lot of [students in the class] did it on health aspects because being in college you tend to have more anxiety and depression. You know because we are on our own. I view it as medicine (Pam, 16 November 2015, Discussion with audience members).

Another audience member at the screening and with proficiency in the digital storytelling approach, inquired about the production process. She asked, "In creating a film that's more for public consumption rather than if you were writing a paper, how did you weigh what you felt comfortable with, like putting in film or putting in a paper; would that have been different, what you would have shared?" Pam responded that digital stories are easier to watch than reviewing an academic paper. "I am so bored. I don't want to read an eight-page paper but I could watch a two-minute video. I am down with it [audience laughter]...put that on Facebook or YouTube or whatever." This exchange shows the connection between pedagogy and learning outcomes, with individuals connecting on a human level over knowledge dissemination and digital storytelling.

Organic Theater

Students in Walsh's "Immigration Politics" course created 8-10 minute skits based upon research they had done into their own ancestral history and traditions. Four groups, consisting of 4-5 students each, built skits around the stories about immigration, identity, and culture that the students gathered from informal oral histories collected from family elders. Many of the students who are the first or second generation in their families to live in the U.S. chose to share stories from their lives that they considered relevant to immigration, identity, and culture. Thus, each skit consisted or three or four short stories blended together in creative ways.

Pre and post surveys were administered to the students in the "Immigration Politics" course that participated in the organic theater exercise. Pre-surveys were administered during the second week of the semester. Post-surveys were administered during the last week of class, after the public performances at El Centro. It's clear from the pre-surveys, which measured the students' previous experiences with organic theater, that very few of the students had any kind of background or knowledge about organic theater prior to the class. In fact, only one answered yes when asked if they had any previous involvement in organic theater. On these pre-surveys, 90% of students rated their level of understanding of organic theater as either below average or average. When asked how prepared the students felt for using organic theater in the classroom, only one replied very prepared. The remaining nine respondents rated themselves as somewhat or not very prepared. The post-surveys revealed a significant shift in students' understanding and comfort with the practice and purpose of organic theater in their education. When asked to describe their level of understanding of organic theater on these post-surveys, all of the students marked average or above average. Only two students described themselves as not prepared to use organic theater in the classroom or community.

Student comments indicate that the purpose of organic theater was clear for most students. One student responded, "I am someone who has to interact with the material in order to learn," describing organic theater as a way to "bridge the learning that happens between teacher and student." Another declared that, because of the theater project, the class was "the only class I have ever had that will have a lasting memory." One student was struck by the way that s/he felt connected with classmates after the plays, writing, "bonding with my group mates was the best part." Another identified the most satisfying element of the project to be "the way we came together in the group and with our professor."

Some students were able to identify a much larger and broader use for organic theater. One declared, "I need to be more personally engaged with material instead of tests." Another identified that organic theater can be a tool for "processing trauma, community development, breaking down social barriers and stigma." This same student wrote of organic theater as:

> so powerful in expanding and engaging individual and group capacities for not only learning information, but feeling, understanding, and relating to experience. It is one very potent tool educators can use to combat the typically alienating, disempowering, and sterile format of institutionalized education (Student in Immigration Politics course, 16 November 2015).

Gently assisting students who feel great anxiety around performing or being on stage is a consistent challenge. A few of the students shared on the post-surveys that they had some initial anxiety around the thought of acting in class. One wrote, "Acting was hard for me, but I'm happy I did it. It was comforting with guidance and structure, so it was a struggle to find my own way." Over the years, I have learned to offer students many options around how they can participate in the project. These include research, writing, assembling background images and music, narration, and of course acting. When presented with these many options, students always find a role that feels comfortable.

All of these themes are consistent with the reactions this author has received from students over the course of sixteen years of using organic theater in history and political science courses at the University of Colorado Denver. During these sixteen years, I have led 104 classes through this exercise, involving an estimated 5,000 students. In all of these courses, students have been required to turn in reflection essays about their experiences with the organic theater projects. This stack of reflections essay is nearly three feet high, and full of important insights about the pedagogical value of this process. The essays have consistently revealed a deep hunger among students for a new way of teaching and learning, one that empowers students to teach from their own world experiences and to be active learners. The following excerpts are just a few examples from these past reflection essays. This reflection of one former student—about a group skit that explored the story of 19th century resistance by a group of Irish miners known as the Molly Maguires—touches on the emotional dimension of theater and the bonds that this creates within the classroom:

> When I learned my group would be learning about the Molly Maguires, I was actually quite ecstatic. I was also excited about dipping my toes in a new kind of learning experience, that of learning through historical theater. The aspect of this project that excited me the most was actually living the history, instead of just learning about it. Instead of sitting in a lecture hall listening to a professor talk on and on about the Molly Maguires with my attention slowly slipping away, I got to go to the front of the class to be a Molly Maguire. By putting myself into the shoes of a Molly Maguire, I not only learned about the facts, but I felt an immediate connection to the Molly Maguires. I gained a deeper understanding of what it is like to be a Molly Maguire, as when I crossed the threshold from 2010 to 1863, the peers in my group crossed the threshold with me and they were no longer my classmates, they were my family (Former student in Immigration History course, 15 November 2006, comments on end-of-semester reflection essay).

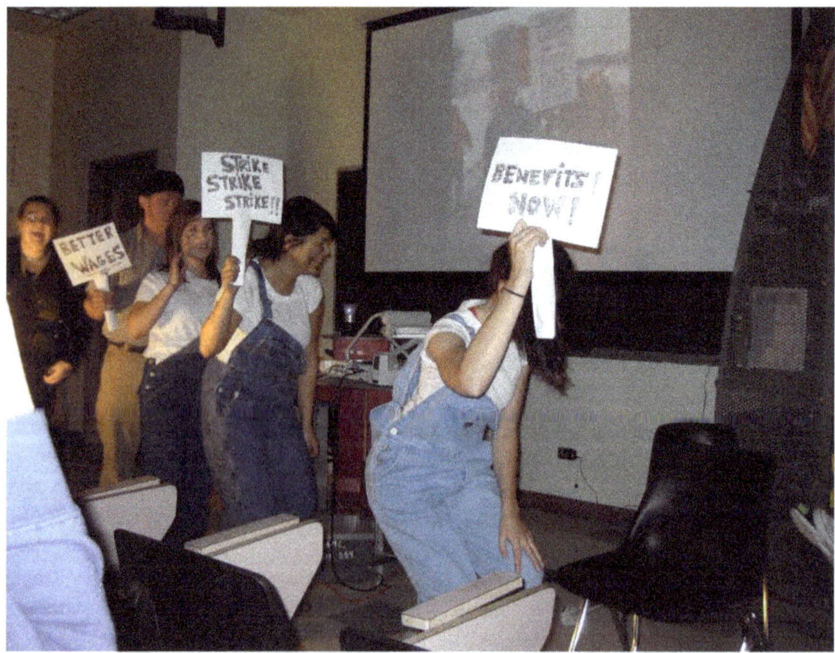

Figure: 10.1 - Students performing Molly Maguire skit; Fall (2006).
Image credit: Jim Walsh

Organic theater offers students a new form of agency in their education and allows them to interpret complex material often in a spontaneous way and in community with their peers. This dynamic and anxiety-provoking experience contributes directly to student retention of information. For nearly twenty years, I have run into former students who quickly mention the character that they played in my classrooms. The following student reflection gives voice to the idea that the arts inhabit a central role in retaining and understanding information:

In my experience with the group project I thoroughly enjoyed it. At first I had my worries just because I am not one to say a lot in class, let alone act. But, it was fun and great way to learn history without having my nose stuck in a book. This activity helped me make a connection with history, making it something a bit more personal than just trying to memorize and learn the facts. While watching the other plays I got the sense of attachment to the characters, and felt I will retain more (Former student in Immigration History course, 15 November 2006, comments on end-of-semester reflection essay).

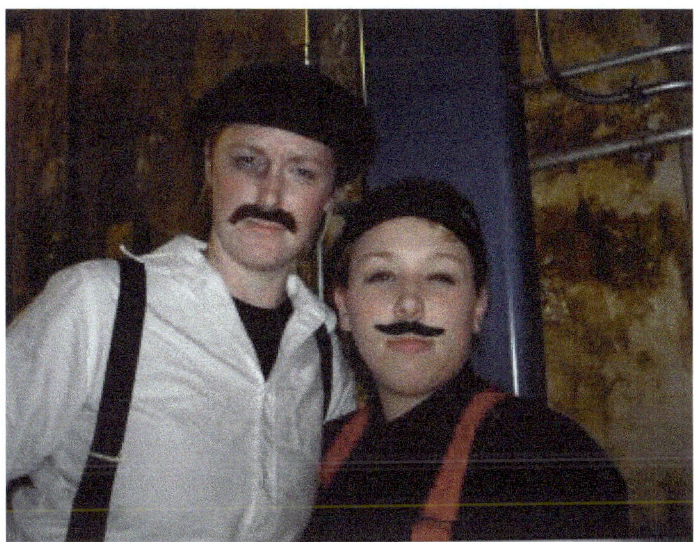

Figure: 10. 2 - Students in Irish in America course prepare for performance, Fall (2006). *Image credit: Jim Walsh*

This student reflection touches on the role that theater plays in developing human empathy and breaking down political issues into their basic human dimensions:

> I began this semester thinking that I knew what to expect from the final historical theater project. I thought that it would be just like it was last semester, but I was wrong—extremely wrong. The stories that lie behind individuals are a lot stronger than those about countries. It's different when you speak about all illegal immigrants than it is when you take one illegal immigrant's life story into account. The presentations took individual stories

> out of the whole and made us relive those horrible moments of history. As human beings, it is easier for us to understand each other on a personal level. For me, playing Javier had a great impact on the way I view illegal immigrants. (Former student in Immigration History course, 15 November 2006, comments on end-of-semester reflection essay).

These reflection essays touch upon important and recurrent themes with organic theater. The most consistent of these themes is transformation. It's clear from the essays that many students find the space for transformation in the creative and challenging process of creating theater for their peers. Nearly all of them begin with the experience of initial skepticism, such as the following essay from a student in 2008. This student highlights the manner in which theater builds a sense of solidarity in the classroom, which enhances the power and potential of the class:

> Almost everyone quickly dismissed the idea that acting could be anything other than stressful and embarrassing or worse. So the thought of acting out a play or teaching about someone's life in front of an entire class sounded positively dreadful. However, what transpired over the course of preparing for and presenting the play was far from the horror I imagined. My group was assigned the life of Paul Robeson, and the fact that I knew nothing about the man made the climb to thespian courage seem all the more uphill. And herein lies the beauty of the project. Acting may not come naturally, and it may be nerve-wracking in the extreme, but the joy that came from researching this man's life far outweighed the difficulty. This seems to be the hidden component of acting that many would not understand—that developing and respecting the character and seeing life through his or her eyes is this rewarding emotionally and intellectually (Former student in Immigration History course, 15 November 2006, comments on end-of-semester reflection essay).

All of the themes mentioned in the above quotations were apparent on the night that the students performed their skits at El Centro Humanitario. The students talked about the importance of working with their classmates in such an intimate way, the power of learning from personal stories, and the way in which the stories challenged them to think about immigration issues with greater empathy, focusing on simply human dignity. They talked about the anxiety in the room, the way that they relied upon each other, and the importance of hearing questions and comments from the audience. In short, they talked about leaving the performance with a better sense of themselves and of their classroom as a community. This is the magic of theater: it can immediately elevate an intellectual exchange into something much greater that is difficult to define but easy to feel.

DISCUSSION

This research project examined digital storytelling and organic theater and their consequences on peer-to-peer teaching and learning outcomes. The significance of the data findings show that students' experiences varied by courses, and that arts-based pedagogies positively influence students' perceptions of themselves as scholars that can have an impact in communities that universities are designed to serve. Study findings are consistent with transformative creative pedagogical approaches to teaching indicated by Freire (1970) and Gubrium (2015). These authors suggest that creative teaching strategies contribute to individuals taking possession of their learning and developing genuine social connections through knowledge dissemination in public settings. Pam and "Knowledge is Power" featured in this analysis is one representative example of the connection between learning outcomes and the digital storytelling process. Her case is emblematic of students who created personal videos and developed research skills to contextualize issues raised in videos. Pam obtained proficiency in media making while situating her work in the relatively underexplored issue of cannabis-related allergens (Armentia et al. 2010; Ocampo and Rans 2015). She identified a personal narrative in a course assignment and shared the video project with peers in a public setting. Pam, in her final project that built on themes in her digital story, interviewed two physicians to deepen her understanding of possible allergens associated with cannabis and advocate for safe adult use of cannabis for individuals who may be allergic or dissatisfied with synthetic drugs.

Pam in her response to one of the ten questions in the post-test suggests that her level of understanding of digital storytelling did not deepen during the semester. This may indicate a poor delivery of digital storytelling training in the course or Pam simply feels she has an average level of understanding of the process relative to her peers who may have displayed a more comprehensive understanding of digital storytelling at the end of the semester. When asked if she was satisfied or dissatisfied with the digital storytelling training she received in class, Pam said, "I was satisfied with the tutorial in class. I personally should have come in for extra help to polish [my] video. It would have nice to spend more time." Her comments partly relate to her comparing herself to her peers (seven out of fourteen in the course) who visited the instructor on three or more occasions (about 30 minutes each visit) for additional technical support and input on their digital stories. It may be that Pam perceived the production quality of videos produced by students who received one-to-one instruction from the instructor as superior to the quality of videos made by her and students who worked independently or visited the instructor only one or two times for hands-on training. Alternatively, Pam, like many new media makers, may have overlooked or undervalued the new understanding of digital storytelling she developed during the semester. These circumstances and data analysis support the argument that instructors who wish to integrate arts-based strategies in courses need to devote an equal amount of class time as well as assignments to traditional text learning and image-based skills development.

Sixteen years of organic theater in large and small classes have taught this author (Walsh) the same lessons that are reflected in the above small sample of reflection essays. First, the arts carry a kind of participatory magic that transforms the power and creative dynamics of a classroom. When students witness this creative freedom from other students, their attention is maximized. When they witness this from other students, they feel permission to push against their own boundaries and to recreate a classroom away from the traditional top-down banking model, the rote-memorization method that Freire critiques so forcefully. Secondly, the bonds created by the creative process are in themselves a very important element of this learning process. Student learning is transformed when they are learning in community, and from each other. Learning in community and through the arts means that the dialogue and the exchange is free of the programming that a more manicured and canned education—usually in the form of a lecture—usually carries. Organic theater is a difficult process, without clear structure, and with its own kinds of anxiety. It's a very difficult road to walk together. When students traverse this terrain together, they feel a deep and authentic sense of accomplishment and community.

Third, organic theater creates empathy and inspires students to seek out the human dimension to large social issues. By engaging students in emotional and even spiritual ways, organic theater transcends the purely intellectual kinds of exchanges that are permitted in higher education settings. It has the potential to create a less hateful citizenry and to allow students to feel solidarity with communities that they do not share any social or cultural connections to. Lastly, most educators do not venture into such terrain as organic theater because it is a risky endeavor. It involves surrendering the podium, relinquishing control and some of our power, and trusting students to take ownership of the class. Organic theater demands dealing with anxiety, personality conflicts, ego, and perhaps the surfacing of ugly ideas that need to surface in order to be confronted. Anything can happen spontaneously when students take to the stage, and educators need to be ready to respond to anything. It's an enormous risk, but the rewards are transformative.

Reflections of the Authors on the Project

Through our collaborative project we discovered the vast rewards of using these art forms in an educational setting. A classroom that involves digital storytelling and organic theater tends to be more student-centered, more engaged, more interactive, more empathetic, and more tuned in to the world that students inhabit. Students in both classes reported a sense of discovery in their projects, a sense that in sharing pieces of their own stories, they were co-authors in their education and co-producers in the content of their classes.

A classroom that offers students the option of doing either a digital storytelling or an organic theater project (or even choosing from other art and experimental forms) will match more students with the art form that gives most effective voice to their experiences and the growth that has come from those experiences. There is also potential to blend the two into the same presentations. Video clips can easily be integrated into skits and short acting pieces can be used to supplement digital stories and highlight certain points and themes. This kind of blended project should be the focus on future research efforts. We witnessed the potential of this blending on the evening that our students performed. Audience members engaged in thoughtful discussions with students and student-artists through their conversations provided deeper thinking on issues presented in their projects. The following week in each of our class debriefings, students who attended the screening praised the work of students in our respective courses and indicated their strong interest to explore both digital storytelling and organic theater as learning strategies in other university courses and in community settings. The common denominator of our approach is escaping the paradigm that dictates that written work is the only valid kind of student learning assessment. The common denominator is the idea that tapping into students' creativity, narrative, and expression ushers a new kind of energy and temporary collective solidarity into the learning process and into the classroom. The common denominator is a desire to break down and dispense with the old banking method model of education and embrace an approach that is rooted in a desire to empower students.

The following anecdote is an example of this goal: In 2005, after five years of using organic theater in classrooms, Walsh began reaching out to former students to create an all-volunteer community organic theater. Named after former Salvadoran Bishop Oscar Romero, the Romero Troupe (Figure: 10.3) is now nearly twelve years old and carries the tradition and mission of organic theater into the larger Denver community. The troupe operates without a budget or director, and on a consensus model. Nearly 400 people have cycled through the troupe and today roughly 100 people are involved. Nearly half of them are Walsh's former students who were introduced to organic theater in the classroom.

The Romero Troupe operates under the same principles as organic theater in the classroom. Every member of the troupe works together as a community to shape the stories that are told. Members frequently tell their own stories and play themselves. We have discovered the cathartic potential in telling personal stories. The vast majority of the troupe's membership is from working class backgrounds and never had any kind of formal theater training. Instead of "acting," we tend to rely on our intuition, our "gut", to inform us about the human story that we are telling. Most of our stories are constructed without a script, sculpted together by dozens of people who never imagined themselves to be artists. The shows are all free and accessible to those communities that have been priced out of professional theater. Actors can change their lines in the middle of a scene. Our audience members sometimes join us on stage, acting in a scene that they have never rehearsed. Romero Troupe audiences are known for being rowdy and loud, with children running through the theater and sometimes through the middle of the play. The purpose of free organic theater for the Romero Troupe is to return theater to marginalized communities, to empower these communities through telling stories of unknown activists and social movements, and to demonstrate how we have built a very strong, large, and diverse community—some might say a movement—around organic theater and the democratic and consensus structures that come with it.

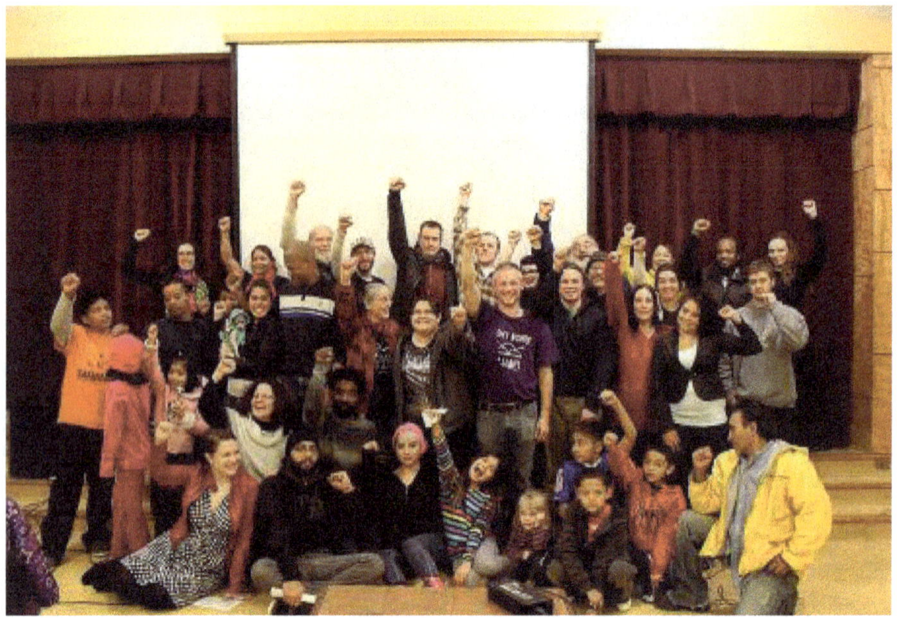

Figure: 10.3 - The Romero Theater Troupe, one of the largest and most diverse arts groups in the U.S, (2013).
Image credit: Michael Kilman.

LIMITATIONS

The authors recognize that these teaching tools are not for every educator. Many times, the digital stories and skits lack a solid narrative, clear connection to the course themes, or any kind of critical analysis. With digital storytelling, instructors need be aware of the possibilities of individuals oversharing personal details or being re-traumatized by revisiting past social problems. Safeguards are to discuss the issues during the introductory part of the assignment and make the public sharing component optional. These may limit any unintended or perceived re-traumatization of individuals who are sharing, sometimes for the first time, painful memories. With organic theater, a skit without much energy or clear message can have a negative and contagious effect on the other groups. It's important for educators to stay as engaged and involved with the groups as possible, during each step of the process. It's also important that educators make themselves available to perform alongside the students if invited to do so. This encourages students to make themselves vulnerable as well and creates a sense of solidarity between the educator and the students. Instructors who use organic theater and digital storytelling in the classroom need watch for negative stereotypes in videos and caricatures in the characters in performances created by students. The remedy is conducting group discussions during pre-screening videos in class and having groups walk through their skits a couple of times before they are performed for the class or the public.

Practical Application to Research Training

Benefits of the study include an increase in knowledge, both in the traditional text form and the visual form, on digital storytelling and organic theater and their influence on students' learning outcomes. Researchers and educators engaged in arts-based teaching strategies may wish to apply digital storytelling and organic theater approaches to contribute to positive class dynamics, humanize social sciences education and increase students' involvement in social and political issues. One of the outcomes of the project was a video produced by UCD of the public screening of student work, http://tinyurl.com/hnsvbc3. The media is publicly available to increase access to project findings and invite researchers and educators to visually document and disseminate innovative pedagogical work. The project video is a resource that complements traditional presentations at professional conferences, text manuscripts, and blog entries and essays about scholarly work shared through social media platforms such as YouTube, Facebook and Twitter.

Future Research

We recommend to educators and researchers in projects that mix different arts-based teaching strategies to apply both strategies in each of their courses. Such classrooms would offer students the opportunity to choose the art form that most closely matches their skills and personality, or develop deep learning and a strong skillset in a specific art form they choose. This would create new levels appreciation and camaraderie among instructors to expand their repertoire of pedagogical tools and community building skills. While the cross-pollination of work may create additional time constraints for instructors in the classroom who seek to develop proficiency in methods, the combination of teaching strategies will open up possibilities for more sharing among students in different classes and community venues. Genuine transdisciplinary work and teaching strategies will help increase parity among didactic styles and more playful activities. Co-authoring study findings is an effective way to share innovative findings, self-reflect on pedagogical practices and build scholarly connections across disciplinary lines.

Conclusion

Digital storytelling and organic theater challenge students to become agents in their education, to merge their own experiences directly to larger disciplines and the issues that these disciplines seek to examine. Inside of this intersection, a transformational contemplation takes place, one that roots student learning in their own experiences. These arts-based strategies also shepherd the learning experience of students into a communal experience, where students are sharing their personal narratives and their connections to the central themes and issues of the class through art and horizontal dialogue. Our study reveals that both processes are deeply contemplative, and frequently transformative, because our students are finding engagement and community and initiative inside of art and the sharing of that art. In order for educators to be comfortable with either digital storytelling or organic theater, they must be willing to surrender much of the structure and focus of a course to the students, while maintaining a rigorous approach to learning outcomes that are consistent with institutional requirements. The rewards for stepping away from a traditional top-down practice of teaching are numerous.

References

Armentia, A., Castrodeza, J., Ruiz-Muñoz, P., Martínez-Quesada, J., Postigo, I., Herrero, M., & Guisantes, J. A. (2011). Allergic hypersensitivity to cannabis in patients with allergy and illicit drug users. Allergologia et immunopathologia, 39(5), 271-279.

Boal, A. (2000). Theater of the Oppressed. New York: Pluto Press.

Benmayor, R. (2009). Theorizing through digital stories: The art of 'writing back' and 'writing for.' In R. Bass & B. Eynon (Eds.), From the difference that inquiry makes: A collaborative case study on technology and learning, from the Visible Knowledge Project (pp. 4-20). Washington, D.C.: Center for New Designs in Learning and Scholarship.

Biella, P. (2008). Elementary Forms of the Digital Media: Tools for Applied Action Research in Visual Anthropology. In M. Strong & L. Wilder (Eds.), Viewpoints: Visual Anthropologists at Work. Austin: University of Texas Press.

Castleden, H., Garvin, T., & Huu-ay-aht First Nation. (2008). Modifying photovoice for community-based participatory indigenous research. Social Science and Medicine, 66, 1393-1405.

Fletcher, C., & Cambre, C. (2009). Digital Storytelling and Implicated Scholarship in the Classroom. Journal of Canadian Studies, 43(1), 109-130.

Freire, Paulo. (1970). Pedagogy of the Oppressed. New York: Bloomsbury Academic.

Gubrium, A., & Turner, K. C. N. (2011). Digital storytelling as an emergent method for social research and practice. In S. N. Hesse-Biber (Ed.), The Handbook of Emergent Technologies in Social Research. New York: Oxford University Press.

Hill, A. (2010). Digital storytelling for gender justice: Exploring the challenges of participation and the limits of polyvocality. In D. Bergoffen, P. R. Gilbert, T. Harvey, & C. McNeely [Eds.], Confronting Global Gender Justice: Women's Lives, Human Rights. London, England: Routledge.

Johnson, J. L. (2008). Therapeutic filmmaking: An exploratory pilot study. The Arts in Psychotherapy, 35, 11-19.

Kilman, M. (2014a). Community Media as a Forum for Resistance: The Case of the Romero Theater Troupe. Anthropology Theses. http://tinyurl.com/zyjzdrt.

———. (2014b). Unbound: The Story of the Romero Theater Troupe [Motion picture]. Director. USA: Loridian's Laboratory. http://tinyurl.com/h6gumu4.

Krippendorff, K. (2004) Content analysis: An Introduction to its Methodology. Thousand Oaks: Sage.

Lambert, J. (2013). Digital storytelling: Capturing lives, creating community, 4th Edition. New York, New York: Routledge.

Maier, R., & Fisher, M. (2006). Strategies for digital storytelling via tabletop video: Building decision making skills in middle school students in marginalized communities. Journal of Educational Technology Systems, 35(2), 175-192

Merriam, S. (1998). Qualitative research and case study applications in education. San Francisco: Jossey-Bass.

Nasir, N. et at. (2013). Pedagogies of Race: Teaching Black Male Youth to Navigate Racism in Schools. In Jocson, K. (2013). Cultural transformations: Youth and pedagogies of possibility. Harvard Education Press.

Ocampo, T. L., & Rans, T. S. (2015). Cannabis sativa: the unconventional "weed" allergen. Ann Allergy Asthma Immunol, 114(18), 7e192.

Otañez, M., & Guerrero, A. (2015). Digital storytelling and the viral hepatitis project,' Chapter 3 in, Participatory visual and digital research in action, Gubrium, A., Harper, K., & Otañez, M. [eds] Left Coast Press: California.

Gubrium, A., Harper, K., & Otañez, M. (2015). [eds]., Participatory visual and digital research in action, Left Coast Press: California.

Otañez, M., & Lakota, W. (2015). Digital storytelling: Using videos to increase social wellness,' in J Cohen and L Johnson, [eds]., Video Filmmaking as Psychotherapy: Research and Practice, Routledge: New York

Roberts, J. (2011). Video diaries: a tool to investigate sustainability-related learning in threshold spaces. Environmental Education Research, 17(5), 675-688

Rony, F. (1996). The third eye: Race, cinema and ethnographic spectacle. Durham: Duke University Press.

Salazar, J. (2005). Digitising Knowledge: Anthropology and New Practices of Digitextuality. Media Information Australia, 116, 64-74.

Tufte, T. (2000). Living with the rubbish queen: Telenovelas, culture and modernity in Brazil. John Libbey Publishing: London, England

Walsh, J. P. (2016). Denver's Romero Theater Troupe: Welcoming Working Class Voices in Higher Education and Revitalizing Class-based Activism through Organic Theater. Labor Studies Journal, 41(1).

———. (2009). Dreams From the Podium. Jesuit Higher Education: A Journal, 1(1), 125-133.

Willox, A., Harper, S., Edge, V., 'My Word': Storytelling and Digital Media Lab, and Government, R. I. C. (2012). Storytelling in a digital age: Digital storytelling as an emerging narrative method for preserving and promoting indigenous oral wisdom. Qualitative Research, 1-21.

CHAPTER 11

Cicada Press: Transforming Dialogues and Applications of Distributed Leadership

Michael Kempson

ABSTRACT

The ideas informing Distributed Leadership (DL) have emerged as an analytical framework evaluating leadership and management systems within schools. DL acknowledges a link between inclusive styles of leadership and the effectiveness of organisations, with potential for implementation in other domains. This chapter offers one practical application of a DL framework in the activities of Cicada Press, a research group at the University of New South Wales Art & Design in Sydney, Australia.

Printmaking is a collective term for a suite of fine art mediums synonymous with the packaging and presentation of ideas for mass circulation. Often marginalised, printmaking is under threat within the fine art programs of Australian universities. Consequently Cicada Press began as a pedagogical experiment to counter this trend. Through a course, unique in Australian universities, artists engage in an educative relationship welcoming students into their creative process, who in turn, contribute as an integral component in this creative partnership. Hence artist, student and course lecturer as custom printer, play an integral and apportioned role in the production of research outcomes.

Using the printed artwork generated in this relationship, Cicada Press fosters exhibitions, academic co-operation and cultural exchange that includes: access programs with remote and urban Aboriginal organisations; oceanic conservation projects in New Zealand; mainstream engagement for artists with intellectual disabilities; and curatorial collaboration with comparable international tertiary institutions and print workshops. The result of this engagement is an enriching collaboration full of informal interaction, community building and networking within and beyond the classroom, incorporating transformative experiences that reinforce the importance of lived experience in learning. Cicada Press works towards a synthesis between an educational philosophy using instructional methods intuitively aligned with DL and a broader social and ethical agenda to assist in empowering the creative leaders of the future.

INTRODUCTION

This chapter addresses the history and ongoing work of Cicada Press (CP), sited in the Art & Design Faculty of the University of New South Wales (UNSW A&D). CP was developed from a series of teaching experiments beginning in the late 90s using collaborative working relationships between invited artists, teaching staff and students to make fine art prints. The model for this work has evolved, over fourteen years since its formal inception in 2004, from modest classroom interactions with a limited selection of artists to numerous comprehensive engagements with many artists, particularly with an Indigenous background, resulting in projects of national and international significance. In response, formal and informal systems involving leadership and responsibility have been developed to facilitate and proselytise the outcomes of these creative interactions.

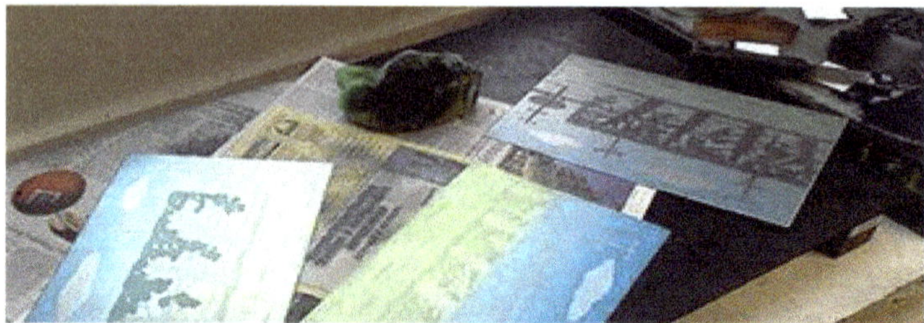

Figure: 11. 1 - Printing plates for Chris O'Doherty aka Reg Mombassa's *Pine Hedge* (2012) etching and aquatint.
Image credit: Ben Rak

The organisational and pedagogical structures used by CP have evolved to respond to issues related to the printmaking discipline or educational delivery, without reference to the theories espoused in the literature of management and leadership. Many of CP's systems have grown in response to the challenges confronted by academic institutions in implementing the educational delivery of skill-based work routines. This has resulted from changes prompted by the cycles of review conducted periodically into existing academic programs. Results of these reviews, apart from a reduction in contact hours and an increase in class sizes, have promoted well meaning philosophical change that stress a generalist interdisciplinarity. Consequently it is harder to align crucial specialist discipline instruction in making with the core conceptual training favoured by most contemporary tertiary art schools. CP offers an organisational structure using an atelier style model that embeds the processes of making as a series of transactions between its participating stakeholders, built around the knowledge, skills and experience offered by the practicing professional artists invited into the dynamic of our activities and the staff who conduct the courses supporting its activities.

However, this chapter also seeks to acknowledge and align scenarios common between CP and the ideas related to systems established in Distributed Leadership (DL) models. There is a considerable body of literature dedicated to DL with varying opinions on the subject. To assist in articulating how DL can occur many scholars in that field have developed taxonomies to describe the nuances of leadership activities. One particular DL framework, proposing six categories of leadership distribution characterised as Formal, Pragmatic, Strategic, Incremental, Opportunistic and Cultural (MacBeath, 2005, p. 357 - 363), is most pertinent in this context.

All of the categories of MacBeath's DL framework have resonance in the work of CP. The Formal model reflects traditional modes of leadership and protocol using deliberate delegation where responsibility is structurally apportioned, carrying with it an attendant expectation of delivery. The Pragmatic model is more informal and reflects a less structured ad hoc approach, most commonly in response to demands generated from unplanned periods of demand or external sources. This can often have some alignment with the Strategic model where the skills and knowledge of new people are embraced to realise specific goals. In fulfilling a strategically important need individual expertise used in support of the team can offer collective strength to an organisation. The Incremental model reflects distribution while ensuring that a person's growth and development is being nurtured and supported. This can result in a scenario where, as one's ability to cope with a designated task develops, more responsibility is given. An Opportunistic model allows for people to take on responsibilities over and above those what has been accepted, giving freedom for individuals to take on tasks, therefore rewarding those with the initiative to lead rather than it being conferred upon them. And finally the Cultural model is responsive in a more intuitive way, seeing roles shared organically as one would expect when responding to the specificity of activities embedded in a cultural context.

> The basic idea of distributed leadership is not very complicated. In any organised system, people typically specialise, or develop particular competencies, [which] are related to their predispositions, interests, prior knowledge, skills, and specialised roles [...] It is the 'glue' of a common task or goal – improvement of instruction – and a common frame of values for how to approach that task – culture – that keeps distributing leadership from becoming another version of loose coupling (Elmore, 2000, p. 14).

The DL model acknowledges that the actions and experiences of people are integral to the functioning of an organistation. The distribution of leadership can therefore reflect a leader's philosophical approach to management and teaching, whether this be intuitive or consciously systematic. In so doing it can be used to establish an environment where there is a shift in focus to embrace an approach to leadership that reflects a more shared model. Thus, DL is represented as relational, inclusive and collaborative and offers an approach that not only transcends conventional roles but goes beyond the broader boundaries of organisations.

> It means generating ideas together; seeking to reflect upon and make sense of work in the light of shared beliefs and new information; and creating actions that grow out of these new understandings (Harris 2003, p. 314).

PRINTMAKING INSTRUCTIONAL MODELS

Printmaking is a technically rich discipline and any serious study of it requires an understanding of its considerable range of materiality and technical process. These techniques include relief printing (woodcut, linocut), intaglio (etching, engraving, mezzotint), lithography, serigraphy (screenprinting and stencilling) and more recently, digital (giclee or inkjet printing, laser cutting, 3D printing). Common to each of these approaches, and true for the production of any art object, is the manipulation of selected materials in particular ways for a specific purpose. Decisions are required of an artist during the production process to find ways to unite material and concept, and for disciplines like printmaking with a range of complex procedural skills this can be a demanding activity. However, without a kinaesthetic comprehension of printmaking's vocabulary of making an artist risks being rendered inarticulate.

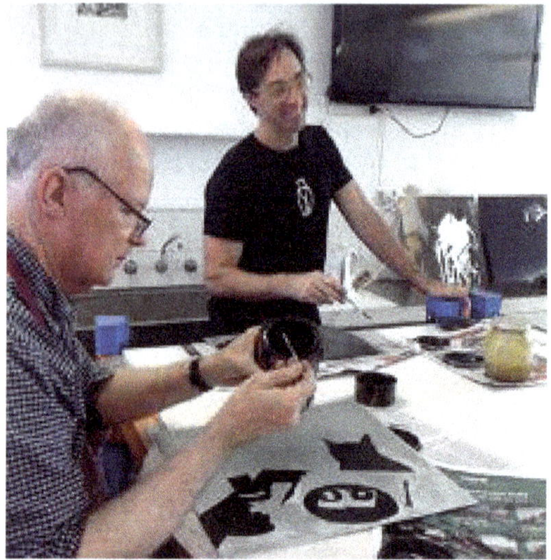

Figure: 11. 2 - Noel McKenna (left) and visiting Canadian artist Mark Bovey develop their printing plates in the etching studio at UNSW A&D (2016).
Image credit: Michael Kempson

Printmaking has endured many cyclical periods of popularity and neglect. As a suite of disciplines within the visual art programs of Australian universities printmaking has always faced considerable challenges. Some academic administrators and curators consider it an old-fashioned, retrograde craft well down the pecking order of the hierarchy of fine art methodologies, resulting in entire printmaking programs or specific print techniques being removed from the curriculum of several significant Australian universities, over the last decade. In this context there must be debate about how educators, committed to printmaking within the tertiary sector, can find relevance for it to provide students with the skill-base and enthusiasm to sustain a practice into the future.

In 2003 at UNSW A&D printmaking was on a downward trajectory and at a crossroads. Appointed as Convenor of Printmaking Studies for the 2004 academic year, I replaced three recently retired long serving senior printmaking academics, and was given one year to resurrect the department. The initial step in this process was a thorough review of all matters pertaining to the discipline. For art schools that continue delivering print programs, one of the most significant challenges faced is that each discipline requires specialised plant and consumables, often in separate purpose built spaces for specific work routines. In addition, highly trained technicians are required with the expertise to maintain the equipment, to ensure compliance with Workplace Health and Safety regulations. There must be a benefit in committing funds for considerable studio space and superseded print technologies, when students have a number of other methodological choices available to them. A rationalist solution ensued in the reconfiguration of the studio layout, identifying parallel working routines common to different printmaking techniques that could encourage multi-purpose uses for the available space, however more was required than changes to bricks and mortar.

Reflecting critically on the effectiveness of teaching and the mechanisms for its delivery is also an important component in any review of academic programs. An analysis of the delivery of the printmaking courses followed, leading to the implementation of Assessment Tasks (AT) that challenged individual student working methods by introducing insights into a fuller range of conceptual and practical approaches to artistic expression. Any solution to the challenges confronting printmaking at UNSW A&D needed to factor in a rethinking of the dynamic of personal and creative interaction within and beyond the classroom. While CP's initial development combined practical common sense, diplomacy, instinctual reasoning and a finely tuned survival instinct, there were parallels with DL's 'post-heroic' paradigm for leadership, which emphasised "human relations-oriented features such as teamwork, participation, empowerment and risk taking" (Oduro 2004).

CP began its operations in 2004, and was the outcome of a series of earlier experiments commenced between 1998 and 2002 at The Northern Sydney Institute of TAFE (NSIT), a Technical and Further Education college at Meadowbank in Sydney's west. The early experiments at both NSIT and UNSW A&D (late 2003 and early 2004) sought to re-invigorate student contact with and experience in, traditional fine art printmaking practice, with a primary focus on the intaglio medium. This was achieved by promoting forms of collaborative print production that would connect an artist with a skilled expert to realise their vision for an image in editionable form. Crucial to this was establishing the formal systems to create the ideal environment for this to occur within an educational institution.

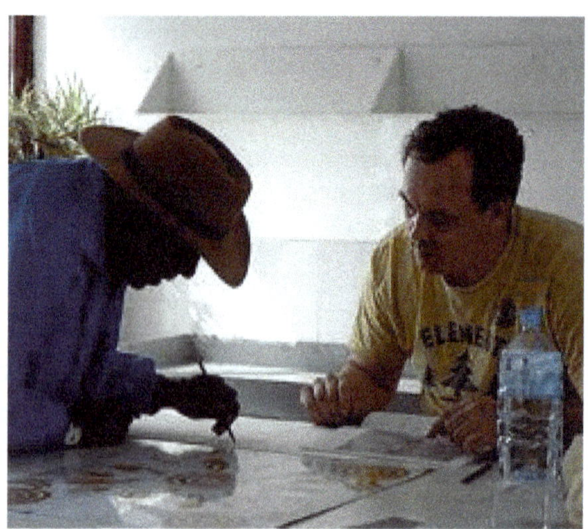

Figure: 11. 3 - Michael Nelson Jagamara (left) working collaboratively with Michael Kempson at Cicada Press (2006) during the first Sydney based Papunya print workshop.
Image credit: Kasumi Ejiri

Print studios offering this kind of service are in abundance around the world and have been since the earliest inception of print technology. In a contemporary context there are several models for print studios. Most are established as commercial operations that are either private or with a facility for public participation, depending upon the funding model. The service of creating prints, with the expertise of a master printer, is normally funded by the artist or by commissioning publishers or galleries, with some workshops maintained by private philanthropy or government grants. Internationally renowned workshops include Crown Point Press in San Francisco, Gemini Editions Limited in Los Angeles and the London Print Studio. In the Asia-Pacific the two notable examples are the Singapore Tyler Print Institute and China's Guanlan Original Printmaking Base offering an application of printmaking as a form of industrial production. In Australia there are several prominent printshops of varying scales of operation with a range of media: The Australian Print Workshop, Lancaster Press and Port Jackson Press in Melbourne; The Art Vault in Mildura; Viridian Press and Megalo Print Studio and Gallery in Canberra; Whaling Road Studio and Marnling Press in Sydney; Basil Hall Editions in country NSW; and Editions Tremblay Print Workshop in Cairns in the far north of Queensland.

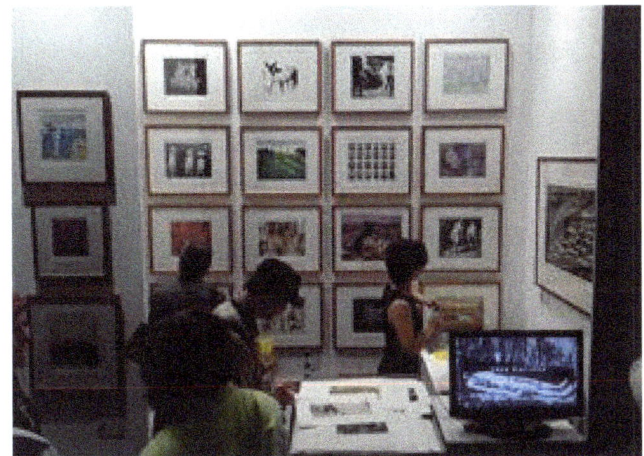

Figure: 11. 4 - The Cicada Press stand in the Paper Contemporary section of Sydney Contemporary 2015 at Carriageworks, Sydney.
Image credit: Michael Kempson

Print workshops affiliated with universities are less prevalent, with the Tamarind Institute at the University of New Mexico in Albuquerque, Anchor Graphics at Columbia College, Chicago and Tandem Press at the University of Wisconsin, Madison in the United States or the Centre for Fine Print Research at University of West England, Bristol in the UK being eminent templates. There has also been publishing workshops, separate from pedagogical service, associated with Australian universities notably Northern Editions at Charles Darwin University in the Northern Territory and Monsoon Publishing at James Cook University in Townsville.

The Pedagogical Structure of Cicada Press

CP as a pedagogical model, while developed with a degree of intuition, has been positioned under the theoretical umbrella of the Brazilian educational theorist Paolo Freire who emphasised dialogue, community, informal processes and the importance of lived experience in learning.

Education either functions as an instrument which is used to facilitate integration of the younger generation into the logic of the present system and bring about conformity or it becomes the practice of freedom, the means by which men and women deal critically and creatively with reality and discover how to participate in the transformation of their world (Shaull, foreword for Freire 2005, p. 34)

CP is a small research group at UNSW A&D that can't be compared to the scale of many of the institutions for which the DL theoretical framework (MacBeath, 2005, p. 357 - 363) has been developed. Despite this CP, in seeking to provide opportunities for students in the arts industry and to assist in empowering our future creative leaders, has developed the potential for individual stakeholders to make contributions outside of the conventional pedagogical structure of a tertiary institution. In so doing it needs to be acknowledged that as the director of CP I perform a pivotal leadership role, giving support and providing mentorship for students and graduates. There is also the challenge faced with the expectations of some academic administrators, and in some instances students, who struggle to accept the consequences of a non-hierarchical leadership structure. However DL isn't necessarily a sharing of formal responsibility, but it is a way of thinking about the dynamics of people, and in this instance, the delivering of educative content that can be open to the contribution offered from an individual participant's skill set. When considering DL the scale of the organisation is not the issue, it is the willingness to acknowledge that learning does not need to be bound by one's past understanding of the teacher/student relationship.

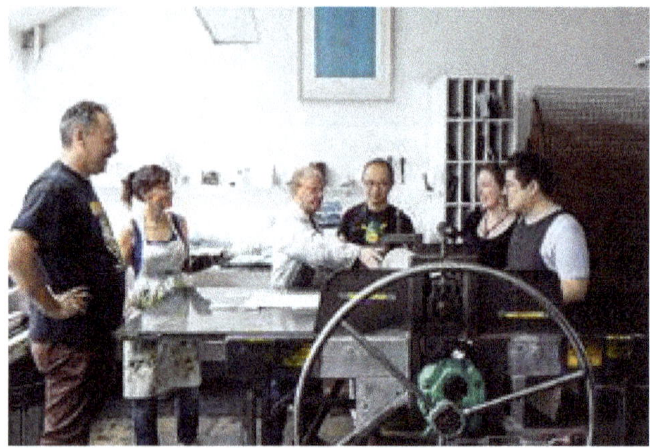

Figure: 11. 5 - Michael Kempson (left) interacts with UNSW A&D students around a printing press (2015).
Image credit: Sally Marks

What distinguishes CP at UNSW A&D is that it has no commercial imperative, being the only workshop in Australian universities using a custom printing model with an educational focus. CP appeared in its current form in 2005, by aligning its activity with an elective custom printing course, open to all undergraduate and postgraduate level students at UNSW. This resulted in students becoming pivotal players, in an apportioned role to this interactive dynamic, variously distributed across a range of encounters and timeframes, for the production of print-based outcomes. CP has developed into a practical example for how the inclusive nature of DL leadership systems, as an analytical framework for evaluating management in the dynamic of educational environments, can have resonance beyond its traditional domain in primary and secondary schools.

Each semester, up to eight nationally respected artists join the Custom Printing Elective, which has been designated by UNSW A&D as a special outreach course. The one Custom Printing Elective comprises a parallel delivery of four courses - an introductory and an advanced stage at both an undergraduate and postgraduate level. While scheduled to run for three hours the class normally spans the whole day, to maximise the time for visiting artists to work within the studio. The students enrolled in the advanced level of the course need to complete the introductory level as a pre-requisite for entry. Those students take on a leadership and peer mentoring role in the class, particularly involving their experience with editioning and matrix development.

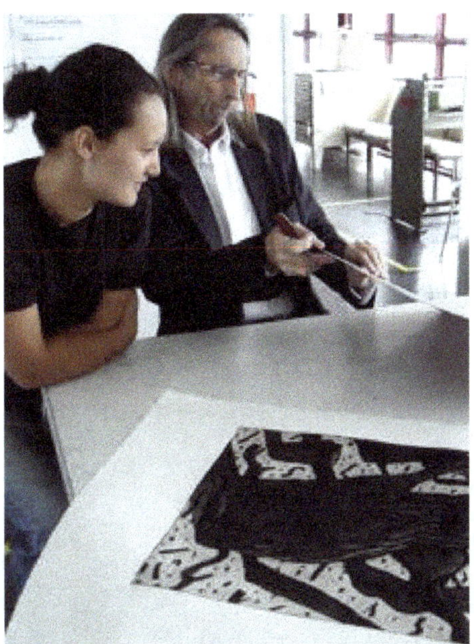

Figure: 11.6 - Chris O'Doherty aka Reg Mombassa with BFA student Kasumi Ejiri (2006).
Image credit: Michael Kempson

The Custom Printing Elective course that underpins the activities of CP was designed specifically to explore the collaborative printer's task of realising the artist's vision. Students achieve a greater understanding of an artist's creative processes, and consequently their own, when they participate in the development and the crafting to completion of work by these invited artists. And sometimes, much can also be learnt from the insight that emerges when working with artists that one might not necessarily understand or appreciate. Hopefully through personal and artistic connection, comes respect and mutual understanding. They also establish personal dialogues from which, one hopes, they gain an understanding of differing creative temperaments and conceptual strategies. It offers a valuable insight into the pace, scope and malleability of printmaking, how it can serve a range of aesthetic expectations, as well as presenting a technical challenge. Rigorous skills training and procedural systems are embedded into the course, so that students are exposed to a full range of methodological approaches needed to produce work at a professional standard.

Structurally the Custom Printing Elective runs over thirteen weeks with three Assessment Tasks (AT). The initial AT informs students, who may have no print experience, of the fundamental principles of printmaking – and specifically how to create an etching plate (matrix) and the procedure for printing it. Additionally there is an introduction to team-based editioning systems and technical procedures, with a fundamental objective of fostering an environment within the workshop supportive of a communal work ethic. The second AT allows for the development of a self-directed student artwork, applying a print process on a collective theme. The student reports to the class weekly on their conceptual and technical development of the matrix, receiving advice and technical direction for its resolution, which is then editioned with the support of colleagues, and distributed so that all participants in the course receives a complete set of images. The third AT involves being available to support the matrix production and editioning of the invited artists. When the second AT is introduced students are divided into groups that position the advanced students in leadership roles. Students in each of the 3 groups are available on a cyclical basis to fulfil the requirements of the third AT, and when not on duty in the other weeks they concentrate on developing their second AT.

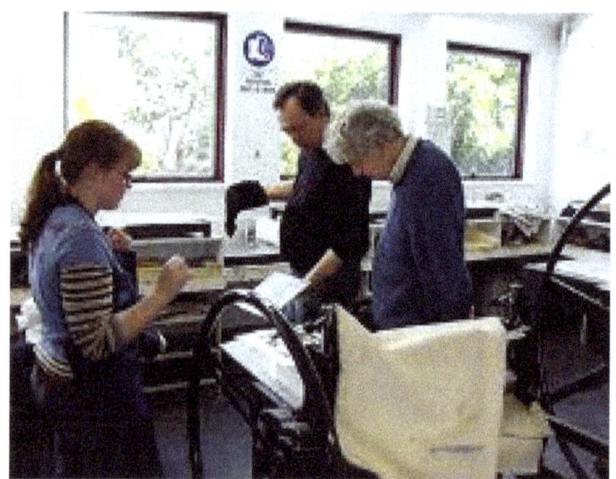

Figure: 11. 7 - Norman Hetherington aka Mr. Squiggle (right) with Michael Kempson and BFA student Tess Barnard (2005).
Image credit: Georgina Gye

Student Participation and Leadership Opportunity

For any organisation to succeed in being productive beyond the short-term, no matter its size, there needs to be an alignment between its goals and stakeholders. Despite a central role in the CP model, I seek to distribute leadership and to empower students so that together, with our invited artists, they become an "emergent property of a group or network of interacting individuals" (Bennett, Wise, Woods & Harvey, 2003, p. 7).

The experiments conducted as a precursor to the implementation of the Custom Printing Elective involved the voluntary assistance of students and there was never a shortage of willing participants happy to spend irredeemable hours working with invited artists. DL's Opportunistic Distribution (MacBeath, 2005, p. 357 - 363) model is an appropriate way of describing this relatively ad hoc contribution. The introduction of the Custom Printing Elective became inevitable for it was essential that there be a course to support CP, that allowed students to gain a formal acknowledgement of their contribution and participation in this collaborative process. The intent of CP and its sustaining Custom Printing Elective is quite different from most courses offered in art schools where the focus is normally on the outcomes of the individual participant. With CP, the student becomes a facilitator: with the support of the academic who supervises the matrix creation and the custom printer who manages the print production, which subsequently requires them to possess a less self-focussed approach.

It was also evident from the very beginning that a substantial workload was being generated, and consequently, consideration was needed for a Formal Distribution (MacBeath, 2005, p. 357 - 363) of leadership roles that arose from contributions from within the Opportunistic Distribution (MacBeath, 2005, p. 357 - 363) model. Motivated students willingly took on further responsibility in delegated roles within the Custom Printing Elective. One particular student, Ben Rak transitioned from being a BFA student who completed both levels of the Custom Printing Elective, into the MFA program, while maintaining a voluntary connection with CP. After completing his post-graduate studies, Rak's intellectual and practical experience applied in fostering his developing career, made for an invaluable casual academic in printmaking studies at UNSW A&D. With the income that was being generated for future projects from the periodic sale of prints left by the artists to promote CP's activities, funds were apportioned to employ an editioning printer. Supplementary to his teaching commitments and editioning work, Rak has contributed to many significant projects, presented CP related issues at international conferences and curated exhibitions that seek to promote CP and UNSW A&D outcomes.

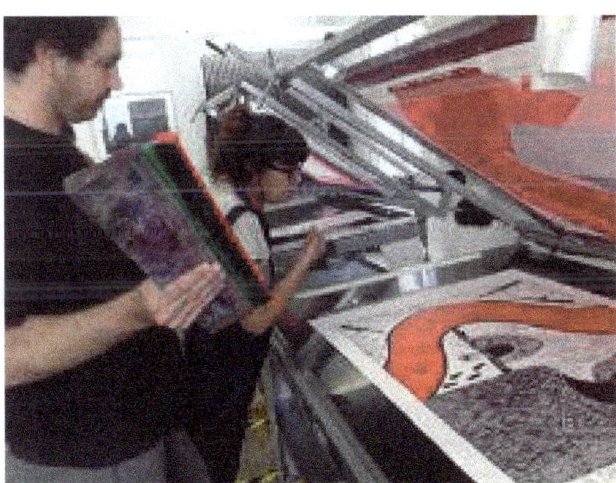

Figure: 11. 8 - UNSW A&D casual academic Ben Rak and Director of Indigenous Programs Tess Allas review a screenprinted layer on Laurel Nannup's *Quirriup,* (2016) linocut and screenprint.
Image credit: Michael Kempson

Additionally in 2012, Rak initiated a different version of a custom printing program, Throwdown Press (TDP) in partnership with another UNSW A&D graduate, Jason Phu. Where CP's scope was connecting students to artists with a national and international profile, TDP was developed to offer residency opportunities for existing post-graduate students within UNSW A&D who had not engaged with printmaking during their studies. Following the CP model, Rak and Phu provided expertise and supervised access to the printmaking studios at UNSW A&D for residency recipients, so that these artists could begin an engagement with printmaking. Ramesh Nithiyendran, an artist gaining considerable national and international recognition in 2016, was one of three of the first participants in a TDP residency.

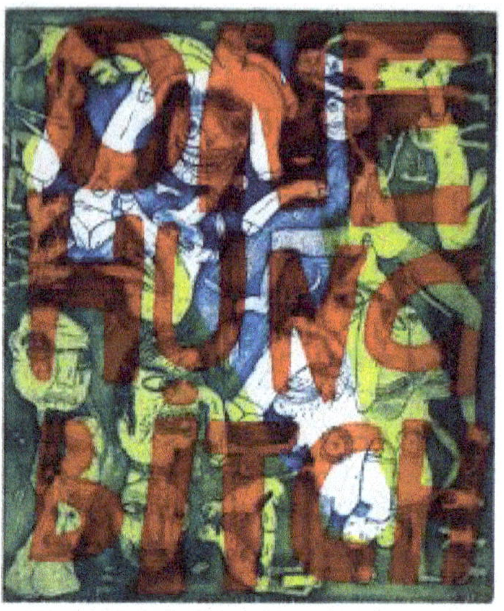

Figure: 11. 9 - Ramesh Mario Nithiyendran *One Hung Bitch* (2013), etching, aquatint and viscosity roll, image size 60 x 50.5 cm, printed at Cicada Press UNSW A&D.
Image credit: Sue Blackburn

Prior to his contact with TDP, Nithiyendran was predominantly a painter but his engagement with etching prompted an interest in another discipline with a long and seemingly dated tradition – ceramics. This connection with ceramic methodologies has catapulted Nithiyendran's practice, resulting in significant awards; including the 2014 NSW Visual Arts Fellowship (emerging) administered through Artspace and Arts NSW and the 2015 Sidney Myer Fund Australian Ceramic Award leading to involvement in Magic Object: 2016 Adelaide Biennial of Australian Art and an upcoming project with the National Gallery of Australia.

> Why have these artists willingly worked with a superseded print technology. Why use an ancient method to speak to such progressive concerns? Perhaps this is answerable to the analogy of artforms as language: In a desire to

> further express themselves, Ramesh, Al and Patrick now have an expanded vocabulary. Old words now have a new currency (Greenhalgh 2013).

Rak and Phu's experience with CP has contributed to their personal development and early career success. Ben Rak continues to generate projects with and independently from CP and in 2015 was able to secure a hotly contested contracted teaching position at the Australian National University in Canberra. In the working relationships established with CP artists, Jason Phu developed a connection with Sydney based painter Noel McKenna, who in turn nominated him to exhibit at the Macquarie Group Emerging Art Prize (2012), one of the most significant awards for emerging artists in Australia. This encouragement led to other successes including a Freedman Foundation Travelling Art Scholarship (2015) and the Sulman Prize (2015) at the Art Gallery of New South Wales. Phu, despite his international engagements, has continued his connection with CP and in the last 4 years has created a print for all Custom Printing Elective students as a component of the first AT encountered each semester.

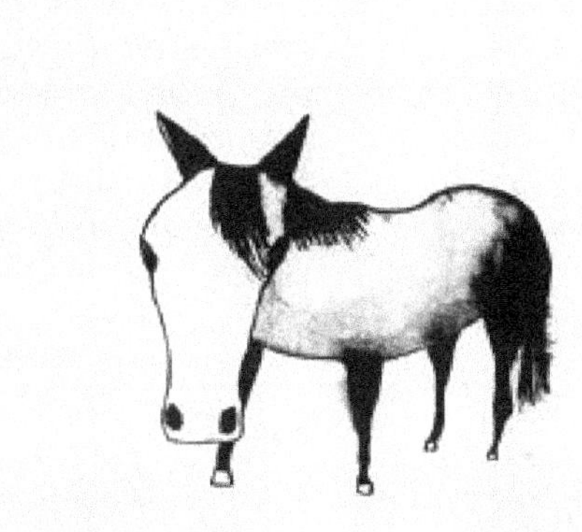

Figure: 11. 10 - Noel McKenna *Horse* (2011) lithograph, image size 38 x 45.5cm, printed at Cicada Press UNSW A&D.
Image credit: Sue Blackburn

The benefits of the Opportunistic Distribution (MacBeath, 2005, p. 357 - 363) model, is also made manifest when considering the career trajectory of one of my first UNSW A&D students, Kitikong Tilokwattanotai, who participated in some of CP's earliest collaborative engagements. Tilokwattanotai's enterprise and dedication to CP projects became the model for his own custom-printing workshop, Chiangmai Art on Paper (CAP Studio). From humble beginnings in a modest studio apartment, to its current home in an upwardly mobile suburb in 2006, CAP Studio has become Thailand's preeminent print workshop. Tilokwattanotai shares his ideas, expertise and staff of local university print graduates with many internationally recognised Thai artists, including Kamin Lertchaiprasert and Kade Javanalikikorn. Tilokwattanotai has participated in many exchange projects with the UNSW A&D, the first being a large exchange exhibition *Thai-Australian Contemporary Prints* held at the Chiangmai University Art Museum (2005), and reciprocated at COFAspace (now A&Dspace) in Sydney the following year. *Confluence of 9* (2008) held at the National Gallery of Thailand, Bangkok, was a project that involved the assemblage of Chiangmai artists with international friends from Australia, Japan and the USA.

Another exhibition project, The International Art on Paper Exhibition – The Faculty of Fine Art and Architecture, Rajamangala University of Technology Lana in association with College of Fine Arts, University of NSW (2011) also included a seminar and workshop. Tilokwattanotai was a member of an international panel Songlines: Community, Connection and Opportunity through Print in the Asia-Pacific' that I convened, presenting Hot and Wet: Printmaking Culture Thai Style - Chiangmai Art on Paper (CAP Studio) at 'Bridges: spanning tradition, innovation and activism, a Southern Graphics Council International conference in San Francisco, USA (2014). He spoke about the development of printmaking in Thailand, many of CAP Studio's projects and of plans with local developers for an international printmaking museum that will become a new focus for the medium in the Asia-Pacific. The most recent exhibition project Interchange: A Printmaking Dialogue between Australia and Thailand in which Tilokwattanotai was an indispensable collaborative partner, was shown at Silpakorn University Art Gallery, Bangkok, Thailand, The ANU School of Art Gallery, Australian National University in Canberra, the Mosman Art Gallery in Sydney and one of regional NSW's most significant print focused galleries Wagga Wagga Regional Art Gallery (2014-15). In May 2016 Ammarin Kuntawong, a staff member and practicing artist from CAP Studio, has been in residence at CP furthering the cyclical connections established through printmaking education by Tilokwanttanotai in 2004.

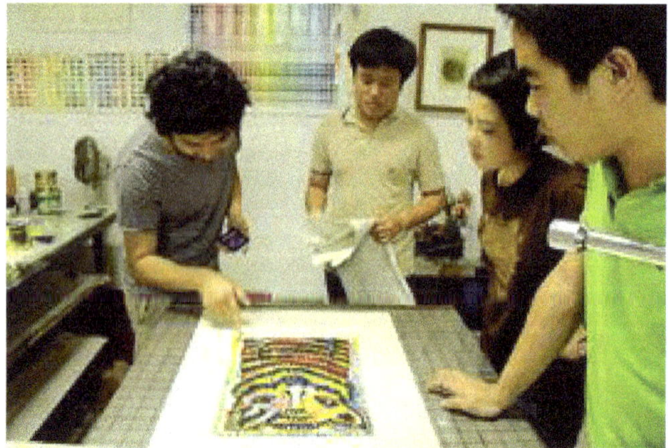

Figure: 11. 11 - Artist and musician Maytee Noijinda (left) discusses options for his print with Yuttana Sittikan, Yuree Kensaku and Kitikong Tilokwattanotai (right) at Chiangmai Art on Paper in Thailand (2011).
Image credit: Surachet Wonghun

THE LEADERSHIP ROLE OF ADULTS

An important element of the Formal Distribution (MacBeath, 2005, p. 357 - 363) component of the DL framework is the crucial contribution of our invited artists. A printer's task is to practically realise an artist's vision by bringing it securely into the world and for custom printing to be a success, it is essential to build a relationship of trust with the artist. Our students experience a working relationship with these artists who in turn must be open to welcoming them into their creative process. This takes a particular generosity of spirit to reveal acts of making in such a public forum, more often performed in the privacy of one's studio. A complicating addition is that most of the artists we invite have little to no experience in printmaking. Consequently, we seek to introduce a way for them to begin a working relationship with the medium. For whilst the artists are confident and in control of their content, they may not be print literate and so need patient and considered support to establish outcomes that reflect their status and reputation.

Every working relationship is different and students revel in witnessing the various nuanced deliberations and idiosyncratic foibles inherent in all the individual creative sensibilities of the diverse range of artists that they encounter. Recently we worked with Guy Warren, who at the age of ninety-five has a career that spans eight decades. He has an enviable reputation as a dedicated painter, critic and innovative arts educator.

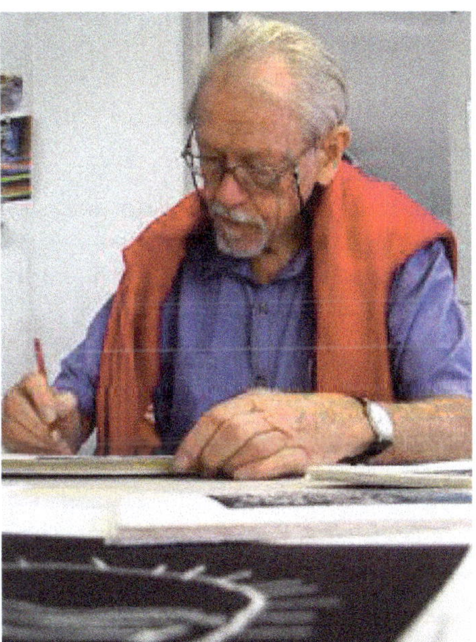

Figure: 11. 12 - Guy Warren signing *Bora Dance* (2006) etching and aquatint.
Image credit: Michael Kempson.

A contrasting practice to Warren's is that of Fiona Hall, Australia's official representative at the 2015 Venice Biennale, and currently one of our nations most prominent artists. With an established reputation in the early 80s as a leading photographer, Hall has expanded her oeuvre to include sculpture, installation, painting, video and now printmaking - the most recent being prints made at CP for the Kermadec project (2011-16) in New Zealand.

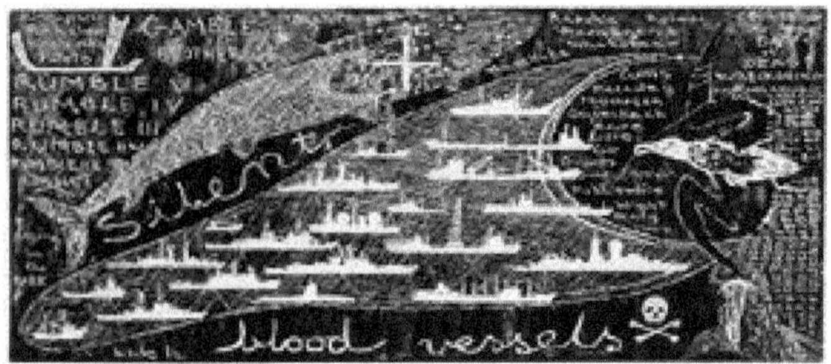

Figure: 11. 13 - Fiona Hall *Lying in the Dark* (2012) etching, aquatint, open-bite and screenprint, image size 50.5 x 101 cm, printed at Cicada Press UNSW A&D.
Image credit: Sue Blackburn

The late Michael Callaghan offered students an insight into passionate motivations and political protest. As a student he produced a series of typewritten concrete poems using the catchphrases of the Vietnam War – 'hearts and minds', 'domino theory', 'defoliate.' His last works were prints combining digital and conventional methods on the military strategies engaged in the Iraq war, featuring the catchphrases: 'Operation Iraqi Freedom'; 'Shock and Awe'; 'Weapons of Mass Destruction.'

Roger Law, the BBC radio broadcaster, cartoonist, satirist and clay modeler behind the satirical puppet television program *Spitting Image* (1980-95), transported himself to Australia and became an international guest at CP. His images of Australian fauna now adorn massive pots made in China, and were exhibited recently in Porcelain City: Jingdezhen at London's Victoria & Albert Museum (2011-12).

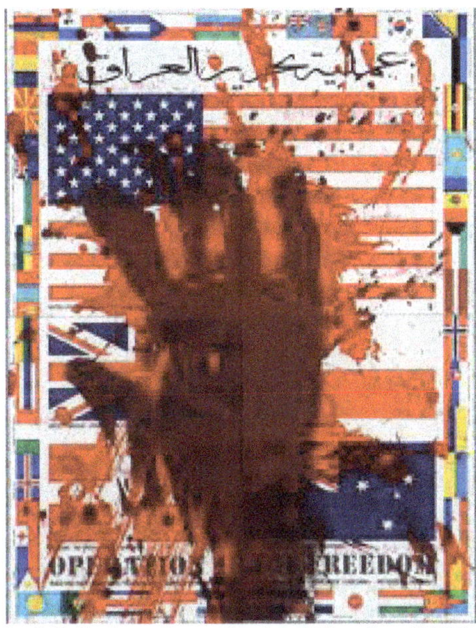

Figure: 11. 14 - Michael Callaghan *Operation Iraqi Freedom* (2009), digital, aquatint and screenprint, image size 136 x 107 cm printed at Cicada Press UNSW A&D.
Image credit: Sue Blackburn.

The benefits of the interaction between UNSW students and our invited artists go beyond the print production activities in the studio. The late Norman Hetherington, who appeared on television in Australia on its very first day in 1956 and notably taught generations of Australian children about the imaginative potential of drawing, opened a student printmaking exhibition in 2006. Performing in the guise of his alter ego Mr Squiggle, he was able to facilitate a regression back to childhood for an audience of 200 cynical art students, along with their parents and also their grandparents.

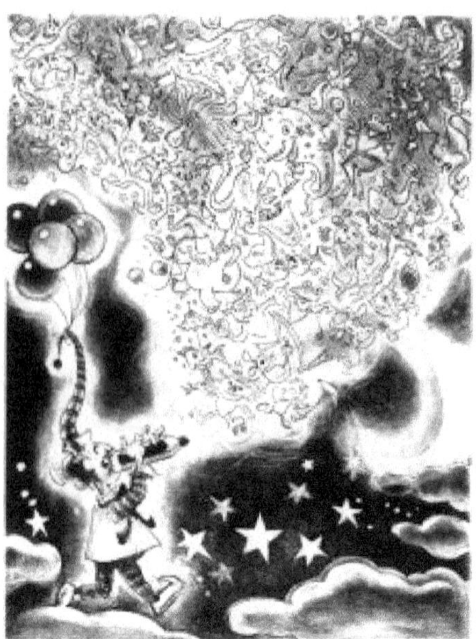

Figure: 11.15 - Norman Hetherington aka Mr. Squiggle The Pied Piper (2005), etching and aquatint, image size 30 x 22.5 cm, printed at Cicada Press UNSW A&D.
Image credit: Sue Blackburn.

DISTRIBUTING OPPORTUNITIES THROUGH PARTICIPATION

Since the inception of CP, over 1500 separate editions have been produced in projects with more than 200 artists, each offering a distinct story to tell and life's experience to convey. The production of every edition with each of the artists at CP requires the integration of many specific functions, some crucial to the outcome, while others are necessary but prefatory. Therefore, in addition to the Formal Distribution (MacBeath, 2005, p. 357 - 363) roles, there is the presence of Incremental Distribution (MacBeath, 2005, p. 357 - 363), where leadership responsibilities are acquired progressively through gained experience. Offering knowledge within a professional environment outside of the collaborative making within the studio has always been a logical extension of CP's broader educational mission. CP has welcomed the contribution of students from the Master of Art Administration program, in curating and hosting exhibition projects. Double Visions at COFAspace (now A&Dspace) and Orange Regional Gallery, NSW (2007), required the coordination between a curatorial class and a hosting venue beyond the confines of the range of UNSW A&D galleries. Many of these Master of Art Administration students have since progressed in their careers, often supporting CP projects once in established positions in cultural institutions around Australia.

There has also been a longstanding partnership with the Arts and Education Faculty of the Australian Catholic University (ACU) in Sydney that involves their Creative Arts and Education students gaining practical experience with all facets of

CP's activities. These internships fulfil an important educational and outreach agenda and add to the range of CP's Incremental Distribution (MacBeath, 2005, p. 357 - 363). ACU Education student Sally Marks, after her internship and graduation, was employed by CP to perform a range of functions that included: participation in editioning sessions; documenting printing projects; pre and post-print management and facilitating liasons with artists to gather biographical information and secure working schedules. These roles then expanded into curating and mounting CP exhibitions in schools around Sydney and then in the bourgeoning array of Sydney's art fairs, as well as coordinating and posting content for CP's social media platforms. The experience and the professional connections Marks established with the expanding network of Australian artists encountered at CP assisted in her securing a full-time teaching position in one of Sydney's most prestigious private schools.

Pragmatic Distribution (MacBeath, 2005, p. 357 - 363) denotes leadership roles and responsibilities that are negotiated and divided between different actors. In many instances this leadership is offered by individual stakeholders within UNSW A&D but in some cases are found within organisations that CP seeks to serve. UNSW A&D graduate Gabrielle Mordy, a fellow author in this book, became the Artistic Director of a Sydney based organisation Studio Artes, which offers visual and performing art activities for people with a range of physical and intellectual disabilities. She initiated a project that fostered mentoring relationships between mainstream art institutions and many of her clients who had long-standing commitments to their artistic practice. CP agreed to provide group residencies that assisted in developing wider artistic networks, and with Mordy's support, Mathew Calandra, an artist with Down Syndrome, was literally shaking with excitement when he started his residency at 'university', participating in the same activities and alongside our other visiting artists. The portraits he produced during this relationship, along with other participants' works, are currently exhibited in mainstream venues across Australia.

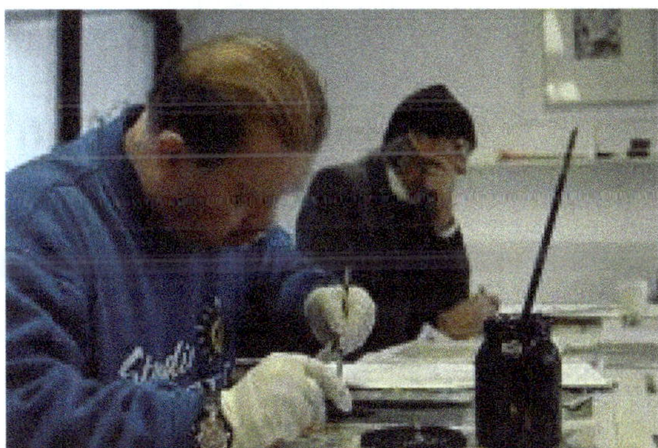

Figure: 11. 16 - Mathew Calandra (left) develops an image while working alongside Chris O'Doherty aka Reg Mombassa at the Cicada Press studio in UNSW A&D (2012). *Image credit: Michael Kempson.*

The outcome of this profound learning experience has secured ongoing relationships and residencies between CP and Studio Artes, with UNSW A&D graduate Jessica

Hodgkinson, who participated in the initial project, taking up an appointment as the coordinator of Studio Artes visual art program. Hodgkinson's role cements and maintains the organisational linkages and expressly affirms the vocational benefits offered by Opportunistic Distribution (MacBeath, 2005, p. 357 - 363).

FORMING INTERNATIONAL ENGAGEMENTS

As UNSW A&D works to expand an international profile, particularly in Asia/Pacific, CP concurrently seeks to support this objective with projects that include residencies with international artists and academic engagements, which include workshops, lectures and seminar presentations with comparable institutions in the region. In conjunction with the outcomes of our domestic engagements, these have been included into a total of 52 exhibitions directly curated under the guidance of CP. As director I have been responsible for many of these projects, however other members of UNSW A&D staff and students who have participated in the Custom Printing Elective, have also been responsible for CP exhibitions. These have been hosted in many venues, from artist run initiatives, commercial galleries, academic institutions and public museums in countries including China, Thailand, USA, Taiwan, Japan, Chile, Tonga, New Caledonia (France), New Zealand, Canada, The Netherlands, India, South Korea, England, Pakistan and the United Arab Emirates.

CP has actively sought an ongoing relationship with artists from New Zealand, with previous residencies involving expats Euan Macleod, Chris O'Doherty (aka Reg Mombassa), Alison Clouston and Locust Jones. In 2008, Jenny Neligan, Director of Bowen Galleries in Wellington, commissioned Crossing the Tasman - a portfolio edition of prints by 14 artists, all of whom located themselves between Australia and New Zealand - for the Melbourne Art Fair (2008). I subsequently developed a strong friendship with Wellington based artist, curator, and poet, Gregory O'Brien, and have collaborated, through CP, with a number of his individual and collaborative projects with fellow New Zealand based painter and poet, John Pule. O'Brien has become a devoted advocate for CP wrote of his experiences in IMPRINT, the Journal of the Print Council of Australia in June 2010:

> Kempson's great skill is to run a workshop where artists can be true to themselves, yet where they can also be shunted forwards or sideways—where they can respond to a medium they may or may not know well. Interactions between artists, academic staff and students are integral to the educational and research nature of Cicada Press. My experience is that such interactions consolidate the thinking rather than serve as a distraction—ultimately, it is a process of learning for all concerned (O'Brien, 2010, p. 39).

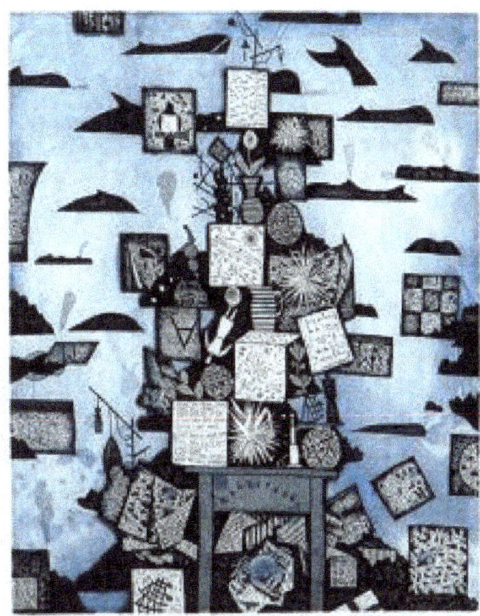

Figure: 11. 17 - Gregory O'Brien *Raoul Island Whale Survey with shipping containers, Astrolabe Reef* (2012-13) etching and aquatint, image size 51 x 41cm, printed at Cicada Press UNSW A&D.
Image credit: Sue Blackburn

Further to O'Brien's advocacy for CP and Pragmatic Distribution (MacBeath, 2005, p. 357 - 363) of leadership was his role in connecting oceanic conservation and printmaking through CP's involvement in the *Kermadec* project (2011-16). Sponsored by the Pew Environment Group, the project included nine artists along with New Zealand's Minister of Conservation on HMNZS Otago. They were bound for the Kermadecs—a 620,000-square kilometre expanse of water, which is one of the least-disturbed maritime regions on the planet. By facilitating the creation of art in response to the voyage, the Pew Environment Group sought to draw attention to one of the world's greatest and least known wilderness zones and lobby to have it named as a World Heritage area. The outcome of the journey was an exhibition that is still traveling concurrently in various forms. A comprehensive show toured major galleries in New Zealand, and travelled to Chile's Museo de Arte Contemporaneo in 2013, while a smaller version tours the nations of the Pacific with supporting educational activities. Central to this project was Voyage to the Kermadecs, a suite of nine prints that have been used as a form of cultural diplomacy for participants, supporters and hosting venues.

This project provided CP with the opportunity to collaborate with New Zealand's most important living Maori artist, Dame Robin White, whose etching Braveheart, uses stylised motifs referencing the complex trade routes between island communities along the Kermadec trench and the greater Pacific. This echoes her larger oeuvre which translates constructed patterns combining Maori, Polynesian and Pakeha motifs onto traditional tapa cloth made with the collaborative support of visual and performing artist Ruha Fifita and female elders from Tongan communities.

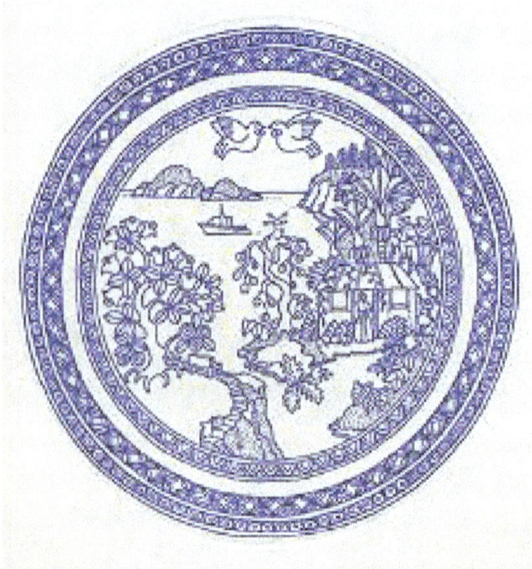

Figure: 11.18 - Dame Robin White *Braveheart* (2011) etching and aquatint, image size 19.5 cm diameter, printed at Cicada Press UNSW A&D.
Image credit: Sue Blackburn.

These New Zealand engagements reveal some of the collective benefits of CP's international experiences for all at UNSW A&D and events are scheduled at least four times a year. All international projects are predicated on developing residency opportunities for visiting artists to CP and/or procuring exchange exhibitions involving prints from CP artists, along with UNSW A&D staff and student work. Examples have included visits to leading schools in the USA, Canada, Thailand, Japan, Taiwan, Korea and several of the most prominent art academies in China. In 2012 with a group of students, I travelled to exhibit and present a paper about CP for the 11th Annual Printmaking Exhibition and Conference for Chinese Academies and Colleges at Guangzhou Academy of Fine Art - the first such invitation offered to an international art school at this prestigious annual event. Other projects have combined Indigenous cultural exchange with the Mohawk First Nation community of Kanawake in Montreal, Canada through to technical workshops and lectures in Lahore and Karachi in Pakistan, with reciprocal visits to CP.

Indigenous Opportunity and Collaborative Relationships

Certainly the most significant application of our research and pedagogical aims, involves CP's very first foray into a group project, conducted with artists from the small town of Papunya in central Australia. This has lead to a substantial engagement with Australian artists with an Indigenous background and provided CP with the inspiration to see that something as fundamental as making a print, and the teaching of it, has a role in the redressing of consequences of historical injustice and civil dysfunction.

In the 1950s the Australian government built a bore for water and rudimentary housing in Papunya to provide room for the increasing number of people who were compelled to leave their traditional life; a life intrinsically linked with this location and its environment. By the early 70s the community had grown to more than a thousand and as a consequence, tensions emerged between tribal groups who, contrary to their custom, were forced together. These circumstances were exacerbated by poor living conditions leading to disease, violence and premature death.

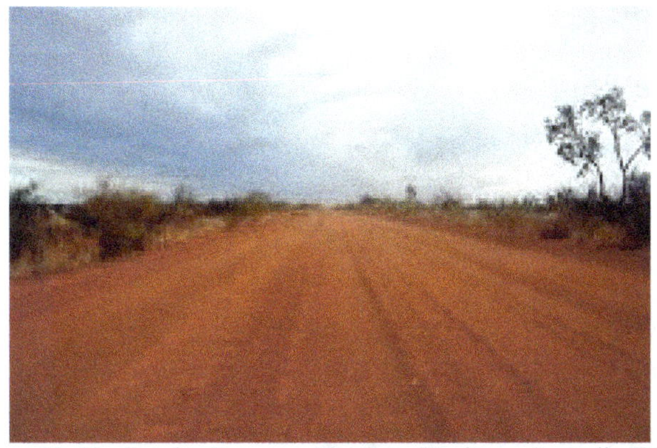

Figure: 11. 19 - Road to Papunya, Northern Territory, Australia (2008).
Image credit: Ben Rak.

It was into this troubled environment in 1971 that a teacher by the name of Geoffrey Bardon, an art education graduate from the institution that was to become UNSW A&D, took up an appointment at the Papunya School. Bardon was sympathetic to these Aborigines, and was to become the catalyst for a painting movement known as Western Desert Art that opened an understanding, appreciation and respect for the culture of these first Australians. He learnt that specific elders of the community had custodial responsibility for particular 'Dreaming' totems, so he encouraged these elders by creating an unprecedented setting for the exchange of ritual knowledge. He assisted in directing this knowledge into artistic expression by shifting their visual thinking from the production of ephemeral images used in communal ceremonial activity, to images on more permanent substrates.

The company Papunya Tula Arts (PTA) was formed in 1972 and today is such a phenomenal cultural and financial success that it is now taken for granted that most Indigenous communities have a vibrant art centre. However, the painting activities of PTA focussed on the Pintupi people when the settlement of Kintore was established 300 km to the west of Papunya. In 1981 the PTA operations bypassed Papunya when new painting studios were built in Kintore to service this large community of artists. Ultimately, those living in Papunya - including the last of the original painters, their widows and descendants – had no place to paint and store their work. Not only did they have no art making facilities - unlike almost every other Indigenous community in Australia – they also had no organisational structure responsive to the needs of the community committed to promoting the now sporadic offerings being produced.

Scholar Dr. Vivien Johnson, whose cultural knowledge, nurtured over decades of interaction with a group of artists from the Papunya community, sought to redress this sad irony for the founders of Western Desert art. In 2006 with the support of local elders, she organised several workshops with Cicada Press, both in the community and in Sydney, to produce work that would contribute to fundraising activities for a new art centre. The Cultural Distribution (MacBeath, 2005, p. 357 - 363) model suggests leadership is naturally assumed by members of an organisation/group and shared organically between individuals. Dr Johnson offered the leadership to achieve the desired outcomes, while several students - Kasumi Ejiri, Simon Taylor, Sian McIntyre and Ben Rak - participated in the workshops and have continued to maintain connections with the community, and supported other Indigenous CP projects.

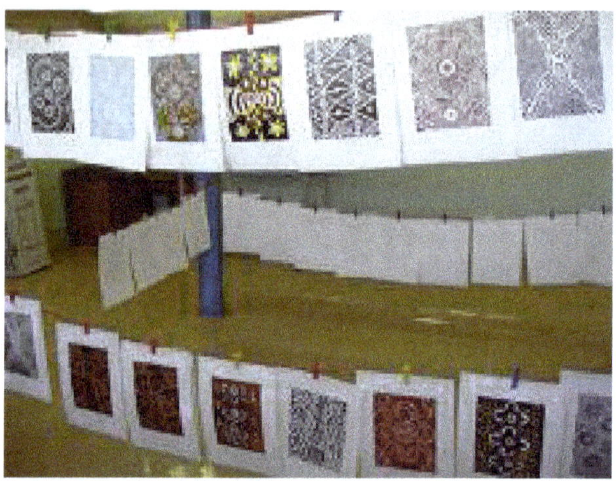

Figure: 11.20 - Reduction block linocuts drying after a session of printing at the Papunya School (2007).
Image credit: Kasumi Ejiri

After the success of the New Beginnings exhibition at UNSW's Ivan Dougherty Gallery (2007), sufficient funds allowed the community to open its own art centre, Papunya Tjupi Arts. Today, it serves over 140 artists, employing Papunya residents in the activities of the centre and producing paintings, along with the prints produced at CP, that form part of a comprehensive exhibition schedule around Australia. UNSW A&D graduates Kasumi Ejiri and Simon Taylor, who participated in the initial workshops, returned to the community as the art centre managers, developing a purpose built art space that serves as a cultural meeting place for the community. Most importantly, at the direction of elders of the differing language groups in the community, Ejiri and Taylor facilitated 'return to country' trips that take the artists, their children and in some instances UNSW students back to significant but appropriate ceremonial sites on traditional lands. In the words of one of Papunya's Warlpiri elders, the nationally famous artist Michael Nelson Jagamara, the goal for the communities cherished art centre is twofold "So that our children will know their stories but also so that our children will have an occupation for the future" (Johnson 2010, p. 1).

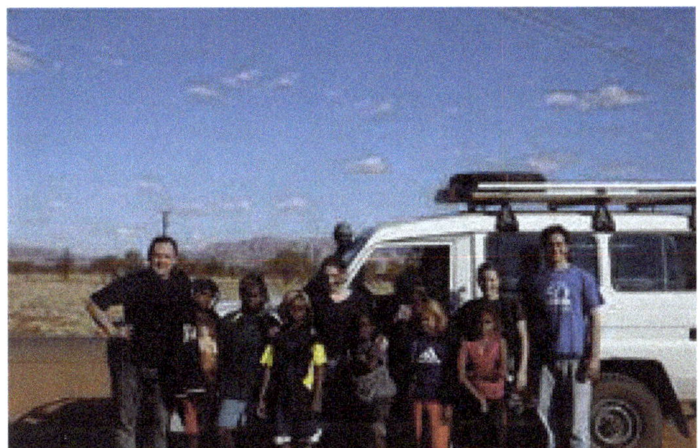

Figure: 11. 21 - Michael Kempson (left) with Jess Bulger, Sian McIntyre and Ben Rak with children from the Papunya School after a print workshop in Papunya (2008).

Further connection continues with UNSW A&D. As well as working with a new generation of Papunya artists, print workshops are scheduled once a year, and often involve UNSW students travelling for a life-changing experience of cultural exchange. They have the significant privilege of working with artists like Doris Bush Nungarrayi, whose work, in its unplanned spontaneity, belies deep knowledge of the land and the subsequent experience of ownership and belonging.

Everyone in Papunya has a Dreaming story and from the very young to those in their 80s, will either sing, dance or make art about them. Participation in these creative activities is taken for granted, as they all have a stake in this human endeavour. Like any educative process they are happy, if permitted, to share this knowledge with CP and our students. This community of painters was the first to break the stronghold of white, colonial art institutions and to demand recognition for a vital indigenous, contemporary art. Their achievement has had a global resonance, and put the issues that underpin their art - land-rights and Aboriginal identity - at the centre of our understanding of the Australian environment.

Telling this story to a broader audience is part of the ongoing work of CP. The most recent exhibition of Papunya prints held in early 2015 was New Narratives: Papunya Tjupi Prints with Cicada Press. Curated by Vivien Johnson and Michael Kempson it was displayed at the Kluge-Ruhe Art Collection of the University of Virginia in Charlottesville in the USA - the only museum in North America dedicated solely to Australian Indigenous art.

> Painting initially on masonite and composition board, and later on canvas, the first generation of artists at Papunya utilized the designs and iconography

of customary art forms like sand drawing and body painting. Now, the new artists of Papunya Tjupi are experimenting for the first time with printmaking, opening a 'new narrative' in the legacy of the Western Desert art movement. The intaglio prints in this exhibition are the result of an eight-year partnership with Cicada Press at the University of New South Wales Art & Design in Sydney, under the direction of master printer Michael Kempson (Johnson 2015, p. 2).

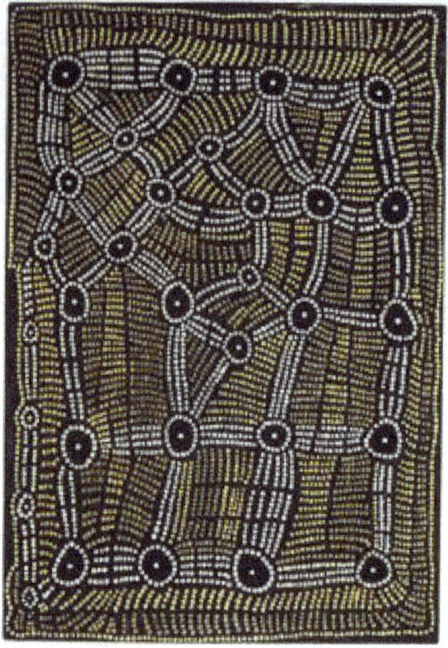

Figure: 11. 22 - Doris Bush Nungarrayi *Untitled* (2011), aquatint, image size 33.5 x 50 cm, printed at Cicada Press UNSW A&D.
Image credit: Sue Blackburn.

Leadership, Strategic Insight, and Aboriginal Workshops

For many Australians and international art audiences the rhythmic use of painted dots, developed in Papunya in the 1970s, simply is Aboriginal culture, however what needs to be understood is Indigenous art, like its broader culture, is much more diverse. The most important ongoing range of projects that have been developed at CP have been in association with Tess Allas, Director of Indigenous Programs at UNSW A&D, artist and independent curator, who initially suggested the need to connect with Indigenous artists with backgrounds other than those from remote communities. This advice to increase the diversity and plurality of CP's scope had evolved through her association with Storylines, a large-scale UNSW research project undertaken by Dr.

Vivien Johnson, Allas and Laura Fisher in conjunction with Design and Art Australia Online.

Allas brought culturally specific knowledge from a broad network within her community. She has been an active participant in CP's Indigenous projects and an exemplar for effective Strategic Distribution (MacBeath, 2005, p. 357 - 363), where new people, with particular skills, knowledge and/or access to resources, are brought in to meet a particular leadership need. Allas, in her formal duties, has overseen a rise in the number of Aboriginal students studying at UNSW A&D, with many of her initiatives including mentoring programs from respected elders, scholarships, securing culturally appropriate spaces for study – all establishing a much needed empathetic environment to ensure the support needed to secure successful course completion. Her commitment to the welfare of Indigenous students has resulted in her providing opportunities for them to garner experience with role models and potential mentors. The disproportionate amount of students with an Aboriginal background who participate in the Custom Printing Elective, or volunteer to support CP projects, clearly affirm the more altruistic motivations driving tertiary Art & Design Indigenous students.

Storylines documented Indigenous art making outside of the paradigm of 'remote' Aboriginal Australia, spanning regions to the south and east of the contentious Rowley Line, the invisible line spanning Australia along an east/west axis and the construct of sociologist C. D. Rowley; dividing Indigenous Australians into two distinct groups of 'settled' and 'colonial.' The research revealed to Allas that many of the artists from below the Rowley Line were not seriously considered, written about, curated into shows or collected, nor did they seem to have the same access to art workshops, studios, equipment as those based in art centres in 'colonial' locations.

With the aim of redressing the imbalance and enabling Indigenous artists access to studio spaces within the University, Allas encouraged a number of residency proposals for artists, either directly with CP or through the initiative of the UNSW A&D Award, aligned with the Parliament of NSW Aboriginal Art Prize. The recipients are given access to the facilities and staff at UNSW A&D to develop an exhibition project that is presented in the A&Dspace gallery on campus. Those artists who have chosen to develop their practice with CP have included Graeme Davis King, Frances Belle Parker, Gordon Syron, Penny Evans and David Nolan. The 2015 recipient Aleshia Lonsdale is currently developing a project with CP.

Allas has assisted as a strategic leader, in facilitating group workshops at CP for artists from Aboriginal cooperative organisations in NSW, including Boolarng Nangami Aboriginal Art and Culture Studio in Gerringong (2012), Euraba Artists and Papermakers in Boggabilla (2012) or Desarts in Alice Springs (2015). Through a pivotal course about contemporary Indigenous practice titled Right Here, Right Now, Allas has also been instrumental in securing individual residencies at CP with practitioners at the cutting edge of Australian's visual arts industry, including Fiona Foley, Vernon Ah Kee, Nici Cumpston, Gordon Hookey and Reko Rennie.

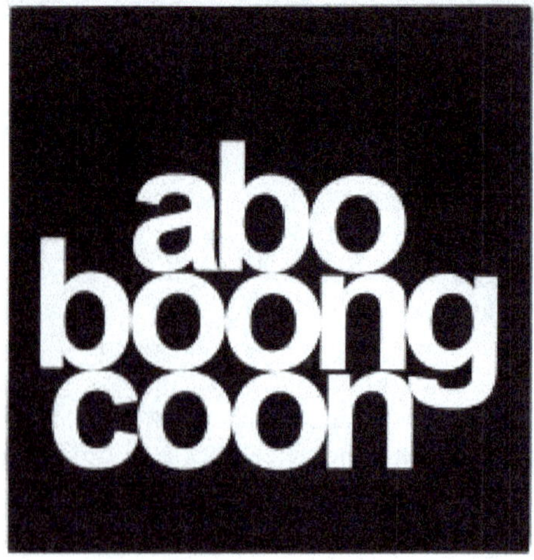

Figure: 11. 23 - Vernon Ah Kee *ABC* (2012), aquatint, image size 32 x 31 cm, printed at Cicada Press UNSW A&D.
Image credit: Sue Blackburn.

The annual Aboriginal Printmaking Workshop (APW), initiated in 2012 is the most significant collaborative leadership project developed in concert with Allas. This was in response to entreaties from Aboriginal artists, particularly the Perth based Laurel Nannup and her son Brett Nannup, who lived a considerable distance from Sydney, and were therefore unable to attend the growing number of short-term residencies offered to artists on the east coast. In keeping with Cicada Press's interests in offering professional development opportunities, the APW often gives access to artists who have an emerging practice, or artists struggling to receive appropriate recognition.

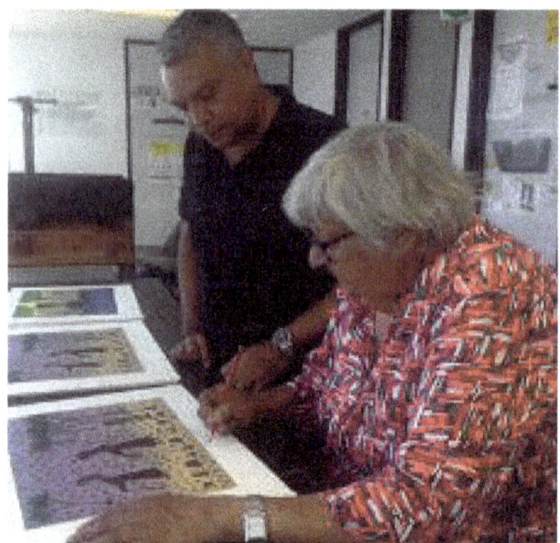

Figure: 11. 24 - Laurel Nannup signs prints with the support of son Brett Nannup (2015).
Image credit: Michael Kempson.

For two weeks each February, a small group of early and mid-career Indigenous artists, from diverse parts of the country, share a studio to test new ideas and participate in new conversations with an unfamiliar medium. This ongoing project has received national recognition, with the Australian Broadcasting Corporation's, Radio National commissioning a program on the 2015 APW. Producer Lorena Allam, who was a participant in the workshop, used the Rowley Line as a central theme.

The line still influences attitudes to Aboriginal people, particularly in the way Australia values and responds to Aboriginal art. The printmaking workshop is part of an effort to erase that imaginary line through collaborative art practice (Allam 2015).

Artists of considerable stature have also chosen to join the APW over the years, aware that it is an empowering way to spend two weeks. Brenda Croft, Dale Harding, Julie Gough and Ryan Presley have worked in concert with others like Bardi artists Caroline, Darrell and Garry Sibosado from Western Australia's Dampier peninsula, Graeme 'Nudge' Blacklock from Guyra and Adelaide's Damien Shen.

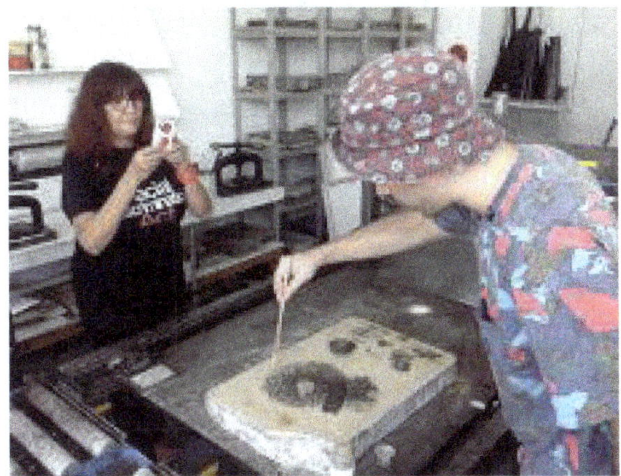

Figure: 11. 25 - Director of Indigenous Programs Tess Allas (left) documents Ryan Presley working on a lithographic stone (2015).
Image credit: Michael Kempson.

Brisbane-based, Dale Harding said of the 2014 APW:

> Collaborating with Michael and Tess to translate some of my works into etchings was entirely like a great conversation between friends in a mutual second language (Moar, 2016, p. 15).

Adelaide artist Raymond Zada, said of the 2015 APW:

> I had never produced art in the presence of anyone else. My practice always involved me working alone and nobody would see works in progress; so it was daunting having people see me work through ideas, which often just involves me staring at a computer screen. However, the workshop was

important for it provided a safe and supportive space for artists to step out of their comfort zone and try new things (Moar, 2016, p. 15).

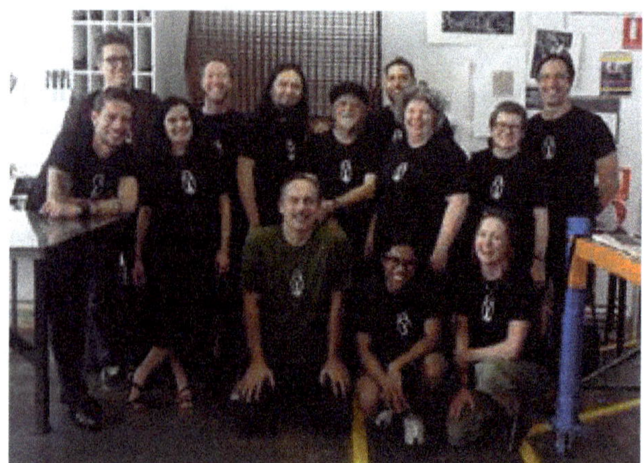

Figure: 11. 26 - Participants and visitors in the Aboriginal Print Workshop (2016).
Image credit: Tess Allas.

Tony Albert, a 2015 APW participant, challenges historical and contemporary ideas of Aboriginal identity and how the Indigenous perspective is reflected in today's society. With *ASH on me* (2008), and later etchings produced at the 2015 and 2016 APW, he transforms seemingly innocuous ashtrays, decorated with kitsch images of Aboriginal people into menacing symbols of racism by highlighting the psychological affront of extinguishing cigarette butts onto the images of Aboriginal men, women and children. Since participating in the workshop, Albert's prints, like those of Harding's and Zada's, have featured in Cicada Press's international and national touring exhibitions.

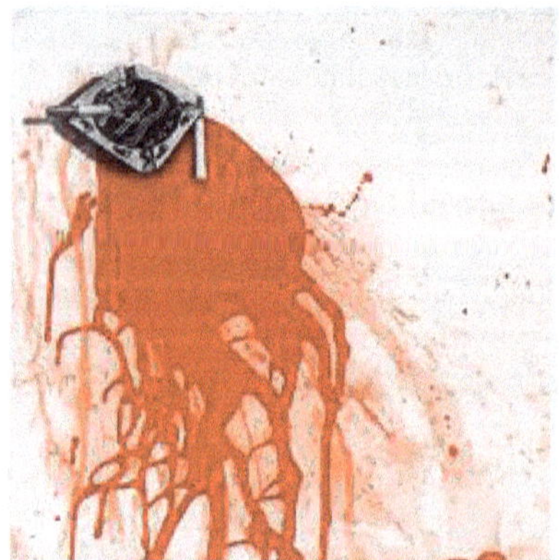

Figure: 11. 27 - Tony Albert *Greetings from Appin,* (2016) etching and aquatint, image size 50 x 50.5 cm, printed at Cicada Press UNSW A&D.
Image credit: Sue Blackburn.

Allas actively encourages students, particularly those Indigenous students doing courses with a predominantly practical focus, to develop mentoring relationships with these artists. However, Tahjee Moar, a recent Art History/Theory graduate, has developed a keen interest in the APW and other Indigenous engagement activities. Moar has volunteered for many of the work routines associated with the making of prints and is one of the new breed of historians with curatorial inclinations, who are willing to engage in the laborious machinations of art practice.

Since its establishment, the Aboriginal Print Workshop has produced something of a development in Indigenous art. It has seen a variety of Indigenous artists inject new voices and perspectives into an often-unexplored medium, becoming part of the ongoing history of printmaking in Australia. Most importantly, it offers an active space for the development of diverse and new voices in Indigenous art practice. As Allas says: ‘it is providing an opportunity for people to see there are stories to tell below the Rowley Line (Moar, 2016, p. 14).

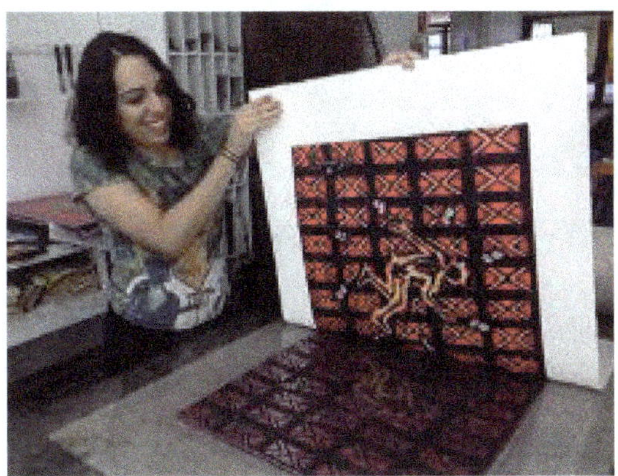

Figure: 11. 28 - Tahjee Moar assists with editioning Ryan Presley’s *dominium* (2015) etching and aquatint.
Image credit: Michael Kempson.

In addition, Moar has contributed to journals such as IMPRINT magazine and the CP blog, reflecting on the scope of our Indigenous projects from her dual perspectives as a student participant at CP with a Torres Strait Island heritage. Allas and I invited and funded Moar to act as CP’s representative to speak at the opening ceremony of the CP exhibition Remember Me: Stories in Print, curated by Georges Petitjean at the Museum of Contemporary Aboriginal Art (AAMU) in Utrecht, The Netherlands (2016). Moar is an example of the fluid nature of DL in the context of CP, as she transitions from Opportunistic to Incremental forms of leadership while eventually fulfilling other roles that could be aligned with MacBeath’s Pragmatic, Strategic and Cultural modes of distribution.

Although making prints is the research outcome for CP, our core business is education and as a constant reminder of that responsibility we welcome our weekly elder-in-residence ‘Uncle’ Vic Chapman. Born in 1932 Chapman, a Yuwalaraay man and ceramicist, travels from his home on the south coast of NSW to act as a mentor to the students engaged with the CP course. His presence, not only as an artist and as an educator of considerable experience, is valuable but it is the precision of his wise counsel to the Indigenous cohort in particular, and to the other local and international students in general, that is incalculable.

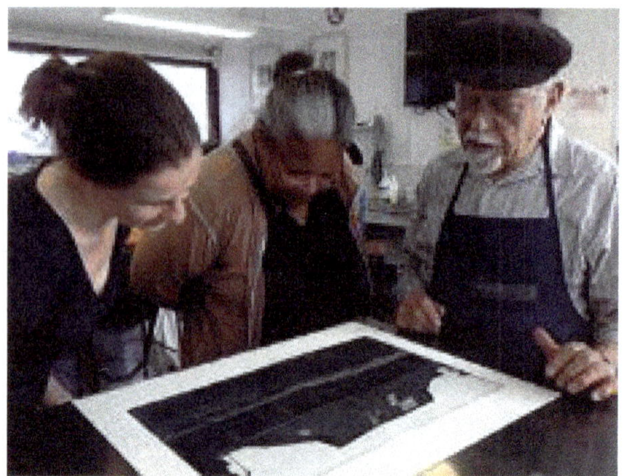

Figure: 11. 29 - MArt student Rachel Dooris and BFA student Ruth Saveka review a proof of 'Uncle' Vic Chapman's *Hebel Hotel* (2016) etching and aquatint.
Image credit: Michael Kempson.

In 1975, Chapman achieved the distinction of becoming the first Aboriginal person in NSW (and possibly Australia) to obtain the status of School Principal at Gwynneville, Berkeley and Thirroul Public Schools until his retirement in 1990. Chapman said of his time as a teacher that "as well as delivering 'readin', 'ritin' and 'rithmetic, I was, like the potter referred to in Jeremiah 18:2-6, given the challenge to refashion lives that threatened to collapse (Allas, 2007).

Conclusion

The pedagogical experiments that led to the development of Cicada Press sought to challenge the ossified norms found in traditional printmaking instruction by providing students with insights into its range of materiality and process. In so doing it was important to align these activities with standards that echoed those of leading examples in the arts industry. Further to this were the benefits accrued by students in the creative interaction developed with invited artists from outside of the institution, an important instructional mode that supported and enhanced the tuition and guidance given by academic staff at UNSW A&D. It would be prescient to suggest the scope of CP's activities today were planned from the outset. The process reflected a more instinctual understanding of how intent works with a combination of other factors like chance, and in concert with goodwill and enthusiasm, can lead to a gradual evolution in the teaching and learning strategies employed.

Time, along with reflection, offers the observer new insights into an event or issue. From a very simple idea CP has morphed into a research group at UNSW A&D that has a considerable national and international profile in the field of printmaking. Underpinning this gradual transformation has been the shared desire from its stakeholders to seek a synthesis between an educational philosophy using instructional methods that can be aligned with the ideas of DL, with a broader social and ethical agenda. One of the significant distinctions between DL and more traditional approaches to managing organisations, is that it 'offered a more systematic perspective on leadership, rather than positioning itself as a distinct theory *per se.'* (Bolden 2011) While DL has been developed primarily for management in schools, the examples outlined in this chapter demonstrate the value of a framework that offers insight into organisational structures and developmental opportunities for the range of people participating in the educational experience that is CP.

MacBeath's framework (MacBeath, 2005, pp. 357 - 363) of Formal, Pragmatic, Strategic, Incremental, Opportunistic and Cultural modes of DL offered common-sense ways to describe the differing leadership roles offered in the interactions performed by each collaborative partner at CP. There is an inescapable reality that CP, while functioning with the support of an accredited course, results in a lecturer apportioning a mark for each student enrolled. While this immediately establishes a traditional or formal leadership model, in the broader context of the relational dynamic of leadership within each CP project, one role within the framework has no precedence over any of the others. The resulting working environment is ultimately relatively open, fluid and collegial. CP, with the insight that DL offers, has harnessed the value of stepping beyond traditional organisational roles and as a consequence created a community of talented people, rich with assorted experiences and expertise, who work with this substantial collective capital towards a common goal.

Inherent in each of the DL roles outlined by MacBeath is the importance of trust, particularly how it is generated within the complex interactions and potential tensions found in the ego-driven pursuit of creative practice. Considerable time is given to establishing a positive environment with open channels for dialogue and problem solving. Initially students need to trust that the teacher can establish a constructively supportive environment conducive to meeting their academic and creative expectations. When students accept responsibility they trust that they have the support, as well as the freedom, to realise cogent outcomes for themselves and others on their own terms. The artists trust that both UNSW A&D staff and students can facilitate the delivery of editioned images that meet professional standards and our external partners trust that we can deliver upon the objectives of each project, on time, for public exhibition or commercial purposes. But in a more holistic sense trust can only be built from the development of honest relationships developed between individuals within the CP organisation and it is only with the crucial ingredients of integrity, competence and respect that a dynamic of reciprocal trust can be sustained.

The artists, the students and the staff that engage in the course that supports CP use a very practical set of scenarios that combine diverse personalities and intergenerational experiences to establish the foundations of a professional network. This is achieved by providing career pathways through the example of making and forming connections with potential mentors, all of which initiate a framework for life long learning. The ideas established in DL and the pedagogical applications that have been gleaned promote positive and constructive learning dynamics within the interplay of the participating players. Most importantly it promotes an environment for sponsored growth for our students and even the artists and teachers who contribute. There is also an ever expanding group of CP graduates and UNSW A&D staff who work to support its activities by generously facilitating connection with their own external networks all provide diverse opportunities for our DL stakeholders to nurture and ultimately test their leadership potential.

Giving students the foundations of a sustainable practice and practical opportunities for personal and professional development is the essential business of an art school. From a situation that presaged a dubious future, to a thriving and altruistic printmaking community, the contribution of CP has been what one should expect of an educational institution with a leadership responsibility. CP offers a modest contribution to the creative sector in the grand scheme of art practice in Australia, but activities like ours are of paramount importance if our pre-eminent universities take their commitment of service to the community seriously.

References

Allam, L. (2015). Erasing the Rowley line: inside an Indigenous printmaking workshop, ABC Radio National – broadcast on *Earshot* 17 June 2015. https://abc.net.au/radionational/programs/earshot/erasing-the-rowley-line/6552106

Allas, T. (2007). Vic Chapman. Design & Art Australia Online. Retrieved from: https://daao.org.au

Bennett, N., Wise, C., Woods, P.A. & Harvey, J.A. (2003). *Distributed Leadership: A Review of Literature.* National College of School Leadership. Spring.

Bolden, R. (2011). Distributed Leadership in Organizations: A Review of Theory and Research. *International Journal of Management Reviews*, *13*, 251-269.

Cicada Press Blog. Retrieved from https://cicadapress.wordpress.com

Elmore, R. F. (2000). *Building a New Structure for School Leadership*, Washington, D.C: The Albert Shanker Institute, 14.

Greenhalgh, D. (2013). *Mirror Mirror: Patrick Cremin, Al Poulet, Ramesh Nithiyendran.* Exhibition review COFAspace 12-22 March (2013). Retrieved from: https://throwdownpress.wordpress.com

Johnson, V. (2010). *Aboriginal Dreams – Paintings, Etchings, Linocuts – Indigenous Art from Papunya Tjupi, Australia.* Indus Valley School of Art and Architecture Gallery, Karachi, Pakistan. Catalogue Essay.

Johnson, V. (2015). *New Narratives: Papunya Tjupi Prints with Cicada Press.* Kluge-Ruhe Aboriginal Art Collection of the University of Virginia, Charlottesville, USA. Catalogue Essay.

Harris, A. (2003). Teacher Leadership as Distributed Leadership: Heresy, Fantasy or Possibility? *School Leadership and Management, 23*(3), 313-324.

MacBeath, J., Oduro, G.K.T. and Waterhouse, J. (2004). *Distributed Leadership in Action: A Study of Current Practice in Schools - Full Report*. National College for School Leadership: University of Cambridge in Collaboration with the Eastern Leadership Centre.

MacBeath, J. (2005). Leadership as Distributed: A Matter of Practice, *School Leadership & Management,* 25(4), 349-366. DOI: 10.1080/13634230500197165.

Moar, T. (2016). Creating a New Movement: Cicada Press and the Annual Indigenous Print Workshop. *Imprint Magazine*, Autumn, *51*(1).

O'Brien, G. (2010). The Glorious Kitchen: Cicada Press, COFA, UNSW. *Imprint Magazine*, Winter, *45*(2), Print Council of Australia.

Oduro, G.K.T. (2004). *Distributed Leadership in Schools: What English Headteachers Say About The Pull And Push Factors*. British Educational Research Association Annual Conference, University of Manchester, 16-18 September.

Shaull, R. Foreword for Freire, P. (2005). *Pedagogy of the Oppressed.* 30th Anniversary Edition, New York: Continuum.

CHAPTER 12

Changing Platforms: How Supported Studios Help Artists with Intellectual Disability Fast-Track Their Career

Gabrielle Mordy

ABSTRACT

You are a talented & prolific artist but you struggle with literacy and/or mainstream communication, how will you access opportunities within the broader contemporary art sector? If you are an artist with an intellectual disability, how can you navigate the competitive professional art system? How can you network with galleries and curators, compose an artist CV and complete grant applications? And who will protect you from corrupt art buyers who may recognise an opportunity for commercial exploitation? This chapter highlights one solution to these problems, the supported studio model. Such studios first emerged in the mid 1970's and have been gaining momentum internationally since. Supported studios offer adults with disability the opportunity to explore and develop their creative skill, and provide professional development pathways. This chapter explores some of the obstacles faced by artists with intellectual disability, and investigates the kinds of assistance supported studios are providing in response. The chapter investigates how supported studios emerge and explores the skills required to sustain such a studio. In particular, it investigates the critical role established artists play as facilitators and directors. The chapter focuses on Sydney based supported studio, Studio A, but also investigates international examples including Creative Growth in San Francisco.

INTRODUCTION

> *"You can do anything here, they let me explore and play and make whatever I want to make."* Artist working at a supported studio, Creativity Explored

How did Judith Scott (1943-2005), a woman born deaf with Down syndrome, become an internationally famous fiber artist, with a solo show at the Brooklyn Museum in

2015? How has she succeeded in an industry that is notoriously competitive and difficult for even non-disabled artists to access?

Scott was a member of a supported studio, Creative Growth. Supported studios have emerged sporadically around the world over the last thirty years and such studios now operate in most major cities. The most established studio is Creative Growth, based in San Francisco. Artwork from Creative Growth is held in significant collections including the Museum of Modern Art, New York. A supported studio is defined by peak advocacy body Accessible Arts as a 'sustained creative environment that fosters and supports the individual practice of visual artists with disability. Facilitated by practising artists, crucial to such studios are the opportunities they offer artists to be involved within wider artistic networks, thereby assisting artists to develop a professional career' (Supported Studio Network website). Supported studios are generally independent and artist led.

This chapter outlines the role and social impact of supported studios, with a focus on Studio A, the only supported studio operating within Sydney. The chapter will investigate how supported studios emerge and foster the skills required to sustain such a studio. In particular, the chapter will highlight the lead role established artists play as facilitators and directors at Studio A. Most studios I have encountered primarily assist people with intellectual disability, however studios are not necessarily exclusive to people with intellectual disability. According to the World Health Organisation (2016), 'Intellectual disability means a significantly reduced ability to understand new or complex information and to learn and apply new skills (impaired intelligence). This results in a reduced ability to cope independently (impaired social functioning), and begins before adulthood, with a lasting effect on development.' This chapter focuses on studios that specifically cater to artists with intellectual and Artistic Director of Studio A, but will also refer to my recent research into and visits to international studios, enabled through an Australia Council travel grant in 2015.

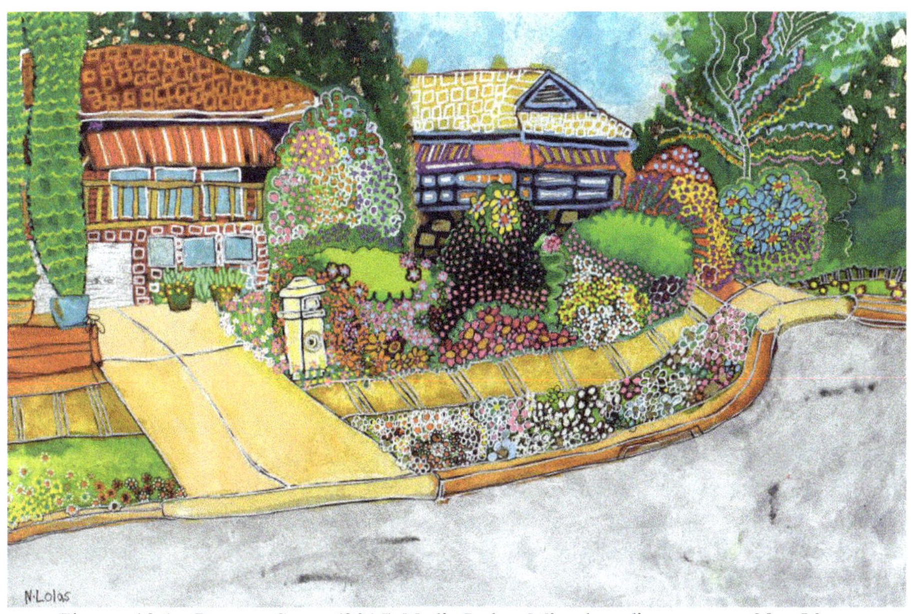

Figure: 12.1 - Ramsay Street (2015) Nadia Lolas. Mixed media on paper, 38 x 56cm.

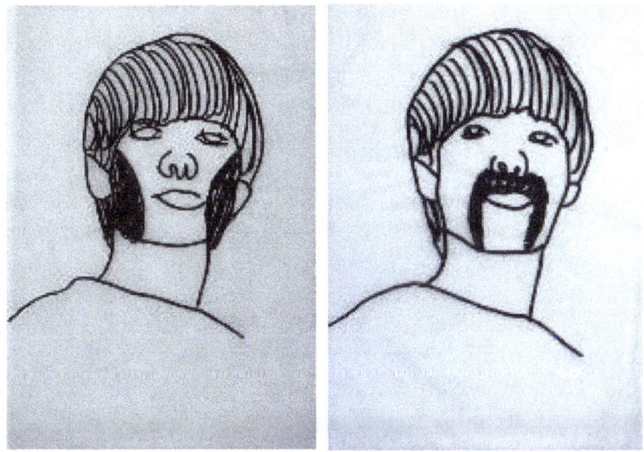

Figure 12.2a (left) - Man with Facial Hair 1 & 2 (2014) Robert Thom Smith, 21 x 30cm (each work), Posca pen on transparency paper.
Figure 12.2b (right) - Man with Facial Hair 1 & 2 (2014) Robert Thom Smith, 21 x 30cm (each work), Posca pen on transparency paper.

THE ISSUE

When out socially I am often asked what I do for work. I reply, "I work with artists with intellectual disability." Almost inevitably comes the response, "Oh, so you are an art therapist." My Studio A colleagues report similar exchanges. I am not an art therapist. I am tertiary trained as an artist, and I am employed at Studio A because of my arts knowledge. Furthermore, I am inspired to work at Studio A because I am interested in the production of art. Studio A employ no art therapists. Artists working within Studio A presumably derive some therapeutic benefits from the activity of art making, just as any artist (disabled or otherwise) likely does. But the artists are not attending Studio A to receive therapy. They are there to make art.

Art therapist Randy Vick (Vick & Sexton-Radek, 2008) describes visiting a series European art centres in 2003. At each centre Vick was met with the same firm assertion "We do not do art therapy" (Vick & Sexton-Radek, 2008, p.1). The studios reaction to art therapy was so vehement, Vick was compelled to undertake a broad formal study investigating fifteen community based art studios in the UK and USA and their relationship to art therapy. The study revealed a consistent aversion from all programs surveyed to any association with art therapy.

I can utterly relate to the firm stance Vick et al describes these studios as having taken in regard to art therapy. The common and immediate assumption that I am an art therapist leaves me feeling extremely frustrated. Whilst I always try to reply politely, I am forthright in my position that Studio A is simply about making art rather than providing therapy. Vick & Sexton-Radek (2008, p.9) quote a Dutch studio explaining their stance, "We do not do art therapy because these people are not sick. As this statement infers, therapy is provided as a healing modality when someone is considered unwell or deficient. Framing a supported studio as an art therapy provider immediately positions the artists involved as people in need of fixing or remedy. Whilst a person with intellectual disability will very likely need assistance in various aspects of their life, not every activity they partake in is about "therapy." The artists I have encountered at supported studios show no desire to be "fixed" or "healed" via their art practice, they are rather simply absorbed and driven by the process of making great art.

Therapy is not the purpose of a supported studio. Unlike art therapy, supported studios prioritize the production and exhibition of artwork, and assist artists to develop professional pathways in the arts. Lucas Ilheim (2013 p.1) writes about the need to get "discussion going about art and disability, beyond the confines of publications focusing on art therapy, mental health and outsider art." Ilheim (2013, p.1) recognizes the role of supported studios as working "to chip away at the paternalism and connoisseurship which often characterise relations within the intersecting worlds of art and disability." The common association of supported studios with art therapy highlights a perception such studios struggle against, that is, that artists with intellectual cannot simply be great artists.

Recognition or evidence of people with intellectual disability making great artwork is not a new revelation. The renowned Outsider artist Henry Darger (1892 - 1973) is just one example of a celebrated artist who likely had an intellectual disability. Darger's work is held in prestigious collections and art institutions internationally. Yet Darger himself never benefitted socially or financially from his artistic success (Cavallaro & Tito, 2015). Indeed, the breadth of Darger's work was only discovered by the art world in his apartment after he had passed away. One can only speculate how different Darger's life may have been if he had the opportunity to exhibit and sell his work during his lifetime. Presumably he would have benefitted financially, but he also may have connected with other like-minded artists, and perhaps felt a sense of pride to see his work so appreciated by audiences. At the 2013 supported studio forum "Possibilities and Potential" held at the Museum of Contemporary Art in Sydney Kris Tito announced "The success of Henry Darger after his death is to be considered a human failing from a supported studio perspective" (Cavallaro & Tito, 2015). Supported studios are about making and sharing great art. They also crucially exist to empower artists with intellectual disability, to ensure they are fairly represented and remunerated from their involvement in the art world.

Current Australian legislation acknowledges significant obstacles that restrict people with disability from being fully involved in all aspects of community life, including the arts. The NSW Disability Inclusion Act (2014, p.1) was passed in 2014, aiming to "dismantle existing barriers so that people with disability can participate fully in their communities, to the advantage of everyone." Specific to the arts, the National Arts and Disability Strategy (2009, p.15) highlights the need to "strengthen pathways into the creative sector and employment opportunities for artists and arts/cultural workers with a disability." Further, the peak federal advocacy body for art and disability, Arts Access Australia (2013, p.1), identified "major barriers to employment in the arts and cultural sector" caused by a "lack of general and disability-specific education, training and mentoring opportunities (which) inhibit the capacity of people with disability to find employment in the arts."

These policies all acknowledge people with disability are distinctly disadvantaged from participating professionally in the arts and, as such, require targeted responses to address the gap. Intellectual disability does not limit the greatness of the art you make. But intellectual disability can limit your capacity to navigate complex art world systems. Typically, to be a recognised professional artist you need to assemble an artist CV, exhibit artwork in galleries, enter art prizes and apply for artist's grants. Hugh Nichols (2012) describes these activities as the necessary 'scaffolding' or structural supports artists with intellectual disability often require. An artist may have a family member or advocate with the resources and skills necessary to provide these supports but if not, how can an artist with intellectual disability hope to access professional art networks? This gap is where the need for a supported studio arises.

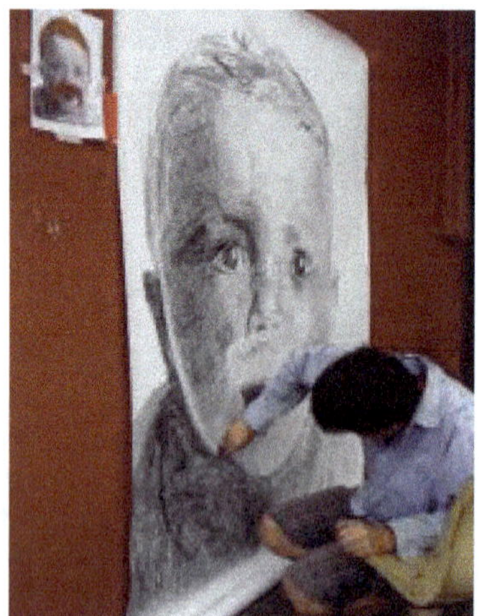
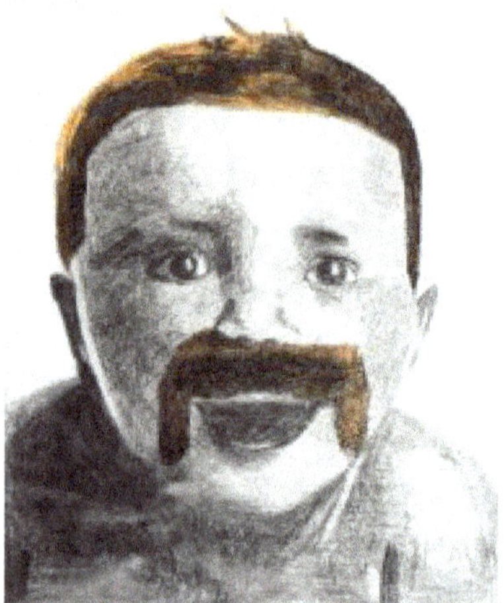

Figure: 12. 3 (left) - Studio A artist Daniel Kim working on portrait (2011).
Figure 12. 4 (right) - Mo Baby (2011) Daniel Kim. Pencil on paper, 140 x 180cm.

Studio A

I first encountered Robert "Thom" Smith on a platform at Hornsby train station in the northern suburbs of Sydney. Unlike the rest of the commuters, Thom was not waiting to catch a train. Instead, Thom was engaged in a performance for the trains. Along the edge of the platform were a series of positioned objects and small sculptures. Thom carefully arranged the objects, then with a broad smile, stepped back. As trains flew by he frantically shifted his gaze from his sculptures to the train carriage whilst energetically waving his arms and yelling 'silvery!' I was not the only commuter mesmerized by this strange happening. Other people on the platform similarly watched on with intrigue. No one approached Thom, rather people gave him a wide berth. The station guards soon appeared and vehemently encouraged Thom to move on.

Move forward five years to 2015 and Thom now has established a reputation within Sydney's contemporary art scene having been awarded several artist development grants, including a $10,000 Emerging Artist grant in 2014. He was an exhibiting artist in the prestigious 2015 Underbelly Art Festival on Cockatoo Island, and features as a performance artist in Carriageworks 2016-17 creative program. What accounts for this dramatic transition? How did Thom transform from a lone eccentric on Hornsby train station to a recognised emerging artist? Like Judith Scott, Thom is a member of a supported studio.

Studio A is an initiative of Studio ARTES. Studio ARTES is a not for profit, independent organization in the outer suburbs of Sydney. Studio ARTES provides creative programs for adults with primarily intellectual disability, including a full time visual arts program. Studio A began on a project basis in 2011 and now manages a separate full time professional development program.

In 2006, I approached Studio ARTES as a volunteer. I was completing my tertiary study in fine arts and anthropology, and thought volunteering would provide some light relief. I imagined lending my creative expertise and 'authority' to people who could benefit from my formal art training. Instead, to my surprise, at Studio ARTES I met a cohort of adults with disability creating strong and compelling bodies of artwork. The work was created with a focus and dedication that far exceeded that demonstrated by my fellow university students. Far from needing my tuition in art making, I felt slightly redundant in assisting the artists with their work. To my further surprise, I realised the artwork emerging from Studio ARTES was only seen by audiences in the local community, who were largely friends and family of the artists. Contemporary art audiences were denied the experience of the work because it was not reaching the other networks, such as inner city galleries and beyond.

Thom Roberts was one of the first artists I encountered at Studio ARTES, I discovered some of Thom's most interesting work on spontaneous display at Hornsby train station. As someone actively involved in the contemporary arts sector, I read Thom's activity through the lens of contemporary art. I saw Thom's activity as a site-specific piece of performance art.

I had an established interest in installation and performance art, so I found Thom's work intriguing. And I suspected contemporary art audiences would similarly appreciate it. Unfortunately, this was not the audience Thom was reaching at Hornsby train station. In fact, rather than applause, on the train platform Thom was more at risk of receiving a formal warning or a fine.

Thom has autism. In 2006, Thom did not describe himself as an artist. He was simply immersed in an activity he loved doing. Thom had never met or worked with a performance/installation artist and it was unlikely he had ever visited a gallery showing such work. Drawing, creating small sculptures, assembling his work, reciting poetry and interacting with his work in a public space were the activities that absorbed Thom, which he did with a compelling and graceful rhythm. It seemed to me there was an art to these seemingly unusual actions, and there was. However, the train platform where Thom showcased his work offered him few benefits and many risks. I wondered whether situating Thom's work within a gallery/art platform would offer him some financial and social rewards. In consultation with Thom and Studio ARTES I explored avenues for linking him with other installation based artists. Through networking within the arts sector, opportunities arose for Thom to be able to make and exhibit work at Sydney College of the Arts. This new opportunity and addition to his CV placed Thom in a stronger position to apply for artist's grants. Thom's intellectual disability precludes him from identifying or completing these applications independently. So, we would brainstorm the projects and applications together, and I would complete the administrative part of the application. Since 2012, Thom has been consistently successful with gallery and grant applications. And his artwork has accordingly developed and expanded. For example, animation is now a staple part of his practice.

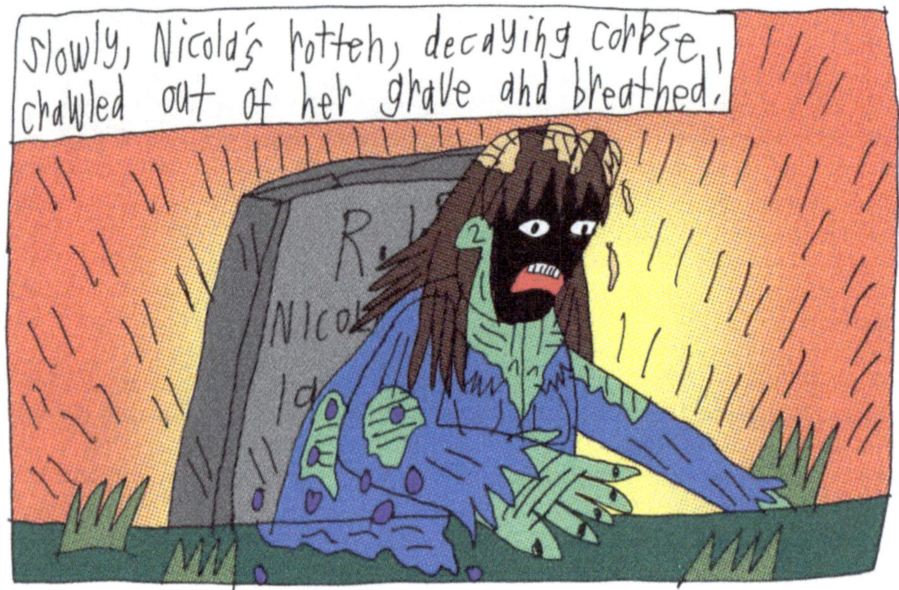

Figure: 12. 5 - Nicola's Return from the Grave (2015) Greg Sindel. Four-colour screenprint on paper, 70 x 100cm.

At Studio ARTES, there were a number of artists like Thom with specific artistic practices and styles. Greg Sindel is a comic artist, Daniel Kim a representational style painter and Mathew Calandra a bold graphic artist, just to name a few. All of these skilled artists had only ever made artwork within a recreational style art program for adults with disability. They had never had the opportunity to connect with mainstream artists with expertise in their specific discipline. Without their intellectual disability, they likely would have accessed an art college and have connected with other like-minded artists.

In response to the need for furthering the practice of artists within the Studio ARTES program, funding was granted by Arts NSW in 2011 to run a mentorship program where five artists with disability were partnered with five relevant established artists, known as 'Studio ARTISTS: Collaborate.' Thom was linked with installation artist Alison Clouston. The project culminated with an exhibition at a mainstream, central Sydney gallery, Gaffa. 'Studio ARTISTS: Collaborate' planted the seed for establishing supported studio, Studio A. The impact of being involved in this project on the artists involved was dramatic and this was not just the artists with disability. As mentor Michael Kempson (Head of Printmaking, UNSW) reported;

> All of us, including myself, who met and worked with Mathew while he was at COFA, might like to flatter ourselves to think of the meaningful contribution we were making to his continuing development as an artist, when in reality it was we who did the real learning (Michael Kempson, personal communication, November, 2011).

The project involved the artists working in new mediums including sound and printmaking, and produced bold new bodies of work. And even beyond the developments in their artwork, they demonstrated profound personal transformations. Artists with autism who have been typically averse to change caught public transport, worked with new artist mentors in new and changing environments.

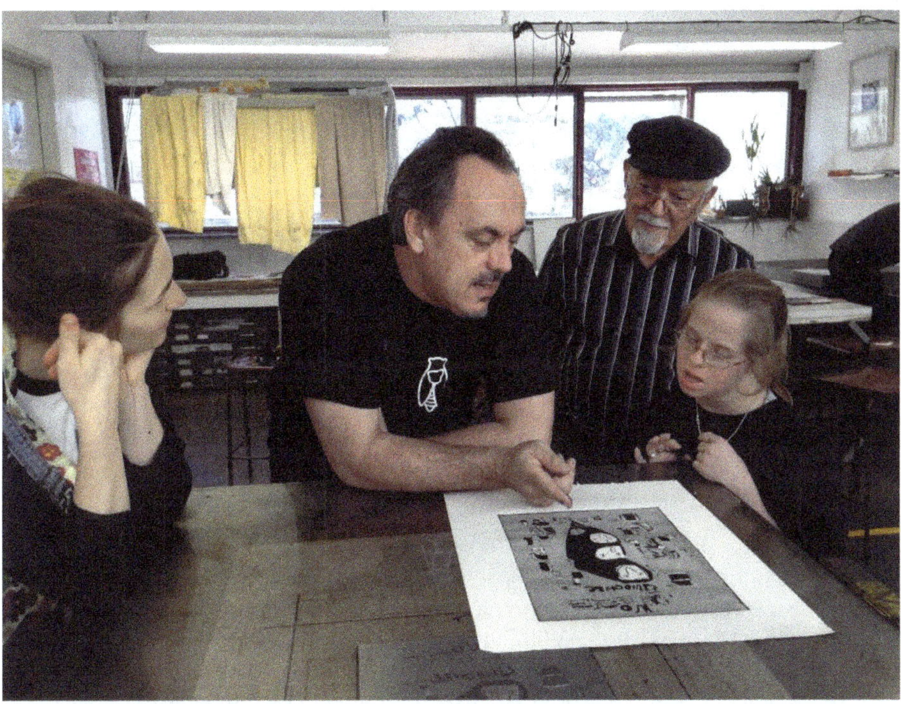

Figure: 12. 6 - Studio A Mentor Printmaker Michael Kempson working with Studio A artist Meagan Pelham in Cicada Press, College of Fine Arts, University of New South Wales (2013) *Image credit: Gabrielle Mordy.*

Since Studio A: Collaborate the demand and interest for this kind of program, which fostered connections between artists with intellectual disability and mainstream art networks has seen the Studio A project expand into a full time program. Currently, twenty artists with disability access the program, and we partner with a range of artists, arts organisations and institutions as mentors and collaborators.

Thom Robert's career has particularly progressed since these early days. Through the various networking channels Studio A has opened, Thom has developed a firm partnership with artist Harriet Body. Under the pseudonym 'Thom and Angelmouse' the two regularly collaborate. They are currently involved in a residency at Hazlehurst Regional Gallery, Sydney. Thom now self identifies as an artist and has a business card that he enthusiastically distributes.

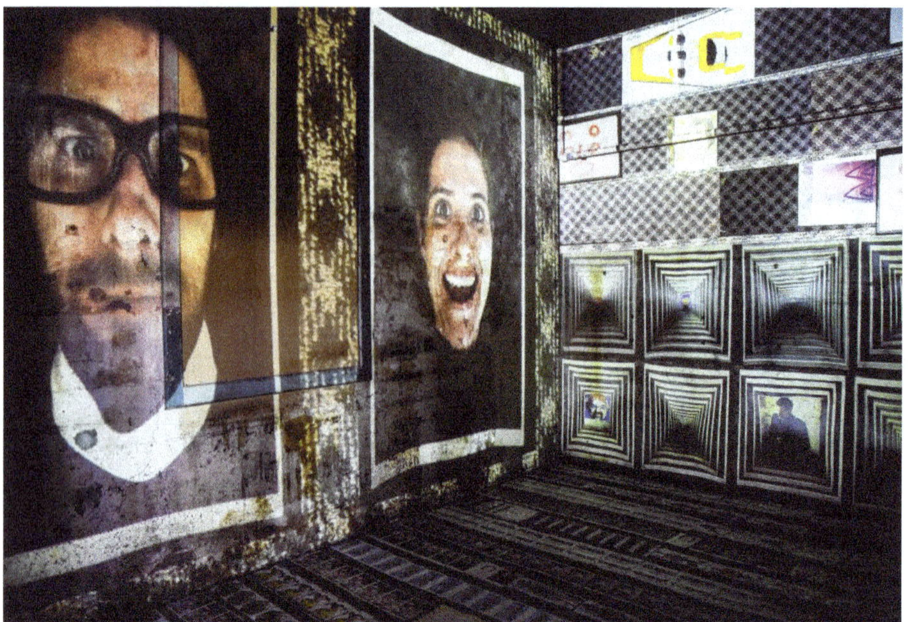

Figure: 12. 7 - City Circle Arrives at Cloud Heaven at Underbelly Arts Festival (2015). Thom and Angelmouse installation.

The professional progress Thom and others at Studio A have experienced has been made through the provision of very specific networking and tangible kinds of support Studio A provides. This includes completing grant applications, preparing artist CV's and networking with galleries. Without Studio A support, these tasks would be near impossible for the artists to manage. But it is these support mechanisms provided by Studio A that have been vital for artists like Thom to win emerging artists grants, and to secure selection in prestigious festivals such as Underbelly Arts. An equally important intangible support that Studio A provides Thom involves taking the art he makes seriously, rather than dismissing his activity on the train platform as strange or as a symptom. A proficiency in art and improved self-confidence means that staff from Studio A recognised Thom's activity as the expression of an artist, and were able to offer Thom further pathways to develop and share his work. In conjunction with the administrative support systems, a fluency in art opportunities is, I believe, key to a successful studio.

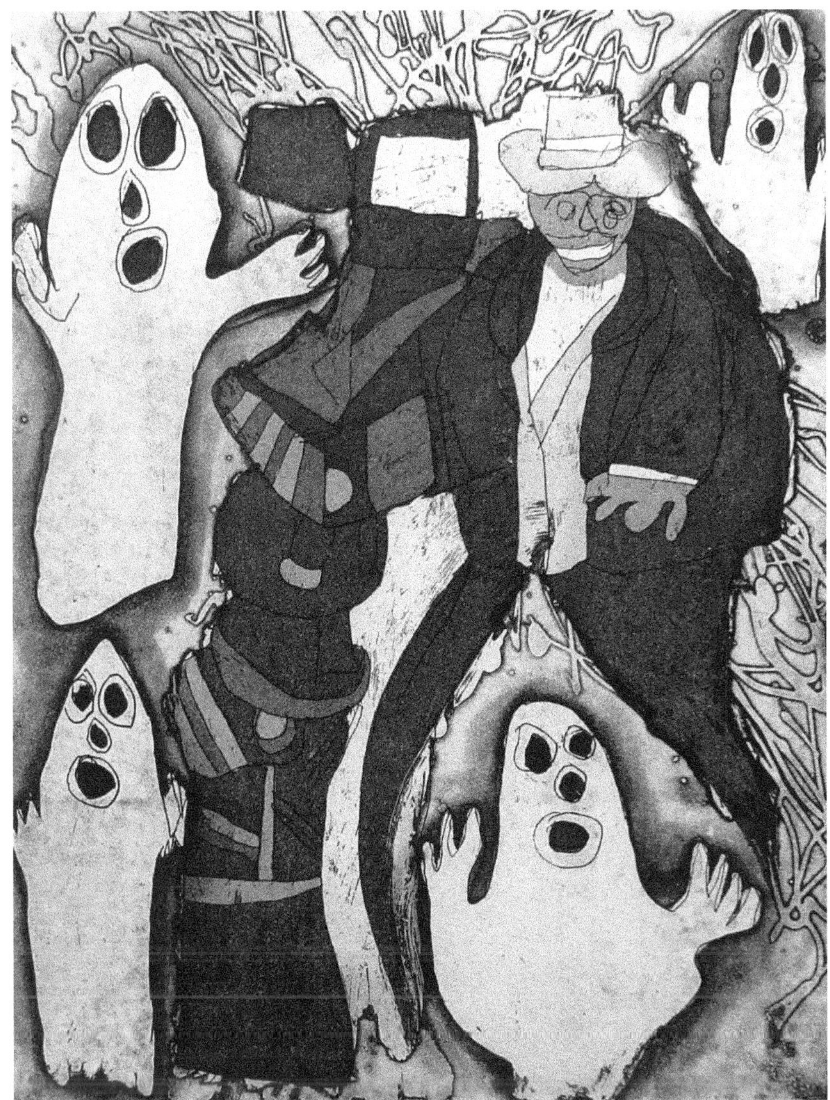

Figure: 12. 8 - Ghost Movie (2013). Mathews Calandra. Etching printed by Cicada Press. 19 x 24.5cm.

SUPPORTED STUDIOS

Supported Studios are distinguishable from other creative programs for adults with intellectual disability in the priority they place on developing artwork. Supported Studios approach adults with intellectual disability principally as potential artists, rather than as individuals requiring therapy or entertainment. Whilst Supported Studio participants may derive recreational or therapeutic benefits from attending the creative programs offered, key to a Supported Studio is the opportunities they offer participants to engage in "art for art's sake." For instance, in his article "An Other Academy: Creative Workshops for Artists with Intellectual Disabilities" Rhodes (2008), compares a selection of international Supported Studios, including Studio ARTES. In identifying a commonality between their working practices, he says,

Despite variations of methodology, all share a belief in the aesthetic value of the product, not only as personally relevant to the maker, but also as being of intrinsic artistic merit. 'Clients' are regarded as artists first and foremost. The fact that they are differently abled is merely the impetus for providing appropriate support for the nurturing and realisation of artistic ambition, rather than their defining characteristic (Rhodes, 2008, p.131).

Rhodes goes onto explain the importance of a Supported Studio as a structure that "not only supports but also *produces* artists" (p.131). Rhodes distinguishes many of the high profile artists to have emerged from Supported Studios from typical 'Outsider' artists. The history of 'Outsider' is proliferated with artists who have created impressive and often monumental bodies of work in solitary, driven by their own determination. In contrast to the typical 'Outsider' artist, Rhodes argues that many of the known artists to have emerged from Supported Studios would never have developed their portfolio of work without the encouragement of this broader studio network.

Describing Supported Studios as 'producing' artists is not intended to detract from the inherent talent of the individual artists who are emerging from Supported Studios. Nor does Rhodes infer that everyone who accesses such a studio will develop into an artist. Indeed, of the one hundred and forty members who weekly access the Studio ARTES program, only a handful of members consistently produce work that would likely catch the eye of curators or collectors. Rather, in 'An Other Academy', Rhodes concentrates on one effect and value of Supported Studios. That is the opportunity it offers adults with intellectual disability to explore, and at times discover, their creative capacity. Rhodes asserts that this capacity would likely lie dormant without the resources and encouragement of what Rhodes' terms 'Other Academies.'

Judith Scott and Creative Growth

The time and space allowed for creative exploration, as highlighted by Rhodes, was vital to the growth of Judith Scott, mentioned in the introduction as an artist from Creative Growth.

Judith's autobiography is almost as famous as her artwork, and much can be read about her personal story through a simple google search. Judith had spent almost a lifetime in institutional care until her sister Joyce Scott had her released. Joyce enrolled Judith at Creative Growth (MacGregor, 1999, p.53). Upon joining the studio, Judith famously sat for two years doing nothing. She showed a steadfast lack of interest in any of the offered activities, until textile artist Sylvia Seventy sparked Judith's interest (MacGregor, 1999, p.57).

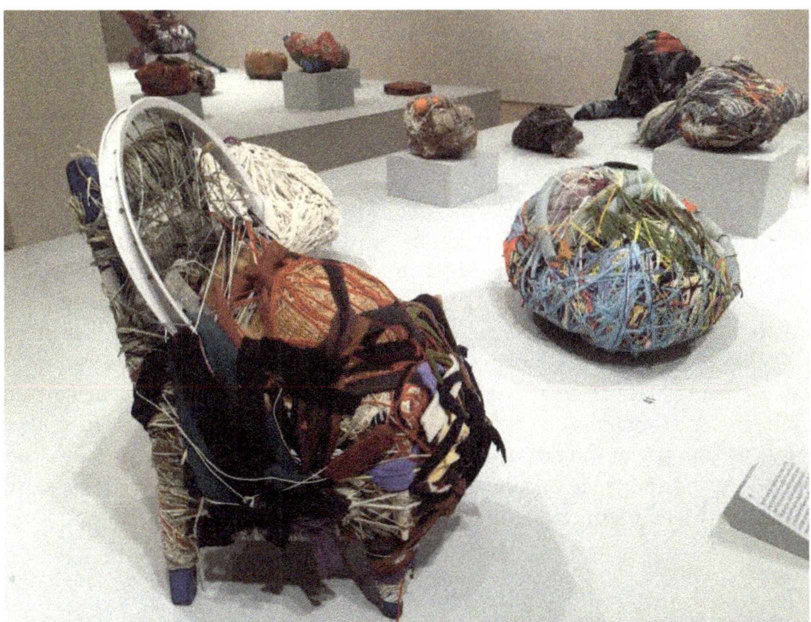

Figure: 12. 9 - Judith Scott's assemblages on exhibition in Judith Scott – Bound and Unbound at Brooklyn Museum (2015).
Image credit: Emma Johnston.

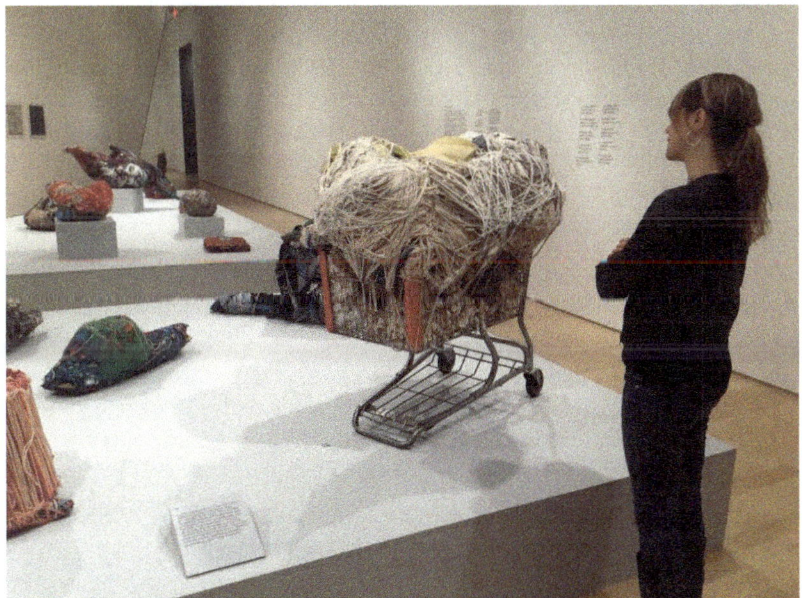

Figure: 12. 10 - Looking at Judith Scott's work on exhibition in Judith Scott – Bound and Unbound at the Brooklyn Museum (2015).
Image credit: Emma Johnston.

Judith made work that was very different to other work at Creative Growth. Using wool and yarn she wrapped found objects including chairs and shopping trolleys into bundled assemblages. Her practice took up lots of space and her activity likely seemed strange.

However, giving Scott space, time and encouragement was one of the first and most important supports Creative Growth offered. They gave her the freedom to explore, and to find materials and methods of working that engaged her. Once Judith was engaged, they gave her the scope and resources to push her practice. Her sculptures were allowed to grow large, she was allowed to incorporate furniture into her artwork. Upon X-ray, keys and mobile phones have even been located inside Scott's sculptures. Creative Growth took what Judith was interested in seriously. They treated her manifestations as artwork, not as purely therapy or recreation. This quality cannot be underestimated as a critical factor for the success of a supported studio. The integrity and journey of the artist must be respected and practicing artists, who respect and understand this creative process, need to be actively involved as staff and collaborators (MacGregor, 1999, xiii).

Visiting Supported Studios in San Francisco

In 2015, I was awarded an Australia Council Career Development grant to investigate how artists with intellectual disability were accessing mainstream art networks internationally. I visited many supported studios in the UK and USA and key on my agenda were the studios Creative Growth and Creativity Explored, both in San Francisco. Both studios were founded in the 1970's by the innovative Florence Ludins-Katz and Elias Katz. Whilst the studios are now entirely independent, they operate with a similar ethos and model. Each has a gallery space positioned beside their active art studios, and both cater to approximately one hundred and fifty artists with intellectual disability on a weekly basis.

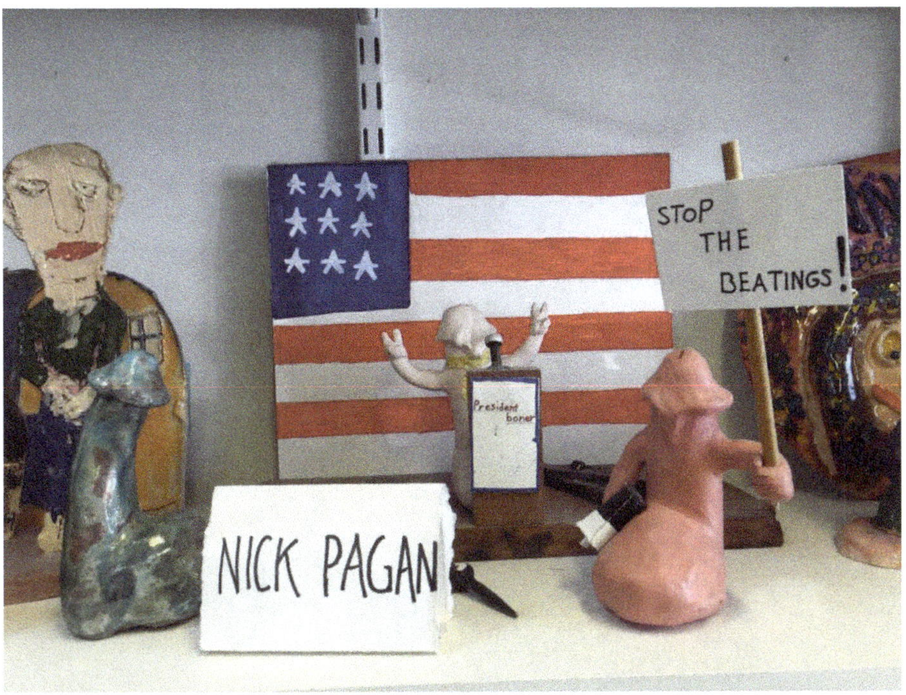

Figure: 12. 11 - Nick Pagan's sculptures in process at Creative Growth March (2015).
Image credit: Gabrielle Mordy, taken with permission of Creative Growth and artist.

In both studios I witnessed artists working in a variety of mediums including ceramics, textiles, woodwork and printmaking. Both studios are committed to supporting their artists to create the artwork they want to make - whether the work is politically correct or not. For instance, an artist working at Creativity Explored explained how he 'loves to come here because you can do anything here, they let me explore and play and make whatever I want to make' (personal communication, March 2015). Particularly compelling was a series of politically motivated ceramic penis' created at Creative Growth's by artist Nick Pagan because they highlight the artistic license afforded to artists in the program.

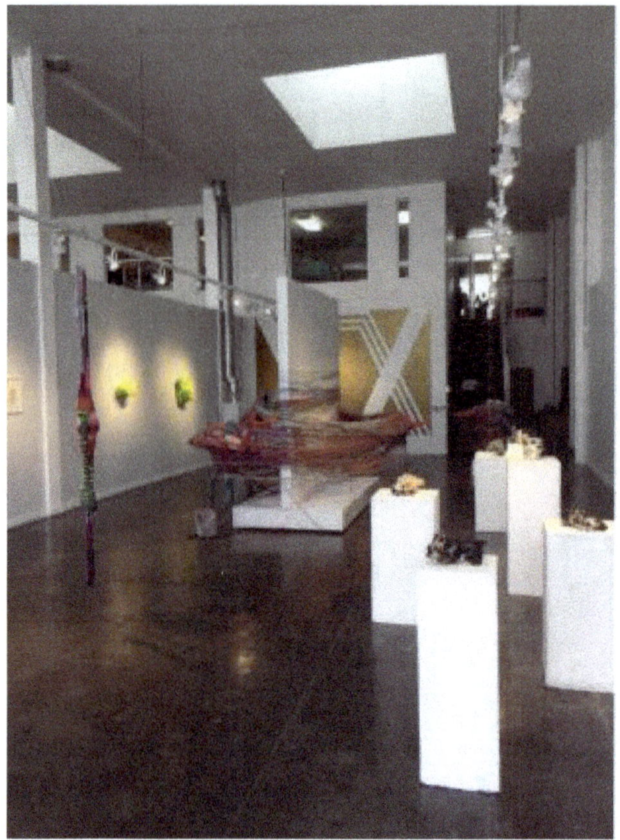

Figure: 12. 12 - Creative Growth gallery space (2015).
Image credit: Gabrielle Mordy.

The studios are located in different zones of San Francisco. Creative Growth sits in Oakland in the San Francisco Bay Area, whereas Creativity Explored is positioned more centrally in the Mission Area. Beneficially, the areas surrounding each studio have both evolved into central arts districts hence galleries, funky cafes and trendy bars now frame each studio. I was fortunate enough to be in town on the first Friday of April, when Oakland hosts its 'First Friday' festival. This involves an evening of open studios, galleries and a rockin' crazy street market. Crowds stream through the galleries and studios, and there are literally traffic jams of people trying to check out the art. It was overwhelming and exciting to see Oakland's appetite for art and Creative Growth of course opened its gallery doors and the crowds streamed through. As I fought my way through the queue in one of Oakland's galleries I casually came across an artwork from Creative Growth. The textile work sat easily beside work made by other mainstream artists. There was no differentiation announcing the work as being by an 'artist with disability.' It was not necessary. The crowds were there to see new work made by local artists, and this work was simply that.

Artwork from Creative Growth is held in prestigious collections and exhibited in leading international galleries. Their Director Tom di Maria was away when I visited managing the studio's exhibition stand at the Tokyo Art Fair. As I traversed the streets of Oakland, I witnessed how involved Creative Growth is in San Francisco's local arts community. Oakland's boutique cinema recently showed film work produced at Creative Growth, and the trendy nearby record store hosted an exhibition of music inspired art works.

Visiting Creative Growth and Creativity Explored I saw artwork from these studios immersed in the local arts community. Their involvement was not framed in bright flashing lights, nor was the work there because the gallery was being 'inclusive.' It rather just seemed to be business as usual. It was encouraging to see how 'normal' and casual the inclusion of artwork from supported studios has seemingly become in San Francisco's edgy gallery districts.

Talking to artist facilitators at Creative Growth, it was clear that opportunities for exhibiting work in local galleries had emerged through networks opened by staff. The artist facilitators were all practicing artists, who all exhibited or worked at local galleries/studio spaces. Hence, they were integral in making introductions and opening opportunities for Creative Growth work to be exhibited. From this experience I learnt that for artwork to be considered for collection by major galleries, it needs to first be seen and active in the more grassroots network of exhibition spaces and galleries. This is where curators and collectors go looking for the next exciting emerging artists. Hence, in delivering professional pathways, a supported studio needs to position artists work in this context.

Some Key Learning and Ingredients for a Successful Supported Studio

1. Culture that values creative exploration and play
2. Practicing artists play a key role in staff
3. Staff are proficient in arts administration
4. Staff and supporters are active in professional art sectors, and can then endorse the quality of artwork and make soft introductions
5. Studio management has advisors from the arts sector
6. Strong and appropriate marketing platforms that speak to the arts sector (this has not been discussed in this chapter, but is an important factor).

Conclusion

My inspiration for working in a supported studio has always been the compelling quality of artwork I have seen produced by artists with intellectual disability, and the artist's commitment to their creative practice. On a daily basis, I witness people involved in productive and meaningful work. Interestingly, when I'm out socially & I tell people I work with artists with intellectual disability, I am immediately assumed to be an art therapist. There seems to be a public perception that if you have a disability, art can only ever be a therapeutic or recreational activity. This perception of course does not reflect the true capacity of these artists, and indeed can limit their artistic potential being realised.

Supported studios, such as Studio A, are drivers of change in this 'mindset' domain. The support mechanisms offered by such studios are allowing artists with disability to engage in art for art's sake, to perhaps discover and develop their talent, and importantly to have their work seen by varied audiences. For me, there is nothing more rewarding than to observe a new audience member experience an artwork from a supported studio, I love to witness their expression as they suddenly realize this artwork is simply really good. In this moment, I see the inspiring capacity of art to change perceptions, connect people and broaden paradigms. Supported studios are key mediums to building these transformations.

References

Arts Access Australia. (2013). *Improving Employment Participation of People with Disability in Australia - DEEWR Discussion Paper*. Retrieved from http://www.artsaccessaustralia.org/resources/submissions/460-improving-employment-participation-of-people-with-disability-in-australia-discussion-paper

Cavallaro, J., & Tito, K. (2015). The Outsider Mirage. *Outside Runway Australian Experimental Art*, 27. Retrieved from http://runway.org.au/the-outsider-mirage/

Cultural Ministers Council. (2009). *National Arts and Disability Strategy 2009*. Australia. Retrieved from http://mcm.arts.gov.au/sites/default/files/arts-disability-0110.pdf

Family and Community Services. (2015). *NSW Disability Inclusion Act* (NSW). Retrieved from: https://www.adhc.nsw.gov.au/about_us/legislation_agreements_partnerships/nsw_disability_inclusion_act/dia-for-people-with-disability

Ilhein, L. (2013). Finding a place in the artworld. *Realtime. (*Dec - Jan). 118, p.6.

MacGregor, J.M. (1999). *Metamorphosis The Fiber Art of Judith Scott.* San Francisco: Creative Growth Art Centre.

Nichols, H. (2012). The Scaffolded Artist: Professionalisation in the supported studio. *un Magazine* 6.2. Retrieved from http://unprojects.org.au/magazine/issues/issue-6-2/the-scaffolded-artist-professionalisation-in-the-supported-studio/

Rhodes, C. (2008). An Other Academy: Creative Workshops for Artists with Intellectual Disabilities. *The International Journal of the Arts in Society,*

3(1). 129-134. Retrieved from: http://aarts.net.au/supportedstudios/wpcontent/uploads/2012/10/An_Other_Academy_by_Colin_Rhodes-The_International_Journal_of_Arts_and_Society.pdf

Supported Studio Network website. http://aarts.net.au/supportedstudios/about/. Retrieved on 10th May 2016.

Vick, R. & Sexton-Radek, K. (2008). Community-Based Art Studios in Europe and the United States: A Comparative Study. *Art Therapy*, 25(1), 4-10. doi: 10.1080/07421656.2008.10129353.

World Health Organisation. (2016). Definition Intellectual Disability. Retrieved from http://www.euro.who.int/en/health-topics/noncommunicable-diseases/mental-health/news/news/2010/15/childrens-right-to-family-life/definition-intellectual-disability

CHAPTER 13

The Process of Collaboration and Contemplation in Examining Public Pedagogies in a Local Makerspace

Lisa Hochtritt

ABSTRACT

This chapter reflects on the collective experience of ten graduate students and a faculty member who together undertook research into public pedagogy through a course offered in the art and visual culture education division at a large, public university located in the southwestern United States. It chronicles our experiences of working together with a local, non-profit maker and hacker community space over the course of a 15-week semester. Data collected in this case study include student generated written reflection papers, input from our class discussions, and personal reflections from the instructor. The chapter is guided by participants' descriptive accounts and snapshots of students' personal learning vignettes and it examines the ways in which a project-based curriculum that included field excursions and collaborative research influenced the conditions of learning. Throughout the course, students designed their own areas of research and self-identified areas of interest and focused on the areas of education, member needs, fundraising, and university connections for examination. The chapter includes the set-up of working with an outside partnering organization within the context of a semester-long course at an institution of higher education including the challenges, benefits, and constraints of such a project. The project confronted traditional student learning and uncovered the unease some students felt when engaging in student-centered curricula. The outcomes of this experience suggest the importance of practice-based projects, student-driven decision making, and learner-centered teaching in university curriculum. It also emphasizes the worth of prioritizing teacher flexibility and trust, as guided by student-articulated needs and interests.

WORKING TOGETHER TO TRANSFORM TRADITIONAL UNIVERSITY PEDAGOGY

What happens when students guide their own learning in a university graduate course? How can a teacher facilitate engagement in a topic? What are the issues when a pre-determined outcome is absent at the start of a graded course? How is student-centered learning beneficial to participants, the local community, and the teacher of higher education course? What are the challenges and benefits in decentralizing the role of the instructor? All of these questions plagued me as I entered into creating the syllabus and setting up the course that I reflect upon in this chapter. As the faculty member in charge I struggled with how much control I should have over the creation and execution of course content based on my own experiences as a teacher and my assumed expectations the students had as they entered into the course. This chapter chronicles the story of an experimental curriculum where I initiated the general project idea, then introduced the students to the organizers of a local, non-profit space, and then left it up to the students to design their own experiences for the semester. I tell this story from my perspective as the instructor of the course with written excerpts by the students. First, I provide some background to the course. Then, throughout the article I include learning vignettes, short reflection papers written by the students at the conclusion of the course. Finally, I suggest implications for practice as gleaned from my students' comments used as data sources to illuminate my findings, along with my personal involvement in the course.

The course where the research project took place was called, *Issues and Recent Research in Art and Visual Culture Education.* It was a required class for master's degree students and an elective for doctoral students; there were 4 master's level students and 6 doctoral level students in the class. Each semester the faculty member who teaches the course chooses the readings, projects, and research topics. I have a great interest in education and learning that occurs outside of the formal classroom and I was anxious to explore with the graduate students' scholarship and practice around the ideas of public pedagogy. Burdick, Sandlin and O'Malley (2014) suggest that the term public pedagogy has taken on various definitions over the years but it can be simply understood as education in public. The text we used in the class, edited by Sandlin, Schultz, and Burdick (2010) encouraged us, as educational researchers, to look beyond the traditional university classrooms and curricula for new ways to understand learning spaces. Through their writings they prompted us to:

> raise critical questions…that center on how we might open our inquiry into the places and people who exist outside of the schoolyard fence or the university campus and how we might address the challenge of recognizing and exploring the very pedagogies that undergird our own private and public lives (Sandlin et al., 2010, p. 1).

Inspired by this challenge, it seemed only appropriate to conduct a course on public pedagogy *outside* of the classroom. In our semester inquiry we placed importance not solely on research papers and article summaries, but on the contextual relationships examined through individual and group reflections, and the experience of co-creating meaning in a negotiated way.

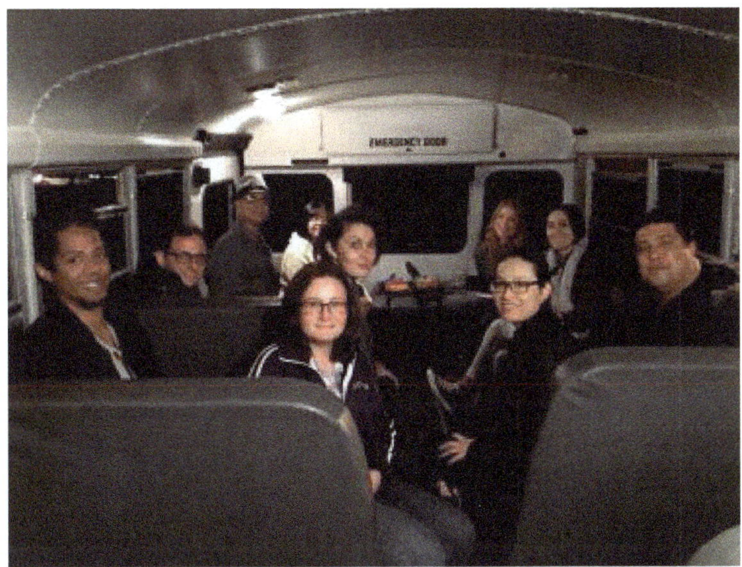

Figure: 13. 1 - Research team in graduate student Michael Barrett's school bus that often doubled as our classroom. 2016.
Image credit: Lisa Hochtritt.

I had taught this course before, but never in this way. In the past I assigned certain chapters from the course text; students read them at home and took notes/wrote personal reflections; the next class one person facilitated the class and guided us through the chapter contents, helping us to make connections to the text. It was fine. But it wasn't dynamic. I found myself a little bored with the general seminar style and I wondered how much the students were gaining from this didactic way of orderly moving through course content? After discussion with my colleagues, I decided to approach this course in a new way, a way in which the students were ideally forming their own content and creating their own educational paths based on their personal interests and educational queries. I kept the intent of the course, but let go of the traditional bounds of what I thought a graduate course should look like.

The major project we embarked upon was a collaborative partnership with Xerocraft, a local makerspace in Tucson, Arizona. This was of interest to me because our university is located in a community with a burgeoning maker and hacker scene and because in recent education literature, makerspaces and the maker movement are gaining attention in schools and communities (Dougherty, 2012; Rosenfeld Halverson & Sheridan, 2014; Sheridan et al., 2014). A makerspace, also referred to as a hackerspace, is marked by a do-it-yourself (DIY) ethos and supports creative production outside of mainstream consumerism. The Xerocraft organization states they are, "a collection of scientists, engineers, tradesmen, artists, or any other hobby enthusiast, but we almost all share one thing in common: curiosity" (Xerocraft, n.d., para. 1) and they encourage their visitors and members to learn from one another. With access to this organization and an open invitation by the director and volunteer coordinator to work with them on projects and research, we included this as the major thrust of our coursework this semester. Mindful of the teaching and learning contexts relative to our goals, we had to be flexible with the changing needs of the participants, partners, and locations. For example, we sometimes held class off-campus in the yellow school bus belonging to a class member (see Figure: 13. 1) and occasionally we met in the active makerspace's dusty basement sandwiched in between laser cutters and drill presses and the youth robotics club's test runs (see Figure: 13. 2). As a contemplative exercise we often talked about how the location influenced the possibilities of what could be created together, the importance of group decision-making, and the need for transparency in organization.

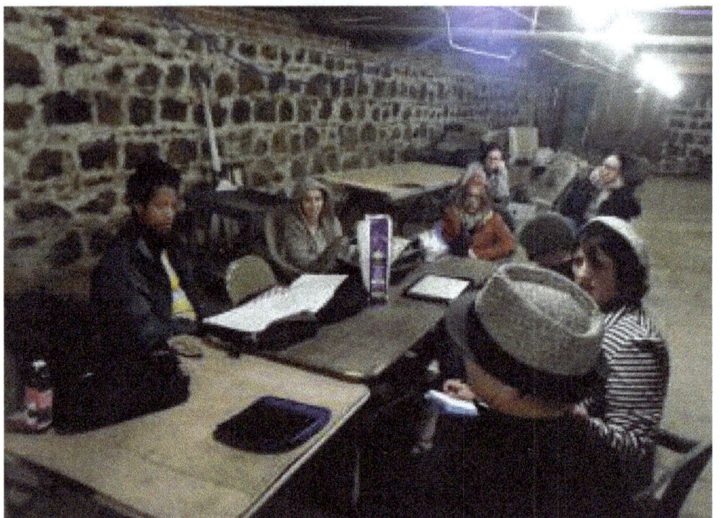

Figure: 13. 2 - Class members in the basement of the Makerspace. 2016.
Image credit: Misha Burstein.

The first time I taught this course I based my syllabus on my colleague's previous one that she generously shared, I decided that the students should read at least 25 chapters in the hefty book, *The Handbook of Public Pedagogy: Education and Learning Beyond Schooling* edited by Sandlin, Schultz, and Burdick (2010). During the semester I assigned case studies, research papers, and a final public pedagogy workshop or intervention. Through classes facilitated by the students on the chapters they read we learned how the book editors and authors critically addressed the topic of learning outside of traditional learning spaces and ways to consider our daily environment as pedagogical learning opportunities. Learning and teaching does not just take place in schools but in communities both in and out of the classroom. Artist Phil Cotton offers up this idea when talking about his work in schools and the importance of looking beyond the designated spaces of inquiry, "My whole concept at the beginning was to get the students to understand that the space of learning was not just a cube – the building, the classroom, the seat – but every aspect from the time you wake up to when you go to sleep is a part of the learning process" (Cotton, Duignan, Lucero, & Sikkema, 2015, p. 103). I thought my assignments were encouraging students to think beyond the cube, but at the time it did not occur to me that the traditional way I was teaching the class was counter-productive to the exciting learning communities they were reading about.

Fast forward to Spring 2016, the second time I taught the course. I stayed with the same book but I decided to reach out to a local makerspace to see how we could put into practice some of the ideas we would be reading about. I was not totally sure what we were going to do there, but I was hopeful that we could figure this out together as the semester progressed. I met with two representatives of Xerocraft in advance of the semester and after sharing with them my hope for the collaboration and they graciously invited us in to their making and hacking spaces with unlimited access. I was excited at this possibility to create something together with the graduate students taking the course but I was unsure exactly 'what' we were going to do and what I was going to expect for grading purposes. I had a lot of trepidation about how I was going to excite the students about this outside of the classroom project and my plan to support them in the design of the semester's coursework.

The Importance of Learner-Centered Curriculum

In deciding to make changes to my previous syllabus for the course I relied on student end of course reviews and also my own instincts. I found out that the students were not enamored with the many reading annotations and associated student-led facilitations I had assigned the first time I taught it. To be frank, I really did not want to read and comment on 250 reading annotations and I decided that adhering to the 25 chapters I had assigned last time I taught it may have not accomplished all I had hoped. What I wanted the students to get out of the readings was a better understanding of public pedagogy. I had hoped that through this experience the students would see the potential of learning and teaching everywhere, not just within the confines of the traditionally designated university learning spaces. What I decided to do the second time was to encourage them to choose their own readings and to annotate them on their own, scanning the five they wanted to share with the class members in our discussions. Rather than feeling relieved about not assigning so much reading and writing, I felt panicked and guilty that I was not doing enough. This feeling was quickly assuaged when students came to class the next session with their list of titles completed and they excitedly shared with each other what chapters they had chosen based on the title and a quick scan of the reading.

The chapters they selected covered topics such as outside curricula, critical public pedagogy, performance art, disruptions of public space, politics of place, decentering teaching, social justice, social media, exposing hegemony, and more (Sandlin et al., 2010). This excitement in choosing their own learning paralleled Weimer's (2002) findings when she encouraged students to pick which assignments and exams they wanted to take instead of assigning everyone the same thing. She writes about the initial confusion and then excitement that the students had in being in charge of their own learning. In her syllabus she had only one required assignment and then a variety of options for them to choose from. Weimer (2002) said she was stunned to see how hard the students were working and how it changed the energy in the class to a productive and positive environment led by students' desire to guide their own learning. In a sense that is what I was doing by providing the students the choice of which chapters they wanted to read. With ten different people in the class with ten different needs, it did not seem feasible or appropriate for me to decide what the best chapters were for all of the participants. Also, given the context of the outside project that required shaping by all of the class participants, not just me, I wanted to give the students the opportunity to help me co-design the course. This made sense to me as a teacher who values and trusts what my students can offer, but it was not readily transparent early on as one of the graduate students explains below.

What follows is the first learning vignette written by one of the graduate students in the course. As this experience was co-created and facilitated by the participants, it was important to me to hear and read their honest feedback about the course, prior to the end of semester course teaching evaluation. Therefore, at the end of the semester and the project with Xerocraft, I asked the students to reflect upon, in a short, written paper, what resonated with them from this experience, and, if they chose, link it to a reading to accentuate a certain idea. These excerpts are the students' exact words and cited in the chapter as personal communication. In the next statement, this student shares her frustration with the course and the lack of structure and detailed requirements. This was one of my guiding questions at the start of this chapter, how will students respond to the hands-off approach I offered? It did concern me that I might not be doing enough or providing enough structure and as you will read, this student started the course aggravated that I was not providing the safe and organized space to which she was accustomed.

Learning Vignette 1

Loss of power, growth of learning

> I was uncomfortable and frustrated early on in this class and with its required project. Everything was up in the air; there was no plan. We were to develop some project about public pedagogy with Xerocraft based on what they wanted from us, and it was to be group work – everyone's favorite kind of assignment. By the end of week one, the syllabus was still vague, the assignment was not even created yet, and expectations were very unclear. "What am I supposed to learn?" I thought. And, I was also frustrated and critical about the idea of public pedagogy, particularly at Xerocraft. After all, the term *public pedagogy* is vague and nebulous, making it open for interpretation, which is problematic (Savage, 2010). And after our initial visit I found Xerocraft, aside from dirty and unappealing to those of us not of its predominant middle aged white male clientele, to also be problematic. In addition to its space and demographic issues, in my view, it is a place very much focused on simply providing materials for individual maker needs rather than social justice focused education for the "public." I thought "How am I supposed to learn about education from a place like that and in a class

like this?" I walked away from the early weeks of this class experience confused and unmotivated.

So, I began this class and my work of looking into the "public" nature of education at Xerocraft with a negative view. From the start I had a mission to prove that what is happening at Xerocraft was not public pedagogy. I was so frustrated that I was not getting what I wanted that I took it out, ideologically on Xerocraft. So, to me, Xerocraft was only a cog in "the current neoliberal order" where "publics are just fictions we recite in the service of private interests" (Sandlin, Schultz, & Burdick, 2010, p. 2). And I was determined to create my own classroom structure and assignment expectations and force them on my groupmates so that *I* had the security of certainty not being provided for me. But in reflecting on what actually happened in this class, I now understand my frustration and experiences through the lens of student frustration and learner-centered teaching.

What I realize now that I did not at the beginning of this class and project is that Lisa was implementing a learner-centered teaching structure in this course. She was trusting us to co-design the class and project to make the experiences more meaningful and educational for us. But, Weimer (2013) notes that students encountering learner-centered strategies for the first time, even advanced students who would be assumed to appreciate all the freedom and shared power structure, often resist learner-centered teaching (LCT) strategies. They often resist, according to Weimer (2013) for four reasons: "increased amount of work, fear, and lack of readiness. And the fourth reason for resistance is that LCT involves loss" (p. 203). And this is certainly why I resisted, without even realizing what I was doing or understanding why.

I needed the security of a provided classroom structure and power dynamic with Lisa. "Classrooms where teachers make all the decisions are safer, simpler places" (Weimer, 2013, p. 204). But little growth happens in safe spaces. Weimer (2013) notes, growth is often the product of loss, whether in educational or personal contexts. And loss often manifests itself as resistance, as it did in my case. I had to give up security of what I expected from Lisa and myself. I had to give up power of responsibility for my success by working not only with a group in class, but also a larger community group. Kloss (cited in Weimer, 2013) argues that whenever you move from one level of understanding to another, "something is lost, something is left behind" (p. 203) and this creates resistance. However, with that loss comes growth. And in my case the growth was a new understanding of myself as a learner. Before this experience I thought I knew what was best for my learning needs. But after this experience I understand that I can and should learn in unexpected situations, even in dirty makerspaces; because,

> that's where my growth happened (R. A. Black, April 26, 2016, personal communication).

Until I read this reflection I had no idea that this student was so strongly opposed to this learning experience at the beginning of the project. I am grateful that she trusted me enough not to drop the course at the onset and that she eventually recognized and worked through the challenges inherent in the learner-centered teaching model. My belief in the importance of this process clouded my recognition of this student's discomfort. I was intuitively present to support the students enrolled in the course, but now after better understanding her experience, I would try to pay more attention to this early on in the semester. The question of how you earn students' trust to encourage them to remain actively engaged in the project is still on my mind.

In the next learning vignette, this student shares the importance of how a multiplicity of voices should be prioritized to get the most from learning situations. Excerpted from his reflection paper, he draws upon scholarship from the course textbook and recognizes how important it is to consider all participants' needs in a learning situation.

Learning Vignette 2

> Having grown up in the San Francisco Bay Area, I was somewhat familiar with the concept of the makerspace. From my experience, the majority of the spaces fit the bill of a typical 'garage like' atmosphere that provides a place where knowledge can give way to creative purposes. It became apparent to me from the very beginning of our work with the makerspace that those near the top were interested and dedicated to change. The director appeared open to addressing current struggles within the program and displayed genuine hope in transforming knowledge into wisdom, while at the same time recognizing the unity in diversity that unites both those on top and near the bottom. McLaren (2010) argues that critical public pedagogy encourages all voices to be considered and most especially, "an infusion of voices from below, a collective expression that leads to a plurality of narratives and conceptions of what constitutes both consciousness and reason" (p. 649) (M. Barrett, April 30, 2016, personal communication).

This student was pointing out how through his research at Xerocraft he found that the main organiser was encouraging of new ideas and supported change; this mirrored current scholarship about critical public pedagogy. His comments made me realize that this trait, to hear and recognize the needs of all participants involved, is essential to galvanise membership. In my own teaching, although I do not think of my students as a voice less important than mine, I do try to constantly remain cognisant of students' needs relative to the course goals and objectives. It is not always easy to juggle the distinct voices and inadvertently someone gets left out, but that is the struggle of a group, learner-centered curriculum and why leaving some segments open to individual student choice is so important.

ISSUES OF STUDENT DISCOMFORT

As you have read, included in the methodology for writing this chapter is the purposeful inclusion of the students' own words as data, collected through their written reflection papers, along with the information gained from our shared in-person class discussions. The next two learning vignettes share how uncomfortable the learner-centered approaches can be for some students and how they can sometimes actively resist such structures. In our debriefing reflection session after the project's end, one of the students shared with us how she did not necessarily trust herself when it came to identifying her learning goals and needs. She said that at first she did not know what she needed to learn best and she was concerned that she was not doing enough to succeed in the course. It can be a point of discomfort for students to be in charge of their own education and some students actually resist it. In the next learning segment, this student reveals how in her undergraduate studies she was never asked her opinion and what a shock it was in graduate school to have small classes where she was expected to talk and share her thoughts.

Learning Vignette 3

> At first, this course fed my anxiety. Seeing that I just stepped out of my undergraduate program, I had become accustomed to having my professors predetermine what we were going to study, how we were going to think and where our studies were going to go – in most cases it would end up is some form of research paper.
>
> But, the first day of class, Lisa gave us choices. We were to decide what we were going to study, and how we were going to go about our research – our personal interests played the key factor in our future success in the course. The guidelines were set in place, confirming that we were going to be working with a local makerspace in town and that we were to going to end with some form of final project, but what we wanted to gain from this experience was specific to ourselves. And Lisa made sure she was there as a helpful support throughout the course.
>
> I felt like I was actually doing something productive with my education and that in some way, what I was doing would benefit someone. I learned more in this class and developed better connections in this class than any other class I have taken (A. R. Urbach Pieterse, May 1, 2016, personal communication).

In the previous student's narrative, she shared how the open-endedness of the assignment caused anxiety as this way of learning was so new to her. In the end, the assignment was perceived to be more meaningful because she was doing something that mattered for others; it was not a theoretical exercise, but a project that meshed together both theory and practice. Another point of importance was that she mentioned the development of meaningful working relationships with other students in the class as a result of collaborating on this project. Building a positive class environment is always one of my teaching goals and in this circumstance it was achieved for this student through a practice-based project. Hers had a positive outcome but there are some students that actively resist a change in the traditional teacher/student, teaching/learning paradigm. For example, a colleague of mine who incorporated collaborative learning strategies in his course told me that students once stated in his teaching evaluation that he was not getting paid to have the students teach themselves. He was the teacher and he needed to start taking charge and tell them what to do. This is not always the case and as you will read in the next vignette: active learning strategies and meaningful class projects can contribute positively to a balanced academic/practical community of pedagogy.

Learning Vignette 4

> As an individual who privileges learning in practical, rather than strictly academic environment, a partnership between the classroom and a community organization yields my ideal learning environment. I am easily unmotivated by standard coursework, however in creating with and for Xerocraft makerspace, I am not only excited about my work, but strive to think more productively and creatively. Because the instructor afforded me the creative freedom to apply theoretical concepts learned in the classroom and through our readings to a real-world collaboration with Xerocraft, I now have experience working with a non-profit organization outside of the museum realm where I generally work (L. Baker, May 1, 2016, personal communication).

This student's example illustrates how she was able to link her needs outside of the course to her own career goals. Since academia typically provides opportunity for students to think deeply into theoretical models and concepts, being able to balance out what she thought to be a practical component seems to have motivated her productivity.

Being Open to Learning

The next student writes about the importance of trust between all parties in the learning process. There were many times during the semester that worried me. Not because of a distrust of students' abilities, but of the lack of trust in myself that I knew what I was doing in this situation. They were out in the field conducting research and they did not come to the weekly class; each group developed their own working timeline. Was I doing enough to help? Were they getting enough support? Did they have what they needed to be successful? These questions were constantly reverberating in my head during the off-site work days. I hoped I had created an environment that encouraged open dialogue between all parties and where they would feel comfortable asking me for what they needed.

Learning Vignette 5

Truth be told, I had not seen it coming. While I have always been very critical of the vertical framework of pedagogy that is typical of formal institutions of learning, I was initially quite overwhelmed by the amount of freedom we were given during the planning, execution and assessment of our public pedagogy research project. I could not believe how perplexed and anxious I felt about the circumstances and possible outcome of our collaboration. For the very first time I was given flexible deadlines, the power to negotiate specific assignments and many liberties in the exploration, format and depth of my contributions, yet still I felt nervous. Was this a taste of what Erich Fromm described as the fear of freedom? I believe it certainly was. You see, my whole education had been quite traditional; traditionally authoritative and constraining, with very little room (if any) for creativity and a critical analysis of society and power. For all our praise of democracy and freedom, most of our classrooms are anything *but* democratic. "Our colleges and faculties of education are certainly not democratic" (Steinberg, 2012, p. 228). According to Shirley Steinberg, professor of Youth Studies at the University of Calgary, one cannot understand democracy without understanding power and how it is created (Steinberg, 2012). These conversations, however, are still not taking place in most of our classrooms. Our teacher of Issues and Research in Art and Visual Culture Education at the University of Arizona, voluntarily gave up much of that power. She certainly took a risk, but by doing so, not only was she sending the message that she trusted us, she was also making us assume a degree of responsibility that extended beyond the individual; the extent of my commitment would have a proportional impact not only in my team's performance, but in the success of the whole project. I argue that this social dimension of interconnection and collaboration is essential in the creation of authentically democratic societies.

Once that moment of anxiety was overcome, I was amazed by the motivation I felt to perform tasks no one was commanding me to do. Driven by a sincere desire to learn and to benefit my teammates' understanding of pedagogical process within the organization, I found myself becoming engaged with the makerspace and visiting the place at times I felt convenient. I attended an organizational meeting to become familiar with their dynamics of decision-making, project-discussion and problem-solving. I observed semi-formal classes taught at the space in order to get a taste of the teaching and learning there. Because I was mostly interested in their philosophy of education, and in the contrast between formal and informal learning environments, my teammates had no objections to the people I chose to interview. All of these were happening at the same time I continued to inform myself by reading the self-selected chapters from Jennifer A. Sandlin, Brian D. Schultz and Jake

> Burdick's (2010) *Handbook of Public Pedagogy*, a collection of essays and studies on applications of public pedagogy.
>
> The opportunity to conduct actual research at a place of public pedagogy was invaluable. Each of us began to build, perhaps unknowingly at the beginning, a relationship of trust with the stakeholders at the place itself. Moving into a new community can be intimidating. Some of our research suggests that identities are not instantly assumed; you do not immediately don the mantle of a maker even if you are already interested in hacking. This confirms research in maker spaces by Kimberly M. Sheridan and Erica Rosenfeld Halverson. "It is not clear that individuals and groups automatically take on identities of participation within the maker landscape" (Rosenfeld Halverson & Sheridan, 2014, p. 502). What all of this means is that there is a social component and negotiation of identities *anytime* we walk within the spatial and social confines of a subculture. We also confronted prejudices and our own bias when bridging the gap between 'formal' and 'informal' education settings. Our findings particularly challenged that dichotomy, and reminded us that a mutually beneficial dialogue can actually take place between the two. This experience is a testament that other models of more democratic pedagogy are possible both at informal *and* formal institutions of education. (L. Garibaldi, April 30, 2016, personal communication).

Entering into this project we were all taking risks: Xerocraft had to trust that we had good intentions and would honor their work in a respectful manner; the students had to trust me to facilitate for them a choice-based classroom that was supportive of free-will and that I was not going to let them fail; and I had to trust myself that I was doing the right thing in teaching the class in this way, to trust the students that they would tell me if they needed assistance, that they would complete the work, and that they would be able to make the connections between our actions and the course goals.

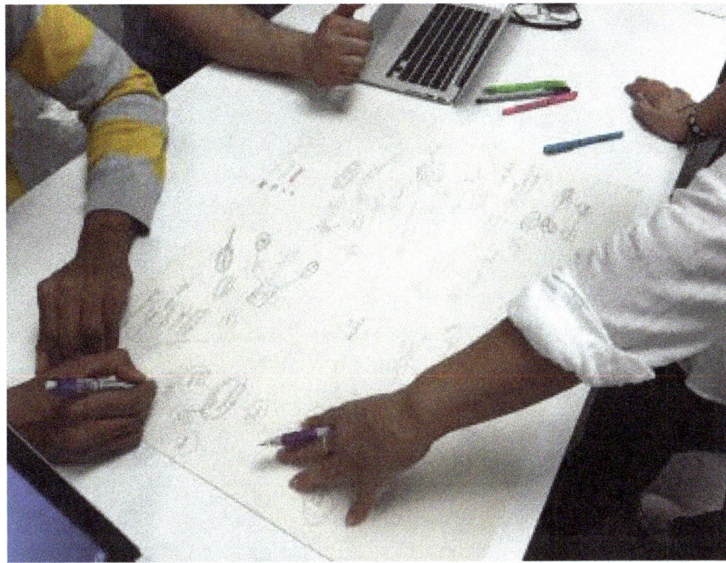

Figure: 13. 3 - Participants in the Education and Public Pedagogy group meet to discuss the mapping of findings, data analysis, and research outcomes. 2016.
Image credit: Lisa Hochtritt.

The next student reflects on important questions related to the collaborative process, uncovering important teaching strategies he thought I employed in the course. As previous students also shared, he discusses how his classmates motivated each other to continue with the project. As pictured in Figure: 13. 3, groups of students would often gather together outside of class time to ensure the group dynamic and workflow was progressing. They called their own meetings and facilitated them independent of the course.

Learning Vignette 6

> One thing that struck me about this class was the strong bond that people felt with each other. As the class continued to develop into a cohesive learning community, I felt that people became more motivated to support each other in the group—shifting focus from individuals being concern about grades and project deadlines to a collective embrace—where students work together in a learning environment supported by concepts of shared power and shared leadership.
>
> As a result, it seems students worked together as a community to finish projects without the stress found in a traditional classroom. I believe this was fostered by the instructor's willingness to experiment with the traditional classroom structure, allowing us to not only study public pedagogy, but to experience it. Specifically, I believe this was shaped through the following pedagogical events:

> - Working outside the traditional classroom and in a public pedagogy space (Xerocraft).
> - Letting sub-groups create their own rules about completing tasks.
> - Letting the class negotiate project requirements and deadlines.
> - Giving the class decision making access about how the curriculum should be shaped and executed.
>
> The literature on public pedagogy supports the idea that power is relinquished from a center figure—one authority or expert, where power is shared, negotiated, and expressed through a collective, who all share a vested interest in the collective outcome (Wenger, 1998). As the class left the traditional classroom and began working in the maker space, students began to experience the conditions of a public pedagogical environment. In turn, students began to re-envision new possibilities for teaching and learning. For example, the following questions came to mind:
>
> - What does it mean to teach in an emergent learning environment?
> - What does it mean to have students completely self-direct their own learning?
> - How does one approach the dynamics of a community of learners as opposed to a classroom of "individual" learners?
> - What happens when students have to command their own learning experiences?
> - What happens when the group has full ownership and responsibility for course and project outcomes?
>
> One other idea I keep coming back to is, did reflective practice impact our class experience? There were moments in during the class called, "check ins" where we reflected on our experiences. I am wondering if this reflection time also helped to shape and support the dynamics of this community? (M. Burstein, April 30, 2016, personal communication).

This student's reflection points to the importance of reflection and he brings forward the idea of an emergent curriculum. During the last class of the semester we reflected on what we learned and what conditions of learning influenced our accomplishments. After reviewing his reflective response, the data he uncovered about successful pedagogical events will inform my future teaching practices. He shared the importance of working outside the traditional classroom; and encouraging students to make decisions about the curriculum including creating their own rules; and negotiating specific requirements and deadlines.

LOOKING BACK AND THINKING FORWARD

In our work this semester we were inspired by ideas about opening up spaces for learning as suggested by Sandlin, Schultz, and Burdick (2010). They state, "expand[ing] understandings of educational spaces and purposes open the possibility of educational discourse that crosses institutional borders and disciplinary fields, and reframes inquiry into the relationships among pedagogy, democracy, and social action – regardless of where these relationships occur" (pp. 3-4). I was also guided by my own desire to make the classroom and active and engaging learning space and one that had malleable walls to the outside world. In the final vignette, this student furthers the discussion about relationships and how a melding of the students and the makers occurred throughout the research.

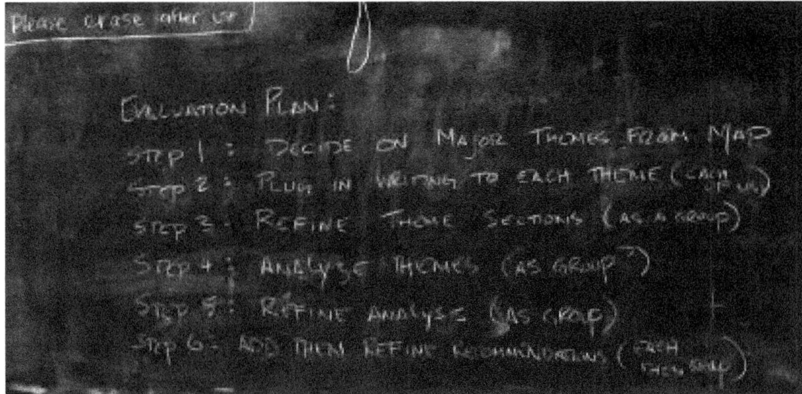

Figure: 13. 4 - The Education and Public Pedagogy group's chalkboard outline for writing the program evaluation review report for makerspace organisers. 2016.
Image credit: Lisa Hochtritt.

Learning Vignette 7

> Xerocraft, our local hackers space in Tucson, was something I was not expecting. When I think of a hacker's space, images of computers in a dark room come to mind. A hacker space is a place where people modified, transformed, altered, whatever they create. Xerocraft did challenge my thinking. While observing the sewing and welding classes, I was pleasantly surprised by knowledgeable the instructors are and how invested the students were. It was not an *us/them* mindset; they blurred the lines and created a *we*. Xerocraft has created a community where help and guiding one another is the norm (B. Longoria, April 29, 2016, personal communication).

At the end of the research, the student sub-groups created a program review document for Xerocraft and presented the results to the organization's leadership team. Teams of students meet separately and outlined their sections (see Figure: 13. 4) and each was responsible for writing a portion of the report based on their research findings. This exercise of writing up their results for an outside organization was another learning experience and the process encouraged many conversations about how one works in a public space.

Practical Application to Transformative Teaching

Examining data from the students' written reflection papers, information garnered from our shared in-class working and discussion sessions, and my own personal observations and reflections, helped me in positioning the findings within the literature. Scholarly writings on public pedagogy and student-centered teaching and learning punctuated the importance of many guiding characteristics including trust, flexibility, and student-centered curricula.

Trust

In their reflections, both here and shared in our class sessions, students spoke of how this class was not what they expected. Because graduate school is oftentimes reading and writing heavy and as faculty we are used to teaching these courses in a particular seminar-based, dialogical way, I struggled with whether I was assigning enough and if the students were learning anything related to public pedagogy. Although I knew that I wanted to have the course driven by student interests it was still delivered within the context of a traditional higher education institution and graded on the quality and quantity of the semester's work, as well as the student engagement with the material that conveys an expectation of things being done in a certain way. I had to trust that students would tell me if they were feeling overwhelmed, confused, or uncomfortable. In restating what one student said of the shift in power between students and teacher,

Voluntarily [Lisa] gave up much of that power. She certainly took a risk, but by doing so, not only was she sending the message she trusted us, she was also making us assume a degree of responsibility that extended beyond the individual; the extent of my commitment would have a proportional impact not only in my team's performance, but in the success of the whole project (L. Garibaldi, April 30, 2016, personal communication).

What this experience taught me, as guided by the student participants, is that risk taking and trusting yourself, your community partners, and your students are critical components in teaching and learning either inside or outside of the classroom.

Flexibility

I learned that sometimes things do not always work out just as you had planned and that it is imperative to embrace flexibility in your teaching. Embracing an emergent curriculum relies on a person's ability to question the power dynamics of the traditional teacher-student roles and organically change with the needs that present themselves, but knowing when to give in and when to stand strong. This awareness of when to bend is still something with which I struggle. I sometimes felt like changing an assignment because students called for it was too forgiving and that I should stick with my plans. These feeling made me question who I was really being unwavering for; me, or my reputation, or the students? I did not want to be perceived by my students as being too easy or having lowered expectations of them, but I truly had to ask myself what the point of a particular assignment was and if the core of the idea could be met in a different way. I had to think of the context and, as stated by art educator Ronald Neperud (1995), "context is that tangled web of relationships among the contents of life that are ever changing and shifting" (p. 12). This openness to consider the relationships of your context and consider new ways of accomplishing course goals, as guided by student input and needs, can be an integral part of facilitating worthwhile experiences for students. This experience with Xerocraft also emphasized the worth of prioritizing teacher flexibility and trust, guided by student-articulated needs and interests.

Student-Centered Curricula

The outcomes of this experience also suggest the importance of practice-based projects and student-driven decision making in university curriculum. The project challenged traditional student learning and uncovered the unease some students feel when engaging in learning-centered curricula. Finding ways to support the students as they make the transformative journey from teacher-driven to student-centered curricula is important to the well-being of the learner. Our work with Xerocraft was an excellent example of a balanced conversation. I started the conversation with the makerspace a few months before the semester began with an unsolicited email to the volunteer coordinator. I am forever grateful to this coordinator for answering my message and trusting that my intentions were good. They provided for us a learning laboratory and they opened up their spaces and introduced us to their makers with open enthusiasm. Artist Scott Sikkema explores the idea of a balanced conversation well explaining the necessity of listening to all of the authors of a learning experience, "In schools, social practice should be unfolded equally by artists and students and teachers; the art, and the learning, never really has one author" (Cotton et al., 2015, p. 101). I know we positively benefited by the Xerocraft project and I hope that we listened enough and that the partnership was mutually beneficial. As a faculty member at a large public institution where I am required to start the semester with a completed weekly syllabus organized for the duration of the course, I will be reminded of the importance of polling my students' interests based on the course description to inform my final curricula requirements. I have noticed a palpable tension at the semester start between conflicting interests such as university expectations for syllabi, students who want everything complete in a tidy package detailing what is necessary for an A grade, and my own organization and content high expectations, yet wanting to leave room for student input. Implementing the student-centered approach is challenging and given the varying participants each semester, it continues to be an exciting, ever-transforming, work in progress.

CONCLUSION

This chapter focused on the lived experiences of the teacher and graduate students involved in a study of public pedagogy and a makerspace located in the southwestern United States. It included the set-up of working with an outside partnering organization within the context of a semester-long course at an institution of higher education, including the challenges, benefits, and constraints of such a project. The findings of our research project helped us to refine our understandings of pubic pedagogy and how this practice can be observed in multiple contexts. Xerocraft, the makerspace we partnered with, provided an exemplary learning studio for the students. The organisation's mission includes a prioritization of opportunities to learn from each other that was a perfect conduit for our research. Our research findings illuminated clearly one of the three readings of public pedagogy suggested by Biesta (2014), "pedagogy *of* the public… located within democratic processes and practices" (p. 22). In other words, education conducted by and within a certain community. The education at Xerocraft was shared through a mixture of structured and informal facilitations and included a trading of skills and expertise by members and visitors to the space. The student researchers noticed this type of public pedagogy in their observations and it was corroborated by readings from our course text. This chapter was guided by learning vignettes written by some of the participants and included students' reflections on the experience of participating in such a non-traditional, project-based format for a traditionally graded course. They also included personal moments of transformation, and the discomfort and gains inherent in self-directed learning and the contemplative process. Although we initially set out to research how a non-profit organization exemplified elements of public pedagogy, the unintended outcomes related to the students' experiences of this project were the most interesting and major findings. Their reflections revealed anxieties of learning in a university space where the outcomes are typically prescribed. The themes they discussed in class sessions and in their writings clustered around the ideas of trust, flexibility, and student-centered curricula through this transformative pedagogical inquiry. This study put into practice the importance of re-orienting conceptions of community engagement and the prioritization of participatory social practice.

ACKNOWLEDGEMENTS

The author would like to thank the following graduate students for collaborating on the writing of this chapter and for sharing their expertise in this project: Lindsey Baker, Michael Barrett, Rebecka A. Black, Misha Burstein, Lino Garibaldi, Jennifer Johnson, Bridget Longoria, Yu-Wen (Eryn) C. Neff, Arielle Rose Urbach Pieterse and Jeffrey Urdang.

REFERENCES

Biesta, G. (2014). Making pedagogy public: For the public, of the public, or in the interest of publicness? In J. Burdick, J. A. Sandlin, & M. P. O'Malley (Eds.), *Problematizing public pedagogy.* (pp. 15-25). New York, NY: Routledge.

Burdick, J., Sandlin, J. A., & O'Malley, M. P. (Eds.). (2014). *Problematizing public pedagogy.* New York, NY: Routledge.

Cotton, P., Duignan, J., Lucero, J., & Sikkema, S. (2015). Engaged education and the schools. In S. Smith (Ed.). *Institutions and imaginaries: Chicago social practice history series* (pp. 101-109). Chicago, IL: The School of the Art Institute of Chicago distributed by the University of Chicago Press.

Dougherty, D. (2012). The maker movement. *Innovations*, *7*(3), 11–14.

McLaren, P. (2010). Public pedagogy and the challenge of historical time. In J. A. Sandlin, J. Burdick, & B. D. Schultz (Eds.), *Handbook of public pedagogy: Education and learning beyond schooling* (pp. 648-651). New York, NY: Routledge.

Neperud, R. W. (Ed.). (1995). *Context, content and community in art education: Beyond postmodernism.* New York, NY: Teachers College Press.

Rosenfeld Halverson, E., & Sheridan, K. (2014). The maker movement in education. *Harvard Educational Review, 84*(4), 495-504.

Sandlin, J. A., Schultz, B. D., & Burdick, J. (Eds.). (2010). *Handbook of public pedagogy: Education and learning beyond schooling.* New York, NY: Routledge.

Savage, G. C. (2010). Problematizing "public pedagogy" in educational research. In J. A. Sandlin, B. D. Schultz, & J. Burdick (Eds.), Handbook of public pedagogy: Education and learning beyond schooling (pp. 103-115). New York, NY: Routledge.

Sheridan, K., Rosenfeld Halverson, E., Litts, B., Brahms, L., Jacobs-Priebe, L., & Owens, T. (2014). Learning in the making: A comparative case study of three makerspaces. *Harvard Educational Review, 84*(4), 505-531.

Steinberg, S. (2012). Democracy and social justice in a capitalist society: Is this possible? A conversation with Shirley R. Steinberg. In P. Orelus & C. Malott (Eds.), *Radical voices for democratic schooling: Exposing neoliberal inequalities* (pp. 223-235). New York, NY: Palgrave Macmillan.

Weimer, M. (2002). *Learner-centered teaching: Five key changes to practice* (1st ed.). San Francisco, CA: Jossey-Bass.

———. (2013). *Learner-centered teaching: Five key changes to practice* (2nd ed.). San Francisco, CA: Jossey-Bass.

Wenger, E. (1998). *Communities of practice: Learning, meaning, and identity*. Cambridge, U.K.: Cambridge University Press.

Xerocraft. (n.d.). Who are we? Retrieved from http://www.xerocraft.org/about.php

CHAPTER 14

Reflections on Transformative Pedagogies and Practice Encounters in the Cultural Sphere

Kim Snepvangers and Donna Mathewson Mitchell

ABSTRACT

This chapter reflects on the scope of community engagement practices, creative partnerships and emergent ways of working in the cultural sphere. Providing an articulation of key ideas significant in creative partnerships this chapter critically reflects on the theoretical framework of 'practice encounters' as a way to re-consider community connectivity related to the visual domain. The significance of creative encounters and the efficacy of participation is an expanding field of discourse in relation to post human professional identity formation, audience engagement and creative industry partnerships. Evidence of transformative pedagogies as strategies to inform practice will be articulated. An examination of the ways in which practices can be considered as living things interdependent and connected in 'ecologies of practice' will be undertaken using contemporary community engagement projects. Evidence of practices as orchestrated transdisciplinary arrangements are described using reflexive accounts to further examine specific projects and how ideas, methods and approaches are situated in relation to the broader field. The implications of ideas presented as "practice encounters" is considered in terms of participatory practice and transformative research methods. We revisit the existing terrain and identify how community engagement encompassing art, education and the cultural sphere can be re-imagined and re-oriented to explore concepts of educational encounter beyond experience, dialogue and pre-determined goals. How social worlds related to art, education and the cultural sphere are prefigured, enacted and reconfigured using permeable boundaries and transformative pedagogy is disclosed. We conclude by speculating on the adaptations and implications of transformative pedagogies and ecologies of practice in art, education and the cultural sphere.

INTRODUCTION

At the outset of this book we asked, within the pedagogic and social turn, is all engagement between community, art and education, transformative, educative, sustainable and linked to democratizing principles that address civic agendas? As we conclude this book there are many ways that we can answer this question and there are many suggested responses. However, it must always be said that such responses are constantly 'in the making' and contingent on approaches to participatory practice, time and space. The significance of creative encounters and the efficacy of participation in museums, galleries and the cultural sphere (Bishop, 2012) alongside the broader fields of community development (Cornwall, 2008) and in social media (Literat, 2012) is an expanding field of discourse in relation to post human professional identity formation, audience engagement and creative industry partnerships. There are clear connections between community engagement, art and education within cultural spheres, yet there remain many questions about the fundamental nature of those connections and their value. Questions generally relate to disciplinary perspectives and focus, the relationship between localised and global praxis and the changing role of art, arts, design and media in relation to community as a socially responsive domain. Authors such as Costandius, Rosochacki & le Roux (2014) highlight key issues in community engagement for institutional and educational institutions. Reviewing their research project about Critical Citizenship Education and Community Interaction in a visual communication design course within a university context, the authors argue that: "student reflections revealed that participating in the project presented a risk of perpetuating deep-seated negative or stereotyped perceptions and attitudes" (p.122). Echoing Apple's (1979, p.63) concerns the authors state: "because educational institutions are 'naturally' generated out of many of educators' common sense-assumptions and practices, educational institutions could unknowingly create, 'conditions and foms of interaction [that] reproduce structures of inequality'" (Costandius at al, 2014, p.123). They are critical of service learning models and note that "a literature review on community engagement reveals that very few self-reflections or critical analyses of service learning modules have been published by lecturers who facilitate these" (ibid). In summary, the authors suggest the significance of consciousness raising, acknowledgement of implicit understandings and seeing the interaction as a chance to network and partner rather than the extraction of information or "viewing the project as a trophy" (pp.123-125).

Such observations about community engagement projects lack of transformational capacity are not dissimilar to the ideas raised by Schatzki (2011, p.4) who argues that just because activities happen does not necessarily mean that those happenings are equivalent to change. Therefore, the performance of an action does not necessarily lead to change and can in fact act to maintain existing stable bodies of knowledge. The authors' and the cases outlined in the preceding chapters continue to investigate the dynamics of practice change. For example, many of the projects share cultural knowledge through a range of practices that show respect for each other's cultures, such as working within Makerspaces, social media and across disciplinary boundaries. Community engagement devices such as the many examples of self-reflection on the lived experience of 'insider practitioners' in this book seek to uncover tensions involved beyond typical sites of service delivery in the tertiary context. When referring to the work of educators, Kemmis (2009) argues that "changing practices requires changing things frequently beyond the knowledge or control of individual practitioners, and frequently outside the individual practitioner's field of vision" (p.38). Similarly, the authors' in this book by pre-figuring encounters, interactions and engagements through the lens of co-participation, co-partnering and at times, co-authoring, seek a critical and self-reflective approach to established hierarchies and social relevance. Transformative pedagogies rely on the visual and practice based dimensions of experience beyond the lecture theatre and "beyond the knowledge or control of individual participants" (ibid).

In considering these questions and exploring this territory, there is a need to consider the existence of art and the cultural sphere in the public domain, and its changing and responsive nature. The public nature of work within this area means that there is a need to consider the aesthetic possibilities of social capital in terms of a socially engaged and informal pedagogical approach. Following this there is importance in re-considering contributions of education and research through transfer of knowledge, skills and expertise across social collectives, partnerships and larger institutional agencies and the consequential impact of such transfer to the development and adaptation of practice. Education has a significant role in facilitating equity and types of participation alongside issues of local and global significance and linking with knowledge pathways. Knowledge pathways have broad significance to the development of social capital within the cultural sphere while also having importance for industry collaborators, cultural custodians, significant sites, policy and funding.

Underpinning engagement in the cultural sphere and the intersection of community engagement, art and education is a focus on social impact and establishing rigorous criteria for partnerships. This is particularly important at a time that is dominated by contemporary neo-liberal funding and educational agendas in which funding and support is contingent on the demonstration of social and economic worth. There is great potential here for critically reflexive visual research methodologies that explore culturally responsive dialogues between artworks, events, sites, publics, adaptive and civic spaces, conceived as practice encounters. Such approaches to research explore non-linear, liminal and temporal engagement and ecologies of practice across relational and professional networks. What is crucial is that the visual artefact, research approach and materiality remains as a core focus uniting those working in the different areas of the cultural sphere. The potentiality of 'practice encounters' is partially derived from Hager, Lee and Reich's (2012) five principles of practice:

1. Practices are knowing-in-practice
2. Practices are socio-material
3. Practices are embodied and relational
4. Practices exist and evolve in historical and social contexts
5. Practices are emergent (Hager, Lee and Reich, 2012, pp.3-5).

Re-considering community connectivity related to art, education and the cultural sphere has focused on the concept of encounter. Contingency, chance elements and encounters conceived as the beginning of new experiences have been shown to have particular educational and transformative value. Accepting the unforeseen and improbability of outcomes and innovation provides a counterpoint to socially static ways of working with communities and the outcomes-based approaches that dominate the educational world. Emergent practices are reported on through the chapters in this book and focus on how interventions and a de-centering agenda can act against neoliberal agendas and institutional practices in the visual and performative domain. Exemplars of working with rather than for a range of diverse communities are disclosed. Localised and contextual practices, highly valued in arts based research co-creation reveal new possibilities in transformative pedagogy.

Of particular interest has been theoretical approaches and innovation in contemporary social spaces, particularly the museum and gallery sphere. Exploring civic engagement through group participatory methods, flow, adaption and connectivity in the cultural sphere, new materialism and research-creation strategies provide a backdrop to challenge audiences, participants and communities in a range of ways and in diverse settings. In examples of practice we can see informal pedagogies considered in relation to socially responsive participatory practice. The role and place of the virtual in social media also signals new relationships between participatory pedagogies, objects, events, display and exhibitions. Effects and meanings central to the work of transformative pedagogy and cultural development research emerge from the projects and examples.

The examples in this book re-imagine sites and situations of learning, culture and place across the life-cycle utilising a range of practices relevant for educators and practitioners in the public domain. There are examples of the application of ecology, practice architectures and site ontologies that reconceptualise professions and pedagogy beyond mainstream or formal educational contexts. This includes examinations of: curriculum design in higher education, transdisciplinarity, transnationality, historical cases, artmaking as research, engagement through digital technologies, the role of the body and affect, artist-led supported studios, community based production and exhibition, multi-literacies, collaborative practices, makerspaces, image making as visual reasoning, design-thinking, cultural planning, leadership, exhibition design, creative practice research, public programs, the use of social media and digital ethnography. In many of these examples, arts-based research is conceived as a network prioritising transitions and becomings to re-conceptualise links. Linking professional networks and agencies to adaptive communities, creates an expanded field of real world and creative partnerships to enable changing pedagogies that have been revealed in differing ways.

What has been revealed through the lived experiences of insider-practitioner's regarding the choice of content, use of artefacts and forms of engagement, as practice reveal examples of "conceptual gateways" (Meyer & Land, 2005 in Land, Rattray & Vivien 2014, p.200) and "transformative" portals of experiences in working with participants. Suspending judgement within transitional and fluid states of liminality, interrupting goal driven accounts and making artefacts in new and fluidly formed communities, creates possibilities to "re-author" forms of beliefs and practices (Ross, 2011 in Land, Rattray & Vivien, 2014, p.201). What is evident is that the practices involved in the examples provided are living things, in the sense that Kemmis et al (2012) suggest. Practices are interdependent on other practices and connected in 'ecologies of practice.' They are orchestrated arrangements that privilege events, networks and relationships. How these ideas engage with contemporary art, design and media is illuminated by exemplars from field-work practices.

TRANSFORMATIVITY THROUGH ECOLOGIES OF PRACTICE

The organisational arrangements and prefiguring of community based engagement from the perspective of insider-practitioners, conceived as 'practice encounters' is the focus of the next section. Following the discussion of practice in the previous section, we would now like to discuss how social and community based 'practice arrangements' (Schatzki, 2002) cognitive patterns and spaces have potentiality for transformation using the concept of prefiguring. Hopwood (2016) discusses the role of prefiguring in a section titled: 'A Schatzskian approach to theorising practice' within a broader discussion of professional practice. What is significant in Hopwood's advocacy of the importance of time, spaces, bodies and things in learning is the articulation of Schatzki recognition that whilst "people and thus practices, are strongly shaped by normativity, there is always the possibility for change" (p.73). Thus, openness, indeterminacy and temporality give rise to a central idea in practice based domains in that "nothing determines what a person does before the act is done" and how "indeterminacy brings questions of agency and prefiguration together" (ibid). This observation signals the qualities and significance of emergent practices as "practices are not determined in advance, and the realities they produce therefore emerge" (ibid). These ideas are useful in the context of developing a knowledge protocol about 'practice encounters' in this chapter focused on the transformative potentiality of community engagement. Even though Hopwood is referring to professional learning and work place settings, in a similar way this book provides the perspective of 'insider-practitioners' working in professional capacities at the edge of institutional and community based learning typically involving informal sites of practice. This signals a shift in practice towards externally facing connections and relations beyond narrow conceptions of the 'workplace' or the 'university.'

Rather than just focusing on the university as an isolated site of practice, recent concepts in the tertiary setting such as 'knowledge exchange', 'community engagement' and social impact' for example, also begin to signal the shift towards externally facing industries, communities and the quality of learning spaces of connectivity in between. The following summary of the value and significance of understanding aspects of practice and the role of prefiguring in a learning encounter, provides a useful set of ideas that can be applied to cultural, material and social projects comprising:

- Stability and change are not exclusive opposites, rather they constantly co-occur;

- Practices unfold amid subtle and less subtle minor and less minor changes;
- Connectedness in action (textures) alters meaningfully altered interpretations (repair, restoration and modification) to produce new textures;
- Simultaneous instability and preservation of practices explore professional learning as people work together
  (Hopwood, 2016, p.73).

The seemingly insouciant and tacit qualities of practice arrangements and bundles identified by Schatzki have resonance with the concept of transformativity in Arnold and Ryan's (2003) definition of transformative experience in educational contexts. They discuss how transformative experiences are "those, which occur with sufficient emotional intensity to be meaningful, and with sufficient cognitive patterning to organize thinking and learning in deeply significant ways" (p. 5). Such cognitive patterning and meaningfulness through intensity is characterised by four factors:

1. Quality of engagement with knowledge;
2. The deepening of teachers' functions, especially as learning mentors;
3. Enhanced capacity for imagination, innovation and creativity;
4. The primacy of relationships as part of the transformative capacity of new learning
(Arnold & Ryan, 2003, p. 5).

In the case study chapters in this book, Arnold and Ryan's four factors: quality engagement with knowledge, deepening mentoring experiences, focusing on imagination and creativity and the primacy of relationships in new learning are all in evidence. These factors will be used to alongside concepts of practice and prefiguring to caste a lens across each project in this chapter, following the next heading and discussion of significance of 'practice encounters' in the visual domain.

Practice Encounters in the Visual Domain

What we are suggesting in this chapter is that meaningful engagement using Arnold and Ryan's' aspects of transformational experience can be enhanced and fostered in the cultural sphere through the concept of 'practice encounters.' An encounter has several meanings and connotations as for example in the Oxford Dictionary, to "unexpectedly be faced with or experience (something hostile or difficult)." The concept of meeting and facing has high salience with educational moments and episodes that may occur in both formal and informal sites of practice. On the one had there is the serendipitous aspects of chance meetings and unexpected encounters with artefacts, events and activities that are highly appealing in experimental and artistic practice. On the other is the opportunity for 'insider-practitioners' to actively plan transitional possibilities through creation of non-fixed meaning states to open possibilities of transformation. Far from being pre-determined, states of 'practice encounters' allow for incremental, iterative and open ended planning in informal or community based sites to seek engagement with contested topics, marginalised communities and what could be perceived as difficult situations and experiences.

Within a framework of emerging media ecologies, the significance of deliberate enactments, artefacts and materiality in visual domain is discussed by Sean Justice (2015), by setting out new ways of seeing digital making and learning as encounter. Whilst focused on media education, Justice outlines how traditional classrooms, Maker Ecologies and new Digital Making and Learning Ecologies have different contact points and foci of attention. For Justice, a focus on encounters anticipates new leaning cultures comprising iterative entanglements, feeling, knowing and recursive spirals of old and new (p.6) to allow a focus on 'presence' and time as intersectional and multi-sourced. These concepts present a conception of educative space that has potentiality to go 'beyond' traditional concepts of community engagement to engage educative and sustainable transformations of practice linked to democratizing principles that address civic and socially just agendas. Experimenting with gaps between formal and informal sites of practice and a "willingness to loosen control of outcomes" (p.17) allows for improvisation and a focus on developing entangled learning. In this way, many of the practitioners, projects and communities identified in this book have moved beyond goal driven deliverables, towards 'sensibility' and 'being' as desirable qualities of communities (Kallio-Tavin,2014).

In the broader educational realm, another example of double-coding using educational concepts such as the authors' use of 'practice' and 'encounter' in this chapter as an overt pedagogical activity, can be seen in the work of Connell (2013). Connell signals the significance of "the creative development of social practice through time" (p.104) whilst simultaneously highlighting concepts of encounter. For Connell, an emphasis on 'encounter' actively involves intervention and interruption in educational contexts to countermand linear social process narratives. Significantly Connell recognises the concept of care (p.104) in this at times, unsettling educational process of engaging complex issues and tensions. Rather than disparagement and maintenance of existing structures and routines, Connell advocates engaging with new educative spaces and diverse changing communities. Many of the chapters in this book anticipate such dual functionality by including a focus on care whilst simultaneously acknowledging diverse often informal spaces and working with marginalised participants. Connells qualities of encounter also include respect, reciprocity, trust, the capacity to shape relationships, discovery as well as the crucial aspect of engagement. Concepts of encounter and engagement encompass a movement from observation towards dialogue and crucially in this discussion dialogic relations with the world. David Seamon's (1979) work in human geography studies describes concepts of rest, movement and encounter in relation to "attentive contact" (Relph, 1980, p. 300). Importantly, encounter can either be enacted across a range of possibilities including oblivion and careful attention. Highlighting the embodied importance of phenomenological accounts of practice, patterns of environmental experience and engagement is another dimension of encounter with salience for this research.

In terms of Australian art history, Janet Hawley's (1993) text 'Encounters with Australian Artists' provides a succinct account of why encounters and encountering have salience with the visual and cultural sphere. For the authors as tertiary educators, it was a revelation for example, in the early nineties to see such a text with actual interviews with artists, which departed from biographical accounts of lifestyles, typically located within exhibition catalogues. Apart from historically reduced scope of the text comprising thirteen male and just one female artist, articulating the stories as 'encounters' enabled Hawley to highlight artistic sensibilities, meeting points, crossroads, reflections and patterns to give a "valid insight into the artist and the artist's work" (p. 10).

In the aesthetic domain, the theoretical concept of encounters and encountering has recently been discussed in the work of Snepvangers & Ingrey-Arndell (2017). In this work, artworks, video and YouTube interviews are presented as case studies of practice that also exemplify shifts required by educators to interrupt the stability of past recording platforms. This work enables the design of learning interventions in everyday routines to countermand prior invisibility of marginalised communities, such as Indigenous Perspectives and International students in tertiary contexts. In the cultural sphere many exhibition projects, such as the National Museum of Australia's recent "Encounters" exhibition (2015), re-envision relationships with past collecting and museological practices to reconnect with contemporary communities through objects and collections. In the exhibition stories of Aboriginal and Torres Strait Islander Objects from the British Museum activities were devised to show how encounter as an organisational and structural device prioritises truncated histories, particularly with regard to colonial and settler histories of Australia.

Whilst it is clear that there are numerous references to encounter and encountering in artistic literature and the realm of embodied and contemplative practices, a small selection has been presented here to show the scope of meaning with relevance for devising educational encounters in the cultural community sphere. The potentiality of 'practice encounters' in the visual domain exists in linking potentialities in transitional spaces. Rather than pre-determining outcomes or throwing out existing practices in their entirety, adaptive and incrementally small changes, prefiguring engagements and tolerating disequilibrium highlight the strength of combining 'practice' and 'encounter' as two conceptually powerful terms.

Concepts of Practice and Encountering in Case Studies

In Chapter 1, Kim Snepvangers and Donna Mathewson Mitchell, examined transformational perspectives of insider-practitioners and extended concepts of individual experience to include dialogic methodologies described by Kemmis as living systems as 'ecologies of practice.' Dynamic conceptions of practice encompassed principles of ecology as networks, nested systems, interdependence, diversity, and flows of development. The mobility of ideas (Creswell, 2012) beyond people and things was suggested as a counterpoint to subjective self-expression, a value typically highly valued in artistic and visual sites and settings. Socio-material engagements with artefacts also signals the primacy of connectedness capabilities and worldly sensibilities. Emergent practices without a necessarily fixed goal in mind were positioned as being at the forefront of community engagement protocols. Encounters regarding embodied and relational arrangements of practice are both serendipitous yet simultaneously well connected signalling key protocols regarding how communities engage. The theoretical concept of 'practice encounters' is introduced as a transformational way to connect learning through lived experience and knowing-in-practice across diverse participants and populations not traditionally perceived as connected.

In Chapter 2, Margaret Woodward investigated the potential for socio-material spaces and artefacts, in the form of a mug, a QR code, events and an exhibition to activate social networks that cross boundaries and borders of geographic isolation through *The Sea is All Around Us*. The concept of 'third space' represents the fusion of the physical, the remote and networked places that can be utilised simultaneously or across other conceptions of time by multiple remote users. In providing practice arrangements that fuse the first space of event and artefact, (exhibition, drawing, drinking tea, talking, souvenir gift) with the remoteness of a second space of mobility on the sea in a ship, a third networked space emerges through the range of encounters activating a third space. Networking practices have evolved, blurring the real and the virtual. Distribution and connection in local and global relations are the primary focus signalling inter-connected space. The primary relationships comprise the global network of missions and seafarer's centres, who as events unfold are joined by artists, designers, and performers enhancing the visibility of some previously forgotten spaces, in this case the maritime work place of seafarers.

Although facilitated by technology using socio-material artefacts the project highlights sensory gestures and embodied participant experiences with tea and cooking alongside more analytic representations of shipping data. This project about journeys of lived experience is still active a year after the launch at the Mission to Seafarers Victoria. The connectedness of the community continues to thrive on new encounters, new geographies and new ideas given the practice arrangements organised in this project. The community of seafarers continues to engage with this project through journeys of lived experience and the mobility of people, things and ideas. The technology facilitates tracing life and days at sea, enabling participants to hover over and immerse themselves in new geographies and destinations, virtually and imaginatively engaging emergent contexts that were not even potentialities before the project.

In Chapter 3, Narelle Lemon explores how new relationships are facilitated by the virtual. #MuseumEdOz is one example of how the online space of Twitter supports the construction and development of a virtual networked environment. This example illustrates the ways in which participatory practice can occur in online environments and thus across time-space to support discussion about pedagogies, new relationships between objects, event, display, exhibition, and knowledge production. As a consequence of the virtual nature of the ways in which participants encounter one another in this online environment, the practice architectures and the practice arrangements are distinct from those that are addressed in other chapters and across other projects. Of course, there are complex connections beyond this environment as discussions consistently make reference to practices that exist and occur in other sites. Lemon uses the concepts of threads, links and knots of lines of digital becoming, visibility, connecting and reciprocity to explore the nature of encounters and connections within the online space and beyond, providing a unique perspective on its growth and contribution. In doing this, importantly, she acknowledges the incompleteness of the story and makes references to reworking the museum in terms of its position in the cultural sphere. The dynamic relationship between practice, learning and change is addressed and the potential of extending conversations and encounters in the online space to support participatory culture in other sites of practice is explored.

In Chapter 4 Jayson Cooper and Maureen Ryan used the dialogue of transformation as they propose framing, hanging, glass on glass, wood on wood, the glass and the frame, as a powerful metaphor for the community engagement that occurs at Gallery Sunshine Everywhere (GSE). Transformation occurs as children's art work, often prepared on cheap butcher's paper and on the back of teachers' strike posters in poorly funded schools, is formally framed for the public gallery context. Transformation also occurs as the young artists express their ideas and are transformed through engagement in the public space of the gallery-cafe where their artworks are exhibited. Importantly, the opening events carry them, their families and teachers from their every day existence, from their usual classrooms to a public space.

In addressing the ideas of glass on glass, wood on wood, the authors are acknowledging that skills and rules support the inherent creativity in the art work displayed. They draw attention to the existence of a work of art as an artefact, a product that is produced through artistic encounters and pedagogical processes in schools and kindergartens and exhibited in particular ways in the gallery context. They further examine the way in which those artworks reflect and represent the embodied and relational states of being in child, youth and adult worlds. They celebrate the everyday, valuing the experience of knowing-in practice and taking the civic, social, economic, cultural, and political worlds of young people seriously.

The authors' acknowledge the double ontologies found in and between youth and adult art encounters, between schools and communities, children and adults, families and neighbourhoods and cultures that occur at GSE. These encounters embrace different ways of knowing, yet are equally celebrated in collaboration, and are accountable through their degree of relationality and connections of care. The notion of care recognises the complex work of teachers as important transformative agents in historical and social contexts, emphasizing the importance of dialogue at the centre of the endeavour, as a way to make connections and value the voices of children and youth. .

GSE involves a relational artistic public pedagogy that maximises connections between little and big worlds, or youth and adults creating what the authors term a contact zone of aesthetic awareness, reasoning and articulation. These are rich encounters between young and old, schools and communities, through positive and inclusive partnerships that then impact on the cultural ecologies of local places. In doing this, the chapter emphasizes the rich opportunities for young people to generate artistic expression and provide transformative insights into the world.

In Chapter 5, Angela Giovanangeli explored the work of the artist Lucien Henry, his belief in social equity and its impact on transcultural flows in education and art. Like Lemon in Chapter 3 and Cooper and Ryan in Chapter 4,, Giovanangeli draws on the idea of the contact zone to examine how Henry effectively crossed cultural borders. The encountering of Henry's ideas with Australian society reflected a contact zone in which complex and unresolved possible meanings emerged as a result of different historical and social contexts. Henry provides an example of one who reflected national ways of understanding the relation between art and community, reflecting his own French cultural background and his developed understandings of art and education. Yet he also invented and constituted a specific way of understanding art education with the aim of transforming the way aesthetic expressions should be understood within Australia, exhibiting an adaptive and emergent approach that demonstrated knowing-in-practice through engagement with new ideas. In this way the fluidity of Henry's concepts and ideas as well his ability to adapt to specific political and cultural concepts, underscore the entanglement and co-presence of trajectories within art pedagogy and community and their relationality. Henry's vision of art education, artistic creation and their relation to the wider public was enmeshed in his concern for the democratisation of the arts and the role art plays locally and globally.

In working with these ideas and engaging with the example of Henry, Giovangangeli further advances transcultural flows, engaging contemporary readers with historical communities in an examination of art and education across time-space. In doing this, she provides us with an encounter to re-think our assumptions about the historical development of practices in art and education in Australia and their local community and international connections.

In Chapter 6, John Rae likewise concerns himself with the role that art plays, centring the discussion on arts-based research. He explores the development of a useful platform for re-imagining the agency of art, examining how 'invisible forces', referred to as forces, flows, energy, connections, emergence and passions, provide a means of getting closer to an answer about how to understand the 'work' of art. In this examination, Rae explores the relationship between researchers, participants, the socio-material artefacts of research such as interviews and transcripts and the social and historical context of research including non-human material. Boundaries are acknowledged and questioned, including boundaries between artist and researcher, between the human and non-human, between the artwork and other material, and between art and other disciplines. The examples that Rae provides explore the removal of these boundaries of practice to examine how encounters in the space between lead to new and emergent ways of thinking about art and about research. As Rae concludes, at the very least, the differences between disciplinary practices, and no doubt a variety of social practices, are counteracted by what they have in common – or, as he states, the company they keep.

In Chapter 7, Gregory Turner-Rahman examined the addition of a student-directed, exploratory and project-oriented class to a traditional art history or visual studies course. The class he describes involves abductive visual reasoning as a type of inference that requires working back from data to a hypothesis of sorts. It requires that we study, recognize, and understand how multiple factors might contribute to a complex collection of interconnected theoretical contrivances, visual products and technologies. In the course used as a case study, Turner Rahman explains how students are encouraged to 'do' critical thinking, to reflect thinking in art practice. He also notes that modelling this kind of thinking is often neglected in terms of how that can be done for art history and theory using methods that mirror practices in the studio. As such he is advocating abductive visual reasoning projects as effectively linking theory to studio production and creative scholarship in an organic manner. Through the act of making or drawing, students learn to recognize the systems contributing to the construction of something- a product, a process, new knowledge. They must then mimic or understand the processes in order to synthesize something new. Finally, they must infer whole systems and interconnected parts. The caveat is that the instructor must shift their role to become a facilitator of sorts and to provide many different opportunities for students to collect, analyse, critique, and ultimately create images

Abduction is a process of discovery shared by the sciences, the arts, and humanities and is therefore a process that crosses disciplines or boundaries as noted in the previous chapter. Through the exploration of such an innovative approach Turner Rahman is moving beyond accepted and assumed approaches to see practice in art history and theory anew, enabling rich encounters that traverse traditional boundaries.

In Chapter 8, Jamie-Lea Hodges and Eleanor Venables discuss how the art of the present activates previously marginalised methods of the past, while materiality informs and inaugurates tradition. The artist's role is to express a way of existing in the world that is not just their own but is that of the collective group or milieu to which he belongs. In addressing *Connective Understanding* as a collaborative artwork, they also observe how it speaks of how culture can express a way of existing within nature, environment and materiality. Community arts projects and exhibitions which highlight collaborative exchange have an authentic potential to engage community knowledge, increase social capital, and reposition a large group of geographically diverse participants into an ecology of practice. Such activities broaden opportunities to revisit a shared understanding of ecological embeddedness and sustain cultural knowledge.

Contemporary arts practice is imperative to keeping and supporting skills in arts practices which are haptic, skilled and technical. Without Indigenous contemporary arts practice or the oral tradition of sharing stories including ecological knowledge, contemporary arts audiences would only be able to view traditional Aboriginal and Torres Strait Islanders artefacts through historical museum collections. Shared knowledge and artistic notions of materiality may be understood in relation to the practice of community arts projects, by unravelling the continuing role of ancient and traditional methods of contemporary artistic production.

This chapter clearly illustrates how participatory interventions may result in effects that were never envisaged at the outset. Community art projects at *Outback Arts, NSW* supported new experiences and connected places where inspiration was facilitated in unexpected ways. In this way the examples show that there is always a way for history to find a way back into contemporary creative practice. Australian

Aboriginal contemporary art, inspired by place, family, community and informed landscape traditions, has the capacity to present a unique ancient history that exists in Australia, particularly in the social and cultural context of a European city like Venice, where much of the architecture, classical art and culture is hailed as being 'old.' As the authors note one is reminded that Australia's cultural history is much older indeed.

In Chapter 9, Jo Higgins and Sarah Coffils utilise a reflective dialogue recorded in 2016 between the authors to make some observational remarks about collaboration and cooperation based on their experiences completing a number of peer-led youth projects. In conclusion the authors contend that cooperation was observed alongside the maintainence of independence for each of the organisations. In terms of the co-presence and premise of collaboration the following issues were discussed as they emerged from the reflective dialogue: asking more of partners aims; responding to difficult questions; collaboration as collision; invisible hours; asking why; balancing work with both individual participants and stakeholders; unexpected agency; necessity of impacting the whole organisation; time to establish collaboration; sustainability and tangible legacies. Acknowledgement and exploration of these issues reflects the ways in which knowing about collaboration came through the practice of collaboration. The discussion further illuminates the degrees to which collaboration is a practice that is embodied and relational, importantly involving the space for emergence to occur over time. Central to the discussion was acknowledgement of people working together yet maintaining independence and space for exploration and criticality and even conflict. Interestingly this sense of conflict, or collision, along with discomfort, are aspects rarely disclosed or interrogated in accounts of practice. Here they are acknowledged in ways that align with ideas of encounters in what can be seen as the contact zone, as previously discussed in relation to a number of other chapters. Encounters in this zone can be both exciting and troublesome in their sometimes seeming impossibility, but often, as noted here, lead to productive generation and co-creation of significance.

In Chapter 10, Marty Ortanez and James Walsh, set out how Digital Storytelling and Organic Theater challenge students to become agents in their education, to merge their own experiences directly to larger disciplines and the issues that these disciplines seek to examine. Inside of this intersection, a transformational contemplation takes place, one that roots student learning in their own experiences. These arts-based strategies also shepherd the learning experience of students into a communal experience, where students are sharing their personal narratives and their connections to the central themes and issues of the class through art and horizontal dialogue. Their study reveals that both processes are deeply contemplative, and frequently transformative, experienced at the level of the body and in relation to one another. They link to powerful ideas within and beyond community, embracing those ideas and making connections that emerge through engagement in practice. As the authors demonstrate these kind of educational encounters require a different approach to teaching and learning, a willingness to surrender much of the structure and focus of a course to the students, while maintaining a rigorous approach to learning outcomes that are consistent with institutional requirements. It is a move away from a top-down approach to a focus on the practice of learning, allowing for significant emergence in and through arts-based methods.

In Chapter 11, Michael Kempson discussed how the pedagogical experiments that led to the development of Cicada Press (CP) sought to challenge the ossified norms found in traditional printmaking instruction by providing students with insights into materiality and process. In so doing it was important that these activities were aligned with standards that echoed those of leading examples in the arts industry. Further to this were the benefits accrued by students in the creative interaction developed with invited artists from outside of the institution, an important instructional mode that supported and enhanced the tuition and guidance given by academic staff at UNSWArt and Design (UNSWAD). The process reflected a more instinctual understanding of how intent works with a combination of other factors like chance, in concert with goodwill and enthusiasm, leading to a gradual evolution in teaching and learning strategies.

This chapter illustrates how time, along with reflection, offers the observer new insights into an event or issue. From a very simple idea Cicada Press (CP) has morphed into a research group at UNSWAD. that has a considerable national and international profile in the field of printmaking. Underpinning this gradual transformation has been the shared desire from its stakeholders to seek a synthesis between an educational philosophy using instructional methods that can be aligned with the ideas of Distributed Leadership (DL) with a broader social and ethical agenda.

As a result of implementation of the DL framework, the working environment at CP is described as relatively open, fluid and collegial. By harnessing the value of stepping beyond traditional organisational roles CP created a community of talented people, rich with assorted experiences and expertise, who work with substantial collective capital towards a common goal. Inherent in each of the DL roles within this model outlined by MacBeath (2005), and as used within CP is the importance of trust, particularly how it is generated within the complex interactions and potential tensions found in the ego-driven pursuit of creative practice. Considerable time is given to establishing a positive environment with open channels for dialogue and problem solving, between students, teachers and artists. As noted by Kempson, in a more holistic sense trust can only be built from the development of honest relationships developed between individuals within the CP organisation and it is only with the crucial ingredients of integrity, competence and respect that a dynamic of reciprocal trust can be sustained. The artists, the students and the staff that engage in the course that supports CP use a very practical set of scenarios that combine diverse personalities and intergenerational experiences to establish the foundations of a professional network. This provides examples of making and forming connections that inform career pathways and initiate a framework for life long learning. The ideas established in DL and the pedagogical applications that have been gleaned promote positive and constructive learning dynamics within the interplay of the participating players, allowing for sponsored growth for students and even the artists and teachers who contribute.

Kempson observes that giving students the foundations of a sustainable practice and practical opportunities for personal and professional development is the essential business of an art school. In this educational endeavor he connects with many of the previous authors, who in accounting for a range of pedagogical approaches, are likewise seeking to promote pedagogical encounters that provide authentic and meaningful experiences of education in practice that then inform future professional practice in the arts.

In Chapter 12, Gabrielle Mordy outlined that her main inspiration for working in a supported studio has always been the compelling quality of artwork produced by artists with intellectual disability, and the artist's commitment to their creative practice. In doing this, she speaks to the investment of working in the arts industry and in educative roles amd its relationship to productive and meaningful work.

Mordy examines how supported studios, such as Studio A, are drivers of change in this 'mindset' domain, changing public perceptions and allowing artists with disability to engage in art for art's sake, to perhaps discover and develop their talent, and importantly to have their work seen by varied audiences. The powerful examples provided demonstrate the inspiring capacity of art to change perceptions, connect people and broaden paradigms.

In Chapter 13, Lisa Hochtritt focused on the lived experiences of the teacher and graduate students involved in a study of public pedagogy and a makerspace located in the southwestern United States. It included the establishment of partnering with an outside organization within the context of a semester-long course at an institution of higher educationhe The findings of the research project helped to refine understandings of pubic pedagogy and how this practice can be observed in multiple contexts. Research findings showed how that public pedagogy is located within democratic processes and practices (Biesta 2014) that engage community members through a trading of skills and expertise. In focusing on public pedagogy within a traditional university course, Hochtritt uses learning vignettes and students' reflections to evidence personal moments of transformation, and addresses both the discomfort and gains inherent in self-directed learning and the contemplative process. In doing so she also acknowledges the challenges, benefits, and constraints of such a project. Although the original intention was to research how a non-profit organization exemplified elements of public pedagogy, the unintended outcomes related to the students' experiences of this project were the most interesting, demonstrating the power of emergence through community engagement. Reflections revealed anxieties about prescribed learning in a university space while the themes discussed clustered around the ideas of trust, flexibility, and student-centered curricula as facilitated through this transformative pedagogical inquiry. This study put into practice the importance of re-orienting conceptions of community engagement and the prioritization of participatory social practice. The tensions highlighted in relation to how such experiences sit alongside university courses, content and grading practices echo some of those noted by other authors in previous chapters. They also act to highlight the importance of such community encounters within education as a means of engaging art, education and the cultural sphere.

CONCLUSION

We conclude by speculating on the adaptations and implications of transformative pedagogies and ecologies of practice in art, education and the cultural sphere. Evidence of transformative pedagogies as strategies to inform practice have been articulated through an examination of the ways in which practices can be considered. Evidence of practices as orchestrated transdisciplinary arrangements have been described using reflexive accounts to further examine specific projects and how ideas, methods and approaches are situated in relation to the broader field. The implications of ideas presented have been considered in terms of participatory practice, research creation and transformative research methods. We can now examine how community engagement encompassing art, education and the cultural sphere can be re-imagined and re-oriented to explore concepts of educational encounter beyond passive observational experience and conceptions of dialogue. How social worlds related to art, education and the cultural sphere are prefigured, enacted and reconfigured using permeable boundaries and transformative pedagogy allows for reimagined community engagement planning.

Engaging with the examples in this book and understanding the connections between community engagement, art and educational potentialities in the cultural sphere can assist in developing new learning challenges and presences using the concept of 'practice encounters.' What is common in all of the chapters is a focus on the skills of divergent thinking, emergence, problem solving, relationality and an approach informed by connectedness and transdisciplinarity. Knowing within specific and localised historical and social worlds and practices highlights the significance of appropriate material and aesthetic artefacts for engagement contexts. Such a juxtaposition of human awareness integrated with qualities of the world is what Seamon (2015) calls "human immersion in world" (p.392). He suggests using the "phenomenon of place [to] provide an organising structure, or "lived emplacement" where "lived relationships come before the human and environmental parts" (ibid) in dynamic interaction. This focus on relationships however, does not merely collapse into relationality, rather the focus is on transformative experience as a movement of ideas.

The visual domain is important because it has the power to communicate knowledge and practice together with meaningful emotional intensity through various lenses of attentiveness as 'practice encounters.' The value of this to education and culture can never be under estimated. To understand the power of the visual image means developing an understanding of domain specificity alongside examples of how to develop prefigured educational encounters. Retaining aspects of serendipity and chance within practice ascribes agency yet, requires certain arrangements within a framework that tolerates inderterminancy. Educators need a clear focus on relationships between the visable content and the skills to be taught in relation to how representational visual forms create connectivity. This involves working with ranges of artistic expertise and sophisticated levels of educational practice, for example as engaged with 'insider-practitioners.' Providing an articulation of key ideas significant in emergent creative partnerships this chapter critically reflects on the theoretical framework of ecologies of practice to re-consider community connectivity related to the visual domain.

REFERENCES

Apple, M. W. (1979). *Ideology and curriculum*. Boston: Routledge and Kegan Paul.

Arnold, R. & Ryan, M. (2003). *The transformative capacity of new learning*. Bundoora, Victoria, Australia: Australian Council of Deans of Education (ACDE).

Biesta, G. J. J. (2014). Making pedagogy public: For the public, of the public, or in the interest of publicness? In J. Burdick, J. A. Sandlin, & M. P. O'Malley (Eds), *Problematizing Public Pedagogy* (pp. 15-25). New York, NY: Routledge.

Bishop, C. (2012). Artificial Hells: Participatory art and the politics of spectatorship. London: Verso.

Connell, R. (2013). The neoliberal cascade and education: an essay on the market agenda and its consequences. *Critical Studies in Education,* 54(2), 99-112.

Cornwall, A. (2008). Unpacking 'Participation': Models, meanings and practices. *Community Development Journal*, *43*(3) , 269–283.

Costandius, E., Rosochacki, S., & le Roux, A. (2014). Critical citizenship education and community interaction: A reflection on practice. *International Journal of Art and Education, 33*(1), 116-129.

Encounter (2017). English Oxford Living Dictionary. Accessed 25 April 2017. https://en.oxforddictionaries.com/definition/encounter

Hager, P., Lee, A., & Reich, A. (Eds). (2012a). *Practice, learning and change: Practice-theory perspectives on professional learning*. Dordrecht: Springer.

Hawley, J. (1993). *Encounters with Australian artists.* The Award –
Winning Interviews. St Lucia, Brisbane, Australia: The University of Queensland Press.

Justice, S. (2015). *Learning to teach in the digital age: Enacted encounters with materiality.* Marilyn Zermuehlen Working Papers in Art Education: Teachers College, Columbia University. Volume 2015, Issue 1.

Kallio-Tavin, M. (2014). Impossible practice and theories of the impossible: A response to Helen Illeris's "Potentials of Togetherness." *Studies in Art Education, 55*(4), 342-344.

Kemmis, S. (2009). Understanding professional practice: A synoptic framework. In B. Green (Ed.), *Understanding and Researching Professional Practice* (19–39). Rotterdam: Sense Publishers.

Kemmis, S., Edwards-Groves, C., Wilkinson, J. & Hardy, I. (2012). Ecologies of practice. In A. Lee, P. Hager & A. Reich. *Practice, Learning and Change: Practice Theory Perspectives on Professional Learning* (Chapter 3, 33-49), Netherlands: Springer.

Literat, I. (2012). The work of art in the age of mediated participation: Crowdsourced art and collective creativity. *International Journal of Communication,* 6, 2962–2984.

MacBeath, J. (2005). Leadership as distributed: a matter of practice, *School Leadership and Management*, *25*(4), 349-66.

Meyer, J.H.F. & Land, R. (2005). Threshold concepts and troublesome knowledge (2): Epistemological considerations and a conceptual framework for teaching and learning. *Higher Education*, *49*(3), 373-388.

Land, R., Rattray, J. & Vivien, P. (2014). Learning in the liminal space: A semiotic approach to threshold concepts. *Higher Education*, *67*(2), 199-217.

Relph, T. (1980). Review: A geography of the lifeworld: Movement, rest and encounter by David Seamon. *Annals of the Association of American Geographers,* 70(2), 300-301.

Ross, J. (2011) *Unmasking online reflective practices in higher education.* Unpublished Ph.D thesis. University of Edinburgh.

Schatzki, T R. (2011, July 11). *The edge of change*. Seminar presented at the Centre for Research in Learning and Change, University of Technology, Sydney.

Seamon, D. (2015). Situated cognition and the phenomenology of place: Lifeworld, environmental embodiment, and immersion-in-world. *Cognitive Process*, 16 (Supplement): S389-392.

———. (1979). *A geography of the lifeworld: Movement, rest and encounter.* London: Croom Helm Ltd.

Snepvangers, K., & Ingrey-Arndell, J. (2017). Spaces of speaking: liminality and case-based knowledge in arts research and practice in Knight L. & Cutcher, L. (Eds) *Arts, Research, Education: Connections and Directions.* Springer Series: Arts Based Education Research.

Contributor Information

Chapter 1 and 14

Dr. Kim Snepvangers is Director: Professional Experience & Engagement Projects and a UNSW Teaching Fellow at *UNSW Sydney: Art & Design*. As the recipient of a 2016 UNSW Strategic Educational Fellowship Grant (SEF#3) titled: *New Approaches to the Development of Professional Identity through Independent Critical Reflection* her research interweaves creative and professional leadership contexts. In her previous role as Head, School of Art History & Art Education (2013-2005) Kim managed the strategic direction of art & design education and art history & theory which gained a maximum 5-star rating in Excellence in Research Australia (ERA). Recent leadership roles comprise: Art & Design representative Women in Research Network (WIRN); Convener Arts Education Research Practice Special Interest Group (AERPSIG) and two competitive grants within the Australian Association of Research in Education (AARE); PhD Scientia Scholarship HDR. Supervisor; Editorial Board *Australian Art Education* and recipient of two Art & Design Innovation Grants. She has extensive management and research experience in developing transitional educative spaces between creative and professional practice.

Dr. Donna Mathewson Mitchell is a Senior Lecturer in Visual Arts Curriculum at Australian Catholic University (2015), having recently moved from Charles Sturt University (2007-2014). She is also an Adjunct Senior Lecturer with the Research Institute for Professional Practice, Learning and Education (RIPPLE) at Charles Sturt University. She has an extensive teaching background, encompassing school-based education and higher education, in addition to maintaining her arts practice. Her contribution to quality teaching & learning, research and community engagement has been recognised through a series of collaborations, projects, awards and nominations. Donna's research addresses art education, teaching practice and teaching and learning in public spaces. She was an invited partner on the cross-institutional OLT Project-Teaching and Learning in Public Spaces (2010-2012) and is currently engaged in a number of collaborative projects. Her research is documented in numerous articles published in high quality international journals and in a series of chapters featured in significant scholarly books. A recently contracted book with Common Ground publishing titled 'Beyond community engagement: Transformative dialogues in art, education and the cultural sphere' will be co-edited with Dr. Kim Snepvangers (UNSW).

Donna's research informs her teaching, providing a foundational focus on the practice of teaching in relation to theory. She has particular expertise in online teaching and learning and distance education. Her ongoing project 'Connections in Teaching & Education' (CiTE) has resulted in a long term collaborative partnership with Bathurst Regional Council, two successful student exhibitions, ongoing virtual exhibitions and a nomination for a Museums and Galleries NSW Imagine Award for Community Engagement in 2014. This project and the associated curriculum design is showcased as an exemplar of practice-based education on the EFPI website (Education for Practice Institute- CSU) and has continued to operate at CSU in a sustainable way. The latest project is with Bathurst Regional Art Gallery and is titled 'Generation Art.

Chapter 2

Margaret Woodward is Associate Professor of Design at Charles Sturt University (CSU). She is a co-founder and leader of the Creative Regions Lab at CSU and a researcher in regional creative industries. Margaret's creative practice investigates the interplay between tourism, design and cultural geography and how designed artefacts frame understandings of landscape and national identity. Her ongoing investigations through souvenirs and cartography include; *Tourism Telemetry (2010 –), Remote Sensing: Sensing The Remote (2012*), *The Sea is All Around Us* (2015) *Fall of the Derwent* (2016) and *Lost Rocks* (2017). More about Margaret's creative practice can be found at: www.apublishedevent.net and http://sensingtheremote.net/

Chapter 3

Dr. Narelle Lemon is an Associate Professor in Education at Swinburne University of Technology, Melbourne, Australia. Narelle's research agenda is focused on engagement and participation in the area of building learner capacity to engage with cultural organisations and community arts programs; arts education; and social media for professional development including Twitter, Instagram, Pinterest, and blogging. She is especially focused on social photography and the generation of visual narratives to shared lived experiences. Narelle blogs at *Chat with Rellypops*, Tweets as *@Rellypops*, and has recently begun a new project to promote stories of how creativity and mindfulness are applied to people's lives from various disciplines in the community. This *Explore and Create Stories* series is curated on Instagram through *@exploreandcreateco*.

Chapter 4

Dr. Jayson Cooper is a music-arts-based researcher whose interests are found in artistic and research practices. Employing auto-ethnography, place-based and land-based education and pedagogies Jayson seeks the dynamic intersections found between cultures, places and communities. Doing so, he articulates his growing sense of how the public sphere is artfully pedagogical.

Professor Maureen Ryan is a Professor in the College of Education at Victoria University where she supervises many higher degree students and is also Director, Gallery Sunshine Everywhere (http://www.gallerysunshine.com). Maureen is committed to collaborative and community focused teaching and research. In her work she continues to explore especially the relationships between education and community, the partnerships possible, the skills and understanding that people working to create and build partnerships need and the particular ways in which arts and activity based projects can enable these things to happen.

Chapter 5

Dr. Angela Giovanangeli is a Senior Lecturer and the Teaching and Learning Coordinator in the School of International Studies at the University of Technology, Sydney. Her research interests include Intercultural Education, Language Policy and French Cultural Studies. She is currently working on a project titled 'Shaping European Geographies' examining cultural initiatives in France as well as a project on the transcultural aspect of the work and ideology of artist and educator Lucien Henry.

Chapter 6

Dr. John Rae is a Senior Lecturer and Associate Head in the School of Biomedical Sciences, Charles Sturt University, Australia. He teaches organisational studies in undergraduate health programs, and creativity, innovation and change in postgraduate health management programs. John uses arts-based research, applying it to his main topic of investigation – the creativity of health services. He also uses art as a teaching strategy. John has worked for 35 years in the public health system in varying roles. Visit John's website at: http://seaofcreativity.weebly.com

Chapter 7

Dr. Gregory Turner-Rahman is an Associate Professor of communication design and new media theory as well as the Interim Program Head of the Virtual Technology and Design program in the College of Art and Architecture at the University of Idaho. His research explores cultural production in the electronic realm, creative communities, and, more recently, visual reasoning. He has contributed to *The Journal of Design History*, *Post-Identity*, *Fibreculture* and *Media Authorship*, an edited American Film Institute Reader published by Routledge. Dr. Turner-Rahman has studied design communities from within as his professional experience spans the disciplines of graphic design, interface and web development, and industrial design. As a member of a creative team, he garnered Apex and Clarion awards for writing and design work. His freelance practice has served clients such as Washington State University, Metro Seattle and Precor.

Chapter 8

Jamie-Lea Hodges is the Executive Director of regional arts development organisation Outback Arts. Born in Coonamble NSW, Jamie-Lea completed her HSC at Coonamble High School and undertook her Bachelor of Art Education at the College of Fine Arts UNSW, with a major in Sculpture and a minor in Photography. Jamie-Lea's focus at COFA was to engage in a variety of arts practices, Aboriginal history and art research courses and then return to regional NSW and work in the arts. In 2009 Jamie-Lea returned to her hometown to take on the role with *Outback Arts*, a not for profit arts organisation in far North West NSW. *Outback Arts* develops and promotes arts and culture in the far west through a broad range of community arts development programs and special initiatives that supports communities that are limited or disadvantaged in terms of access to arts and culture. Her artistic practice is a reflection of her family's Aboriginal history and tracing knowledge lost within the family through traditional weaving techniques using natural and contemporary materials. Jamie-Lea's work has been exhibited as part of *String Theory: Focus on Contemporary Australian Art 2013* which brought together over 30 Aboriginal artists and artist groups from across the country at the Museum of Contemporary Art Sydney and also in *Country: Connective Understanding: A Focus Through Contemporary Aboriginal Ar*t a Collateral event at 56th Venice Biennale, 2015. Her passion towards community practice has played an integral role in her own artistic achievements in the role of Regional Arts Development Officer.

Eleanor Venables is a Sydney born museum educator who has developed educational events and resources for institutions such as the National Trust S.H. Ervin Gallery and the Campbelltown Arts Centre. Undertaking study at UNSW Art and Design (formerly COFA) she received a Bachelor of Education (Hons) and after graduating in 2000 she began her art education career teaching into secondary schools both in Sydney and the UK. Eleanor has been involved in UNSW Art and Design since 2011, through her sessional lecturing and tutoring and more recently with her research work on UNSW Learning and Teaching projects with Kim Snepvangers and Tess Allas (*Indigenous Learning Ecologies – Bending the Twig* 2013 & *Evolving Curriculum* 2014). She has written and presented seminars for Visual Arts teachers focusing on unpacking the artist's practice and methodology. Her paintings, drawings and prints explore figurative and abstract dimensions of human fertility and have been included in various exhibitions in Sydney. Eleanor also teaches programs for Pine St Creative Arts Centre (City of Sydney) and is passionate about projects that link current issues about culture, philosophy, visual arts, contemporary practice and encouraging public engagement in creative disciplines.

Chapter 9

Jo Higgins is a published art writer and consultant specialising in gallery and peer-led youth education and arts partnership projects. She holds a B. Art Theory (Hons) and a B. Arts (History) from UNSW and a MA Contemporary Art from Manchester University. From 2008-2013 she lived in London, where she wrote the survey publication *21st Century Portraits* for the National Portrait Gallery. From 2011-2013 she worked as the Young People's Online Editor at the South London Gallery on the Louis Vuitton Young Arts Project. She was also the UK Contributing Editor for *Artlink* magazine during this time. Since returning to Sydney, Higgins has worked for the University of Sydney, UNSW Art & Design, Biennale of Sydney and with Kaldor Public Art Projects, for whom she developed and delivered a Pilot Regional

Engagement Program in partnership with the Western Plains Cultural Centre in Dubbo. Since 2017, she has been the Young Creatives Coordinator at the Museum of Contemporary Art Australia.

Sarah Coffils is the Head of Education at the South London Gallery (SLG), an internationally acclaimed contemporary art space in South London. Providing opportunities for innovative collaborative projects with the local community is at the centre of the SLG's core mission. The original marquetry floor, designed by Walter Crane in 1891, bears the inscription "The source of art is in the life of a people." From 2008-12 she was project manager of the Louis Vuitton Young Arts Project, an ambitious collaborative programme between the SLG, Tate, Whitechapel Gallery, the Southbank Centre and the Royal Academy of Arts. Other notable projects include Double Take (2007-8), which saw the SLG's contemporary collection exhibited in purpose-built spaces in two secondary schools in South London, and the establishment of a peer-led youth programme. Previous roles include Education Manager at the Stanley Picker Gallery, Kingston University, working with Turner Prize- winning artist Elizabeth Price, Juneau Projects and art and architecture practice Public Works to develop education programmes for local schools.

Chapter 10

Dr. Marty Otañez is a California-born cultural anthropologist, tobacco control advocate and documentary filmmaker in the Anthropology Department, University of Colorado Denver. Otañez' research and advocacy extends to digital storytelling. Digital stories are three-minute autobiographical videos with photographs, narration and background music. In 2009-17, he conducted twelve digital storytelling workshops with over fifty community members and administered university courses with digital storytelling assignments, creating over 325 digital stories. Workshop themes covered tobacco use, cancer survivorship, cannabis cultures, gentrification, and viral hepatitis among Latinos and other disenfranchised communities. The purpose of Otañez' digital storytelling research is to determine the ways people make sense of wellness issues and how digital stories can influence behavioral change, community engagement, youth leadership development, and public policy. His publications include 'Digital storytelling: Using videos to increase social wellness,' in Cohen and Johnson, eds., *Video Filmmaking as Psychotherapy: Research and Practice,* Routledge: New York; and 'Digital storytelling and the viral hepatitis project,' Gubrium, Harper and Otañez, eds., *Participatory Visual and Digital Research in Action*, Left Coast Press: California. Dr. Otañez is the producer of the public access television show through Denver Open Media called Getting High on Anthropology: A Story-Based Approach to Cannabis Research, Education and Funding, http://fsandgreen.org.

Dr. James P. Walsh is an Assistant Professor, C/T, in the Political Science Department at the University of Colorado Denver, where he has taught for the past eighteen years, specializing in Labor, Immigration, Community Organizing, and Irish American History and Politics. Walsh began using *Organic Theater* in his classroom sixteen years ago and the experience inspired him to found the Romero Theater Troupe, an all-volunteer organic community theater that resurrects unknown stories of activists and acts of resistance. The Romero Troupe is now eleven years old and has been nationally recognized, winning the *Cesar Chavez Civil and Human Rights Award* in 2015 from the National Education Association. The troupe has performed hundreds of community workshops and dozens of original plays about local human rights and social justice struggles. The purpose of Walsh's research is to assess how organic theater in a classroom setting can transform teacher/student dynamics and contribute to student engagement and empowerment. His publications include "Denver's Romero Theater Troupe: Welcoming Working Class Voices in Higher Education and Revitalizing Class-based Activism through Organic Theater," *Labor Studies Journal*, 2016.

Chapter 11

Michael Kempson is a Senior Lecturer and Convenor of Printmaking Studies at the University of New South Wales Art & Design in Sydney, Australia. Michael was the International Member at Large for the US based Southern Graphics Council International (2014-2016); a visiting professor at Xi'an (2012) and Tianjin (2016) Academies of Fine Art in China; and a resident artist at Alfred University, New York, USA (2017). He is a member of the advisory committee of the International Academic Printmaking Alliance, formed by the China Central Academy of Fine Art (2016). Exhibiting since 1983 with a total of 26 one-person exhibitions and over 200 group exhibitions, in addition Kempson initiates printmaking projects in the Asia-Pacific in his position as Director of Cicada Press, working with over 200 significant artists and curating 56 exhibitions. These have included: *Seoul-Sydney: Contemporary Korean and Australian Prints,* Galleries UNSW in Sydney and Chugye University for the Arts, Seoul, South Korea (2014); and *Interchange: A Printmaking Dialogue between Australia and Thailand,* at venues including Silpakorn University Art Gallery, Bangkok and Mosman Art Gallery, Sydney (2014-2015). Kempson exhibited in *Kyoto Hanga 2014: Australia and Japan* at the Kyoto Municipal Museum, Japan (2014) and curated the Australian component of the *International Academic Printmaking Alliance Exhibition,* Imperial Ancestral Temple, Working People's Culture Palace, in Tiananmen, China (2016). Kempson's work is represented in the Museum of Contemporary Art, Bangkok, Thailand; National Taiwan Museum of Fine Arts, Taipei; National Gallery of Australia, Canberra, and many Australian state and regional galleries.

Chapter 12

Gabrielle Mordy is the Artistic Director of Studio A (www.studioa.org.au) with over nine-year's experience working with artists with disability. Her achievements in this field were recognised by the National Association for the Visual Arts through the 2011 Curatorial Mentorship Initiative award. In 2014 Mordy was awarded a Churchill Scholarship and an Australia Council Career Development Award to undertake international research into the supported studio sector. Mordy regularly presents at conferences on the emergence and impact of supported studios, and have written several articles including 'Outsiders Collaborating? How creative relationships at Studio ARTES are opening doors for artists with intellectual disability' (published in Collaboration in Experimental Design Research Symposium: Conference Proceedings. University of NSW, June 2012) and 'Being Seen to be Heard: The Language of Lynda Strong' (published in Das Platforms Emerging & Contemporary Art, December 2011). In 2009 Mordy worked as research assistant to Professor Colin Rhodes (Dean, Sydney College of the Arts). She contributed eighteen entries to Professor Rhodes Encyclopaedia on Outsider Art and helped to manage Callan Park Gallery. Mordy is a founding member of Accessible Arts 'Supported Studio Network'(SSN). SSN provides a framework for visual art studios that support the professional development of artists with disability. SSN aims to connect these studios to foster knowledge, research and information sharing. Mordy holds a Masters of Fine Arts & a First Class Honours degree in Anthropology. In 2010 she was awarded an Australian Postgraduate Scholarship. Mordy is also a practicing artist working with a range of media including textiles, printmaking, drawing and sculpture.

Chapter 13

Dr. Lisa Hochtritt is an Associate Professor in the Division of Art and Visual Culture Education (AVCE), School of Art at the University of Arizona (UA), Tucson, Arizona, USA. She obtained her Doctor of Education (Ed.D.) degree in Art and Art Education from Teachers College, Columbia University in New York City and her Master of Arts (M.A.) degree from San Francisco State University in Creativity and Creative Arts Education. Hochtritt is the co-editor of the Routledge anthology *Art and Social Justice Education: Culture as Commons* (2012). She has worked with participants of all ages in schools, museums, and community settings and received awards for her teaching and service to the field including the National Art Education Association Higher Education Art Educator of the Year, Pacific Region (2014); and the Colorado Art Education Association Colorado Art Educator of the Year (2011). The chapter co-authors and collaborators are graduate students at the University of Arizona: Lindsey Baker, Michael Barrett, Rebecka A. Black, Misha Burstein, Lino Garibaldi, Jennifer Johnson, Bridget Longoria, Yu-Wen (Eryn) C. Neff, Arielle Rose Urbach Pieterse, and Jeffrey Urdang.

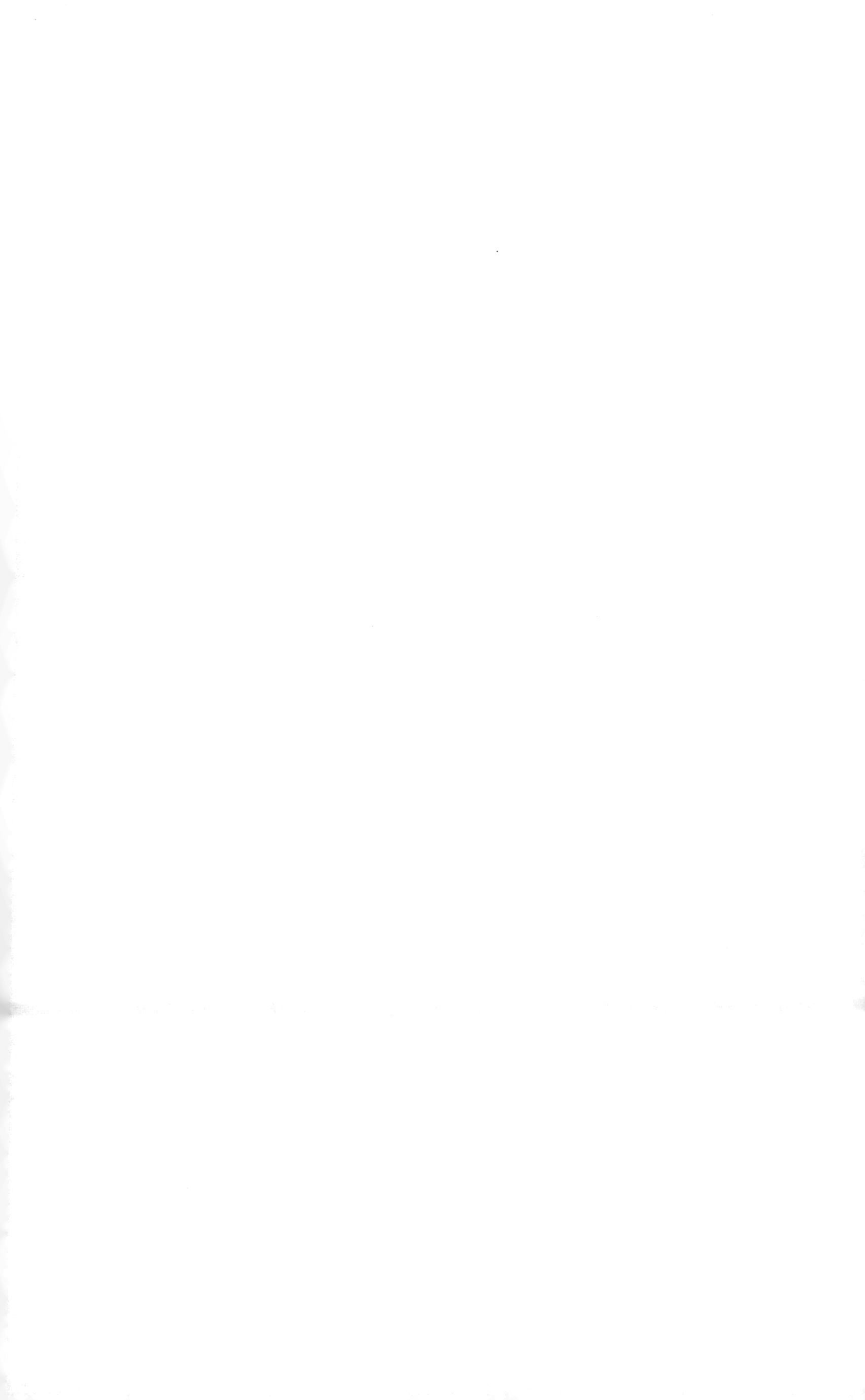

CPSIA information can be obtained
at www.ICGtesting.com
Printed in the USA
LVHW061733080119
603170LV00008B/352/P